PETER DILLON'S
MAJOR VOYAGES IN THE SOUTH SEAS

Calder ⎯⎯ 1823-25 ⎯⎯⎯⎯⎯⎯
St Patrick ⎯ 1825-26 ••••••••••
Research ⎯ 1827-28 ⎯⎯⎯⎯⎯⎯
Jess ⎯⎯ 1837-30 ⎯⎯⎯⎯⎯⎯

The two-way voyages of *Calder* and *Jess*
between Sydney and the Bay of Islands
are not shown

SAMOA
Uea
(Wallis)

Vavau
TONGA
Tongatapu

Aitutaki
COOK IS
Atiu
Rarotonga

Chile

to Chile *(first voyage)*

J. W. DAVIDSON

Peter Dillon of Vanikoro

CHEVALIER OF THE SOUTH SEAS

Edited by O. H. K. Spate

MELBOURNE
OXFORD UNIVERSITY PRESS
LONDON WELLINGTON NEW YORK

Oxford University Press, Ely House, London, W.1

GLASGOW NEW YORK TORONTO MELBOURNE WELLINGTON
CAPE TOWN IBADAN NAIROBI DAR ES SALAAM LUSAKA ADDIS ABABA
DELHI BOMBAY CALCUTTA MADRAS KARACHI LAHORE DACCA
KUALA LUMPUR SINGAPORE HONG KONG TOKYO

Oxford University Press, 7 Bowen Crescent, Melbourne

This book is copyright. Apart from any fair dealing for the purposes of private study, research, criticism or review, as permitted under the Copyright Act, no part may be reproduced by any process without written permission. Inquiries should be made to the publishers.

© Oxford University Press 1975

First published 1975

ISBN 0 19 550457 7

PRINTED IN AUSTRALIA BY JOHN SANDS PTY. LTD. HALSTEAD PRESS DIVISION

40990

*Dedicated to the many friends of
JIM DAVIDSON
in the Islands, in Canberra,
and wherever they may be*

Editor's Introduction

It is a strange and very sad irony that in our salad days at the Australian National University, around 1951-52, Jim Davidson's disappearances to the coast 'to finish off Dillon' were already as it were a family joke between us; twenty years later the old jest came up in our last conversation; and now there is left to me the melancholy duty of preparing for publication the work that had been spread over half his lifetime. The failure to complete the book was in no sense due to any dilettantism on Davidson's part, nor even to that perfectionism, the best being the enemy of the good, that has stifled so many works of scholarship—he was a perfectionist, but not to that self-stultifying degree. Rather it was due to the subordination of an abiding private interest to his activity in the public weal—the weal of his students and his Department, of the Research School and the University, and above all of those Islands peoples, from Micronesia and New Guinea to Samoa, whom he loved, and who loved him.

The manuscripts which came into my hands were divided into two unequal parts: a book structurally near complete, but in detail very far from that. The first fourteen chapters were in an advanced form, though with marginal or interlinear queries, and comments by colleagues, to be worked in. There was a proem which, according to a note by Davidson, bore only a 'shadowy relationship' to the much longer introduction he had intended; this has been retained. It was clear, however, that if the last six chapters (on his revised plan of twenty) were to be on this scale, the book would be much longer than a publisher would care for. Some deletions were called for; for instance, the details of the actions of the rival Sultans of Atjeh, and of Governor Arthur's machinations against the Van Diemen's Land press, which could be excised with no significant loss to the story of Peter Dillon. For the rest, the editorial task in this part was relatively easy—the checking of references, the silent emendation of a very few infelicities of phrase or errors of insignificant detail. These matters do not seem to call for specific notice in the text.

The later chapters were in different case, being in places very rough-hewn. There was a draft, double-spaced on quarto, but this was obviously very preliminary, with many notes on the versos indicating possible corrections, deletions, additions, recastings, and especially clues and suggestions to follow up. These notes were not always easy to decipher, and quite often they were difficult to weld into a coherent narrative; on the other hand they usually gave references or indicated where references might be found. From these indications it was possible to revise the draft into a form which, as it seems to me, at least more closely resembles Davidson's ultimate intent. The drafts and my recension are filed in the Department which he founded.

In these later chapters there is in one or two cases a considerable rearrangement. The eight chapters of Davidson's last outline have been reduced to four: for one there were only two brief manuscript notes; three were virtually sub-sections which could be subsumed under the title 'Finale in the South Seas', and the concluding chapter seemed rather brief to stand on its own. In Chapter 18 I was able to take advantage of a suggestion of Davidson's for an introductory paragraph setting out the topics to be dealt with in this very compound chapter, and following on this to bring, for example, Dillon's affair with the Wesleyans into one sequence. There is some deletion, in Roger Therry's stories and in the account of Luke Dillon's amatory misadventure. In total there is probably a little more addition than deletion, but practically all that is added stems from Davidson's own suggestions, though here and there I have inserted, without signalling it, half a line or so to point up an analysis or a situation. I have also added occasionally to the notes, identifying additions by square brackets, and have supplied a bridging passage (pages 278-9) for the missing chapter and an Appendix on Dillon's Rock.

There were two cases which gave me some difficulty. In the discussion of the Wesleyans' reaction to Dillon's attacks, Davidson had noted that they had sent two missionaries, having no connection with Tonga, to inquire into the allegations; but he had not incorporated any of their findings. These are constrained: apart from flat denial of some of Dillon's more outrageous charges, the emissaries naturally enough tried to put the best face they could upon a situation which equally naturally and very rightly gave them grave unease. As the draft stood, however, it could be taken as presenting fully only the anti-mission side, which would certainly not have been Davidson's intention. Rather than attempting to rewrite, thereby risking an undue obtrusion of my own views, I have indicated some specific points in the Wesleyan response by attaching their words to Dillon's in clearly editorial footnotes.

The epilogue presented a different problem. Both the beginning and the end of Davidson's text were obviously only first faint foreshadowings of what he would have wished to write, and it is clear from one of his marginalia that he intended to round off the book with an assessment of Dillon's character; this refers to some other manuscript notes, but to my great regret I have been unable to find them in his great mass of Dilloniana. To some extent he had already written such an assessment in *Pacific Islands Portraits* (1970), and at one time I thought of trying to incorporate some of this essay in the conclusion. But, although I have taken two or three hints from that source, this method seemed on reflection awkward and artificial. I have therefore slightly expanded Davidson's last two or three pages, using my own words more than I could have wished, but so interwoven with Davidson's that it would be typographically ridiculous to try to distinguish; but all the points—except the irresistible quotation from *Julius Caesar* —are based on scattered notes and jottings in the files. I have had the concurrence of good judges in these procedures, but the initiative and the responsibility are mine.

Documentation presented a more mechanical problem. I was myself quite unfamiliar with the archival sources and their notations, and the always tricky and tedious task of checking would have been quite impossible without the skill and devotion of Mrs Honore Forster, who had worked on the book with Davidson. In spite of all our efforts, and ready assistance from many archivists, a few references may yet be found faulty. It may be noted here that in all passages quoted directly from Dillon's own writing, his own spelling has been preserved, free from the intrusive [sic], in all its idiosyncratic charm. 'I', 'me', 'my' in the notes refer to Davidson.

The task of revision has been a labour of love, arduous and sad. Yet it has been fascinating to watch, page by page and note by note, the emergence of this flamboyant personality, in whom the elements were so strangely mixed—an intense practicality with delusions of grandeur, ultra-combativeness and self-centred unfairness in pursuit of advantage with a basic generosity and human feeling. Dillon did indeed take the tide at the flood: where the average captain finding the relics at Vanikoro would have talked in the tavern, perhaps written to the papers or at best to the French Government, Dillon pressed on to a serious effort of discovery with intelligence and single-minded persistence; but the flood did not lead on to fortune.

In part this was due to sheer bad luck: for example the supersession of his French Consulship by the July Revolution—though one may suspect that its annals would have been much more stirring than constructive. But more must be put down to his own failings and his incurable ineptness in the arts of handling bureaucracy. In his devotion to the main chance of the moment he offered his services to British and French—even Belgians—with abandon. At times his projects came near to sharp practice—the New Zealand land sales prospectus, the plagiarism of Coxe. There is extenuation: he surely deserved more tangible reward for the Vanikoro exploit, and men were knighted for no greater service; no doubt the Establishment was a comfortable club dispensing jobs for which none but gentlemen need apply—and yet Dillon, claiming ever to be a gentleman, battled so wildly that in effect he wrote himself off as a wild Irish outsider, a mere adventurer. Yet his intellectual curiosity brought him the friendship of intelligent and cultured men, and despite his tremendous rows with the missionaries, he became a useful and respected member of the Aborigines' Protection Society—a testimony that his sympathy for Islands people and ways was not just a tactical one, put on for the useful occasion, but something more deeply rooted in his own persona.

Dillon seems to be superb raw material for either (the choice is difficult) Dickens or Thackeray. Reading through those endless petitions and 'memoirs', one sees him, almost visually, as a figure by Cruikshank or Phiz, very firmly rooted in the early Victorian world, with its idealisms and its pomposities, but above all its energies.

These remarks doubtless go beyond an editor's duty; their excuse is that after three months of intensive living with both Dillon and Davidson, the fascination of the man had seized within me, and must out. I can only hope that I have succeeded in shaping from an incomplete torso, a book worthy of the friend whom I so greatly admired as a scholar, and loved as a man.

O.H.K.S. *Canberra, January 1974*

Acknowledgements

THANKS ARE DUE to the following, whose names are drawn from Professor Davidson's Dillon correspondence file. Designations are in general from this source; to any who may be inaccurately styled, and to any who have been inadvertently omitted, the editor proffers his apologies.

The Reverend J. E. Bell, S.M., Rome; Mr A. E. Browning, State Librarian, Tasmania; Dr John Cumpston, Canberra; Professor J. L. Davies, Macquarie University; Mr Claude Dillon, Mosman; le comte Dillon, Besnaux, France; Mr Gerald Dillon, Rose Bay; the late Messrs John Peter and Joseph Napoleon Dillon, Sans Souci (great-grandsons of the Chevalier); Mr R. Dods, Commissioner, Northern Division, Fiji; Captain Brett Hilder, Sydney; Mr M. G. Hitchings, Hocken Library, Dunedin; Mr A. E. Hobson, Vaucluse House, Woollahra, Sydney; Mr D. K. R. Hodgkin, Australian National University; Dr Hugh Laracy, University of Auckland; Dr Sione Latukefu, University of Papua New Guinea; Lieutenant-Colonel M. H. S. Lawes, Sussex; the late Dr Ida Leeson, Mitchell Library; Mr C. C. Legge, Chicago Natural History Museum; Mr P. D. Macdonald, Public Service Commissioner, Fiji; Mr R. Mahuta, University of Auckland; Miss Phyllis Mander-Jones, Mitchell Librarian; M. Emile Michel, Ministère des Colonies, Brussels; Mr E. H. Milligan, Friends' House, London; the late the Most Reverend Archbishop Eris O'Brien, Canberra; Dr John Owens, Massey University; Sir Thomas Ramsay, St Kilda, Victoria; Dr O. M. Roe, University of Tasmania; the late Mr G. K. Roth, Chairman, Fijian Affairs Board; Mrs G. K. Roth, Cambridge; Mr M. J. Saclier, Principal Archivist, Tasmania; Mr. K. E. D. Scott, Australian Embassy, Brussels; Mrs G. M. Strathern, Hocken Library, Dunedin; Professor A. P. Thornton, University of the West Indies; M. de Vaux de Forestier, Archives de la Seine, Paris; Professor R. G. Ward, Australian National University.

The editor would like to express his gratitude to the following colleagues from the Department of Pacific and Southeast Asian History at the Australian National University: Dr W. N. Gunson, Mr H. E. Maude, Mr D. Munro, Mr R. A. Langdon and Dr Deryck Scarr; and also to Miss P. Croft of the A.N.U. Press. Thanks are also due to Fr Jean Coste, S.M., Padres Maristi, Rome, Mr D. J. Cross, Senior Archivist, New South Wales; Miss Jean Dyce, Mitchell Librarian; Messrs M. G. Hitchings and D. C. McDonald, Hocken Library. The assistance of Mrs Honore Forster, who worked with Professor Davidson on the original drafts, was invaluable. Thanks are also due to Mr Ian Hayward, of the cartographical section, Department of Human Geography, at the Australian National University, for the care and skill devoted to the maps; and finally to the typists, Mrs Robyn Walker and Mrs Ann Prudames, who typed from drafts which, for the last four chapters at least, were distinctly messy.

Contents

		page
	Editor's Introduction	vii
	Acknowledgements	xi
	List of Plates	xv
	List of Maps	xvii
	Abbreviations	xix
	Proem	1
1	The Setting	5
2	Pacific Apprenticeship	13
3	The Path to 'Dillon's Rock' 1813	28
4	A Man of Consequence in Australia 1813–16	42
5	Calcutta and the 'Country Trade' 1816–23	54
6	To South America and the South Seas 1823–25	78
7	Dillon in Mid-Passage 1825–26	94
8	The Search for La Pérouse: persuading Bengal	118
9	The Search for La Pérouse: the voyage out	134
10	Vanikoro	170
11	Return from Vanikoro	190
12	In Quest of Recognition: London and Paris 1828–29	207
13	Dillon's Narrative	219
14	A Chart for Catholicism 1829–30	235
15	In the Wake of Success 1830–34	241
16	Interlude in New Zealand 1834–36	259
17	Finale in the South Seas 1836–38	265
18	An Uneasy Londoner: Petitions and Polemics 1839–47	280
	Appendix I Books, Pamphlets and Printed Letters by Peter Dillon	310
	Appendix II Dillon's Rock	312
	Notes	316
	Index	343

List of Plates

		facing page
1	The affair at Dillon's Rock from Dillon's *Narrative*, 1829	44
2	Korolevu and Dillon's Rock from the sea	45
3	The brig *Calder* from George Bayly's Journal, by courtesy of the Hocken Library, University of Otago, Dunedin, N.Z.	60
4	The wreck of the *Calder* in Valparaiso Bay from George Bayly's Journal, by courtesy of the Hocken Library, University of Otago, Dunedin, N.Z.	61
5	The *Research* under East India Company colours off the coast of 'Arracan' in 1825 from the *Sydney Morning Herald*, 15 August 1931, after a copy of a water-colour by Captain J. G. F. Crawford of the *Research*	188
6	Dillon's Chart of Vanikoro from Dillon's *Narrative*	189
7	The village of Manevai, Vanikoro from Dumont d'Urville	204
8	The inauguration of the monument to La Pérouse at Vanikoro by Dumont d'Urville, March 1828 from a painting in the Rex Nan Kivell Collection, by courtesy of the National Library of Australia	205

List of Maps

Endpapers Peter Dillon's major voyages in the South Seas
The track of the *Research* has been constructed from positions given in Dillon's *Narrative*; the other routes shown are generalized courses.

1	The Fiji Islands	35
2	The Tonga group and the Society Islands	81
3	Northern New Zealand in Dillon's time	261
4	The location of Dillon's Rock	313

[Names underlined on Maps 1 and 2 are of islands known to have been visited by Peter Dillon.]

Abbreviations

ADB	*Australian Dictionary of Biography*, Melbourne, 1966—
AIML	Auckland Institute and Museum Library
AL	Australia Letters, London Missionary Society records, London
AMAE	Archives du Ministère des Affaires étrangères, Paris
ANL	National Library of Australia, Canberra
ANM	Archives Nationales: Série Marine, Paris
APM	Archivio Padri Maristi, Rome
ATL	Alexander Turnbull Library, Wellington
CMS	Church Missionary Society records, London
CO	Colonial Office records—Public Record Office, London
CSO	Records of the Colonial Secretary's Office, New South Wales—State Archives of New South Wales, Sydney
CSO(VDL)	Records of the Colonial Secretary's Office, Van Diemen's Land—Archives Office of Tasmania, Hobart
EC(VDL)	Records of the Executive Council's Office, Van Diemen's Land—Archives Office of Tasmania, Hobart
EIC	East India Company
FO	Foreign Office records—Public Record Office, London
GO(VDL)	Records of the Governor's Office, Van Diemen's Land—Archives Office of Tasmania, Hobart
HL	Hocken Library, University of Otago, Dunedin
HRA	*Historical Records of Australia*
IOL	India Office Library, London
LMS	London Missionary Society (now Congregational Council for World Mission)
ML	Mitchell Library, Sydney
MMS	Methodist Missionary Society records, London
NZC	New Zealand Company
PRO	Public Record Office, London
SC(VDL)	Records of the Supreme Court, Van Diemen's Land—Archives Office of Tasmania, Hobart
SSJ	South Seas Journals, London Missionary Society records, London

Proem

'I AM THE Captain Dillon . . . who was so unfortunate as to discover the fate of the French Expedition commanded by the unfortunate but far famed Count de la Perouse.' Thus, four months before he died, Peter Dillon addressed himself to the Marquess of Normanby, summing up his career in words that he had used much earlier in the times of disenchantment in which much of his later life was spent.

In a sense, they were true. Brave, intelligent, imaginative, driven by an unassailable conviction that he had been born to command, he had overcome many of the handicaps of a humble upbringing. He had risen quickly from seaman to master, to shipowner and merchant. He had gained the friendship, and won the active support, of men of wealth and influence in Calcutta, Sydney and Valparaiso. When a chance call, on one of his trading voyages, provided him with the essential clues that led him on to the complete unravelling of the mysterious disappearance of the eighteenth-century explorer La Pérouse, he was well on the way towards an established position in the world of commerce. But the discovery changed the direction of his life. It brought him loss of fortune—but also modest fame, the honour of appointment as a Chevalier of the Legion of Honour, a pension from the French Government, and acquaintance with men of affairs and of letters in both London and Paris. The more substantial recognition that he thought was his due, however, eluded him. He felt that his achievement identified him with men of substance and influence; and the *élite*, he believed, looked after its own. He sought an appointment appropriate to his standing, of the kind that the powerful conferred on their less affluent relatives; as a consul or colonial official in the service of Britain or France. But he was disappointed in his expectations; and his later years were ones of financial struggle, made more embarrassing by the need, as he saw it, to maintain a façade of gentility.

Yet, in more important senses, his assessment of his life was false. As a young seaman, he had been more deeply involved in seeking to understand Fijians and Polynesians than in the performance of his formal duties—though his rapid advancement shows that he did his work well. As a sea-captain, he made himself an authority on the history and ethnography of the Pacific. When he returned to Europe with proof that La Pérouse had been wrecked on Vanikoro, in the Solomon Islands, he wrote a *Narrative* which portrays Pacific Islanders with wit and sensitivity and expounds opinions on race relations which were in advance of their times. In pamphlets and letters he set forth his views, forcefully, on many subjects relating to the Pacific: the work of Christian missions, the colonization of New Zealand. In his final years he was active in the affairs of the Aborigines' Protection Society. When he was dead, his name, and his vivid, erratic and passionate personality, were remembered with warmth—mainly of affection but, in a few cases, of detestation—by men and women in the islands and in Europe.

But, despite his achievements, he was not—in the ordinary use of the term—a 'great man'. It is difficult to believe that the course of events in the Pacific would have been in any perceptible manner altered if he had not exerted himself as he did. Even the achievement that made him publicly known, the ascertaining of the fate of La Pérouse, was of little significance in the history of the Pacific, though an important event in Pacific historiography.

Biographers most commonly find their subjects in men of a kind different from Dillon—in the lives of those whose individual actions appear to have affected directly the public weal, through their attainments in politics, in science or in the arts. Such men are, indeed, fit subjects for biography: an assessment of their role is both important to scholarship and of general interest; and the records of their lives are more likely to have survived than are those of other men. But a 'great man' is not necessarily the most rewarding subject for the biographer, any more than he is for a sculptor commissioned to produce his marble likeness, to be set on a granite plinth in some public square.

To write a biography of Peter Dillon is to essay the task of creating a human portrait. Dillon's personal qualities and the range of his experience make him an admirable subject for this endeavour. But a life of Dillon can be something else besides. It can attempt to describe the colour and texture of life in the times and places in which he lived. To students of Pacific history—a group to which he himself belonged—his fitness for biographical study resides in his life as a mariner, as a writer, and as a participant in public affairs, reflecting the changes in the Pacific between the end of the age of exploration and the beginning of the age of empire.

ONE

The Setting

In 1788, when Peter Dillon was born, the intellectual climate of Europe was changing. The urbane spirit of the Age of Reason was giving way to a mood of romanticism and revolution. In France the passionate voice of Jean-Jacques Rousseau had both extended and contradicted the more measured teaching of Voltaire and the Encyclopaedists. In England Dr Samuel Johnson had died four years earlier, and his friend Sir Joshua Reynolds had reached the end of his active life. William Blake, who was about to publish his *Songs of Innocence*, and the youthful Wordsworth, Coleridge and Southey, who were approaching manhood imbued with a love of nature and of liberty, reflected the attitudes of a different age.

Men who rejected the claims of the traditional social order, who rejoiced in the newly-gained freedom of the United States and were soon to welcome the outbreak of revolution in France, were also eager for knowledge about pre-literate societies beyond the frontiers of the Christian world. Shortly before he died Dr Johnson said of a collection of *Voyages to the South Sea:* 'A man had better work his way before the mast, than read them through . . . There can be little entertainment in such books; one set of Savages is like another'.[1] But his was a voice from the past. Philosophers and men of letters were reading narratives of exploration in search of models of beauty and virtue, and men of science were doing so in pursuit of exact knowledge.

This interest was not, in essence, a regional one. But, between the close of the Seven Years War in 1763 and the outbreak of hostilities between Britain and revolutionary France thirty years later, the opening of the Pacific was the major achievement of European exploration. It was thus towards the islands and peoples of the South Seas that much of the literary and scientific attention of Europe was directed.

EUROPEANS had first crossed the Pacific during the southern summer of 1520-21. From the Straits of Magellan—so named, retrospectively, in their discoverer's honour—they had sailed north-west through almost empty seas till, after ninety-eight days, they had reached the island of Guam. Thence they had continued westward, to the Philippines.

Magellan had been seeking a route that would open to Spain the riches of the Moluccas and those of the unknown lands that might lie within the Pacific. The rigours of his voyage showed that the passage through the Straits and the long north-westwards crossing of the ocean placed an excessive burden upon both men and ships. But his success in reaching the borders of Asia provided knowledge that was used by many other Spanish navigators, sailing from the ports of Mexico and Peru. In 1565 Spain established a settlement at Manila, from which goods from China, Japan and the Indies were shipped to Acapulco, in Mexico. More important geographically, however, was the series of voyages from Callao, in Peru, in search of *Terra Australis Incognita*, the great southern continent which it was thought must lie in the southern half of the ocean. In 1567 Alvaro de Mendaña sailed upon this quest and discovered the Solomon Islands. In 1595, when seeking to return there, he found the Marquesas and eventually reached Santa Cruz, to the south-east of the Solomons. In 1606 Pedro Fernandez de Quiros, who had served under Mendaña, discovered a number of islands between Ducie and Henderson—to the south-east of the Tuamotus—and Espiritu Santo, in the New Hebrides.

During the 150 years following Quiros's voyage, many European navigators traversed the Pacific and sighted previously unknown islands. But the most important contributions to geographical knowledge were made by the Dutch. In particular, the discoveries of Abel Janszoon Tasman, in his great voyage in 1642-43, included Tasmania (which he named Anthony van Diemen's Land), New Zealand, Tonga, and the outskirts of Fiji. And eighty years later Jacob Roggeveen reported the discovery of the Samoan group and of Easter Island and several atolls in the Tuamotus.

By the second quarter of the eighteenth century a few islands at least in most of the major archipelagos had been visited by Europeans; and information about them had been published in books and maps, recorded in official reports, or passed on orally in the seaports frequented by Western mariners. But much of this information was inexact. The explorers had possessed no satisfactory method of ascertaining longitude. They had frequently been compelled to retreat from newly discovered coasts because of deficiencies in their ships, the ill health of their crews, or conflict with the local inhabitants. Moreover, they had generally approached their task without the later scientists' passion for exact knowledge: the Spaniards had been preoccupied with the expansion of empire and of Christendom; the Dutch with that of trade. Islands—like the Solomons, whose distance from the American coast Mendaña had under-estimated by two thousand miles—had been found and lost again. Great tracts of ocean had remained untraversed.

When Swift published *Gulliver's Travels*—in 1726—he was able to place Brobdingnag and Balnibarbi within the boundaries of the Pacific. And forty years later it was still possible to believe that a rich and populous continent might lie in the southern half of the ocean. The European image of the Pacific contained a mixture of fact and fantasy.

The voyages that were undertaken—mainly by the British and the French—in the second half of the eighteenth century marked a new phase in the history of exploration. Their leaders—and those in Europe who sent them out—had absorbed the attitudes of the Age of Reason. Exploration was still concerned with the interests of trade and empire. It was concerned—till the hypothesis had been disproved—with the search for *Terra Australis Incognita*. But to those old objectives it added a new one: the exact description of the ocean, of the lands it contained, and of the peoples who lived in them.

The first important additions to knowledge were made by the expedition which sailed from England in 1766 under the command of Samuel Wallis. On entering the Pacific, through the Straits of Magellan, Wallis's ship became permanently separated from the sloop accompanying her. The latter, under Philip Carteret, followed a more southerly course than any earlier vessel had done in the eastern Pacific; Wallis's most important discovery was Tahiti. Within a year of the visit by Wallis, Tahiti was reached independently by another explorer —Louis-Antoine de Bougainville, a Frenchman of resolute character and diverse interests, whose voyage took him westward across the Pacific, through Samoa and the New Hebrides, till he sighted the barrier reefs off the unknown east coast of Australia.

Yet the achievement of Bougainville was little more than a prologue to that of James Cook, who, in the three definitive voyages which he undertook during the ensuing decade, gave to the map of the Pacific something like its modern form. Cook was a navigator and surveyor of exceptional skill, a careful observer, and an able leader. He devoted himself, with an unwavering diligence, to maintaining the seaworthiness of his ships and the health of his crews, so that he was able to remain in the Pacific for longer periods than his predecessors had done. And he was accompanied by scientists and artists.

Cook first sailed for the Pacific, in the *Endeavour*, in 1768. The voyage had two objectives: the observation, at Tahiti, of the transit of Venus; and the continuance of the work of exploration. The *Endeavour* remained at Tahiti for three months, during which Cook and the group of naturalists and artists led by Joseph Banks made a more detailed study of the island and its people than had previously been attempted anywhere in the Pacific. From Tahiti Cook sailed to the islands of Huahine, Ra'iatea and Taha'a, in the Leeward group of the Society Islands, which had not been visited by Wallis or Bougainville. Thence he sailed south; and, when he had reached 40°S without encountering land, he turned west. This course brought him to New Zealand, which had not been sighted by Europeans since Tasman's discovery in 1642. The *Endeavour* remained in New Zealand waters almost six months. During this period Cook made a complete survey of the coasts and, with his colleagues, studied the resources of the country and the way of life of the Maori people. When work in New Zealand was completed, he decided to sail for the East Indies but to attempt, *en route*, to resolve another geographical problem. Mariners had gradually built up an outline of the west and parts of the north and south-west coasts of Australia, and Tasman had discovered Van Diemen's Land; but no European had yet sighted its eastern shores. Cook reached the unknown coast in April 1770 and followed it northward, surveying and recording details of the country.

A year after his return to England, in July 1771, Cook sailed again. The primary purpose of the second voyage was the solution of the problem of *Terra Australis Incognita*. The absence of any large land mass north of the Antarctic was proved by two great traverses of the southern ocean. But, in the course of the voyage, Cook also made many discoveries and rediscoveries and examined in detail island groups that had previously been visited only briefly or described imprecisely. Substantial parts, at least, of Tonga, the Tuamotus, the Marquesas, the New Hebrides, New Caledonia, and several lesser groups and islands were studied and surveyed.

On his third voyage, which began in July 1776, Cook was concerned with another of the major problems of geography: that of the North-West Passage. By examining the Pacific coast of North America he

The Setting

sought to discover whether there was a navigable passage to Hudson's Bay. On his way there he found the Hawaiian Islands—the first recorded sighting of them by Europeans. They impressed him as a place where men could recruit their strength after an arduous voyage, and so he returned there from the American coast to spend the winter. On this occasion, relations with the Hawaiians became less amicable than they had been during the first visit, and on 13 February 1779 Cook himself was killed.

By the time of Cook's death European knowledge of the Pacific was vastly greater than it had been ten years before. Narratives of his first two voyages and those of his immediate predecessors, based on their commanders' journals, had been published; and some others who had been on board had published accounts or commentaries. The navigators themselves and many of those who had gone with them had been questioned by public men, by scientists and men of letters. Moreover, both Bougainville and Cook had brought a Tahitian back to Europe with them; and these two men, Ahutoru and Mai, had delighted the *salons* of Paris and London.

Educated Europeans were now able to form a clear impression of the South Seas: of the pattern of land and ocean; of the beauty and fertility of many of the high islands and the limited resources of the atolls; of the contrast between the bronze-skinned Polynesians, whose company the voyagers had greatly enjoyed, and the darker-skinned Melanesians, with whom they had established only more tenuous contacts. They were able to plan, as some did, a closer involvement in the life of the Pacific. But, for a greater number, the islands provided a model that they could use for passing judgement on their own civilization.

For these, Tahiti possessed a preponderant interest. Wallis, Bougainville and Cook showed the Tahitians to be happy and admirable people, unaffected by many of the inhibitions and frustrations characteristic of life in Europe. Others—such as Philibert Commerson, the naturalist who accompanied Bougainville—were less restrained in their eulogies. Commerson, who described himself as the island's '*adorator perpetuus*', wrote emotively of the beauty and accessibility of the women and avowed his belief that he had found in Tahiti 'the state of natural man, born essentially good'.[2] Since Tahiti became known in Europe when educated men were beginning to reject the claims of reason, it came to symbolize that state of primitive simplicity which Rousseau had described as 'the happiest . . . of epochs', 'the real youth of the world'.[3] Its significance in European thought helped to create a lasting market for books about the South Seas.

In the year of Peter Dillon's birth two events occurred at Botany Bay, on the east coast of Australia, that were eventually to determine the shape of his career. In January 1788 Captain Arthur Phillip, with a body of convicts, arrived in the bay to found the settlement of New South Wales. And in early March a French exploring expedition commanded by Jean François de Galaup de La Pérouse sailed from it, never to be seen again by European eyes.

At the time of Cook's death, there was much work in the Pacific for explorers and surveyors still to do. Broad stretches of ocean had not been sailed over; many coastlines had been sketched only cursorily; the position of innumerable islands had to be verified, and even their existence proved; and winds, tides and currents needed careful study. The performance of these tasks extended over many decades. But there were several even more basic geographical problems that remained unresolved. In the North Pacific, Cook had not finally settled the question of the North-West Passage. And, in the South, Mendaña's Solomon Islands had not yet been identified. Two years later, however—in 1781—a solution to the latter problem was propounded by a French geographer, Jean Buache. He argued that they must be the islands between Santa Cruz and New Guinea which had been visited by Bougainville and subsequently by another French explorer, Jean-François de Surville.

The search for a North-West Passage and the verification of Buache's hypothesis were both included in the instructions issued to La Pérouse. In 1786 and 1787 he examined the North American and Asian coasts and then, moving south, touched at Hawaii and Samoa. When he sailed from Botany Bay, he was bound for the Solomons.

La Pérouse's voyage represented a continuance of the work that had brought earlier Europeans to the Pacific; the arrival of Phillip reflected the dawning of a new age. Despite the gaps in geographical knowledge, Europeans were now able to settle in the Pacific and to sail its waters in relative safety. In about 1785 traders had begun to visit the American north-west coast for furs and to call at Hawaii to rest their crews and obtain provisions. In 1787 Lieutenant William Bligh was sent to Tahiti in the *Bounty* to procure breadfruit trees for transplantation to the British West Indies. From 1789 British whalers were working in the Pacific, and by 1792 they had reached Polynesian waters from

Sydney, calling for refreshment at islands such as Tahiti and Tongatapu and at the Bay of Islands and other ports in New Zealand. In 1797 the London Missionary Society—an undenominational Protestant body—landed missionaries in Tahiti, in Tongatapu and in Tahuata (in the Marquesas).*

The settlement of New South Wales—which Phillip had decided to base at Sydney Cove, in Port Jackson, rather than Botany Bay—soon began to affect European penetration of the Pacific in a variety of ways. Its existence provided mariners with a port of call controlled by men of their own culture. Its convict population included many who eventually found their way to the islands to become beachcombers. Above all, it became a centre for the development of whaling and sealing and of trade with the islands.

Whalers and sealers began to sail from Sydney in the 1790s; and in 1801 two new ventures were started. A group of Sydney businessmen visited the Firth of Thames, in New Zealand, where Cook had declared that masts might be cut 'such . . . as no country in Europe can produce'.[4] Although they obtained a satisfactory cargo, their success was not followed up for some years. But the other new venture—the despatch of a government vessel to Tahiti for salt pork—led to the establishment of a continuing trade.

Far more important commercially than the pork trade, however, was the discovery of sandalwood in Fiji and a few years later in Hawaii. For centuries Europeans had traded in 'the scentful sandalwood', collecting it on the Malabar Coast and in Timor and selling it in the cities of India and at Muscat and Canton. It was burnt in temples, used in making fans and small articles of furniture and in cosmetics. Supplies from Malabar and Timor were not large; and the demand was keen—the merchants of Malabar were receiving almost £75 a ton from the agents of the East India Company. The Fijian discovery thus held out the prospect of large profits to those who were first to exploit it.

Europeans seem to have learnt in Tonga that sandalwood was growing somewhere in the little known, and largely uncharted, islands of Fiji. The actual location was discovered as a consequence of the wreck, in 1800, of a schooner bound from Canton to Sydney on a reef between the two groups of islands. A survivor, Oliver Slater,

---

* The London Missionary Society was known simply as 'The Missionary Society' till 1817. For simplicity, I have referred to it as the London Missionary Society (or LMS) throughout.

made his way to Bua, in Vanua Levu, where he found the tree growing abundantly. When the Sydney party that had been at the Firth of Thames chanced to call there in 1801, *en route* to Manila with their cargo of timber, he reported his discovery. Circumstances made any action impossible for several years; but in 1804 the first vessels sailed from Sydney for Fiji. Those who had been informed of Slater's find tried to keep the knowledge to themselves—both to maintain a monopoly of the source of supply and because of restrictions placed on the activities of British-registered vessels by the East India Company. But the secret did not survive for long. In 1807 the trade began to develop rapidly, and in 1808 the Fiji sandalwood rush was at or just past its height, when five colonial vessels, a London-registered ship previously engaged in sealing, three American vessels and one from India arrived in the islands. On the last of these Peter Dillon seems to have reached the Pacific.

PETER DILLON arrived as a seaman; but he was a man of unusual qualities of intellect and imagination, of courage and perseverance. He became a sea-captain, a shipowner and an independent trader. He became an authority on the history of the Pacific, a perceptive student of the ways of life of island peoples, and an acid commentator on the foibles and pretensions of their Western invaders. In later life, as a writer and the companion of scientists and scholars in London and Paris, he joined that body of men—including his hero, Cook, and the impressionable Commerson—who had sought to explain the Pacific to the European world. He lived his life—in more than one respect—between two worlds.

TWO

Pacific Apprenticeship

PETER DILLON was born in Martinique on 15 June 1788.[1] He was the son of an Irish immigrant from County Meath, also named Peter, who is said to have been a former member of the Dillon Regiment, which for many years had garrisoned the island.[2] The period following his birth was marked by revolutionary disturbances throughout the French West Indies, which culminated in the mass rising of mulattos and negro slaves in Saint-Domingue during 1791. At about the time of the rising, Peter was taken home to Ireland, where he spent the remainder of his childhood. Then, by his own account, he entered the Royal Navy to be trained as an officer and 'had the honour to serve at the battle of Trafalgar'.[3]

In his later years, Peter Dillon occasionally claimed a connection with the Dillon family of Martinique.[4] This was a family of considerable eminence.[5] Its head at the time of Peter's birth, Comte Arthur Dillon, was a great-grandson of the founder of the Dillon Regiment, the seventh Viscount Dillon. The regiment had been raised in Ireland to fight for James II; but, after the latter's flight to France, it had been transferred to the service of Louis XIV. Arthur Dillon's elder brother had succeeded to the Viscountcy and lived on the family estates in Ireland; but he himself had made his career in the French service. He had become colonel of the Dillon Regiment and, in 1786, been appointed Governor of Tobago. After service as deputy for Martinique in the States-General and as commander of the Army of the North in the early stages of the revolutionary wars, he was guillotined during the Terror.

As his second wife, Arthur Dillon had married Marie de Girardin (Comtesse de La Touche), a first cousin of Marie-Josephe-Rose Tascher de La Pagerie, who became Mme de Beauharnais and, eventually, the Empress Josephine. By her he had a daughter, Frances (known as Fanny), who married Henri-Gratien Bertrand, the companion of Napoleon's final years in St Helena.

Peter Dillon mentioned his kinship with the Dillons of Martinique only in private letters, not in his published writings, and only when circumstances made it useful to do so. His claim seems likely to have had a firmer basis than the identity of name, since in his own years of fame he was in touch with the Bertrands and with many of Fanny's Irish relatives.[6] But the connection was probably remote and perhaps soured by illegitimacy at no distant point in his ancestry.

This background—of descent and of naval service—was important to Peter Dillon, however, in his private imaginative life. It seems to have lain behind his essentially aristocratic conviction that it was his role to command and that he was at least the equal of all whom he met. It probably provided him with a justification of his own readiness, in his later years, to enter the service of any of the European Powers. It accounted, in part at least, for the high regard in which he held service in the armed forces, in politics, and in diplomacy. It added intensity—and almost intimacy—to his veneration of Napoleon.

IN ABOUT 1806 Peter Dillon sailed to the East.[7] This part of his career —like his childhood—is full of obscurities. His failure to describe his early years may contain no hidden meaning, since he never attempted to write sustained autobiography. But this is unlikely. If he had entered the navy—probably as the servant of an officer or petty officer—why did he leave it as a youth of seventeen or eighteen? For most of his life, Dillon was susceptible to sudden losses of self-control, when he was capable of acting with disastrous violence. Many years later one of his officers who had been exposed to these excesses expostulated with him. He immediately became calm[8]—perhaps remembering some incident in his past. His departure from the navy may well have followed the commission of an act of violence that he found it painful to recall. There may also have been another reason for his virtual silence about this phase of his life. As an older man, when he devoted much of his time to writing, he was obsessed with gentility, so that the humble capacities in which he was obliged to work as a youth probably became matters that he deemed it needless, or even undesirable, to record.

He seems to have gone to Calcutta, for he became 'intimately acquainted' at this time with an Irish sea-captain based on that port. This was Anthony Burnsides, the master of the ship *Clyde*, which ran from Calcutta to Bombay, Colombo, Penang and the ports on the west coast of Sumatra. It is likely that Dillon sailed with him. And it is not unlikely that, through Burnsides, he made other contacts that were useful to him in his subsequent career: the *Clyde* was owned by the Calcutta firm of Campbell & Company, which had a branch in New South Wales, managed by one of its partners, Robert Campbell.[9]

PETER DILLON was reticent about the circumstances of his arrival in the Pacific. When he was writing for publication, he appears to have intentionally concealed them. But in a letter he stated that he had been acquainted with the South Seas since October 1808, and he referred elsewhere to his presence in Fiji during that year.[10] These statements make it almost certain that he was on board the ship *General Wellesley*, owned by David Dalrymple & Company of Madras, which sailed from Calcutta early in May and, after a call at Penang and a slow voyage round the south of Australia, arrived at Bua Bay, on the coast of Vanua Levu, on 6 October.[11]

The *General Wellesley* had passed through Fiji a year earlier, *en route* from Tahiti to Penang; but, on that occasion, her master had been unable to discover in what part of the group the sandalwood tree was growing. During 1808 the sandalwood boom had reached, or perhaps passed, its peak. In Bua Bay, where the trade was centred, accessible stands had been largely depleted. More importantly, much of central Fiji was in a condition of turbulence and disorder. Moreover, the arrival of the traders had provided a powerful new motive for local warfare. Chiefs who organized working parties for them—particularly the Buli Bouwalu, the highest ranking chief in south-western Vanua Levu—benefited substantially. They received payment for their services in European goods; on occasion they might gain the help of armed boat-crews in subduing their enemies. By October 1808 the Buli Bouwalu and his allies were beginning to be subjected to attack by their less fortunate neighbours.

When the *General Wellesley* reached Bua, one other vessel lay at anchor—the brig *Favourite*, from Sydney, commanded by Captain William Campbell.[12] On the day of her arrival, the *Favourite*'s boats were about to sail northward to Naurore Bay, on the north-west coast, where it was hoped to make an agreement with the local people for the supply of sandalwood. Some days later one boat returned with a load of wood; but two others failed to follow her. Eventually Campbell was told that their crews had been massacred and eaten. In retaliation he attacked a village in the north of Bua Bay which had allied itself with the enemies of the Buli Bouwalu. While he was there, he was joined by one of the men he believed to have been killed and was told that the boat crews had been captured by a hostile canoe fleet. The fleet, which contained a contingent from as far away as Bau, a small island on the coast of Viti Levu, intended to enter Bua Bay the following morning. Thus warned, the two ships and the fort of the Buli Bouwalu were able successfully to resist attack; and, after some desultory skirmishing, the release of all the remaining captives was obtained.

At about the end of October the *Favourite* sailed for Sydney, under charter to the captain, David Dalrymple, and the supercargo of the *General Wellesley*. On the voyage from Penang, they had lost 'upwards of twenty' members of the crew 'by sickness'. (Dalrymple himself was still seriously ill and died before reaching Sydney.) At Bua, at least one man—and probably more—had left the ship. The principal purpose of the *Favourite*'s voyage was to recruit replacements.[13]

Dillon later wrote that many sailors left their ships in Fiji at about this time; 'some deserted, and others were regularly discharged by their commanders'.[14] In May 1808 the American brig *Eliza* had been wrecked on a barrier reef off the island of Nairai. She had been carrying a large quantity of Spanish silver dollars, a substantial proportion of which had become dispersed among the islands. The sailors remained in Fiji—to quote Dillon—'with a view of enriching themselves'. It seems very likely that Dillon himself may have followed their example. It is clear that, at this period in his life, he developed a strong liking for the Fijians.

When the *Favourite* reached Sydney, it was reported that a European known as 'Peter, who formerly belonged to the "Wellesley"', was living among the Fijians in Vanua Levu.[15] It is possible that this was a man who left the ship in Fiji during her earlier visit;[16] but it may have been Dillon. Twenty years later Dillon wrote of his four months residence in Fiji at this period, 'during which time, being in the habit of associating very much with the natives, I made considerable progress in learning their language'.[17]

Dillon's warmth of feeling towards the Fijians seems to have been returned by them. There is evidence that, in later years, he enjoyed a popularity and was accorded a measure of respect only rarely offered to visiting sailors and traders. Even as a young man of twenty, he possessed many of the attributes that accounted for his later standing.

Physically he was impressive, six feet four in height, heavily built, with a mop of red hair. But it was his qualities of mind and spirit that principally distinguished him from the common run. He possessed both great courage and the instinct of command, was calm and effective in times of danger. He possessed intelligence and imagination that enabled him to gain a ready understanding of indigenous society. Above all, he possessed the capacity to appreciate pre-literate people in their own terms, unencumbered by a sense of cultural superiority. He judged them as individuals, not as types produced by a 'savage' culture. Some of the men with whom he worked, and of the women with whom he slept, thus became his firm friends.

Dillon seems to have remained, for most of his time at least, in the region frequented by sandalwood ships and to have been employed in obtaining cargoes for them. He later wrote that he was able to collect 150 tons within a period of three weeks.[18] But, though he liked the Fijians and was in touch with Europeans, his way of life was not one that could bring him lasting satisfaction. He was, in effect, a beachcomber, dependent for his survival upon the successful deployment of his personal talents and upon the goodwill of his Fijian associates. Moreover, the months when he was there are those in which Fiji passes from the dry season into the wet. In October, the south-east trade is blowing; days are usually sunny; rainfall and humidity are low. But by about the end of the year conditions have normally changed. Humidity rises, and heavy rains impede outdoor work and make tracks slippery or impassable. The attractiveness of island life—even to a young man of romantic inclinations—is sensibly diminished.

In December, or early in January 1809, the brig *Perseverance* called at Bua for sandalwood.[19] It is likely that Dillon assisted her master to obtain a cargo and highly probable that, when she sailed, he travelled in her to Sydney.

The *Perseverance* was owned by Robert Campbell, of the Calcutta firm that had employed Dillon's friend, Captain Burnsides. She had called at Bua on her return from a voyage to the Society Islands. But Campbell was apparently encouraged by the evidence he received on the future prospects of the sandalwood trade. The brig was at once prepared for a further trip to Fiji. Less than a week after she reached Sydney, on 20 February, a government notice was issued listing those who were about to leave the colony in her; it included the name 'Peter Dellon' (a fairly obvious misprint for Dillon).[20]

The *Perseverance* finally sailed on 27 March.[21] In May Campbell despatched a second small vessel to join her. This was the *Hunter*, commanded by Captain Robson, and owned by Campbell & Company of Calcutta.[22] It was intended that the sandalwood acquired by the *Perseverance* should be transferred to her, for disposal in China, and that the brig should then collect a second cargo to bring back to Sydney. But Campbell's expectations were not borne out by events.[23] The *Perseverance* returned to Sydney on 15 September without cargo, her master reporting that all the wood he had been able to obtain had been loaded on to the *Hunter* but that, when he had sailed from Vanua Levu on 8 August, Robson had still been attempting to complete his cargo.[24]

DILLON remained in Sydney till mid-October. Anthony Burnsides, who had arrived in the colony shortly before the *Perseverance* had sailed in March, was still there, awaiting a passage to England.[25] But it was another Irishman with Indian experience, Thomas Reibey, who provided Dillon with his next employment. Reibey was joint owner, with Edward Wills, of the *Mercury*, a schooner of fifty-three tons, which was being sent to the Society Islands for a cargo of salt pork.

Colonial vessels had been visiting Tahiti and the other islands of the Society group for more than eight years; and whalers and traders bound for Sydney from more distant parts of the Pacific had occasionally called there. Many of them had engaged Society Islanders as seamen. Moreover, Sydney had become the centre through which the London Missionary Society maintained contact with its workers in the Pacific. Though the mission stations established in Tongatapu and Tahuata in 1797 had been abandoned, that in Tahiti had survived. The Reverend Samuel Marsden acted as the Society's New South Wales representative, and missionaries going to or leaving the field generally visited Sydney. Information about the islands quickly passed into circulation—through merchant houses and taverns and the pages of the *Sydney Gazette*. The early descriptions of Tahiti by Cook and others were thus supplemented by detailed accounts of more recent events.

For many people in Sydney interest in the Society Islands had a primarily professional emphasis. Merchants and mariners were interested in the prospects of profitable trade, government officers in the conduct of British seamen and the apprehension of escaped convicts. But the effective pursuit of these interests required an understanding of local affairs. In particular, the changing fortunes of the chief Pomare

II of Tahiti affected the whole range of European relations with the islands.

At the time of Wallis's visit in 1767 and of Cook's first visit two years later, Pomare II's father and grandfather had been chiefs of Pare, a district immediately to the south of Matavai Bay, where both explorers anchored. Before Cook's second visit, however, they had gained paramountcy over Te Porionu'u, a major division of the island comprising Pare and the district to the north of it, which included Matavai. Of Tuamotuan origin in the male line, their family had built up its standing through a succession of advantageous marriages in Tahiti. Pomare II's grandfather, Teu, had further enhanced the family's position by marrying a daughter of Tamatoa, the paramount chief of Ra'iatea. When Cook found Teu's son, Tu Vaira'atoa, treated with supreme deference at Matavai, he seems to have assumed that he was king of the whole of Tahiti. And from that time onwards Tu—who later took the name Pomare—used the friendship of Europeans as an additional means for the attainment of his dynastic ambitions.

Bligh, who was sent to Tahiti to transplant the breadfruit tree to the British West Indies, and Vancouver, who called there on a voyage of exploration, similarly made their headquarters at Matavai, as did the missionaries in 1797. Pomare benefited from the respect that was shown him and from the gifts that were bestowed upon him. He was able to negotiate new alliances; and, when the *Bounty* mutineers returned to Tahiti after the disastrous termination of Bligh's first expedition, he enlisted them in his forces.

The foundation of a mission settlement changed the context of Pomare's association with foreigners, rather than its basic character. The missionaries came to recognize that Pomare was not 'king' and that his rise had created bitter antagonism among other chiefs and their supporters. But they were forced by circumstances to become even more firmly committed to his cause than their naval predecessors had been. Pomare well knew the value of friendship with Europeans. He helped and protected the missionaries, as did his son, Pomare II, after his father's death in 1803. The existence of the mission, in turn, encouraged the growth of commerce. The masters of whalers and of trading vessels soon came to regard Matavai as the safest port in the South Seas. The people were always eager to barter hogs, fruit and vegetables for European clothes, tools and firearms; and the missionaries were available to act as interpreters or to remove misunderstandings. The importation of muskets and gunpowder presented the missionaries with something of a moral problem, but not with a practical one. They could not prevent the trade and therefore contented themselves with ensuring that firearms were acquired principally by the Pomares.

This further encouragement of the Pomares' ambitions exacerbated earlier tensions. There were minor skirmishes from time to time and frequent rumours of imminent major conflict. Finally, in November 1808, there was a large-scale rising against Pomare II. The brig *Perseverance* was then at the island, about to sail for Fiji. Her departure was delayed, to give the missionaries time to decide whether to remain or to embark in her. In the event, most of them requested a passage to Huahine, in the Leeward group.[26]

The great knowledge of the literature of Pacific exploration that Dillon subsequently possessed was almost certainly acquired at a later stage of his career. But he cannot have been unaware, at this time, of the classical portraits of Tahitian society, for stories of the explorers' visits and of Bligh and the mutiny on the *Bounty* had become part of the European heritage. Of more recent events he must have heard much from the men on the *Perseverance* and probably also from other sailors, including Tahitians, encountered in Fiji and in Sydney. The total impression made upon him by these varied accounts cannot have been other than powerful. Curious, sensual, passionate, responsive to the claims of alien cultures, he seems certain to have embarked on the voyage to the Society Islands with high expectations.

Thomas Reibey himself may have talked to Dillon about the islands, for some two years earlier he had sailed as master of the *Mercury* on her first voyage in the pork trade. Like many mariners bound from Sydney for the tropical South Pacific, he had called at the Bay of Islands, in northern New Zealand, to purchase fresh provisions (particularly potatoes). Thence, presumably, he followed the usual course and sailed before the westerlies till he reached the longitude of the Society Islands before turning north. The first part of the *Mercury*'s cargo was obtained in Tahiti. Then she had proceeded to Huahine and Ra'iatea. Good relations were established with Pomare II and with leading chiefs in the Leeward Islands. Tapoa, an important chief of Borabora who had also attained great influence in Ra'iatea, where he had kinship ties with Tamatoa, was especially helpful. When Reibey decided to have the schooner hove down before sailing for Sydney, Tapoa had a storehouse built to contain everything that had to be unloaded. On less practical grounds, as well, Reibey was pleased with his venture. At Ra'iatea, he was shown a medallion bearing the inscription 'Resolution and Adventure MDCCLXXII', which had been given to its owner's father; and, when the *Mercury* was hove down, he was told he had moored her to the tree chosen by Cook for the same purpose over thirty years before.[27]

The plan for the *Mercury*'s second voyage in the pork trade was based upon that of the first. On this occasion the schooner sailed from Sydney on 17 October 1809, with Theodore Walker as master and James Tait as mate.[28] Dillon shipped as a seaman.[29] Among the other members of the crew was a Society Islander known as 'Bolabola'—presumably a native of Borabora.

Early in November the *Mercury* reached the Bay of Islands. Four other vessels lay at anchor; and Maori canoes were constantly passing back and forth, visiting the shipping and travelling between the settlements that dotted the islands and intricate shores of the Bay. Dillon went ashore several times. He was pleased with this first experience of New Zealand. He liked the Maori people whom he met and considered them dignified, courteous and helpful. He also had talks with a Tahitian named Jemmy who, in Marsden's words, 'could speak English exceedingly well'. Jemmy had lived for some time with John Macarthur, one of the most prominent men in New South Wales. At this stage, he was on the point of taking as his wife the daughter of a chief of the Aupouri tribe and of settling permanently in New Zealand.[30] The establishment of this contact with Jemmy was characteristic of Dillon, who, throughout his career in the Pacific, always sought the acquaintance of islanders of character and wide experience.

Walker, meanwhile, was attending to the business of the schooner. He had no difficulty in buying fish from canoe parties that visited her, or in obtaining labour for the cutting and loading of firewood. But in relation to the major purpose of his visit—the laying in of potatoes for the voyage—he was unsuccessful. He was at the Bay two months earlier in the year than Reibey had been. The people insisted that they had no potatoes ready to sell; and Dillon understood that the crop had not yet matured. But Walker did not comprehend, or would not accept, this explanation. One evening, Dillon said later, when Walker was 'in a state of intoxication', he compelled Dillon and two other members of the crew to accompany him ashore.

> We rowed to a piece of ground planted with potatoes. We landed on the Beach and walked a little way thro' the Bush to the Ground. We had a

Bucket and a Bag. We pulled up several of the stalks of the potatoes—some had potatoes to them—some had not. What with pulling them up and walking over them we destroyed the greatest part of them. I was armed with a musquet and ammunition . . . Walker had a carbine. Towards the middle of the night we returned on Board.[31]

A day or so later, Walker decided to seize a supply of potatoes that he believed a local chief had in store.

The chief was Te Pahi, a man of high rank and much influence. Although he had complained to the Governor of New South Wales of misconduct by whalers, he was recognized as a good friend to Europeans. Several years earlier, he and his sons had visited the colony, where they had stayed with the Governor and been introduced to some of the leading settlers. Samuel Marsden wrote of him:

> He possessed a clear, strong, and comprehensive mind, and was anxious to gain what knowledge he could of our laws and customs. He was wont to converse much with me about our God, and was very regular in his attendance at church on the Sabbath. . . [32]

Marsden counted upon his support for the mission he hoped to establish, and New South Wales officials regarded his sympathetic interest in commerce as a factor conducive to peaceful relations between Maoris and Europeans at the Bay of Islands.

Te Pahi's position did not affect Walker's decision, however, when he sent an armed boat crew, under James Tait, to raid the chief's storehouse.[33] On this occasion, Dillon volunteered his services, intending to desert, he said, as soon as the boat reached the shore.[34] But his offer was refused, and he continued to the Society Islands.

Because of the report of civil war in Tahiti, the *Mercury* sailed direct to Huahine, where she cast anchor on 8 January 1810. Like all the larger islands in the group, Huahine is mountainous and forested to the shore. The white coral sand of the beach is partially covered by a luxuriant growth of convolvulus. Behind the beach, thatched houses lay scattered among groves of coconut palms and breadfruit trees. The physical setting was well suited to the gracious and unhurried way of life described by the explorers.

The visitors soon learnt, however, that the political situation remained disturbed. Pomare was awaiting the arrival of reinforcements from the Leeward Islands before attempting to reassert his authority. Some months earlier a small Sydney schooner, the *Venus*, had been seized by the Tahitian 'rebels'; the mate had been killed and the master and crew taken prisoner. The *Venus* had subsequently been recaptured, and her company released, by William Campbell, now master of the *Hibernia*. But the missionaries had been so depressed by developments that most of them had embarked in the *Hibernia* for Sydney.[35]

When the *Mercury* arrived at Huahine, it was still possible to contract with the people for the supply of salt pork. The chiefs were committed, however, to providing military assistance to Pomare; and, before the schooner was a quarter laden, they issued a general call to arms. At that stage Walker decided to sail to Borabora, the westernmost of the major islands of the Leeward group.

Even at Borabora there were repercussions of the Tahitian war. As the *Mercury* entered the lagoon, she was boarded by an islander, who handed Walker a letter signed by Pomare.

> Sir,
> In consequence of a rebellion that has taken place on the Island, you will do well to be cautious where you anchor: but if you will follow the bearer's direction, he will pilot your vessel where you will be under my protection.
> I am, Sir, Your sincere friend,
> Pomarre,
> King of Taheite.[36]

Walker acted on the proferred advice, which he later concluded had probably made the difference between commercial success and the seizure of the schooner.[37] And he found Pomare's allies, who were the followers of Tapoa, to possess 'a greater share of honesty, and a more zealous inclination to render service to a stranger' than any others in the islands. When the *Mercury* returned to her home port, on 3 May, she was considered by the *Sydney Gazette* to have made an 'expeditious voyage', despite 'the conditions that prevail'.[38]

FOR Dillon, the pleasures of return were soon clouded by ill news. Shortly after the *Mercury* had sailed from the Bay of Islands, the ship *Boyd* had called at Whangaroa, a harbour some distance farther north, on her voyage to England. There she had been seized by Maoris and nearly all those on board had been massacred. Among them was Anthony Burnsides.[39]

Dillon appears, at first, to have seen the tragedy primarily in terms of the loss of life it had entailed. And he later wrote:

There was an East-India captain named Burnsides, who was a passenger in her, and who having by industry accumulated a fortune of £30,000, was on his return to end his days among his friends on the banks of the Liffey. This was an object poor Burnsides had always kept in view: it was the goal of his long and arduous exertions; a subject to which with much fondness he constantly reverted, during the period I had been intimately acquainted with him. But, alas! he was doomed to end his days far otherwise than among his friends: he never again beheld the populous banks of the river Liffey, but was murdered on the savage shores of the Wangerao.[40]

Some time later Dillon heard other stories about the massacre. The masters of whaling and sealing vessels which were on the New Zealand coast shortly afterwards believed that Te Pahi, of the Bay of Islands, had ordered the attack, and they had sent an armed party to his settlement in search of possible survivors. Fighting had ensued, in which over sixty Maoris were killed and Te Pahi himself was mortally wounded. Dillon was told that the chief had turned against Europeans because of the destruction of his potato ground by men from the *Mercury*.[41]

The story of Te Pahi's involvement caused some perturbation in Sydney. Marsden disbelieved it: he thought Te Pahi had been confused with another chief possessing a not dissimilar name.[42] Dillon's initial attitude is less clear. He had a strong sympathy towards Polynesians and seems already to have been forming the opinion that they were often the victims of European callousness and brutality. The problem continued to trouble him; and many years later he obtained an explanation from a Maori that exonerated Te Pahi. But he was a complex man. His humane opinions were firmly held; but they were expressed most strongly in circles where they would be acceptable. And he did not allow them to obstruct him in the pursuit of his immediate interests. Now twenty-two years of age, ambitious, and fascinated by the islands, he agreed to serve again under Theodore Walker.

Wills and Reibey had been pleased with the results of the previous voyage. They entered into an arrangement with Isaac Nichols, a government official who was also engaged in commerce. Nichols was the owner of the fifty-eight ton *Endeavour*, which was to accompany the *Mercury* on a further visit to the Society Islands. James Tait became master of the *Mercury* and Walker transferred to the *Endeavour*. In the list of those about to depart in the latter Dillon's name appeared next to Walker's—as '*Mr.* Peter Dillon', a dignity bestowed only on a mate or supercargo.⁴³ On the outward voyage he almost certainly served as mate.

The two vessels sailed from Sydney on 20 July 1810 and arrived on the coast of Tahiti about the beginning of September.⁴⁴ This was Dillon's first sight of the island and of its neighbour, Mo'orea, ten miles to the west. With their heavily eroded peaks rising like gigantic, crumbling battlements and pinnacles from deep, shadowed valleys and dank forest, their summits often hidden in cloud, they present a memorable spectacle to the weary seafarer. As he comes nearer, the scale changes. He sees the groves of coconut palms, the smoke of fires, the canoes of fishermen, inhales the perfume of trees and flowers; hears the dull roar of the ocean breaking upon the reef. If he is a man of Dillon's temperament, he experiences something of the exhilaration described by Commerson—and so actively responded to by the *Bounty* mutineers.

The *Endeavour* and *Mercury* were welcomed with the traditional signs of friendship. As they entered a bay towards evening, canoes came out and invited the visitors ashore to trade. But, as the people were understood to be 'rebels', it was decided that no one should land till next day. At dawn the beach was crowded with pigs. They were, however, apparently intended as a snare. Walker and Tait later reported that, at this stage, a 'worthy female by stratagems found timely access to them' and told them 'the dreadful secret of a plot to decoy the crews on shore, there treacherously to surprise and murder them', so that possession might be obtained of the schooners. They decided to leave Tahiti and sail to Mo'orea. But even this action had to be taken with care, lest the Tahitians should see them preparing to depart and attempt to seize the vessels.⁴⁵

Pomare was then living in Mo'orea, in company with Henry Nott, one of two missionaries who had remained in the islands. Tait delivered a sword to him, presented by Wills and Reibey, 'as acknowledgement of past kindnesses', and a letter to Nott, who was believed to have proposed, and probably to have drafted, the letter of warning to mariners visiting Borabora. The owners of the *Mercury* thanked Nott 'for his advice and very able assistance on her last voyage, without which she would very probably have fallen into the hands of the rebel party'.⁴⁶

Dillon and his colleagues heard the news of the islands from Pomare and Nott. Pomare's military position, though still not secure, was gradually improving. Trading vessels were continuing to visit him and bring him firearms. In the previous month a large group of Leeward Islanders, led by two chiefs of Borabora, had arrived to join his forces. But a larger group, under Tapoa, was still detained at Huahine awaiting suitable weather for sailing to the Windward Islands by canoe. A little earlier Tapoa had proposed the seizure of a visiting American ship; but the rulers of Huahine, who saw that their own people would be blamed, declared that he would have to meet them in battle first.[47] The visitors also heard another story which, although it was unconnected with the war, similarly emphasized the uncertainties of life in the islands. Michael Fodger, of the *Trial*, who was making Mo'orea his base while he traded for pork, pearl-shell, bêche-de-mer and sandalwood, had left a pearling gang of four Europeans and several islanders ashore in the Tuamotus. Three of the Europeans had subsequently been killed but only—Pomare insisted—after they had themselves committed murder.[48]

Dillon's contact with Society Islands affairs had been substantially widened by the abortive call at Tahiti and the visit to Mo'orea; but his association with them was soon to become much more intimate. From Mo'orea, it appears, the *Endeavour* sailed to Huahine and brought back Tapoa and a party of nearly three hundred warriors to join Pomare's forces.[49] Then she proceeded to Borabora, where Dillon was put ashore.[50] He was to purchase pigs and prepare canoes of salt pork, first for the two vessels on their present voyage and, later, for other callers.

Borabora is one of the most striking, and most beautiful, islands in the South Seas. From Huahine, the easternmost of the Leeward Islands, it appears like a gigantic obelisk rising almost sheer from the ocean. In fact, the central mountain rises from a lower range of hills falling to a narrow coastal flat, and coconut-clad islets occupy much of the reef which encircles the broad lagoon. On the west a passage leads to safe anchorage off the village of Waitape.

The visual dominance of Borabora had been paralleled, in recent years, by its political role. The steep slopes of the mountain provided effective positions for defence during local wars and in case of attack from other islands. Tapoa had taken advantage of the apparent security of his home base and of his ties of kinship with important families in the neighbouring islands to attain a temporary primacy in Taha'a and, as Reibey had found in 1807, to some extent in Ra'iatea. But his long absence had encouraged his rival, the chief Mai, in Borabora. The resultant unsettlement, as well as the Tahitian war, almost certainly contributed to the situation that had existed during the *Mercury*'s visit early in 1810. The *Endeavour* and *Mercury* did not sail for Sydney till March 1811. The latter returned towards the end of the year.

Dillon lived for more than a year on Borabora in the family of 'the most powerful chief' in the Leeward Islands. This was Tapoa, whose adopted son he stated that he became.[51] During this period he was in intermittent contact with visiting traders—at least two other vessels visited the islands for pork—but he spent his time mainly with the local people, becoming fluent in their language and acquiring knowledge of their history and customs.

No doubt news of Pomare's peaceful visit to Tahiti early in 1811 filtered back to Borabora—not least because of the dignified reception reputedly accorded to Tapoa by the Tahitian rebels. And Dillon himself seems to have travelled to other islands of the Leeward group. He became a friend of Fenuapeho, the leading chief of Taha'a and a man deeply committed to traditional ways. One of Fenuapeho's daughters apparently became his mistress.[52]

The understanding that Dillon gained through involvement in the daily lives of the people must be largely inferred, since he later referred only in passing to this part of his career. But he clearly learnt of the ties of kinship that led the chiefs of the Leeward Islands to go to Pomare's support. He must have learnt, too, that this common action was not inconsistent with the survival of intense rivalries between the leading chiefs. Tapoa's long contest with his kinsman, Tamatoa, for influence in Ra'iatea, and the chief Mai's thrust for dominance in Borabora, had not prevented all three from taking their followers to join Pomare's forces. Yet Tapoa's association with the Tahitian rebels suggested that his loyalty to Pomare was limited by his own ambitions. One consequence of Dillon's residence in the Leeward Islands is, however, fully attested by later events: it created ties between him and several important chiefly families that long survived his departure.

Dillon later wrote that he lived in the islands 'from October 1810 till March 1812'.[53] If this statement is correct, he must have sailed in the *Mercury*, which left Borabora on 17 March, with Henry Nott as passenger. After calling at Norfolk Island, the *Mercury* reached Sydney on 27 May.[54]

THREE

The Path to 'Dillon's Rock'

1813

DILLON's movements in the months following his return to Sydney remain obscure. He later referred to a meeting at this time with Fa'aanuhe, a Ra'iatean 'commonly known among Europeans by the name of *Big Jack*'. He said that Fa'aanuhe had been taken aboard the *Endeavour* by Captain Walker at the end of 1810 and that he had first met him when the brig returned to Borabora. Subsequently Fa'aanuhe had left the *Endeavour* in Sydney because Walker 'would give him but little for his services'. For this action he had been gaoled and put on a diet of bread and water. Later he had been returned to the *Endeavour*. He was reluctant to work again for Walker, however; and, when the captain refused to have him landed in the brig's boat, he had jumped overboard and swum ashore. Fa'aanuhe told him this story, Dillon said, when he came to see him on board the *Trial*.[1]

The brig *Trial*, in which Captain Fodger had been trading among the islands, had returned to Sydney in September 1811; at the end of 1812 she was under repair.[2] In the intervening period—when her movements are unrecorded—it is not unlikely that she was engaged in the coastal trade. Dillon may have served in her—or merely have lived on board. By about the end of the year, however, he was at Norfolk Island.

At that period ships were visiting Norfolk Island to move the inhabitants to Van Diemen's Land. Whalers also put in there, as did traders bound from Sydney for the South Sea Islands. The manner of Dillon's arrival is unknown; but the circumstances of his departure are both recorded and of particular relevance to his later life. In January 1813 the *Hunter*, of Calcutta, called at the island on her way to Fiji. Her master, James Robson, may already have been acquainted with Dillon, since they had been on the coast of Vanua Levu at the same time during 1809. In any event, he offered him the position of third mate, which Dillon accepted.³

The appointment—as an officer in a vessel such as the *Hunter*—represented professional advancement for Dillon. But, on the voyage northward, he heard stories that disturbed him. In August 1809, when the *Perseverance* had sailed from Vanua Levu, with Dillon on board, Robson had been having difficulty completing his cargo of sandalwood. None the less, he had returned to Fiji two years later. It emerged that he had finally resolved his problem by entering into an alliance with the chief Vonasa, of Wailea village, in Naurore Bay. He had repaid the people of Wailea for their work in cutting and loading sandalwood by helping them to make war on their neighbours, some of whom, according to Dillon, had been 'cut up, baked, and eaten in his presence'.⁴

On the present voyage the *Hunter*'s difficulties began even before she reached her destination. Most sandalwood traders entered Fijian waters from the east, thus passing through the islands of Lau and Lomaiviti *en route* to Vanua Levu. Robson apparently followed a more direct course from Norfolk Island. This brought the *Hunter* to the almost unknown south-east coast of Viti Levu, where, in the vicinity of Laucala Bay, she ran aground on a reef and there 'lost her false keel and sustained other Material damage'.⁵

NAURORE Bay, which was reached on the afternoon of 19 February, is a deep inlet in the north-west coast of Vanua Levu.⁶ It is protected to the north and north-west by the mountainous island of Yaqaga, which lies several miles off the coast. The bay is bounded on the west by the jagged and irregular mountains of the Naivaka Peninsula. Farther east—beyond a strip of low land adjoining the peninsula—it is bordered by mangrove swamp, intersected by streams. Behind the mangroves, valleys and low ridges merge into higher hills and plateaux, which are broken by massive outcrops of black lava. As the afternoon advances, and the sun moves behind Yaqaga and then Naivaka, the deeply shadowed mountains form an increasingly dramatic backdrop to the placid waters of the bay.

The *Hunter* anchored about a quarter of a mile off the entrance to a creek that led through the mangroves to Wailea, Dillon's 'Vilear'. Even before the anchor was dropped, Vonasa's brother came aboard to welcome Robson; and he was soon followed by the chief himself. On Vonasa's invitation, Robson visited the village, accompanied by

Dillon. They were received with formality and presented with a pig, yams and coconuts.

This welcome was not wholly the expression of simple friendship. Vonasa related that, soon after the *Hunter*'s departure in 1811, the villages which had been conquered with Robson's help had risen in revolt, in alliance with Dreketi,[7] a district farther east. He hinted that these enemies would strike again, if the men of Wailea were dispersed in small parties cutting sandalwood, and asked the captain to join him at once in a new campaign. Robson declined. But over the ensuing six weeks, as sandalwood came in very slowly, Vonasa and his associates continually repeated the request. They promised that the ship should be loaded within two months of a military victory.

Eventually Robson capitulated, and at the beginning of April an armed force set out for Dreketi. Three of the *Hunter*'s boats, one mounted with a cannon, contained twenty musketeers. A fleet of forty-six canoes carried, at Dillon's estimation, a thousand armed men; and a still larger Fijian force travelled overland. On the morning of 4 April the flotilla entered the Dreketi River on its way to Bekavu, a fortified islet several miles upstream. As it passed the mouth of the river, Dillon relates, it was 'saluted by showers of arrows and stones from slings by the enemy who were standing on its banks'. When it reached Bekavu, the cannon opened fire on the fortifications; and the defenders of the island fled to the mainland, where they were pursued with musket fire. The flotilla then proceeded farther up the river 'and destroyed the towns and plantations on its banks'.

That evening the war party camped beside the river. Eleven of the Dreketi people had been killed during the day and their bodies recovered. One corpse was 'despatched in a fast-sailing canoe' to Wailea, to provide a feast for those who had stayed at home. The remainder were prepared for the warriors. Dillon observed the scene.

> The dead bodies were placed on the grass and dissected by one of the priests. The feet were cut off at the ankles, and the legs from the knees; afterwards the private parts; then the thighs at the hip joints; the hands at the wrists, the arms at the elbows, the shoulders at the sockets; and lastly, the head and neck were separated from the body. Each of these divisions of the human frame formed one joint, which was carefully tied up in green plantain leaves, and placed in the ovens to be baked, with the *tara* [taro] root.

Several days later the war party returned to Wailea.

The *Hunter* had already been visited by three foreigners living near by—two Europeans and a Lascar, who had been discharged from sandalwood ships. Early in May a party of Europeans arrived by canoe. These men lived under the protection of Naulivou, the Vunivalu of Bau. The chiefs of this small island on the coast of Viti Levu had attained great power in much of coastal Fiji, through the prowess of their warriors at sea and through marriage into important chiefly families in other parts of the group. Naulivou had further strengthened the position of Bau by enlisting the services of Europeans, who were proficient in the use and servicing of firearms. For several months each year these men worked for the sandalwood traders in order to keep themselves supplied with liquor, tobacco, tools and other European goods. Robson engaged them at a wage of £4 a month, payable in trade goods.

Shortly before the arrival of the party from Bau, the *Hunter* had been joined by the *Elizabeth*, a cutter of thirty-four tons which Robson had brought from Calcutta in frame and had launched in Sydney.[8] As sandalwood was still not being received in satisfactory quantities, Robson decided to augment his cargo with bêche-de-mer. He heard it was plentiful on the reefs near Kaba Point, on the coast of Viti Levu, a few miles south of Bau. He therefore formed a party consisting of the Europeans from Bau and several members of the crew, placed it under Dillon's control, and landed it from the *Elizabeth* at Kaba Point.

Dillon and his party remained at Kaba for over three months and prepared about two tons of bêche-de-mer for shipment.[9] Fijians from Bau and villages associated with it were employed to collect the 'fish' from the reef, while the Europeans manned the boats and attended to the curing. This process—of which no details are given by Dillon—was usually carried out in a house specially built for the purpose. Shallow trenches were dug along each side of the house and platforms covered with reeds constructed above them. As the bêche-de-mer came in, it was spread out on the platforms and a slow fire kept burning in the trenches below. The preparation of a cargo of bêche-de-mer was thus an occupation that required considerable care and vigilance. But for Dillon—who later planned to write a history of Fiji 'from its first discovery to A.D. 1825'[10]—contact with the chiefs of Bau and with the Europeans working under him almost certainly provided the major interest of the months at Kaba.

One of the beachcombers from Bau was, indeed, a man of some local note. This was Charles Savage, a Swede, who had been in Fiji since the wreck of the *Eliza* in 1808 and had lived in Tonga before that. He seems to have been the first, and certainly became the most valued, European armed with a musket in the service of Naulivou. He took part in the conquest of Verata, the powerful northern neighbour of Bau. Subsequently, in equally successful campaigns to the southward, he was said to have used his musket from the security of a kind of sedan chair constructed of coconut sinnet, in which he was carried to within firing range of the enemy. Savage, it appears, further enhanced the reputation he gained from his military prowess by maintaining a degree of detachment from the domestic affairs of Bauan commoners. He was rewarded with a chiefly title and given two women of high rank as his wives.[11]

The other Europeans with Dillon were more typical beachcombers. Two of them were able to give him first-hand accounts, however, of an incident of which he had already heard. At Naurore Bay he had been told that the foreigners at Bau had made themselves extremely unpopular.

> Such was their bad and overbearing conduct, that the natives rose on them one day and killed three of them, before the king of Bow [Bau] had time to suppress the wrath of his people, who wished to destroy all the Europeans on the island.

One of the two was John Graham, who had first sailed to Fiji from Sydney as a youth in 1809 and later returned as an interpreter.[12] The other was Martin Buchert, a Prussian from Stettin, who had been in Fiji since 1810, and was later to play a significant role in Dillon's career.[13] Graham and Buchert had saved themselves from the consequences of the Fijian anger by swimming out to sea.[14]

Dillon was also in contact with Naulivou and other chiefs of Bau. Kaba and Bau are separated by a relatively short stretch of protected water, over which, for much of its distance, a canoe can be propelled by a pole. Moreover, the people of Nabouwalu village, at Kaba Point, owed allegiance to Naulivou, who held the title of Tui Kaba. Movement between the two places was thus frequent and easy; and Dillon formed a close relationship with Naulivou and his brothers.

Dillon's period at Kaba came to an end when the *Elizabeth* returned late in August. As Robson had brought no trade goods to pay for the work that had been done, the Europeans also travelled in the cutter to Naurore Bay, and a party of over 200 Fijians accompanied them in two canoes.

Nearly five months had now passed since the chiefs of Wailea had promised to complete the *Hunter*'s cargo of sandalwood within two months of the victory at Dreketi; but they had brought in only 150 tons—no more than a third of a cargo. Even worse, they had 'declared their inability to procure more wood', as the forest had been so largely cut out in supplying earlier traders. Relations between them and Robson had consequently become tense. Dillon later wrote:

> The chiefs and men of consequence kept away from the ship, being apprehensive they might be detained as hostages until their engagements ... were completed. Captain Robson was very much displeased at this trick played on him by a savage and cunning people, and vowed vengeance against his old and faithful allies, whose stomachs he had so often helped to glut with the flesh of their enemies.

Shortly after Dillon's return, the Waileans declared that a large quantity of sandalwood was ready for loading at Macuata Island, some forty miles to the eastward. Robson and Dillon therefore set out in the cutter, accompanied by a number of Wailean canoes. But, when they reached their destination, they found that the sandalwood amounted only to 'three small boat Loads'. Soon after they had made this discovery, Charles Savage arrived in a Bauan canoe, with a message for Robson from the *Hunter*'s first officer. This seems to have been a warning that an attempt might be made to seize the cutter, for Robson detained one Fijian and sent seven or eight others back by canoe with a note that they should be confined on board the *Hunter*.

A day or so later, when the *Elizabeth* was returning towards Naurore Bay, she encountered a fleet of canoes, manned by armed warriors. On Robson's orders, it was attacked. Some ten canoes were sunk, and one Fijian was killed. That evening a letter was received from the first officer, in which he reported that he had set fire to part of Wailea village and killed some of its inhabitants.

It was now impossible to continue trading for sandalwood. Neither vessel was yet ready to sail, however, as both the *Elizabeth* and the *Hunter* had been aground. Robson deemed it prudent to have repairs made to both vessels before they continued their respective voyages; and, in the case of the cutter, he proposed that these should be undertaken by hauling her ashore. He recognized, however, that this proposal would be difficult to execute in the midst of hostile Fijians. He resolved his dilemma by accepting the advice of the Bauans that before work on the two vessels began a landing party should destroy the Wailea canoes that had not already been sunk.[16]

On the morning of 6 September three boat-loads of men, all armed with muskets, were rowed ashore from the *Hunter*.[17] They included the *Hunter*'s officers (Norman, Cox and Dillon), crew members from the snow and the cutter, and the beachcombers who had been with Dillon at Kaba. They were joined by about a hundred of the Fijians from Bau, under the leadership of their chiefs, a brother and a nephew of Naulivou. The party landed at a place known as the Black Rock, the only point on the eastern side of the bay where the shore was not screened by mangroves. The boats and canoes were then taken out into deep water to prevent their grounding at low tide.

When the party had assembled on shore, Norman, the chief officer, declared that the tide had already fallen too far to permit the Wailean canoes to be removed from the creek so that they could be sunk. It was therefore agreed that the party should proceed towards the village.[18] At this stage, to Dillon's disquiet, 'the Europeans began to disperse into straggling parties of two, three, and four in a group'. The leaders, including Norman and Dillon, walked for some distance along a level track and then ascended a hill, at the top of which they were cursorily challenged by a few Fijians. At this point, Norman turned on to a path that led to a small hamlet, towards which he was followed by Dillon, the Bauan chiefs, and some others. Here, the group was challenged again, but this time 'in a threatening Manner', with the brandishing of spears and clubs.[19] In retaliation, some of the intruders discharged their muskets, killing one of the defenders, and set fire to the houses, all of which 'were in flames in a few seconds'.

Soon afterwards, Dillon recounts, they heard the beating of a Fijian drum and 'dreadful yells and shoutings' from the track below them. They learnt from the Bauan chiefs that the commotion indicated that members of the landing party had been killed. 'We determined', Dillon continues, 'to keep close together and fight our way back to the boats'. But, when they reached the top of the track running down the hill, they realized that the Waileans must have called in their allies from many parts of the coast, for the land between them and the boats was 'covered with thousands of infuriated savages, all armed'. At their feet was the body of Terence Dunn—an Irishman living at Wailea—'with his brains beaten out by a native club'. Overwhelmed by the situation the young John Graham ran off into the bush, where he was pursued and killed by Fijians. A moment later Norman was struck by a spear 'which entered his back and passed out of his breast'.

Dillon fired at Norman's killer. When he had reloaded his musket,

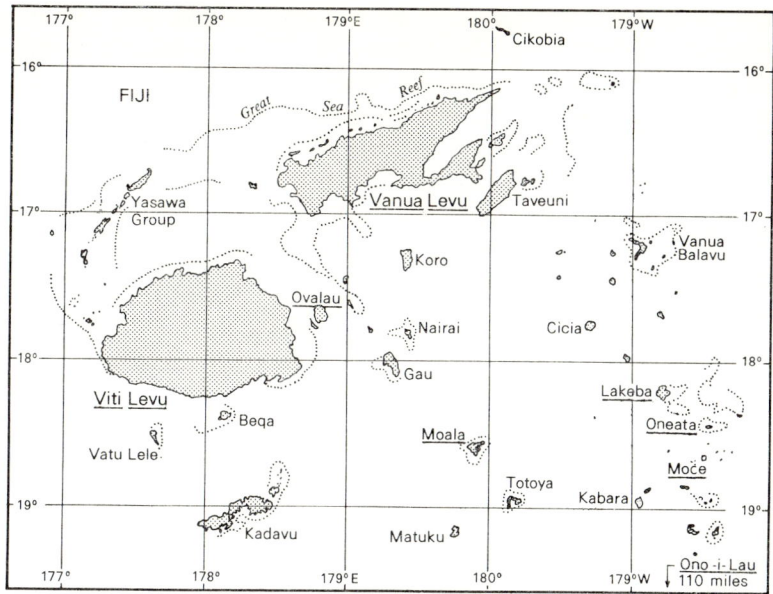

1 The Fiji Islands

he found he had been deserted by the rest of the group and therefore concentrated on the preservation of his own life.

> Taking advantage of the absence of the natives, who had all quitted the path and pursued our unfortunate flying men, I dashed along with all the speed that was possible, but had not proceeded more than a few yards when I came on the dead body of William Parker [a European from Bau], who was prostrated across the path with his musket by him, which I took up and retreated with.
>
> About this time the natives observed me and gave chase. One of them came up so close to me that I was obliged to throw Parker's musket away, as also a pistol which I had in my belt. In a moment after this I reached the foot of a small steep rock that stood on the plain.

Dillon had by then joined other members of the landing party. As it was impossible to get back to the boats, he concluded that the best chance of safety lay in attempting to climb the rock and called out to his companions 'take the hill!'

The most probable site of 'Dillon's Rock' is on the seaward flank of Korolevu, a great flat-topped hill which dominates Naurore Bay (Plates 1 and 2). It is a hillock composed of black lava, which rises precipitately on three sides from the surrounding country. To the north it stretches out in a narrow spur, broken by one or two steps and with sheer faces on either side; on the top there is a flattish space from which the whole of the Bay is in sight, as well as the land below. There is thus little dead ground and, as may be seen from the map in Appendix II, it forms a commanding position readily defensible by a few men.

Of those who responded to Dillon's call, several were struck down by the Fijians and only five reached the summit with him: Charles Savage, Martin Buchert and 'Luis a Chinaman', all from Bau; and William Wilson and Thomas Dafny, both seamen from the *Hunter*. Dillon took command of this little group. Dafny was wounded and unarmed; the others possessed only a limited supply of ammunition. They soon found, however, that they were safe against attack from the flat land below them. Spears and stones hurled from slings could not reach the top of the hill, while arrows were turned from their course by the wind. Dillon therefore ordered that shots should be reserved for Fijians who climbed up to them and that only one or two muskets should be fired at a time.

After several Fijians had been killed, the attack was suspended; but to those on the hill this offered no more than a respite. Below them, preparations were being made for a cannibal feast:

> Fires were prepared and ovens heated for the reception of the bodies of our ill-fated companions, who, as well as the Bau chiefs and their slaughtered men, were brought to the fires in the following manner. Two of the Vilear [Wailea] party placed a stick or limb of a tree on to their shoulders, over which were thrown the bodies of their victims, with their legs hanging downwards on one side, and their heads at the other. They were thus carried in triumph to the ovens prepared to receive them. Here they were placed in a sitting posture while the savages sung and danced with joy over their prizes, and fired several musket-balls through each of the corpses, all the muskets of the slain having fallen into their hands. No sooner was this ceremony over than the priests began to cut up and dissect these unfortunate men in our presence. Their flesh was immediately placed in the ovens to be baked and prepared as a repast for the victors . . .

Dillon had hoped that Robson might attempt to rescue the survivors, with the help of the Bauans who had not been included in the landing party; but this hope was destroyed when he saw their two large canoes heading for the open sea. Instead of possible rescue, he now faced the danger of insubordination, as he overheard Savage proposing to Buchert that the two of them should climb down into the mangroves and attempt to swim to the ship. Only a threat to shoot the first deserter kept the group—for the time being—intact.

At this stage, discussions began with the Fijians. Dillon reminded them that eight men from the village were still held prisoner on board the *Hunter*. He said that they would be released if he and his companions were allowed to return to the ship. Eventually, after a priest had climbed the hill to negotiate with them, it was agreed that Dafny should deliver a message to Robson. According to Dillon, this was a proposal that four of the Wailea people should be sent ashore immediately and that a promise should be given that the remainder would be released and presented with 'a large chest of ironmongery, whales' teeth &c.' as soon as the men on the rock were safely on board.

After Dafny had passed unmolested through the Fijian warriors, several chiefs came up the hill. They protested their friendliness towards Dillon and the others and promised they would be safe if they left their retreat. Eventually Savage prevailed upon Dillon to allow him to accept the offer. He was convinced that, with his experience in Fiji and his fluency in the language, he could successfully make peace. He did, indeed, talk amicably for some time with Vonasa and other chiefs. Meanwhile, Luis had surreptitiously gone down the other side to place himself 'under the protection of a chief with whom he was intimately acquainted, and to whom he had rendered important service in former wars'. The chiefs then called out to Dillon, in Fijian: 'Come down, Peter, we will not hurt you: you see we do not hurt Charley!' When Dillon again refused to move, however, this semblance of friendship was at once abandoned.

> Charles Savage was seized by the legs, and held in that state by six men, with his head placed in a well of fresh water until he was suffocated; whilst at the same instant a powerful savage got behind the Chinaman, and with his huge club knocked the upper part of his skull to pieces.

As soon as they were dead, the two men were cut up and placed in the ovens.

The attack on the hill was then resumed with added ferocity. Of the three remaining defenders only Dillon and Buchert were competent marksmen; but, as they possessed four muskets between them, Wilson was able to have one loaded for each of them as soon as it was required. In this manner they fended off the attack. Buchert, Dillon writes, 'shot twenty-seven of the cannibals with twenty-eight discharges, only missing once'. Finally, when the defenders' supply of cartridges was almost exhausted, the Fijians desisted and shouted repeatedly that they would take the three men with ease as soon as it was dark. 'I was bespoken', Dillon writes, 'joint by joint by the different chiefs, who exultingly brandished their weapons in the air, and boasted of the number of white men each had killed that day'.

The Fijian expectations of imminent victory seemed, all too obviously, to be soundly based.

> Myself and companions, seeing no hope of mercy on earth, turned our eyes towards heaven, and implored the Almighty Ruler of all things to have compassion on our wretched souls... The only thing which prevented our surrendering quietly was, the dread of being taken alive and put to the torture.
>
> These people sometimes, but not very often, torture their prisoners in the following manner. They skin the soles of the feet and then torment their victims with firebrands, so as to make them jump about in that wretched state. At other times they cut off the prisoner's eye-lids and turn his face to the sun, at which he is obliged to look with his bare eyes: this is said to be a dreadful punishment. From the fingers of others they pull off the nails. By all accounts, however, these punishments are very rare, and only inflicted on persons who have given the greatest provocation; such as we had done this day, by shooting so many men in our own defence.

Dillon, Buchert and Wilson decided that, when darkness fell, they would discharge their final rounds into their own hearts.

By now the afternoon was well advanced, a time at which the offshore wind usually falls away. The sun, sinking behind the shadowed mountains of Yaqaga and Naivaka, illuminates a motionless landscape. This was the scene in which the three men on the hill-top awaited their fate against a background of exultant shouts from the Fijians feasting on human flesh below them. It was a classical setting for tragedy. And, when Dillon and his companions saw a boat pull out from the *Hunter* and land all eight of the hostages at the Black Rock, the end seemed inevitable, and near. 'I could not imagine how the captain could have acted in this strange way', Dillon later wrote, '... all hope seemed now fled ...'.

As soon as the former prisoners had rejoined their compatriots, they came up the hill, accompanied by the priest who had earlier talked with Dillon. The prisoners had received the chest of ironmongery, the priest said, and Robson had sent instructions that the Europeans were to hand over their arms and be escorted to the boat.[20] Once again, Dillon refused to leave the hill unarmed.

Then a plan of escape occurred to him:

> I tied Charles Savage's musket with my neck-handkerchief to the belt of my cartridge-box, and presenting my own musket to the priest's head, told him that I would shoot him dead if he attempted to run away, or if any of his countrymen offered to molest me or my companions. I then directed him to proceed before me to the boat, threatening him with instant death in case of non-compliance.

With Dillon walking behind the priest, and his armed companions on either side,[21] the little party 'passed along through the multitude'. As they went, the priest exhorted the Fijians not to harm 'Peter or his countrymen', since, if they did, his own death would follow and the gods would punish the transgressors. 'I had recourse to this dreadful expedient', Dillon later suavely commented, 'being aware of the influence and sway which the priests in all barbarous nations have over their votaries'.

When they neared the shore the priest refused to proceed farther. He declared that he would rather be shot than do so because—as he told Dillon—'you want to take me on board alive, and put me to the torture'.

> We then walked backwards to the water-side, and up to our breasts in water, where we joined the boat, and had no sooner got into her than the islanders came down, and saluted us with a shower of arrows, and stones from slings.

They rejoined the *Hunter* just as the sun was setting behind the Naivaka Peninsula.

THE events of 6 September 1813 are the only ones from Dillon's earlier life of which he wrote a detailed account for publication. Their horror, of course, engraved them for ever on his mind. 'Auch! an' it's not iv'ry one', he was wont to say, 'that's had the j'ints of him bespoke for supper by the haythin cannibals'.[22] But it was probably their consequences, rather than their innate quality, that led him to describe them so fully in his book, for many years later they led him to a discovery that transformed his life.

Back on board the *Hunter*, he learnt further details of the tragedy.

From the ship and the cutter, not only the chief officer but also the second, Charles Cox, had died, together with four others. Among the foreigners who had joined them in Fiji the loss had been heavier: those killed included six Europeans, Luis (the Chinese) and a Tahitian. And the Bauans had fared worst of all. Of the hundred who had joined the landing party only about forty had got back to the canoes, and many of these had been 'desperately wounded'. The remainder, including the two chiefs, were presumed to have died.

In view of what had happened Robson decided to sail at once for Canton. One difficulty that confronted him was the presence on board the *Hunter* of several men and women who did not wish to leave Fiji but could not safely be landed on the shore of Naurore Bay: Martin Buchert and his Fijian wife; a Lascar known as Joe; and two other Fijian women who had been living with Europeans. These five were ordered to embark in the *Elizabeth*, of which Dillon became master; and it was decided that, as she passed Bau, they should be transferred to a canoe which she carried on her deck. For six days after the weighing of the anchors, the two vessels were hindered by lack of wind. Then, as they neared Bau, the weather became tempestuous and the canoe could not be launched. The *Hunter* and *Elizabeth* therefore continued their voyage—towards the north-west.

A week later they sighted a small island, on which Buchert, whose wife was pregnant, and the Lascar expressed a wish to be landed. At first they believed it to be uninhabited; but, as they came nearer, canoes put out from the shore. It was the island of Tikopia, a Polynesian outlier of the Solomons. The men in the canoes were found to be friendly but unaccustomed to contact with Europeans.

> They came on deck without reserve, seized upon bars of iron from the forge, and jumped overboard with that metal, as also a frying-pan, the cook's axe, knife, saucepans, &c. The firing of a musket in the air had not the least effect upon them. I became alarmed on account of the smallness of the cutter in which I was, as they had only to make one step out of their canoes on board of it. On flourishing a light-horseman's sword, however, and cutting a piece out of the rail, it alarmed them. Those on deck jumped overboard, excepting one, who was carrying off our compass, when one of the Beetee [Fiji] girls on board became alarmed at our danger, and therefore seizing him by the throat with one hand and by the privates with the other, in this way got him under her, where she certainly would have strangled him, had I not interfered.

Order was finally restored when 'an elderly chief' came on board.

Dillon then went ashore, accompanied by the chief, Buchert and Joe. Buchert was introduced to the paramount chief. He gave him some presents and, 'by signs, words, and gestures', indicated that he and others wished to remain on the island. As the chief 'appeared much pleased with this arrangement', the two intending settlers returned to the cutter to pick up Buchert's wife and their personal possessions. Later, Dillon landed the party finally on Tikopia.

The *Hunter* and *Elizabeth* continued westward and next morning were in sight of 'a large high island', which Dillon later came to know was Vanikoro. Here they parted. The *Elizabeth*, carrying the other two Fijian women, who had been unwilling to remain on Tikopia, sailed for New South Wales. She reached Sydney on 22 October, just a month after leaving the *Hunter*.

FOUR

A Man of Consequence in Australia

1813-16

THE Sydney to which Dillon returned was a different place from that which he had first visited four years earlier. In 1809 the town had not outgrown the characteristics of its founding years. Public buildings were modest in scale and generally unimpressive in design. Many private houses and stores were constructed of unsawn logs or of wattle-and-daub. The roads, largely unmade, were waggon-rutted tracks, often impassable after rain. Pigs wandered freely on them and rubbish remained uncollected. The Tank Stream, which provided the town's water supply, was polluted by refuse and used for washing clothes. At night time, robberies and assaults were relatively commonplace. Moreover, because of the lack of roads, the town's connections with its environs were difficult and limited.

In 1809 New South Wales had been under the administration of Colonel William Paterson, of the New South Wales Corps, following the deposition of the Governor, William Bligh. By October 1813 it had experienced nearly four years of strong and energetic rule. Lachlan Macquarie, who had been sworn in as Governor on 1 January 1810, had shown himself to be devoted, with a passionate intensity, to the pursuit of order and of progress. He introduced a new street plan and directed that, wherever possible, streets were to be of a minimum width, with footways on both sides. The streets were signposted and the houses numbered. Leases of town sites were converted into permanent grants to encourage the construction of substantial buildings, the plans for which now required official approval. The erection of many new public buildings was begun and a new public market established. Police districts were organized, each centred on a watch-house, for the more effective maintenance of law and order, and a scavenging service was introduced to keep the town clean. Outside Sydney new townships were founded, and roads were built linking them and other near-by areas with the town. The population of Sydney itself—at about 5,300—seems to have somewhat declined, as a consequence of the greater dispersion of settlement. But, in terms of the ambitions and pretensions of both government and settlers, Sydney was now more recognizably the centre of a growing colony, the hub of a country that Macquarie was to recommend—several years later —should be known henceforth as 'Australia'.

Dillon was, of course, already familiar with some of these changes, since he had been back in 1810 and again in 1812. But, during his absence in Fiji, the character of the new Sydney had significantly developed, as plans reached fruition or action towards their implementation became apparent. He may have been conscious of this evolution as the *Elizabeth* entered Sydney harbour, for the newly completed road to the signal station at South Head had become popular with sightseers keen to observe the movements of shipping. It must have been brought home to him when she entered Sydney Cove. On the water's edge, to the west, stood the stone commissariat store, four storeys high, begun before Macquarie's time but only recently completed, and near it a new customs house. On a ridge, on the eastern side, the big new hospital was beginning to rise in Macquarie Street. Beyond the head of the Cove—in the heart of the town—many new buildings were under construction, mostly in brick.

When Dillon stepped ashore, he was confronted by much ampler evidence of the colony's development. Shortly before his return new currency had been introduced to smooth the working of the economy. Some months earlier—in May—three settlers, Blaxland, Lawson and Wentworth, had succeeded in crossing the Blue Mountains, west of Sydney, and thus shown the way to a vast expansion of colonial pastoralism. And scarcely less important was another development that had occurred more gradually: the change in status of the time-expired convicts or emancipists.

In 1809 officers, and former officers, of the New South Wales Corps had dominated the colony, economically as well as socially. Robert Campbell, with whom Dillon had had associations, was conspicuous, even as a free settler of substance and talent, through being outside their circle. Some emancipists had, indeed, been highly successful as merchants and farmers; but their social position, particularly in the eyes of government, continued to be determined by their past as convicts, not by their present role as responsible settlers. Macquarie early concluded that the leading emancipists constituted 'by many

Degrees the most useful members of the community'.[1] He therefore took action to improve their standing, not only in matters such as land grants, but also by appointing several of the most prominent of them as magistrates and entertaining them at Government House. Macquarie's policy towards the emancipists was opposed by the old establishment, strongly but, in the main, unsuccessfully. In effect, it provided New South Wales with the foundations of a new middle class, not exclusive in its criteria of acceptance but open to all men of talent.

If Sydney was a different place in 1813 from what it had been in 1809, so also was Dillon a different man. Then he had landed as a young seaman in a strange port. Now he arrived as the master of a vessel —even if only of a very small one. More importantly, he was the bearer of a dramatic and distressing story in which he himself played the leading part. The day after his return the *Sydney Gazette* carried an article headed 'Massacre at the Fejee Islands'. It began with the words: 'From Mr. Dillon, master of the *Elizabeth* cutter . . . we receive the melancholy information . . .'.[2] Dillon was a fine raconteur, and his vivid account of Robson's conduct and its tragic consequences attracted attention to his own courage and right thinking. During the bland spring days that followed, he was received by leading members of the Sydney community as a man of consequence.

Several of those who had been killed at Naurore Bay were members of Sydney families or were well known in the colony. One of these was Charles Cox, to whom Dillon later referred as 'a young man for whom I had a great regard'. On the morning after the massacre Dillon had obtained Robson's permission to his pulling close in shore with two of the *Hunter*'s boats in an attempt to recover Cox's bones. When his Bauan interpreter explained his purpose to the Waileans, 'They replied that they had neither the flesh nor the bones to spare, as they had all been devoured the night before'.[3] Cox was the son of a prominent settler, Captain William Cox, formerly paymaster of the New South Wales Corps and a successful farmer.[4]

But Dillon's story was examined in a broader context than that of personal loss. Since the beginning of the century senior government officers and men such as the Reverend Samuel Marsden had been worried by the lawless conduct of whalers and traders among the islands and by the likelihood of local retaliation. Their concern had been intensified by the *Boyd* massacre of 1809, and it was evident that, since then, the situation had been worsening rather than improving.

1 The affair at Dillon's Rock

2 Korolevu and Dillon's Rock from the sea

On 6 November Dillon made a deposition before a Justice of the Peace regarding the *Hunter*'s period in Fiji.[5] Three days later the brig *Endeavour* arrived from Tahiti with news that was perhaps even more disturbing.[6]

The *Queen Charlotte*, under the command of William Shelley (a former missionary), and the *Daphne*, commanded by Michael Fodger, had both been captured by Society Islanders employed as pearl divers. Captain Fodger and a number of others had been killed during the mutiny on board the *Daphne* and the two mates and another European during that on board the *Queen Charlotte*. Both brigs had subsequently been sailed back to Tahiti by the mutineers, where the *Queen Charlotte* was restored to the control of her master through the influence of Pomare and the *Daphne* was recaptured by Captain Walker of the *Endeavour*. Even in outline this was a sombre story; but, as detail was added, it became increasingly darker. Macquarie eventually concluded that Fodger's death had been 'but too just a Retaliation for Numerous Cruelties, which he had been guilty of to the Natives on every occasion of his Visiting those Islands'.[7] But, before that conclusion was expressed, two facts emerged that were deeply disturbing. One related to a matter on which no direct action could be taken: the leader of the mutiny in the *Queen Charlotte* had been Fa'aanuhe, the Ra'iatean who had earlier been harshly treated by Captain Walker. The other was of a different character: after the recapture of the *Daphne*, Walker had been told that a Lascar seaman still on board had supported the mutineers and had thereupon hanged him from the yard-arm. It was officially considered that Walker, who had returned to Sydney in the *Endeavour*, should be charged with murder.[8]

Samuel Marsden, who was a Justice of the Peace, initiated the move against Walker by obtaining statements concerning the killing of the Lascar.[9] Dillon assisted him by providing information about some of Walker's earlier actions. He made a deposition regarding the latter's conduct at the Bay of Islands in 1809 and a statement of what Fa'aanuhe had told him in Sydney in 1812.[10] But, despite the conclusiveness of the evidence, Walker was never convicted, because the New South Wales Supreme Court concluded that it lacked jurisdiction to try him, and a proposal that he should be sent to England for trial was not acted upon.[11]

The surge of opinion that had first been created by Dillon's story of events in Fiji did not end, however, in complete inaction. On 1 December the Governor issued a General Order requiring the master (or owners) of every British vessel sailing from Sydney for the Pacific Islands to enter into a bond on behalf of her company to refrain from acts of trespass or war against islanders and from interference in local disputes or in the exercise of indigenous religion. They were bound also to obtain the consent of chiefs and parents before accepting islanders as sailors or passengers. Macquarie fixed the penalty for a breach of the bond at £1,000.[12] He recognized that the order would be difficult to implement but hoped by the severity of the sanction imposed to frighten potential offenders. Three weeks later, on 20 December, a public meeting was held in Sydney, at the behest of Samuel Marsden and others, and a decision taken to form a New South Wales Society for the Protection and Civilisation of the Natives of the South Sea Islands. Marsden became the Society's secretary.[13]

DILLON was not present in Sydney when these later actions were taken. On 25 November he had sailed in the *Elizabeth* for Hobart Town, in Van Diemen's Land.[14] But soon after his return, on 20 January 1814, he was again in touch with Marsden.

For some years Samuel Marsden had been anxious to extend Christian missionary work to New Zealand through the agency of the Church Missionary Society. When he was in England some six years earlier, he had obtained the Society's approval of the proposal and the appointment of the first two members of the new mission. These men, William Hall and John King, sailed for New South Wales with him in the ship *Ann* in August 1809. Also on board was a young chief from the Bay of Islands, where the first mission station was to be situated. This was Ruatara, who, like his uncle, Te Pahi, became a good friend of Marsden. Soon after the party reached Sydney, however, news was received of the *Boyd* massacre and the subsequent killing of Te Pahi and many of his people. These events caused Marsden to postpone the execution of his plan, but not to abandon it. On the arrival in Sydney of a third member of the proposed mission—Thomas Kendall, a schoolmaster—in October 1813, he concluded that the time for action had at last arrived.

Marsden decided that he and two of the future settlers, Kendall and Hall, should pay a preliminary visit to the Bay of Islands to obtain the agreement of the local people and to assure themselves that the missionaries' wives and children could safely live there. He tried to charter a vessel for the voyage but was unable to do so on satisfactory terms. He therefore purchased the *Active*, a Calcutta-built brig of about 120 tons.¹⁵ He then discovered that memories of the *Boyd* massacre still cast a shadow over the New Zealand coasts, for he offered the command to several mariners, who declined from fear 'of being murdered and eaten', before he approached Dillon, who accepted.¹⁶

Years later Dillon wrote: 'With regard to my religion . . . I am a Catholic, but not an enthusiast'.¹⁷ And this seems to have been his position in 1814. He did not share Marsden's enthusiasm for turning Maoris into Anglicans or his views on sexual relations between Europeans and indigenes, though he was sympathetic to his desire to bring peace to the Bay of Islands. More pertinently, he was attracted by an offer that would give him both professional advancement and the prospect of interesting experience.

A crew was engaged—including a Hawaiian, a Tahitian, a Boraboran and a Maori, as well as Europeans of various nationalities—and Dillon was given his instructions. He was to sail first to Hobart Town to unload some cargo that had been on board the *Active* when Marsden bought her; then he was to proceed to the Bay of Islands. Marsden continued:

> The main object of this voyage is to promote a friendly intercourse with the natives of New Zealand. You will do all you can to prevent any quarrel between the natives and the ship's company. If Duaterra [Ruatara] or any other chiefs wish to come to Port Jackson you will receive them on board when you finally leave the island—or if they wish to send any of their children to be instructed, or a young man or two, these you may bring. I wish the natives to be treated with the greatest kindness while you remain there . . . On the Sabbath Day I wish Mr. Kendall to read on board, when the weather will permit, the prayers of the Church, and when you arrive at New Zealand I desire that you will be very particular in the observance of the Sabbath day; not buy or sell anything on that day, but all the sailors to be clean and do no work.

In a postscript he added: 'you will not suffer any of the native women to come on board, as this voyage is for a particular object'. One part of the instructions was more consistent, however, with Dillon's previous experience. Marsden was anxious to recoup the cost of the voyage, as far as possible, through the import of New Zealand products to Sydney. Dillon was therefore instructed to seek a return cargo: flax, timber, 'Pork, if it is to be obtained', *kauri* gum, salt fish. And Marsden concluded meticulously: 'I wish you to fill up with potatoes; they had better be kept in the baskets in which the natives bring them, as I think they will keep better that way'.[18] Marsden was a hard taskmaster, but Dillon carried out his duties to his employer's satisfaction.[19]

By the time Marsden wrote the instructions, he knew that he would not himself be sailing in the *Active*. The other passengers—Kendall and Hall, and several for Hobart Town—embarked on 7 March. But the brig lay in Sydney Cove for another week, awaiting an improvement in the weather. Even so, she had not travelled far down the coast before running into a gale. She proved a poor sea boat, according to Kendall, incapable of sailing close to the wind. Shelter was sought in Jervis Bay, where she remained till about the end of the month. Those on board made contact with the local Aborigines, who, in return 'for a few biscuits and a little tobacco', supplied them with fish and oysters. The Aborigines were friendly, though cautious (in particular, keeping their women and children away from the visitors); but eventually two young men were persuaded to visit the brig, where they climbed a mast, to show their brethren on shore how well they were received.[20]

Dillon seems to have been on good terms with both his missionary passengers. He presented a quadrant to Kendall, who was showing an interest in navigation. He talked to them about the Bay of Islands, a subject on which the Maori seaman, Tui, a youth of chiefly family who had been living at Kendall's home near Sydney, was also well informed. But relations between the two missionaries were uneasy.

On the morning of 12 April the *Active* entered the broad and placid waters of the River Derwent, along with the brig *Spring*, which had sailed from Sydney a fortnight after her.[21] In the late afternoon the two vessels cast anchor off Hobart Town. The principal settlement in Van Diemen's Land had been founded in 1804 and was now a town with a population of a little over 1,400, of whom about a quarter were convicts.[22] The town was built on sloping land backed by the dramatic bulk of Mount Wellington. It was surrounded by lush green country, well suited to agriculture, and possessed, in the Derwent, a magnificent harbour. But it still lacked well-made roads, and few of its buildings were of permanent construction. In part, this lack of development was a consequence of earlier deficiencies in its administration, which had been only slightly lessened by the arrival in 1813 of a new lieutenant-governor, the amiable but indolent and untalented Thomas Davey, of whom it was written, kindly rather than with acrimony: 'He shared in common a taste for spirituous liquors, and was not unwilling to participate wherever he was welcome as a guest'.[23] In part, it was a consequence of the prevalence of bushrangers in the surrounding countryside. And, in part also, it derived from the fact that the Derwent —like Port Dalrymple, in the north of the island—had only been opened to general commerce in June 1813.

The arrival of a vessel was thus still a notable event in Hobart Town. The chaplain, Robert Knopwood—a conspicuous *bon viveur*—noted each one in his diary as carefully as he recorded the dinner parties he gave and attended. During the six weeks the *Active* lay at anchor, he entertained Dillon, as well as Kendall and Hall, several times.[24] The Lieutenant-Governor also acted as host to the two missionaries, and perhaps to Dillon; but the latter's main contacts were probably with the leaders of the close-knit commercial community, with some of whom he was to remain associated for many years. Two Maori seamen, both from the Bay of Islands, welcomed the arrival of the *Active* even more warmly, for it seemed to offer the prospect of a passage home. One of them, who was serving in the *Spring*, could not obtain the termination of his articles from her owner, Edward Lord, or her master, William Bunster.[25] But the other, who had walked overland from Port Dalrymple, joined the *Active*'s crew.[26]

Dillon sailed from Hobart Town on 23 May and reached the Bay of Islands on 8 June. The *Active* anchored off Te Puna, on the northern side of the bay; but after about a week she was moved, at the request of the elderly chief Tara, to his village of Kororareka, on the southern side, where she remained till shortly before her departure. Tara and Ruatara were handed letters from Marsden explaining his plans for the mission and asking for their help in the loading of the brig. The most powerful of all the local chiefs, Hongi Hika, took up residence on board, where he was later joined by two of his sons. He and the captain apparently found one another's company congenial, for—in Dillon's later words—he 'continued one of my most sincere friends up to the day of his death'.[27] The chiefs directed the cutting and loading of spars and flax, as they had been asked to do. The people generally were friendly and seemed well disposed towards the future mission. And on Sundays some Maoris were always present at the church services held on board.

The sensitive Kendall was well pleased with his first experience of Maori society, though he recognized that it had 'been for ages lost in heathen darkness'.[28] He was much less favourably impressed with the influence and attitudes of Europeans. One day, when he reproved his protégé, Tui, for swearing, the latter replied that Europeans used expressions such as 'Damn your eyes' and 'God damn you, you bugger', Kendall was also displeased with Dillon. He considered that the captain was lax about Sabbath observance and, even worse, that he showed contempt towards Maoris. One day Tara's brother had been refused permission to come aboard and had 'burst into tears'. And he added, as a further example:

> It has also been a custom in other vessels which have put into the Bay of Islands for the Captain to invite the chiefs to sit down at his Table but in the Active which was sent out expressly for the purpose of 'bearing [tidings] of goodwill', they have been taught to feel their inferiority.[29]

He thought he saw signs of a declining friendliness on the part of some chiefs, as a result of the attitude which he attributed to Dillon.

Despite the presence on board of Hongi and his sons, it is possible that Dillon was over-cautious about admitting Maoris to the brig and over-conscious of the dignity of the captain's table. He was new to the responsibilities of command. His memories of the plan to seize the *Hunter* and *Elizabeth* at Wailea and of the seizure of the *Queen Charlotte* and the *Daphne* by Society Islanders were still fresh in his mind. He was aware that many Maoris had been given as good cause for disliking Europeans as had Fa'aanuhe. Ruatara, for example, during his years at sea, had several times been swindled out of his wages, had been stranded on Norfolk Island without food, and had been landed in England without money or adequate clothing, as a result of which his health had been permanently undermined.[30] Beyond this, he knew how strongly seafaring Polynesians were tempted by the chance of taking a European ship. When he had gained more experience as a master, he always combined friendship with caution, and he never confused sympathy with sentimentalism.

At the end of the third week of July, Dillon concluded that the objects of the voyage had been attained. Hongi and two of his sons, Tui and his elder brother Korokoro, and Ruatara and Tinana (a chief of Kerikeri) embarked for Sydney and were emotionally farewelled by their relatives. On 25 July the *Active* sailed. As she was getting under way, Kendall was struck by the main boom and knocked overboard. He could not swim, but was picked up by a Maori and suffered only a bruised leg.[31]

This was not quite the last of Kendall's tribulations. On 5 August the *Active* met the brig *Campbell Macquarie* bound from Sydney for Fiji. Dillon hailed her, and he and the two missionaries went aboard. They drank with her captain, Richard Siddins, till Kendall, as he confided to his Journal, 'was quite overcome with Liquor'.

> In the Evening I had some very unpleasant conversation with Captain Dillon and as I am informed made use of very improper language for which he struck me. I know it is my duty as a man professing godliness to take hold to what I say even in the sight of mine enemies. I therefore notwithstanding the blow made an apology to Captain Dillon. I have also sinned against God.[32]

Dillon, at twenty-six, was nearly ten years younger than Kendall; but he possessed already some of the gravity of a commander, as well as the quick temper that was a lifelong affliction.

On 22 August the *Active* entered Port Jackson. For Dillon the return to Sydney was more than the end of a voyage.

AMONG the Sydney families Dillon came to know was that of Patrick Moore. Like Dillon, Moore was from County Meath; but, unlike him, he had reached New South Wales as a convict. He had probably been convicted of an offence connected with the agrarian disturbances of 1796, as had a majority of those who travelled with him from Ireland in the ship *Britannia*.[33] In any event, he seems always to have been regarded as a man of good character, and within a few years of his arrival he was granted a free pardon. After a period of employment by the government, he entered business on his own account in Pitt Street, as an ironmonger and box-maker.[34] He also obtained a grant of land near Cook's River, which he developed into a profitable farm.[35] Moore did not belong to the small group of affluent and influential emancipists who had gained the Governor's patronage; but he was a man of substance, one whose support was sometimes sought for public causes. At this time, he was in his mid-forties.

Patrick Moore and his wife, Rose, had two sons, John and Peter, and a daughter, Mary, who was several years older than either of her brothers.[36] Mary had attended the school—or 'academy', as it was styled—run by John Pascoe Crook during his temporary withdrawal from the Tahitian mission. There—at a cost to her father of one shilling a week—she had acquired a fluent hand and other genteel accomplishments.[37] She was now a young woman of seventeen.

On 22 September 1814 Peter Dillon and Mary Moore were married. Like Dillon, the Moores were Catholics; but, in the absence of a Roman Catholic chaplain, the ceremony was performed according to the rites of the Church of England, at St Philip's, in Sydney.[38]

Dillon's marriage provided him with a base in middle-class Sydney society: with a home to which he and Mary—and later their children—could always return; with a father-in-law who was always able and willing to act for him in matters of business. It also cut him off, for some years, from the life of the islands. He did not remain in command of the *Active*: his appointment had been limited to the preliminary voyage.[39] It is doubtful whether he served at sea during the months immediately following his marriage, as the next reference to his movements was in March 1815, when it was announced that he was 'about to depart for the Derwent'.[40] He probably sailed once again in the cutter *Elizabeth*, which left Sydney on 12 March, with a cargo of merchandise.

In Hobart Town he was not received as a stranger. In May, for example, he served as a juryman at an inquest into the death of a settler who had been fatally injured in an affray with bushrangers.[41] He visited Robert Knopwood and others whom he had met during the previous year.[42] He seems, in particular, to have been in touch with Edward Lord and William Bunster, the two men who had refused to allow a Maori seaman to return home in the *Active*, for by September, if not several months earlier, he had accepted employment as mate in Lord's brig, the *Spring*.

Dillon had probably not returned from Van Diemen's Land when, on 26 June, Mary gave birth in Sydney to a son. He was present, however, when the child was baptized and named 'Peter', at St Philip's, on 14 September.[43] But his time with his family was brief; and during his next absence, which extended to eight months, Mary had not only to care for her infant but also to mourn the death of one of her brothers. Four days before Christmas John Moore was bitten by a snake as he was returning home from his father's farm; he died next day. The story of his death was told in great detail by the *Sydney Gazette*. Even the snake was described, though with a prefatory apology: 'It may seem frivolous to combine with so melancholy a narrative a description of the wretched reptile that cut the thread of this fine youth's destiny'.[44]

Dillon himself had left for Hobart Town, as mate to Captain Bunster, a few days after his son's christening. In November he had sailed in the *Spring* to Port Dalrymple; and from there he had set out, with Bunster, upon an enterprise which was a pioneering one in the commercial life of Van Diemen's Land.[45] They had sailed for Kangaroo

Island, off the unsettled southern coast of the Australian mainland, for a cargo of salt.

The *Spring* reached her destination on 23 December and anchored in the Bay of Shoals, in the north-east of the island. Near the bay is a shallow salt-water lagoon which dries out under the heat of the summer sun. Bunster found that he had arrived too early in the season and decided that the crew should be employed catching seals till the salt had crystallized. For this purpose, Dillon set out with the brig's boats on a circumnavigation of Kangaroo Island and a visit to Althorpe Island, farther north; some 600 sealskins were obtained. Subsequently, the *Spring* visited Thistle Island and Port Lincoln, in Spencer's Gulf. When the lagoon had dried, between forty and fifty tons of salt were collected. But at this point the inexperience of Bunster and Dillon ruined the enterprise: after only seven tons had been taken aboard, the remainder was dissolved in a shower of rain.

In the middle of March 1816 the *Spring* sailed for Hobart Town. The voyage had not been without interest for Dillon: he had observed the new country with care, noting the varied forms of vegetation and the prevalence of kangaroos; he had looked north from Althorpe Island over the 'verdant plains without timber' of Yorke Peninsula; he had visited wells dug by the explorer, Matthew Flinders. But a life in the coastal trade of Australia was not his choice. When he returned to his family in Sydney, he prepared to sail for India.

FIVE

Calcutta and the 'Country Trade'

1816-23

SOME of the sea-captains trading, by licence of the East India Company, between Bengal and New South Wales owned the vessels that they commanded. These men did not necessarily possess any substantial capital, since mariners whose reputation was sound could borrow the purchase money from one or other of the Calcutta agency houses. Moreover, if they wished to trade on their own account, as they commonly did, they were also able to obtain their cargo upon credit.

For an owner thus indebted, a voyage to New South Wales was a highly speculative enterprise. His outgoings were heavy. He paid a high rate of interest on his borrowings and a high premium for the insurance cover that the lenders required. His expenditure on manning and maintaining the vessel was considerable. Furthermore, his initial estimates could be confounded if sustained bad weather delayed the voyage or caused damage to the ship or her cargo. And, if he should suffer the ultimate disaster of shipwreck, he could find himself saddled with heavy debts not covered by insurance. On the other hand, if nothing untoward occurred and the cargo was satisfactorily disposed of, he was likely to make a handsome profit. This was his primary expectation, but not his only one. As the owner of his ship, a captain was free to change his itinerary as he chose, in order to accept freight or a charter whenever an attractive offer was made to him. Beyond that, for an independent-minded man, the fact of being his own master, in this fuller sense, was itself of substantial value.

At Sydney and Hobart Town, Dillon had seen these privately owned 'country' ships lying at anchor; and he seems certain to have talked with their captains. Indeed, unless he left the *Spring* at Port Dalrymple, he is likely to have travelled back to Sydney from Hobart Town in one of them—the *Lynx*, owned by Captain G. F. Read, or the *Bridgewater*, owned by Captain W. T. Jones.[1] It is highly probable that, even at this early stage, he had set his heart on becoming a ship-owner himself.

On 1 June 1816 the *Sydney Gazette* carried an announcement that Dillon and his family were leaving the colony. They were, in fact, travelling to Bengal and probably embarked in the *Lynx*, which weighed anchor on 10 June.[2] She was bound for Calcutta but, on her passage through the Indies, made a call at Batavia, where Captain Read accepted the offer of a return cargo for Sydney.[3] If the Dillons were on board, they must have transferred there to another vessel. But, whatever the circumstances of their journey may have been, it is clear that before the end of the year they were in Calcutta, which was to remain Dillon's headquarters till 1828.

CALCUTTA, the capital of British India and the seat of a wide-ranging commerce, presented both great opportunities and great perils to ambitious men such as Dillon. Fortunes could be quickly made and as quickly lost. Some Europeans eventually returned home extremely wealthy, while others were reduced to penury or succumbed to tropical fevers or the excesses of an indulgent life.

Built on the low-lying banks of the Hooghly, Calcutta revealed something of its essential quality to the traveller even before he landed. Indian boats, noisy and clamorous, thronged the broad river, and ships from many parts of the world lay at anchor. On the east bank, the massive citadel of Port William bore witness to the military strength of the East India Company. The Esplanade, which ran north from it towards the centre of the city, was backed by mansions designed in the neo-classical style then favoured in Europe, white-plastered, with wide colonnades. The most magnificent of the buildings in this style was Government House, set in large grounds close to the central square of the city and not far distant from the principal public buildings and the offices of the leading private merchants.[4]

This was Calcutta as it was known to most Europeans; but it was only a part of the rapidly expanding city, with a population of half a million or more. Farther north lay 'the black town'—as the British commonly referred to it—with its narrow, unpaved streets, its poor buildings, its thousands of small shopkeepers and hawkers, and its overcrowded tenements. Moreover, Calcutta lay at the centre of a densely populated region, which was estimated to contain more than two million people within a circumference of some twenty miles.

The commercial world of the Calcutta merchants, as of the East

India Company, extended from England to China. Ships from Calcutta carried merchandise from Europe and Bengal to the ports of south-east Asia and to Canton and Macao. They returned with the products of eastern Asia—such as tea, sugar, silk and spices—for shipment to Europe. Because of the large profits to be made, mariners and those who employed or financed them readily faced the special risks of Asian commerce—the danger that a ship would be captured by pirates or, on the coast of China, by government officers; the uncertainty of trading in markets not organized on Western lines. But, at the time of Dillon's arrival to seek his fortune, one risk had recently been removed. The Napoleonic Wars had ended, so that British merchantmen had no longer to elude the ships of foreign navies.

Much capital—Indian, as well as foreign—was invested in the commerce of Calcutta. The administration of this capital, through banks and insurance companies, as well as agency houses, was a complex operation. The leaders among those who were involved in it were men of wealth and power, whose influence permeated the whole fabric of non-indigenous Calcutta society. They included not only the senior members of the principal British firms but also many men of non-British origin, particularly Portuguese and Armenians. They were always able to pick and choose from the large number of young men seeking employment or financial backing. But, in the years following the Napoleonic Wars, their field of selection was unusually wide, as many former officers in the army and navy came to India in search of a civilian career.

Dillon nowhere explained the circumstances of his own acceptance by the Calcutta community; but his standing ten years after his arrival was described by a local newspaper as that of a man 'well known to us all' and by Lord Combermere, then Commander-in-Chief in India, as that of one who 'was considered by the public functionaries, and the Merchants, as a Man of excellent character'.[5] His passing references to his contacts in Calcutta are, in some cases, more tantalizing than illuminating. For example, he later referred to having relatives in the city, who were apparently of some respectability, since he introduced them to Combermere;[6] but their identity remains unknown, as does their period of residence. It is thus impossible to tell whether he was helped by introductions from a kinsman of his or perhaps of Mary's. But several of his contacts are, at least, somewhat less problematical. He became a Freemason.[7] He seems likely to have early made the acquaintance of Calcutta journalists, for the *Government Gazette* published an account of the Dillon's Rock episode soon after his arrival,[8] and he was later in close touch with men writing for papers that supported the merchant interest. Moreover, he was at that period an avid reader of books on Asia and the Pacific; and this interest not improbably gained him the friendship of merchants and government officers who belonged to the Asiatic Society—an institution of which he later became an active member. Most importantly of all, he possessed first-hand knowledge of Australian and Pacific waters that, with his taste for over-statement, he is bound to have presented to his listeners in impressive terms.

Campbell & Company, to whose New South Wales branch Dillon had become well known through his service in the *Perseverance* and the *Hunter*, no longer operated in India; but his contact with it may still have been useful to him, for in 1820 he gave the office of John Gilmore & Company—a firm with which Campbell's had been closely associated—as his Calcutta address.[9] It was, however, another of the agency houses—that of Joseph Barretto & Sons—with which his fortunes were eventually most closely linked.

The Barretto family had been in India for more than two hundred and fifty years. In the sixteenth century, Francisco Barretto and Antonio Moniz Barretto had both held office as governors of the Portuguese possessions. Subsequently, members of the family had grown wealthy in commerce. Their ventures were based on India; but, before the end of the eighteenth century, they extended from Lisbon to Canton and included banking and insurance, shipowning and general merchandising, and the trade in opium.[10] William Hickey described Luis Barretto, with whom he sailed from Lisbon for Madras in 1782, as 'a man endowed by nature with extraordinary talents and elegant address, though under the unfavourable circumstance of an extremely dark skin, indeed nearly black'. At Trincomalee, in Ceylon, which was then occupied by the French, Barretto's ship was taken as a prize because she was deemed to be British and her owner a British subject (he had been born in Bombay). Through the seizure of the ship and her cargo, Barretto lost a fortune, Hickey relates, but at the time of his death in 1806 he was again a wealthy man. Hickey was present in the Roman Catholic cathedral in Calcutta for his funeral which was, he wrote, 'performed . . . with the utmost pomp and splendour and was altogether a very grand exhibition'.[11]

The Barrettos were on terms of close friendship with senior officers of the East India Company, such as David Scott, who was its chairman for some years.¹² In Calcutta they were known not only for their business acumen but also for the scale of their public benefactions.

Their munificence had, indeed, made possible the completion of the Roman Catholic cathedral; and in 1813 the will of Luis's son provided for a charitable trust—John Barretto's Calcutta Charity—which for many years assisted both Catholic and Protestant churches in the city.¹³ After Luis's death, the most noted of them was his brother Joseph—the senior partner in Joseph Barretto & Sons—a man whom, it is said, many Indians believed to possess the power of transmuting base metals into gold.¹⁴

When Dillon arrived in Calcutta, Joseph Barretto's partners were his sons Joseph and Luis, John Da Cruz, and Edward Brightman, an Englishman of Indian birth. In addition to membership of the agency house, these men had interests in a number of banks and insurance companies and in shipping. Outside the commercial field, they were active on committees concerned with education and religion and in the Asiatic Society.¹⁵ They were apparently impressed by Dillon, for in 1819 Joseph Barretto & Sons financed his purchase of a ship and, over the succeeding years, the firm and its partners individually remained closely associated with him.

DILLON's employment for about a year after his arrival in Bengal is unknown. He may have served in ships sailing on the Indian coast or beyond it, possibly as far as Macao or Canton, or he may have earned a living on shore. His first recorded movement is in September 1817, when he sailed from Calcutta as first officer of a brig bound for Hobart Town and Sydney. This was the *Greyhound*, of 246 tons, owned and commanded by Thomas Ritchie, a Scot of about Dillon's age, who had recently left the Royal Navy, with the rank of lieutenant, to seek a career in civil life.¹⁶ She carried a general cargo of English and Indian goods, which was added to *en route*, and a party of prisoners in charge of a military guard.

From the Hooghly her course was laid for the mountainous coast of western Sumatra, where a call was made at the East India Company settlement of Benkulen, a source of pepper and nutmegs. Founded in 1684, just after the Dutch had finally excluded the company from Bantam, Benkulen had known few periods of real prosperity. Its links with the hinterland were impeded by mountains and by swampy ravines, which were prolific breeding grounds for malaria-carrying mosquitoes. Now, its buildings were dilapidated, its streets overgrown with grass, and indeed in a few years—1824—it was to be exchanged for Malacca. Company officials were ill paid, in ill health, and fearful of attack by the local people who lived amongst them. To European visitors such as Dillon, it displayed the East at its most threadbare.[17]

After leaving Benkulen, the *Greyhound* passed through Sunda Strait and followed the coast of Java to Batavia, where she remained for three weeks in December. The city was probably already known to Dillon from his journey of the preceding year; but it was a place that vied with Calcutta in interest to the traveller. From the roadstead, sheltered by off-shore islands, it appeared as a vast canopy of trees and palms pierced, here and there, by the towers of major buildings. When observed from within, its canals, its gardens, and the style of its mansions and public offices gave it the character of a city nostalgic for the Netherlands, as was Calcutta for eighteenth-century England. It was the capital of the Dutch empire in Asia; and at this time, when the British occupation of the war years had not long ended, its rulers were busy planning the future of their rich domain.

After leaving Batavia Ritchie made two more calls in the Indies. One of them was in the island of Bali—probably at Karangasem—where he purchased fresh provisions for the long, unbroken voyage from Lombok Strait to the Derwent. At this season, winds were more favourable and the weather off the coast of Australia more clement than they had been when Dillon earlier crossed this stretch of ocean, in the *General Wellesley*, during the southern winter of 1809.[18] The *Greyhound* thus made a good passage and anchored off Hobart Town on 25 February 1818.

There Ritchie placed his cargo on sale 'for ready money or wheat' during the following weeks.[19] But for him, even more than for Dillon, the visit to Hobart Town was also an opportunity for mixing with local people. Though he had not previously been in Van Diemen's Land himself, his brother had served as commandant at Port Dalrymple; and he was much entertained by the official community.[20] When he sailed, two members of this group—Lieutenant Hector Macquarie, a nephew of the Governor of New South Wales, and George William Evans, the Deputy-Surveyor—joined the *Greyhound* as passengers to Sydney.[21] The latter was a man of unusually wide interests and of varied talents, a painter and a writer and, in his professional capacity, a participant in some of the most important journeys of exploration in New South Wales since his arrival there some fifteen years earlier. Dillon's contact with him, which on this occasion was unexpectedly lengthened when the *Greyhound* put into Adventure Bay for repairs to a yard-arm,²² continued in later years.

Dillon had brought his wife and son with him in the *Greyhound*, and in Sydney they spent two months among their relatives and friends before the brig was ready to sail again for Calcutta.²³ Captain Ritchie was still a bachelor; but, at this time, he formed an association with a girl of about seventeen, named Hannah Harris. She was refused permission to leave the colony with him. But, on the morning of 10 June, while the *Greyhound* was passing through Sydney Heads, and Dillon was on watch, she came aboard from a rowing boat. Hannah became the mother of Ritchie's children and eventually also became his wife. When he returned to Sydney in 1819, however, he was convicted and heavily penalized for taking her illegally to India. The authorities were unimpressed by his statement that he was unaware of her presence on board till her boat 'was almost out of sight' and by Dillon's that 'he had something else to do' than to send her ashore.²⁴

Late in August, the *Greyhound* called at Madras, whence she proceeded to Calcutta.²⁵ Mary Dillon was pregnant again, and about February 1819 she gave birth to a daughter whom they named Mary Martha.²⁶ It was a bad year for the parents of young children to be in the city, as a cholera epidemic of great severity ravaged Bengal;²⁷ but the Dillons remained unaffected by it while Peter made plans to sail again for New South Wales. He purchased from Joseph Barretto & Sons a ship of 170 tons, which was known henceforth as the *St Michael*. She had been built in Bordeaux and now lacked a register, though she had been given a 'pass' by the East India Company.²⁸ Since Dillon possessed no capital, it seems that Barrettos retained a mortgage over her to substantially her full value. An indication of Dillon's financial difficulties is conveyed in a statement—made twenty years later—by Samuel Horton, then an officer in a Bengal 'country' ship. Horton was a hostile witness—a prominent Methodist, anxious to discredit Dillon, who had strongly criticized the Methodist mission in Tonga not long before he wrote—and his statement is not wholly accurate in detail. None the less, his reference to a meeting with Dillon 'about the year 1818' is not without interest.

> I remember the individual coming on board to borrow something & I was in his company some time—after his leaving I made some inquiries respecting him as he appeared rather eccentric—I was told he was familiarly called 'Paddy Dillon' that he had charge of a small Bengal coasting Brig & that

3 The brig *Calder*

4 The wreck of the *Calder* in Valparaiso Bay

she was generally fitted out by what he could beg or borrow from all the ships in the harbour.[29]

Dillon was able, however, to obtain a cargo upon credit; and, towards the end of June 1819, he sailed from Calcutta—upon his first voyage as a shipowner and a merchant.[30]

At this season of the year, that of the south-west monsoon—he later wrote—it was usual for ships sailing from the Hooghly into the southern hemisphere to 'beat to windward along the coast of Orissa, Golconda, and Coromandel, until they reach the fifteenth or sixteenth degree of north latitude; they then stand across the Bay of Bengal to the south-eastward with the wind at south-west, until they cross the line'. But this route, he declared, was both slow and 'attended with great difficulty, such as ships getting dismasted, springing of leaks, being obliged to return with their cargoes damaged, and the hulls of the ships so much injured as to be condemned by the underwriters as unfit for further service'. In the *St Michael* he followed the eastern side of the bay, passing to the leeward of the Andaman Islands, where the monsoon became 'moderate and fair'. As a result, he made far better time.[31] But he did not, in fact, avoid one of the perils of the alternative route, for in the rough weather north of the Andamans the *St Michael* sprang a leak; and he had to take her into Penang for repairs.[32]

As a port of call, the settlement of Penang—or Prince of Wales Island—had many merits. The harbour was both commodious and well sheltered. The town, whose red-roofed buildings were shaded by trees and backed by densely forested hills, presented a restful contrast to Calcutta, far quieter, less intensely hot because of the breezes off the sea, and free of the dreaded cholera. Moreover, since the settlement was administered by the East India Company, Dillon was able to arrange that ten convicts whom he was transporting to New South Wales should be lodged in the fort while the *St Michael* was under repair.[33] But, for a man with Dillon's thirst for knowledge, perhaps its greatest merit was its quality as a sounding board for news of the Indies. Malays, Chinese and Indians, as well as Europeans of various nationalities, lived within the town. And during the five weeks Dillon was there nearly forty vessels anchored in the port.[34] Many of them arrived from the coasts of the Malay peninsula, Sumatra and Java, others from India, Burma and the Philippines. Their masters included Malays and Arabs, Englishmen and Portuguese.

F

One of the principal topics of discussion in Penang seems certain to have been the politics of Atjeh—the *St Michael*'s next port of call—a subject on which Dillon showed himself to be well informed when he reached Hobart Town.[35] Atjeh, at the north-western tip of Sumatra, had been for centuries an *entrepôt* for commerce between East and West. Though its role was a more limited one in the opening years of the nineteenth century, it remained important—especially to Penang —for trade with the Sumatran coast. The main port, off the mouth of the Atjeh River, was a collecting point for pepper and betelnut, in particular, and other ports on the adjacent coasts were within the jurisdiction of the Sultan of Atjeh; Penang Malay merchants, resentful of the ruler's attempts to maintain a monopoly, had backed a rival claimant. Only recently Stamford Raffles, then the Lieutenant-Governor of Benkulen, had settled the matter by exerting the East India Company's influence.

On 6 September the *St Michael* left Penang to sail across the Straits of Malacca to Atjeh.[36] Dillon's purpose in visiting this politically turbulent region is fairly clear. Penang imported much of its food and prices were therefore high. Atjeh, on the other hand, with its fertile soil and large population, produced an abundance of rice, of cattle and chickens, of fruit and vegetables. It was thus an excellent place at which to lay in supplies for the long voyage ahead. Dillon probably intended also to buy Sumatran goods, such as pepper, for sale in the colonies. Since the *St Michael* seems to have remained at anchor for nearly three weeks, it is likely, though not recorded, that he went by boat up-river, through groves of coconuts and bamboos, to Banda Atjeh, the capital, dominated by its fortified royal compound and great mosque and with thousands of houses of rough timber and bamboo, many raised on stilts, a typical Malay town, unlike any place in the Indies he had previously visited. It is apparent from later statements that he followed with interest the fortunes of the rival sultans. Saif, 'the Usurper'—the Hobart Town newspaper reported several days after Dillon's arrival —had moved from Atjeh down the coast to Pidie, as a consequence of the Raffles treaty, and Jauhar, 'the legal Sovereign', appeared in the port with a fleet of five vessels while the *St Michael* lay there; he was expected to land on the day she sailed.[37]

The *St Michael* left Atjeh on 29 September and reached Hobart Town forty-two days later, on 9 November. Her voyage, the *Hobart Town Gazette* noted, was 'the shortest passage ever made to this Territory'. Dillon remained in Hobart Town for eleven days offering his cargo for sale—unlike Ritchie, 'for ready money only'—before moving on to the larger market of Sydney.[38]

In Sydney he learnt that a small schooner had been built, under instructions from the British Government, for presentation to the King of Hawaii, in fulfilment of a promise made by the explorer George Vancouver twenty-five years before.[39] He wrote to the Colonial Secretary suggesting that he should deliver her in the *St Michael*. Since the latter was 'a very fine vessel for Sailing' and a visit to Hawaii would merely involve her in a longer return voyage to India, this arrangement seemed preferable to despatching a ship specially from New South Wales. Moreover, he was unusually well qualified to undertake the mission, because he had been 'for many years past in [the] habit of visiting and conversing with the Natives of the North and South Pacific Islands, and understanding their customs and languages, which on such an Expedition would be of very material benefit in promoting the object in view'. He would be prepared to receive his charge for this service, which would be £1,000, in the form of a remission of duty on 3,000 gallons of spirits that he had in bond.[40] But the schooner, it seems, was not yet ready—she did not reach Hawaii till 1822—so that Dillon could not be given the opportunity of increasing the profits of his voyage and his knowledge of Polynesia.

He thus sailed direct for Calcutta in January 1820. On this occasion Mary Dillon was accompanied by her infant daughter and by two personal servants, an Indian whom she had brought with her and Margaret Chamberlain, a girl of eleven who was being taken out of New South Wales 'by the personal Consent of her Mother'.[41] Her son Peter, now four, was left with his maternal grandparents, with whom he subsequently made his home.

DILLON's first venture as an independent trader was a success. In Calcutta he began to look for a larger ship. About June 1820 he sold the *St Michael* to Henry Marsh, who had served with him as first officer, and James Hobbs, a former resident of Van Diemen's Land.[42] In her place, he acquired a vessel of 259 tons, launched at Cochin four years earlier.[43] When Dillon owned her she was usually called the *Phatisalam*. But several variants occur, of which one, given by Dillon to a man who sailed with him some years later, *Futta Salam*, was probably the original form of her name.[44]

During his time in Calcutta Dillon took up a matter not directly related to his mercantile interests. Excusing himself by reference to his past service as master of the *Active*, he wrote to the Reverend Joseph Pratt, the Secretary of the Church Missionary Society, in London. The subject of the letter—a claim to land in Ireland—is interesting because it relates to his little known early years. Its form is no less so. Dillon never learnt to spell; but in later years, when most of his writing was done, this was concealed by his common recourse to an amanuensis. In later life, too, he had come to possess, through reading and through contact with men of affairs and of letters, a flexible and sophisticated vocabulary. In his letter to Pratt, of 13 October 1820, he revealed himself as he then was, a man of little formal education, expressing himself through a crude phonetic rendering of his Irish brogue. 'Sir', he wrote,

> I beg you will excuse the liberty an intire stranger takes in addressing you on the following subject.
>
> the Person who addresses you is Capt P Dillon of the Hon East India Company Country Service who formerly commanded the Misshionary Brig Active . . . .
>
> I will be extreamly obliged if you will caus one of your Servants to see the Inclosed letter delivered, or to see if the person to home it is directed is living or dead, or if he has left London or not. I have frequently writ to the person for hom the outher letter is, but Could neveur get and answer, his existence is a matter of the greatest Conciquence to me as I intend to go to Europe if he is a live and inter an Ackchiom for the Recovery of som[e] landed property which I have been deprived of, my Counseler writs from Dublin if I can procure this mans evidince I will gean the property in dispute. I have writ to him by sevoural and directed outhers to inquire but was all ways disceaved which is the Caus of my thus intruding on youre time by the advice of one of your Misshionarys in this part.
>
> and answer to the above inquiry will confer a great Obligeachion me pray Direct as underneath
>
> > I am with much
> > Respect yours Obed
> > Servant
> > Peter Dillon
>
> To Capt P Dillon, kear of Me[ssrs]
> John Gilmore and co Calcutta
>
> PS the person I inquire after is James McCabe a Native of Ireland who lived at No 36 East Lane Barmunsey London he was in the Employ of Mr Frinch of that pleas . . . ho kept a Rope Walk [45]

In due course Pratt found McCabe and sent a letter from him to Dillon, who presumably received it on his next return from the Australian colonies. But whether or not the letter encouraged Dillon to persist with his claim is unknown.

The *Phatisalam* sailed from Calcutta on 25 January 1821, carrying several passengers and a party of convicts, in addition to a cargo worth some £8,000.[46] His liabilities were thus substantial, since they included not only the immediate expenses of the voyage but also the payment of interest on the money he had borrowed and a high premium on the insurance policy he had lodged with his creditors.[47] His expectations, however, were no less so. He had been able to draw on earlier experience in planning his present speculative voyage; and he now commanded a ship that was almost new and was leaving the Hooghly at the most favourable time of year, when, with the wind from the north-east, he could reasonably count on a rapid passage to the Line.

Dillon seems to have sailed in a confident mood, for, undeterred by the dangers of a lee shore, he kept to the western side of the Bay of Bengal and anchored, on 15 February, in the exposed roadstead at Madras.[48] Once at sea again, all went well until the Equator was passed, when the ship began to leak, and he realized that she must have sustained greater damage than he had previously suspected when she had gone aground—under the control of a pilot—coming down the Hooghly.

By the time the *Phatisalam* reached 15°S., she was making six inches of water an hour; and the leaking rapidly increased as she sailed southward into south-easterly winds. When she finally ran into the westerlies—in the unusually high latitude of 46°S.—she was making between sixteen and eighteen inches an hour. The position, for those on board, was by then desperate. The members of the crew, nearly all Lascars, were unaccustomed to the cold weather, and their resistance had been further undermined by the labour of constant pumping and by shortage of food and water. Many of them were ill; several had died. Dillon estimated the ship's position as being about 2,500 miles from Van Diemen's Land and 1,400 from the unsettled south-west coast of the Australian mainland. He doubted whether even with the westerlies behind her, she could be brought safely into the Derwent by her debilitated crew and therefore altered course to bring her to the nearest point on the Australian coast.

On 21 May—almost three months after sailing from Madras—the *Phatisalam* anchored in King George's Sound. There, her freshwater tanks were re-filled; but, in the absence of shore facilities, the damage to her hull could not be effectively repaired. And she was nearly 2,000 miles from the closest point at which her company could obtain succour. Dillon, with his interest in maritime history, must surely have wondered how many ships had been lost without trace on this isolated coast.

When he took the *Phatisalam* to sea again, in June, it was already winter, the same season of cold and rough weather as that in which he had first seen this stretch of ocean from the deck of the *General Wellesley* in 1809. But, on this occasion, conditions were immeasurably worse. Soon, according to his later report, the ship was making about twenty inches of water an hour, 'varying in quantity as the wind blew'. As she staggered across the Great Australian Bight, she was often in imminent danger of foundering. After she had crossed it, Dillon tried to put in to Kangaroo Island and, later, Port Phillip; but he was foiled by the winds. He then turned towards the southern shores of Bass Strait and found refuge off the Hunter Islands, at the north-western extremity of Van Diemen's Land. For several days the ship lay precariously at anchor—probably in the passage between Hunter and Three Hummock Islands—but on the night of 8-9 July, when the wind increased in strength, she was driven on shore.[49]

Those on board were all safely brought ashore; but they were on an uninhabited island, with little food except some 'damaged rice' and no shelter except that which they could contrive for themselves. Dillon's responsibilities as a commander were added to by his personal ones, for both Mary, who was again pregnant, and the two-year-old Martha were with him. And the nearest settlement was George Town, at the mouth of the Tamar some ninety miles to the east. The first attempt to reach it in an open boat was terminated when the boat capsized on leaving the island. All those on board, except the officer in charge, were drowned in this mishap; and—adding a further element of horror to the situation—their bodies, which were recovered and buried, were soon 'rooted up and devoured by wild dogs'.[50] Later in July, however, Dillon and seven of the least unfit seamen succeeded in leaving the island. At this time of year waves of considerable height build up in Bass Strait and temperatures are low, both day and night. The boat crew, Dillon wrote, 'endured the greatest privations and sufferings from a tempestuous Winter';[51] but on 6 August—after a voyage of twelve days—it reached its destination.

The commandant of northern Van Diemen's Land, Gilbert

Cimitière, was stationed at George Town. With his help Dillon was able to charter the schooner *Little Mary*, owned by Captain Joseph James, at a cost of £200, to rescue those whom he had left on the island. Her log clearly indicates the kind of weather prevailing on the coast at the time, for, though she sailed almost immediately, she was unable to get beyond the mouth of the Tamar River for several days or to return with the marooned crew and passengers till 23 August.[52]

While awaiting her arrival, Dillon turned his attention to some of the other problems of the wreck. Though his personal capital—which cannot have been large—had almost certainly been lost in the disaster, he had to take what action he could to preserve his standing with Calcutta business houses and to save himself from immediate destitution. The earlier damage to the *Phatisalam* had not been irreparable, if tools and materials had been available; and she appeared to have suffered little further damage in going ashore in the Hunter Islands. He believed there was a good chance of salvaging her,[53] though he lacked the financial resources for undertaking the task himself. Moreover, much of her cargo was unharmed. He decided to offer both ship and cargo for sale by auction at Launceston, the principal town in northern Van Diemen's Land, and despatched a notice of his intention to Hobart Town for insertion in the local newspaper. The sale was to be held on 18 August and to be for cash, which would provide him with ready money, but its proceeds were eventually to be applied 'for the benefit of the Underwriters'.[54]

The auction was a failure. The highest offer for the ship was £525, so Dillon retained her by bidding £600.[55] He acted similarly in respect of the cargo.[56] His financial predicament was thus worsened. But, in an effort to resolve it, he was forced to incur additional expenditure: he chartered a second vessel, the *Glory*, to remove the *Phatisalam*'s cargo.[57] His anxieties were reduced when Mary and Martha and their companions arrived safely from the wreck and the people of the little settlement of George Town—to quote the *Sydney Gazette*—'vied with each other in their tender expressions of kindness towards the unfortunate sufferers'.[58] But his relief was not complete, for he was told that the master and crew of the *Little Mary* had looted the *Phatisalam*.[59] And this news merely marked the beginning of a series of setbacks that made the ensuing months one of the most miserable periods of his life.

He had believed, and the amiable Cimitière had apparently agreed, that the government would pay for the charter of the *Little Mary* and the sustenance and repatriation of his crew. All those who had been shipwrecked were British subjects. Furthermore, he had been carrying mail from Bengal and the Carnatic, without payment but under a bond that he would forfeit if he failed to ensure delivery. The Lieutenant-Governor, William Sorell, however, would not accept the obligation, nor would he agree to a compromise proposed by Dillon: that payment should be made in spirits, valued at current market rates, when the *Glory* returned from the wreck. In a succession of letters dictated to an amanuensis (possibly Mary) Dillon argued his case with knowledge, citing British help to mariners wrecked 'on the Coast of Barbary' and elsewhere for precedent and quoting relevant sections of British law. But neither the Lieutenant-Governor nor, subsequently, the Governor-in-Chief, Lachlan Macquarie, were persuaded by his argument.[60] 'If I have to provide for the subsistence of the Lascars, in Conjunction with the paying Captain James's demand', he wrote, 'it will be the total ruin of me and my family'.[61]

Meanwhile, Dillon's position in Launceston, where he and his family were living, was becoming increasingly unpleasant. In part, this was a consequence of the auction. Local bidders, confident of obtaining the ship and cargo at bargain prices, had been angered by his intervention. And an error in the announcement of the sale in Hobart Town had created further ill will. He had sent a draft of the advertisement across the island to his friend James Kelly, the pilot and harbour master on the Derwent, with a request for its publication. This did not reach Kelly till 13 August, too late—or so the latter seems to have concluded—to enable interested persons to reach Launceston by the eighteenth. He therefore altered the advertisement, so that, in its published form, it stated that the sale would take place 'on or about Monday, the 20th Instant'. A group of Hobart Town businessmen who acted on this information and chartered a vessel to salvage the wreck and take off the cargo thus arrived in Launceston too late.[62] Though Dillon had been unaware of Kelly's action, and embarrassed by the absence of acceptable offers, he was publicly censured by the intending purchasers.[63]

In part also, the attacks on Dillon were generated by his efforts to recover the property looted from the wreck. David Smith, who had served as master of the *Little Mary* on her voyage to the Hunter Islands, was summoned to appear before a bench of magistrates, who committed him for trial in the Criminal Court.[64] The schooner, meanwhile, had sailed for Sydney under the command of her owner, Joseph James.

Since Dillon had not recovered his property, he inserted an advertisement in both the Hobart Town and Sydney newspapers offering a reward of £50 for information as to its whereabouts[65]—an inducement well calculated to produce an informer. Among the small traders and farmers, the schooner captains and sailors, in the Australian colonies there were many men of little principle. The stigma attaching to convict origins was often well deserved. Men such as Joseph James, David Smith, and Jonathan Griffiths—the owner of the *Glory*, who was later suspected of similar pilfering from the *Phatisalam*[66]—were concerned primarily with evading the law, rather than with observing it. Dillon had, literally, fallen among thieves; and they, in retaliation for his attempt to bring them to justice, spread scurrilous stories about him.

The most bizarre of these stories alleged that Dillon had run the *Phatisalam* ashore intentionally in order to collect the insurance.[67] It was also said, regardless—or in ignorance—of his prior ownership, that he had issued a false advertisement in Hobart Town so that he could buy the ship and her cargo for a song at the auction. Perhaps to give credence to this story, it was claimed that, when he sold the *St Michael* to Hobbs and Marsh a year earlier, he had not possessed a clear title to her. Still another allegation—one that must have hurt him deeply—was that the wreck was brought about by his negligence and incompetence. The charges were all of a kind easily dreamed up by men such as Smith and James and their cronies. Strangers to professional standards, venal and undisciplined, they could themselves well have been guilty of any of the offences, had they possessed the opportunity of committing them. But, as allegations against Dillon—passionate and, at times, devious, as he was—they were the product of malice.

Dillon did not lack supporters. Edward Lord, one of the most influential men in the colony, and Thomas Simpson, a landowner and magistrate living in Launceston, signed a statement that the rumours were being spread by men frightened that he would prosecute them for piracy.[68] Two army officers who had travelled as passengers in the *Phatisalam*, Captain J. Smith and Assistant-Surgeon J. Jackson, addressed letters to him.[69] Smith referred to the allegations 'whose intention it seems to be to prejudice you in the opinion of the world, and which if permitted to pass without notice, may prove highly injurious to you in your professional capacity'. He continued, ungrammatically but without essential ambiguity:

> I am happy to have it in my power to state, that the disastrous result was by no means owing to any neglect or want of conduct on your part, but on the contrary your seaman-like behaviour, as commander, in every point relative to the duty of the ship, and the interests of all concerned could inspire, was invariably made by you. . .; and that every possible endeavour, consistent with the exhausted and helpless state of the crew . . . was used by you in the last arduous struggle. . . .

Jackson referred to Dillon's being 'unjustly slandered', 'you, a man who underwent uncommon fatigue to save the ship and crew'; 'you persevered', he declared, 'to save the lives on board your ill-fated ship, at periods[?] when every hope was despaired of'. Dillon himself dealt with the charge concerning the *St Michael* in a statement before a magistrate, in which he set out the circumstances of his purchase of her.[70]

Dillon's hardships were mitigated also in more material ways. When the *Glory* had returned from two trips to the wreck, he had in his possession a substantial part of the *Phatisalam*'s cargo, including some thousands of gallons of spirits.[71] Edward Lord, who was acting as agent for the underwriters, agreed to sell part of this cargo for him in Van Diemen's Land, while Dillon retained responsibility for sales in New South Wales.[72]

But his tormentors had not yet quite done with him. In October official surveyors visited the *Phatisalam* and destroyed her by fire, contending, in their subsequent report, that she could not have been refloated. But there were rumours—which circulated in Hobart Town for years—that one of their number had become implicated in the looting and was concerned with covering his tracks.[73]

The Lieutenant-Governor still held Dillon liable for the charter of the *Little Mary*; but he offered to let the claim stand for six months provided Dillon bound himself to pay if his appeal to higher authority failed and subject to his obtaining a guarantor. Edward Lord accepted the latter role; and Dillon signed, but only—he wrote—from 'the fear of being detained in this dreadful place'.[74]

The Dillons were thus able to embark for Sydney at the end of October, taking with them part of the *Phatisalam*'s cargo and the surviving Lascar seamen.[75] The brig in which they travelled, the *Haweis*, presented Dillon with an ironical reminder of his more carefree years, for she had been built in the Society Islands to serve the missionaries and was now owned by Robert Campbell, in whose employment he had first sailed from New South Wales for Fiji.

Sydney was not yet a large town; but its atmosphere was less constricting and, to Dillon's nostrils, far less contaminated than that of Launceston. His old friends, and men such as the editor of the *Sydney Gazette*, followed his movements with sympathetic interest. Patrick Moore, dependable and experienced, was always ready to help him in any way he could. And on this occasion those who were there to welcome him included Edward Brightman, of Joseph Barretto & Sons, who was on a visit from Calcutta. By this time Mary had given birth to another son; and Brightman showed his continuing friendship by acting as sponsor at the infant's baptism. That Dillon's flamboyance had not been quelled by misfortune was demonstrated by his endowment of the boy with the name 'Napoleon'.[76]

But Dillon was not free for long from the business of the wreck. In August he had written to Moore asking him to have the *Little Mary* searched when she arrived in Sydney. Helped by the expected appearance of an informer, Moore had obtained the issue of a search warrant and gone aboard with three constables. They had found ten muskets, 'under . . . [James's] bed-cabin' and rolls of textiles and other cargo elsewhere in the schooner, in addition to a sail and ropes and blocks belonging to the *Phatisalam*. Moreover, the informer told them that, when the *Little Mary* had been forced to put into Jervis Bay, James had distributed the muskets among the crew as protection against marauding Aborigines but warned them not to mention the fact, since they came from the wreck. On 7 November Dillon went to the Police Office to have the matter examined, in the presence of James. The latter agreed that stolen property had been found on board his schooner but claimed he had not known that it was there. This statement destroyed Dillon's equanimity, and he said to James: 'You are the biggest little villain in the world. You received these goods, my property on board your vessel and you knew it and you'll be hung for it'. According to James, who later complained that he had been defamed, Dillon repeated these remarks, with some verbal variation, several times.[77]

Dillon's main interest, however, was in improving his financial position. On 24 November he addressed a memorial to the Governor, Lachlan Macquarie, appealing against the decision that he was himself responsible for the charter of the *Little Mary* and the support of the Lascars.[78] Consideration of his case was probably not helped by the fact that Macquarie was on the point of relinquishing office in favour of his successor, Sir Thomas Brisbane; but he was promised, and eventually received, reimbursement for his expenditure on behalf of the seamen, on his signing a bond to repay should the claim be disallowed in London.[79] Meanwhile, he was also engaged in selling the spirits he had imported and placed in bond. A letter from him to Lord, setting a price of 7s 6d a gallon, with the purchaser paying the duty,[80] probably reflected the normal conditions of sale; but the amount of cash he received cannot be estimated, since it depended not only on the quantity sold but also on the amount of credit he was required to give.

After the New Year, Dillon's principal concern was in returning to India. This presented him with fresh difficulties. One was overcome when Moore agreed to act as guarantor of his bond to the New South Wales Government.[81] Joseph James, however, gave notice of his intention to bring an action for defamation and sought to have him detained. Not till 26 January, when his written undertaking to return was accepted, did he obtain permission from the Judge-Advocate to leave the colony.[82] Five days later he sailed as a passenger in the *Lady Hungerford*, which reached Calcutta on 18 April.[83]

THE loss of the *Phatisalam* had not destroyed confidence in Dillon. Indeed, his strenuous efforts to protect the interests of his backers may even have increased it. Brightman's friendship to him in Sydney proved a portent of his partners' attitude in Calcutta. Joseph Barretto & Sons financed his purchase of another ship. She was the *Calder*, a brig of about 200 tons, 'a very strong teak-built vessel' (according to one of her officers), 'a good specimen of the Calcutta builder's workmanship' (in the words of her new owner).[84]

On 29 June 1822 Dillon sailed in her from Calcutta, accompanied by Mary and their two younger children. He took more than a fortnight dropping down the Hooghly, this time without mishap. On the evening of 1 August he arrived off Atjeh and anchored in the roadstead next day. He remained there for three weeks. Though his primary concern was with trading and taking in water, his knowledge of both the history and the contemporary circumstances of the Eastern world was steadily expanding, and he, no doubt, observed with interest Sultan Jauhar's continuing failure to re-establish himself in the capital.

The *Calder* reached Hobart Town on 28 September, only thirty-five days after sailing from Atjeh, thus setting a record for the passage a whole week shorter than that established by the *St Michael* in 1819.[85]

Hobart Town had changed over the years Dillon had known it, most significantly since his last visit three years ago. The arrival of Sorrel in 1817 had placed the government of Van Diemen's Land in the hands of an efficient administrator, a man keen to give practical expression to Macquarie's ideals of progress and order. By 1822 the results of his work were clearly evident in the capital. A new wharf had been built in Sullivan's Cove, where the *Calder* lay at anchor; the streets in the town had been regularly laid out; and buildings of brick or of the golden-brown stone of the area were replacing the former temporary structures. Using convict labour, the government had built barracks, a gaol and a hospital, and the handsome church of St David's, not far from the Cove; and some of the more affluent residents now occupied houses as substantial as those of their counterparts in Sydney. The population had grown from the 1,400 of 1814 to over 3,500.[86]

The new urbanity of the town was in tune with Dillon's buoyant mood on these crisp spring days, when his situation was so different from what it had been at Launceston a year earlier. Little evidence remains of his social life during the six weeks that he remained at Hobart Town, apart from the unexpected statement that he paid several visits to the home of the Methodist minister, William Horton —a cousin of Samuel, the ship's officer whom he had met in Calcutta— and that he was believed to have contributed to the funds for the chapel that Horton was then building.[87] But his mercantile pursuits are well attested by the advertisements he inserted in the local newspaper.[88] He obtained space at 'the Warehouse of Mr. Bostock, near the King's Wharf', and there he 'expose[d] for SALE by Wholesale and Retail' a 'most choice Investment'. This comprised a wide range of piece-goods and clothing, including such items as 'gentlemen's long cloth muslin frilled shirts' and 'spotted and coloured silk handkerchiefs'; tea ('Imperial Pinco hyson' at £12 a chest and 'fine hyson-skin' at £7), sugar, rice, soap and saltpetre; 'Good strong Bengal rum' and 'superior brandy'; silverware ('warranted Dollar Silver, at 7s 6d per Ounce'); 'wax candles for the approaching Christmas'; and much else. He offered 'A Deduction of several per Cent' on purchases of £100 or over.

The *Calder* sailed from Hobart Town on 10 November and reached Sydney on the twentieth.[89] Dillon had been expected for several weeks, as he had written from Van Diemen's Land to the editor of the *Sydney Gazette* informing him of his own activities and of other matters of interest.[90] His unvarying practice, it may be noted, of providing journalists with news—often by giving them papers from the ports at which he had been—made him a welcome visitor and assured him, particularly in the news-starved Australian colonies, of a sympathetic press. On arrival he said that his destination was Lima, in Peru, and that his stay in Sydney would be short.[91] But he had several matters to attend to: repairs to the *Calder*'s bowsprit; a further sale of merchandise; and the completion of his unfinished business with Joseph James.

Dillon's advertisement of his wares gave greater emphasis to luxury items than had that issued at Hobart Town: 'camels' hair shawls . . . ; jewellery . . . ; Port and Madeira; together with some real Irish whiskey'. It is impossible to estimate the profit made during these sales or even the turnover, except as a crude approximation. On this occasion Dillon paid duty on general merchandise valued at £4,484 10s. In addition, he imported spirits to a value that cannot be ascertained because he left them in bond till a sale was made, when the purchaser paid the duty. Three thousand gallons of spirits—a modest estimate of his sales—would have produced a return of about £900. If retail prices on general merchandise were well above customs valuation, as seems certain, his total sales in Sydney may thus have considerably exceeded £5,000—a substantial sum at a time when colonial sea-captains were receiving £200 a year and the seamen in the *Calder* £2 10s a month.[92]

On 30 November the case of James *versus* Dillon came before the Supreme Court. The hearing was something of an anticlimax. Before his return to India Dillon had retained one of the most highly respected Sydney lawyers, Frederick Garling, who had been brought to New South Wales some years earlier, along with William Henry Moore, as a crown solicitor. At the hearing itself he was represented by both Garling and Moore. James was represented by a solicitor; but, with discretion, he had remained absent from the colony since the inquiry into his possession of stolen property. Dillon pleaded not guilty, arguing justification for the words he had used. The Court found in his favour, and the judge added: 'if the plaintiff himself were here, I do not know what might be the consequence'.[93]

After the case Dillon lingered in Sydney, at peace with the world. He attended a meeting to form the Sydney Bethel Union Society, with which Samuel Marsden was associated, and which planned to establish an undenominational Protestant chapel for seamen. He made donations to the Roman Catholic chapel, in his own name and those of Joseph Barretto and Edward Brightman. He gave a bag of sugar and a half-chest of tea to the Benevolent Society. In January 1823 he further delayed his departure by sending the *Calder* to Newcastle, under the command of his first officer, William Worth, for a cargo of timber and coal.[94]

Dillon was seldom lucky with his ships. At the end of the month he received word that the *Calder* had gone aground when entering the Hunter River. He immediately travelled north, where he found that the brig had been abandoned by Worth and the crew. Three weeks later, with help provided by the commandant (whom he publicly thanked), he succeeded in refloating her.[95] But the mishap created fresh problems for him, of which the most urgent was that of preparing the *Calder* for the long voyage ahead of her. On 30 April he informed the Colonial Secretary that he had 'nearly completed her repairs with the exception of some lead work which she cannot possibly do without'. The government foundry was the only establishment in Sydney possessing the necessary material. He therefore asked—and the Colonial Secretary subsequently agreed—that he should be permitted to purchase it from the foundry, despite the normal ban on such assistance to private persons.[96]

The unavoidable postponement of his departure was, however, embarrassing to him. When the *Calder* arrived in Sydney, he had gone with his family to live ashore. One morning, when he returned on board, he found that members of the crew—which, on this occasion, contained more Europeans than Lascars—had been 'very insolent' to Worth. He summoned the ringleader, Peter Barnes, to see him in his cabin; 'he appeared not inclined to come to me, I laid hands on him to pull him in; when he drew from his Pocket a clasp knife'. 'Being indisposed at the time', he had 'allowed the Matter to stand for a few Days'. Later, when he brought it before the court, Barnes and another seaman had refused to continue serving in the *Calder*. Since they were forbidden by law to obtain their discharge in New South Wales, they were committed to prison, where Dillon was required to pay for their custody and subsistence. By May—when he wrote to the Colonial Secretary—they had cost him more than £100. He expressed doubt as to whether the regulations were intended, in his loaded phrase, 'to enrich the Gaoler, the Chief Constable'; but his scepticism regarding the rights of the two officers was not shared by the authorities.[97]

These difficulties, like the need to replace Worth, who either resigned or was dismissed, were not sufficient to cause Dillon to change his plans. He proposed to sail to South America before the strong and steady westerlies that blow in the 'Roaring Forties'. In Peru and Chile he would dispose of the remainder of the merchandise from India and of timber loaded in New South Wales. Then, after taking on a return cargo for the Australian colonies, he would use the south-east trades to cruise through the islands of the tropical Pacific.

On 2 July the *Calder* was cleared by the Naval Officer, although she did not leave the harbour for another two weeks. In addition to her cargo she carried a number of passengers, including Peter Moore (presumably Mary Dillon's brother) and John Florence (a mariner who had recently arrived in the colony).[98]

A LITTLE more than a month earlier, on 15 June, Dillon had had his thirty-fifth birthday. In the ten years since he had turned twenty-five —at Kaba, collecting bêche-de-mer with Charles Savage and Martin Buchert—he had developed into a man of rather formidable qualities.

Even in youth, of course, he had been conspicuous for his physical presence, his intelligence and imagination, his sensitivity in personal relationships, and his instinct for command. But he had used his innate qualities to good effect. He mixed easily, and on terms of equality, with men and women of diverse rank and cultural background. A born story-teller, with wit and a ribald sense of humour, he had delighted many with accounts of his experiences; and he had enlivened many evenings with his singing of Irish songs. An insatiable seeker of knowledge, he had gained an impressive understanding of the intricacies of commerce, as well as of navigation. Furthermore—and less likeably— he possessed a streak of ruthlessness that made him a man who could not be ignored. He sailed for South America as a merchant and ship-owner who had won the respect of men as various as the Midas-rich Joseph Barretto and the piously powerful Samuel Marsden.

From the harvests of the years since Kaba he had also gleaned much self-knowledge. At 'Dillon's Rock' and again during the voyage of the *Phatisalam* he had remained in control of his emotions. He had learnt that, through example and the exercise of leadership, he possessed the power to save his own life and that of others in periods of great peril. At a more mundane level, he had not permitted himself to become discouraged when he had been seeking employment or the backing of business houses, or when he had sustained severe financial loss. He had learnt that he could surmount difficulties with greater buoyancy than most.

Since 1813 he had made only one voyage into the Pacific—that to

New Zealand, as master of the *Active* in 1814; but his mind had remained preoccupied with the island world. The character which that preoccupation had assumed was, indeed, the most striking of all the facets of his mental development, the one that was to have the greatest effect upon his later life. He had become an absorbed student of the history of the Pacific. He had mastered—perhaps mainly on the long passages between India and Australia—the narratives of the explorers and sought to re-create their experience in his own mind. That his interest in documentation was much more than that of a casual reader is suggested by his offer in 1820 of 'an extremely liberal price' for a 'SET of SYDNEY GAZETTES for the Year 1814'.[99] But, for him. Pacific history was far more than the record of European endeavour He was interested no less in the canoe voyages made by Polynesians and in the cultures evolved by island peoples. He was thus concerned with understanding forms of human behaviour and experience about which relatively little could be learnt from documents. From his travels, and perhaps from his contacts with men such as Joseph Barretto (who was an Orientalist of some note), he had acquired an interest more disciplined than that of his youth in the study of languages and cultures and in the collection of artefacts. When he sailed for South America and the islands, he was in search of more than the profits of a successful speculation.

SIX

To South America and the South Seas

1823-25

DILLON intended to sail direct to the South American coast. But, when he had been a week at sea, he discovered four stowaways, of whom he believed three to be convicts. He therefore decided to call at the Bay of Islands in the hope that he could arrange for them to be taken back to Sydney.[1]

Conditions in northern New Zealand had greatly changed since his visit in the *Active*. At the end of 1814 Kendall and Hall had returned to the Bay of Islands accompanied by the third of the intending settlers, John King. Marsden had travelled with them and remained for two months supervising the establishment of the mission. During the eight and a half years that had since elapsed, the mission had grown in size and gained acceptance as a permanent part of the local scene, though it had not yet obtained its first convert. Because it was there, mariners had come to regard the Bay as a safe port of call; and whalers, in increasing numbers, were putting in to rest their crews, take on water, and purchase pork and potatoes.

Maori interest in this growing commerce was based upon the opportunities it provided for acquiring firearms and ammunition, which the missionaries, as well as visiting sea-captains, supplied in exchange for the food and the services that they needed. As a result the people of the Bay area—the Ngapuhi—soon possessed many hundreds of muskets. Thus equipped they were confident of their ability to achieve victory over tribes not similarly blessed with access to Europeans.

The most remarkable of the Ngapuhi leaders to avail themselves of the new opportunities was Hongi Hika, the man whom Dillon regarded as one of his 'most sincere friends'. Hongi's high standing as a chief, his dignity, intelligence and charm, had all been apparent when he lived on board the *Active* and travelled in her to Sydney. Subsequently, his goodwill had been an essential factor in the survival of the mission. In 1820 he accompanied Kendall to England to act as an informant during the compilation, at Cambridge, of a dictionary of the Maori language. When he returned to the Bay of Islands in July 1821, he brought with him not only a wider experience of the world but also several hundred muskets and some more exotic military accoutrements, including a scarlet uniform, a helmet and buckler, and a suit of chain-mail.

Hongi well knew the grievances of his people, the defeats and the insults they had suffered: he was deeply steeped in tradition and had himself fought in former wars. He now saw it as his duty, as well as his pleasure, to wreak vengeance upon their enemies. Less than two months after his return, he set out for the Hauraki Gulf, to the southward, with a fleet of canoes carrying more than two thousand warriors, of whom almost half were armed with muskets. Near the banks of the Tamaki River this force attacked the Ngatipaoa and, according to report, killed at least a thousand. It then sailed into the Firth of Thames, where it inflicted similar punishment on the Ngatimaru. When it returned to the Bay of Islands in December it brought with it— according to the missionaries—about two thousand prisoners. During 1822 Hongi and his army fought in the Waikato. In 1823 they embarked on a third campaign that took them as far as Rotorua, inland of the Bay of Plenty, and were still away during the *Calder*'s visit.[2]

The battles fought by Hongi and his contemporaries were, at this stage, the most disturbing consequence of European contact. Unlike traditional warfare, they were grossly unequal struggles, which resulted in an unprecedented welter of killing and provoked a marked increase in cannibalism. But they were not its only consequence. The presence in New Zealand—particularly in the vicinity of the Bay of Islands— of escaped convicts and of men who had deserted or been put ashore from ships was also an unsettling influence, as was the ill treatment of Maoris by visiting mariners and their recruitment as seamen without the consent of their chiefs. In these cases, responsibility lay directly with Europeans—and mainly with British subjects. For this reason, and because European lawlessness invited Maori retaliation—as incidents such as the *Boyd* massacre had shown—Governor Macquarie had sought means of exercising some control. In 1814 he had commissioned

Kendall as a Justice of the Peace, and five years later he had similarly appointed another member of the mission, John Gare Butler.

Dillon intended to surrender his stowaways to the two magistrates, so that they could be placed on board the first vessel bound for Sydney. He could not persuade Kendall and Butler to accept them, however, since they possessed no lock-up and, unlike the gaoler at Sydney, lacked the power to claim maintenance for anyone they might detain. He therefore handed the men over to his friend Towai, a son of the late Te Pahi.

At about the time of Dillon's arrival, Marsden also reached the Bay of Islands with the new head of the mission, the Reverend Henry Williams. Dillon wrote to him about the stowaways, addressing his letter—rather in the style of a bygone age—to 'The Revd. Samuel Marsden Clerk .[3] He asked him to arrange a passage for them to New South Wales, in order 'to rid this unprotected place of such desperadoes, as they are'. Men of this kind, he added, were 'accumulating in numbers every day, and will I have every reason to apprehend seize upon and carry some vessel off very shortly, unless their numbers are reduced'. He also asked him to inform the Governor of 'the necessity there is of having a different class of persons to search the ships from those at present employed . . . who for a trifling remuneration would allow all the convicts in New South Wales to escape'. Though Marsden was interested in Dillon's letter—not least because one of the stowaways was a former servant of his own—and had a talk with him about it, he took no effective action to return any of the men to Sydney[4].

Before the *Calder* sailed, she was boarded by 'two oppressed and enslaved chiefs, from the district of the River Thames',[5] who had been brought to the Bay of Islands by Hongi's men. Dillon agreed to give them refuge and to take them with him to South America. The words 'district of the River Thames' were used, at that time, to refer to an area stretching from the Waikato in the west to Coromandel Peninsula in the east. Dillon's description could thus have applied to chiefs of any of the tribes whose members might be met with on the southern shores of Hauraki Gulf or those of the Firth of Thames. One of the refugees, named Hinaki, however, was almost certainly of the Ngatipaoa, as probably was his unnamed associate. In any event, they came from a part of New Zealand rich in *kauri* forests. It was, indeed, the district that Cook had pointed to as a future source of the finest masts and spars. Now, when many of its people had been massacred because of their lack of firearms, it was

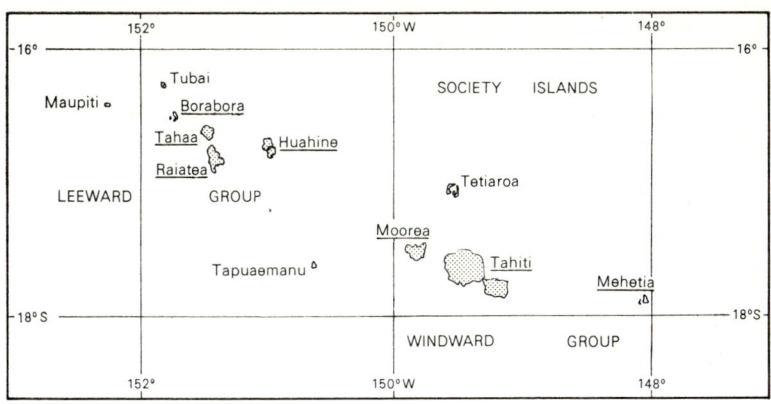

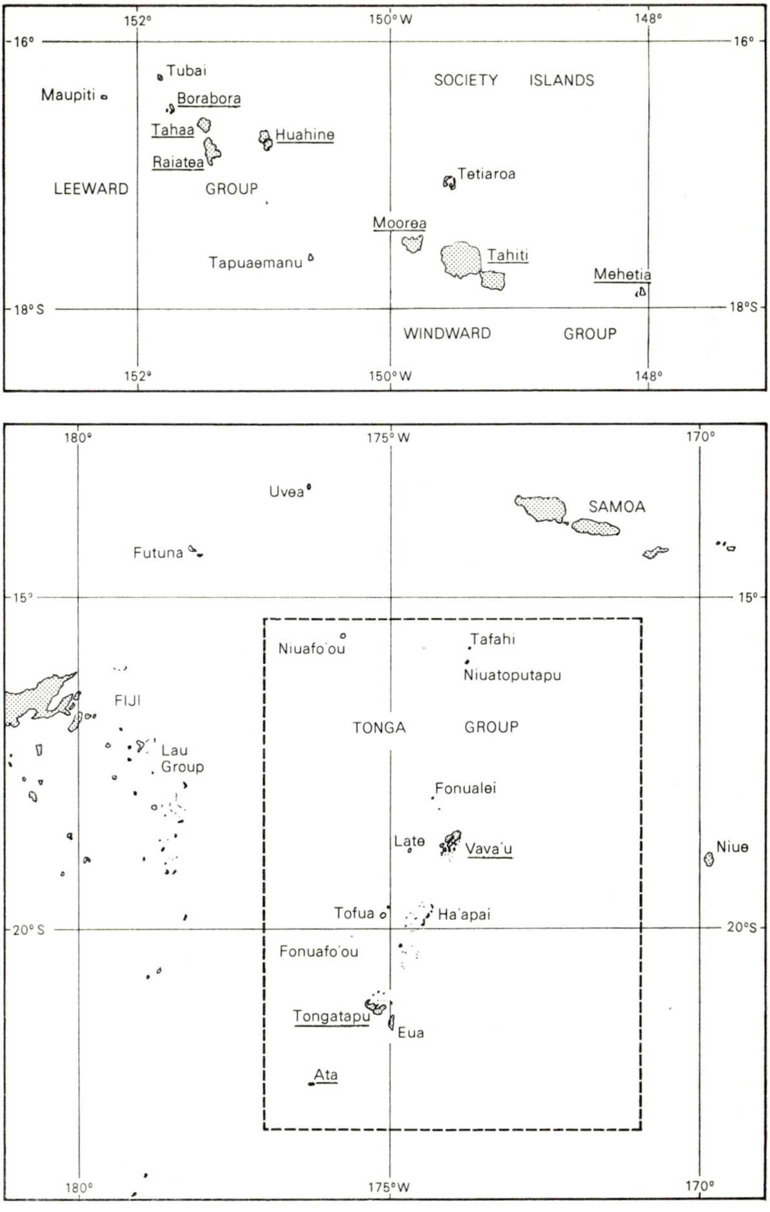

2 The Tonga Group and the Society Islands

ripe for exploitation. By befriending the two chiefs, and promising to bring them back from Peru and Chile laden with muskets and powder, Dillon created for himself a promising commercial opening.

From the Bay of Islands the *Calder* sailed before the westerlies to the South American coast. Dillon made a call at Talcahuano, in Chile, where he loaded wheat and wine. He then followed the coast northward and reached Callao, in Peru, on 18 December 1823.[6] This visit to Callao—the port from which Mendaña had sailed over 250 years before—brought Dillon an unexpected reward in near-by Lima.

A contemporary traveller has described the route from port to capital, thronged with pack-mules escorted by muleteers in 'immense brimmed hats':

> The approach to Lima, especially by the gate of Callao, is very inviting: the bright spires and towers of various churches and public buildings are seen rising from the bosom of orange and lime groves, and contrasting beautifully with their verdure. The summit of the cathedral, the dome of San Augustin, and the towers of San Francisco and San Domingo, are most conspicuous. In the back ground are the Andes, which seem in some situations to approach so near the city as to block up the principal streets.[7]

Dillon was much impressed by 'the really christian conduct of the benighted ministers of the catholic religion at Lima';[8] but he was most excited by his meeting with the widow of Máximo Rodríguez.

One of the mysteries of Pacific history that had interested him was the evidence of two Spanish voyages to Tahiti between Cook's several visits there. It seemed, too, that Roman Catholic ceremonies had been performed on shore. What had been the purpose of the visitors and whence had they come? Cook himself had wondered, and so had the LMS missionaries, and so had Dillon. Now he heard that in the city of Lima an old woman was still living whose husband had gone on those two voyages. He therefore set out for the capital.

In the spring of 1772 the Viceroy, Don Manuel de Amat y Juniet, had despatched the frigate *Aguila* from Callao. She had remained in Tahiti for a month, in November and December, and had then returned to Peru. Rodríguez had served on this voyage as a foot-soldier or marine. In 1774 the *Aguila* had sailed again, accompanied by a second vessel, the *Jupiter*. On this occasion two priests and their attendants had been left in Tahiti for about a year. Rodríguez, acting as interpreter, had been one of these attendants. He had kept a journal of his experiences; and Dillon obtained a copy of it from his widow. Two accounts of these voyages had, in fact, been published in Spanish, and one of them had subsequently appeared in German translation. But these accounts had remained generally unknown in the English-speaking world. It was from Dillon's summary of the Rodríguez journal, published on his return to Calcutta, that later historians began to build up their knowledge.[9]

From Callao, the *Calder* beat south for Valparaiso. This was Dillon's first visit to Valparaiso; but he was following in the wake of other Indian 'country traders', who had been making the voyage from Calcutta since 1816. The port of Valparaiso is a curving bay, exposed to winter storms. The town is built along a narrow coastal strip and on the steep slopes of ravines that penetrate the higher land behind. In 1824 it was being rebuilt after a disastrous earthquake. But it was the centre of much commercial activity. Following the wars of independence in Spanish America, it had been made a free port and had become the principal *entrepôt* for the Pacific coast as far north as Acapulco, in Mexico. The English community was estimated by the British consul to number between 1,000 and 3,000. It included substantial merchants and small traders, tavern-keepers and sailors, and a large group of adventurers who had been drawn to South America by the revolutionary wars.[10]

Dillon had no difficulty in making commercial and social contacts. Even the governor of Valparaiso, José Ignacio Zenteno, who had consciously adopted an English way of life, soon became his friend. In this congenial environment, his commercial ambitions expanded. He decided not to delay his exploitation of the Thames till he was ready to return to New Zealand in the *Calder*. He bought a second vessel, in partnership with a local merchant—a ship of about 430 tons,[11] renamed her *St Patrick*, and placed her under Chilean registry.[12] John Florence was appointed master and a crew engaged. The two Maori chiefs joined her as passengers; and, loaded with muskets and powder, she was despatched for a cargo of spars.

Dillon himself, in the *Calder*, seems to have made a trip round the Horn and to have visited the Falkland Islands. The purpose of this visit is not clear. He may have called in the course of a voyage to Montevideo or Buenos Aires; or he may have gone specifically to the Falklands—perhaps for a cargo of livestock. But, whatever the circumstances, he obviously spent some little time there, for he 'sketched out a Chart' of the islands. And, from this time, the tangled history and the future prospects of the Falklands became one of his minor interests.[13]

Back in Valparaiso, Dillon loaded the *Calder* with a mixed cargo, in which copper and tobacco were the most valuable items; and, apparently towards the middle of August 1824 he sailed on his return voyage to New South Wales by way of the Pacific Islands.[14]

DILLON's approach to his work, as a mariner and as a merchant, was practical but essentially professional. He seems always to have provided himself with the most authentic charts and pilot books that were available. One of his several accounts of the wreck of the *Phatisalam* makes it apparent, for example, that he was then in possession of Matthew Flinders's chart of Bass Strait; and, in his later writings, he occasionally emphasizes a point of detail by referring to the charts of earlier sailors or particular publishers.[15] Looking back on his early service in the *Calder*, a sea-captain of high standing in his profession wrote of Dillon: 'He was a very shrewd navigator by dead reckoning, worked the chronometers, but never troubled himself to obtain the longitude by lunar observations'.[16] Though Dillon was probably inclined to ignore procedures that he considered inessential, he took great pains to ensure the accuracy of his observations when the situation so required. He displayed unusual interest, for example, in surveying and chart-making.

As a merchant he was always well informed. At the time of his death he owned a copy of William Milburn's *Oriental Commerce*, the most authoritative guide to trade in all the recognized parts of eastern Asia and on the continental shores of the Pacific.[17] This was the edition of 1825; but it is likely that he possessed or, at least, had read its predecessor of 1813 when he began trading on his own account. Moreover, in his correspondence and statements to the press, he displayed a wide knowledge of Asian and Pacific commerce. His competence in matters of business was, indeed, implicit in Combermere's assurance of his standing with the merchants of Calcutta and in a statement of his own, in 1828: 'I had been established and was well known as a Merchant, and Ship owner in India, as well as in South America, where I had formed many connections'.[18]

But, for the Pacific Islands, there were as yet no manuals on trade, no pilot books, and—for many archipelagos—no charts, apart from those published with accounts of exploration. Like other mariners, Dillon used the narratives of the explorers as guides to navigation. Like other merchants, he examined them for information on the islands' resources. When he sailed from Valparaiso, he was 'in search of sandal-wood',[19] which he already knew to be present in several island groups other than Fiji. But the successful conduct of a trading voyage through the islands represented, for him, little more than the overt framework of a far deeper personal experience. With the narratives of the explorers open before him he lived again the lives of Wallis, of Bougainville, of Cook. He followed the movements of sun and stars, inhaled the breezes blown off island shores with the concentration and excitement of the Polynesian navigators of many centuries before or of their modern successors who were spreading Christianity through the eastern islands.

Land was first sighted in the Tuamotus★, the chain of atolls that stretches through nearly ten degrees of latitude and fifteen degrees of longitude on the eastern border of Polynesia. Narrow, low-lying strips of land prolific in coconut palms enclosing placid lagoons, they resemble gigantic wreaths flung upon the ocean. Some of the lagoons can be entered by ships; and at one of these the *Calder* touched for rest and refreshment before continuing her voyage to the Society Islands.

She reached Tahiti on 13 September 1824. Dillon was now back among friends of his youth. But much had changed in Tahiti, and the remainder of the Society Islands, since his departure in 1812. After long years of warfare the islands were at peace; the people had become Christians; and modern systems of government had been established. The island governments were guided by the missionaries of the LMS, many of whom Dillon had previously known and one of whom, William Pascoe Crook, had been Mary's schoolmaster in Sydney. When Crook learnt of Dillon's arrival, he hastened to Matavai, where the *Calder* was anchored, and found them at the house of his colleague Charles Wilson.[20] But it was Dillon's old friendship with still another member of the mission, Henry Nott, that proved most fruitful.

Dillon was informed that Teehuteatuaonoa (or Jenny), one of the women who had accompanied Fletcher Christian in the *Bounty* in 1789, had returned home. The settlement that the mutineers and their Polynesian companions had formed on Pitcairn had been discovered by an American sealing captain in 1808; and, after its rediscovery by

---

★Before this, the *Calder* may have visited Pitcairn. The *Bengal Hurkaru* (5 September, 20 October 1826) refers to a visit by Dillon to the island, which, if made, could have been only at this time. However, the knowledge of events there in the early twenties which Dillon certainly possessed could equally well have been gained from contact with other mariners.

H.M.S. *Briton* and *Tagus* in 1814, the outlines of its history had become widely known. But, except for one narrative based on a discussion with Jenny, the accounts that had been published all depended on the testimony of John Adams, the only one of the mutineers to have survived the first ten years of violent disputes. Jenny had been the wife of Adams himself and, subsequently, of Isaac Martin. In 1817 she had obtained a passage to South America, whence she had eventually returned to Tahiti. On 23 September Dillon and Nott arranged a meeting with her, during which she recounted her experiences. This narrative, which was taken down by Nott, is the best account that exists of events between the departure of the *Bounty* from Tahiti and the discovery of the Pitcairn settlement nineteen years later. It was published by Dillon in Calcutta in 1826 and later elsewhere.[21]

About the beginning of October the *Calder* sailed for the Leeward Islands. Before Dillon left Sydney he had written to his friend of earlier years, the daughter of Fenuapeho, of Taha'a. He had sent her some presents and a message that he would be visiting her island to buy pigs; and she had duly prepared for his return.[22] But his experience in the pork trade had also convinced him that the islands could become producers of beef. He had therefore brought from Chile two cows and a bull, together with horses and donkeys. This livestock was landed on Taha'a, where, in the course of time, it greatly multiplied.[23]

On a visit to the neighbouring island of Ra'iatea, Dillon met the missionary John Williams, a man whom he subsequently held in high regard. Williams had first arrived in the Society Islands some years after Dillon's residence there. He was of humble origin and not physically robust; but he possessed both the power of leadership and a restless spirit. 'For my part', he wrote, 'I cannot content myself within the narrow limits of a single reef'. He had already played the principal role in the extension of the mission's field of work to the Cook Islands, where, through the guidance of the chief Rongomatane, of Atiu, he had reached the important but uncharted island of Rarotonga. Polynesians, when setting out on a voyage—he later wrote— 'do not leave from any part of an island, as we do, but invariably have what may be called starting-points'. Rongomatane had therefore directed that Williams's schooner should be taken to a particular place on the coast of Atiu and lined up with the accepted landmarks. She was then, he explained, pointing in the direction of her destination.[24] Though Williams's claim to being the European discoverer of Rarotonga was incorrect, his extensive voyages through the islands gained him the comradeship and respect of men such as Dillon.

When the *Calder* sailed from the Society Islands, late in October, she was bound for Fiji. But two calls were made *en route*, at Atiu and at Tongatapu. The first of these provided Dillon with interesting evidence on the range of Polynesian drift voyages. Williams had told him that, some six months earlier, his boat had disappeared while returning from a visit to Tahiti. He believed its crew must have perished. At Atiu, however, Dillon found the boat and its crew. They had been, he wrote, 'drifting about at sea for three months' before they finally made land five hundred miles from their starting point.[25]

At Tongatapu, Dillon was put on the track of an experience remarkably similar to that of Williams during his voyage to Rarotonga. 'I bought a valuable kind of pearl shell', he wrote. 'I enquired from whence it came, and was given to understand, from an island three days sail to the westward from Tonga.' Takai, a minor chief of Lakeba, in the Lau group of Fiji, who was then in Tongatapu, told him he 'had been drifted there once on his way to Tonga by foul weather' and could find it again. Taking Takai as pilot and a Tongan named Langi, Dillon sailed towards the west.

Takai first directed Dillon to the island of Ogea, in southern Lau, where 'he got the vessel's stern placed opposite to a bluff . . ., and directed me to steer in the direction of her head'. A hundred miles to the southward, the expected landfall was made.

> I discovered a fine fertile and verdant island, cultivated and inhabited from the water's edge to the tops of the hills, which were moderately high and abounding with yams, some of 30 lb, weight; tarra [taro], sweet potatoes, bananas, sugar cane, cocoa nuts, and various tropical fruits, were in great abundance. There were likewise plenty of pigs, fish, and fresh water; the circumference of the island is about nine or ten leagues, surrounded by a reef and no anchorage. On the N.W. side there is a good boat passage and landing place. The natives appear friendly, and speak a dialect nearly similar to that spoken by the natives of the Fidgees.

The people told him that they had not previously seen a ship but that one had been wrecked 'a long time ago' on the small islands of Tuvana, a day's sail to the southward, from which they had 'got a pistol and some glass beads, both of a foreign manufactory, being either of a Spanish or Russian make'.

Dillon believed that the island was a new discovery, since his

'General Chart for 1823, by John Purdy, Hydrographer', showed unbroken seas in this latitude and longitude. He therefore 'called the island . . . Joseph Barretto's Island, in respect to my patron, Joseph Barretto, Esquire, merchant of Calcutta'.[26] It was, in fact, Ono Levu, the major island of Ono-i-Lau, which had been visited by a Russian expedition, commanded by Bellingshausen, four years earlier. But, to a mariner who travelled with stories of the past always in his mind, the sight of a fertile and inhabited island where none was generally known by Europeans to exist was, in itself, no inconsiderable experience.

Towards mid-December the *Calder* reached Bua Bay, where the *General Wellesley* had anchored fifteen years before. Dillon was unsuccessful in his quest for sandalwood: 'after a stay of three weeks', he wrote, '[I] procured about 500 lbs, of Sandal Wood; whereas I had in the same space of time in 1808 procured 150 tons of that valuable wood'.[27] But Fiji, like the Society Islands, had a firm place in his affections. He remembered his warm friendships with Fijians and discounted even his moments of terror on 'Dillon's Rock'. 'The Fejee Islands, . . . leaving Christianity out of the scale', he said on his return to Sydney, 'make the nearest approximation to civilization,' of any of the South Sea Islands. And during this visit he was treated with 'the utmost attention and kindness'.[28]

The leading chief of the district—the Tui Bua—named a son 'Peter' after him.[29] More importantly, his old friend Naulivou sent his three brothers on the hundred-mile journey from Bau to greet him. No doubt they told him of the war parties that had been sent to Naurore Bay to avenge the massacre of 6 September 1813. But they also brought him a message that Naulivou wished Dillon to live with him and would give him his daughter as a wife. Dillon relates that he declined this proposal, explaining that he was unable to remain in Fiji at that time, but said that he would like some land, so that he might return later. He was then given, he states, the island of Makogai, with its people and its products.[30]

When Naulivou's brothers returned to Bau, they were accompanied by a young American, David Whippy, who had joined the *Calder* on the South American coast. Whippy carried presents from Dillon to Naulivou. It was intended that he should remain at Bau for some months collecting bêche-de-mer and tortoise-shell for Dillon, after which he would rejoin the latter on his next visit. But it was thirteen years before Dillon was again in Fiji. Long before his return Whippy had decided that he did not wish to leave the islands. He was well received by the Vunivalu; and, over the years, he enjoyed the support of many other chiefs. He founded the settlement of Levuka and came to exercise a considerable influence over relationships between Fijians and foreigners. When he died in 1871 he left a large family of part-Fijian descendants.[31]

At about the time Whippy landed at Bau, on 6 January 1825, the *Calder* sailed for the New Hebrides. On the fourth night out from Bau, the island of Futuna was sighted. The following day the brig anchored at Port Resolution, on the east coast of Tana. Dillon had not previously visited the New Hebrides. He arrived therefore as a seeker of knowledge, with Cook's narrative of his visit in 1774 as his guide.

At Port Resolution he noted: 'It seemed to me that no Ship had been there since Captain Cook left it . . .'.[32] In fact, his impression was erroneous—not surprisingly, since no one on board spoke the local language—though only one intervening caller, the Russian explorer Golovnin, in 1807, is known. But, imaginatively, it was important to him as he sought to reconstruct the visit of his illustrious precursor. He obtained two of the medals Cook had distributed and persuaded himself that 'a few of the old natives' could still pronounce 'the memorable name of Cook', as well as those of Wales, the astronomer, and Forster, the naturalist. He compared the scene that lay before him—the lush surroundings of the sheltered harbour and the gaunt volcanic peak of Yasur rising behind them—with Cook's account of it. The volcano was 'sending forth throughout the day and night immense columns of fire and smoke', as it had been when Cook was there.

Dillon concluded that Tana was 'more numerously inhabited than any of the islands' he had previously visited in the Pacific. But, from the time when a canoe came out from Port Resolution as the *Calder* approached, he was somewhat disenchanted with New Hebridean culture.

> The canoe contained fourteen naked young men, armed with formidable clubs, bows, arrows, stones, and slings; both the canoe and arms were far inferior to those of my friends the Fejees . . . , and bespoke the inhabitants of this island to be many years behind them in point of civilization.

Later, after he had left the New Hebrides and compared his observations with 'the collateral testimony of others', he reached an even more unfavourable conclusion.

... I may safely assert without incurring the hazard of contradiction, that the Natives of the New Hebrides are by many shades further removed from civilization, and that their general disposition indicate[s] a more permanent attachment to barbarous feelings and habits than has hitherto been found in any part of the South Sea.

He supported his contention by citing two examples chosen from the 'many curious facts' that had come to his knowledge. The people lacked delicacy, since 'those parts of the human body which are almost always concealed from view are completely exposed by the males'. And they had failed to develop beyond a primitive level of material culture, since 'holes in the earth or caverns amongst the rocks serve for their habitations, and this in a country beautifully supplied by nature with every requisite for the construction of comfortable habitations'.

But the New Hebrideans were not altogether lacking in likeable traits. Dillon described an incident whose outcome revealed one of these. Soon after the *Calder*'s arrival in Tana, the cook's mate, 'a very small Chinaman', rushed to him in terror exclaiming 'the savage want kill me, take my clothes, want pull me in canoe'. Accepting the story, Dillon fired at the retreating canoe and wounded one of its occupants. When he learnt that the visitors had merely attempted to steal shirts that the Chinese was hanging on a line, he 'regretted exceedingly' his rash action. A little later the wounded man returned to the brig; 'I then probed and dressed the wound', Dillon wrote, 'and sent my patient on shore, who, to my great surprise and joy returned ten days after completely recovered, and presented me with some baskets of fruit and fine fowls . . . '. Nowhere else in the Pacific, he considered, would such an incident have had so happy an outcome.

Another characteristic of the people of Tana that Dillon noted was a fondness for anything highly scented, like flowers or herbs. One day he was visited by a Tanese with a piece of sandalwood tied to one arm. Dillon's purpose in coming to the New Hebrides had been to search for sandalwood; but his early inquiries had been fruitless. Now, he learnt from his visitor that it was abundant on the neighbouring island of Eromanga.

The *Calder* sailed for Traitor's Head, on the east coast of Eromanga, where 'Captain Cook anchored, and had a fight with the natives'. But, as the wind was blowing from the east into the open bay, Dillon decided to sail to the lee side of the island. When the brig was off the lava cliffs and broad fringing reef that make much of the south-west coast inaccessible, a large open bay was seen to the northward. The boats were sent in and found good anchoring ground. Next morning an attempt to move the *Calder* into the bay—subsequently named Dillon Bay—was foiled by lack of wind. A party was sent ashore, however, armed and carrying axes, to look for sandalwood. Towards noon it returned with a substantial quantity of sandalwood and a report that the tree was growing plentifully close to the shore. In the afternoon a watering party was landed, and Dillon made a sketch of the anchorage.

Dillon Bay, with a vigorous stream flowing into it and thus inhibiting the growth of coral, is the only good anchorage on the west coast of Eromanga. By discovering it and the existence of sandalwood near by,[33] Dillon had opened up the possibility of a new development in Pacific trade. None the less, he decided to sail next day; and he never returned to the New Hebrides. The reasons for his decision were several. He had found the people 'not to attach the least value to any of our goods', so that they had no incentive to cut sandalwood for him. Moreover, while the watering party was ashore, it had been attacked with spears and arrows and with stones thrown from slings. But, as was not infrequently the case, Dillon seems to have been influenced not only by sense but also by sensibility; he was a warmhearted man who had always thought of Pacific Islanders as his friends, and he did not like the New Hebrideans.

From Eromanga, the *Calder* sailed 'for New Caledonia', though it is doubtful whether she did more than skirt its eastern coast. Thence, her course was laid for the Bay of Islands, where Dillon could expect to receive news of the *St Patrick*. In fact, he narrowly missed falling in with her, for when he reached the Bay, on Wednesday 9 February, he learnt that she had sailed for Valparaiso on the preceding Thursday.[34] His major question regarding her voyage was, however, satisfactorily answered: she was carrying a full cargo of spars.

The sailing of the *St Patrick* was not without interest in another way, for Thomas Kendall and his family had embarked in her as passengers. In August 1823, when Dillon was at the Bay of Islands *en route* to South America, Marsden had handed Kendall a letter dismissing him from the service of the Church Missionary Society.[35] Now he was travelling to Valparaiso where, Captain Florence had told him, the English community was seeking a clergyman. He had been found guilty by his employers of drunkenness and adultery, and—like his colleagues in the mission—he had traded in firearms. Weaknesses in his complex personality, of which Dillon had gained some experience in 1814, had largely brought about his fall from grace; but the disturbed state of Maori society—epitomized in the destructive ambitions of Hongi Hika—had helped to precipitate it.

On this occasion Dillon found the Bay of Islands even more unsettled than it had been in 1823. A plundering party had returned from Whangaroa a few days before his arrival, and a large force led by Hongi and another local chief, Te Whareumu, was assembling for a further expedition to the southward. These conditions were not conducive to amicable contacts between visiting mariners and the local people, for, as soon as the *Calder* had dropped anchor, she was rushed by a crowd of Maoris, who, according to the missionary William Hall, 'immediately began to steal and take away every thing, they could lay hold of'. Intervention by Dillon's friend Towai temporarily halted the pillaging, but later a musket was stolen by a half-brother of Towai, who was himself held hostage by Dillon till it was returned two days later. This was not, however, the final affront inflicted on Dillon, whose temper seems often to have become frayed during the latter part of a long voyage. When two other Maoris were discovered stealing a copper chain from the rudder, he had them brought to the quarter-deck where, after examination before Maori witnesses, they were punished with two and three dozen lashes respectively.[36]

Dillon's call at the Bay of Islands was a brief one. On 25 February he reached Sydney, where the *Sydney Gazette* warmly welcomed the return of 'this old Commander out of Australia'. He gave the *Gazette* an account of his voyage, and of events in many of the places he had visited,[37] and contributed an interesting letter to its newly-founded rival, the *Australian*, on his discovery—as he still believed it to be—of 'Joseph Barretto's Island'.[38]

The *Gazette* took a particular interest in Takai, whom Dillon described as a Fijian admiral, and his Tongan companion, Langi. In successive issues it described Takai's entertainment by some of 'the most respectable inhabitants', his visit to 'Mr. Dickson, of the steam engine' (whose wondrous machine he regarded with awe), and his quest for goods that would be useful to him when he returned home.[39] In reporting the chief's first meeting with the merchant Robert Cooper, it added a comment on Dillon himself. Takai, it declared, believed that Cooper must be the '*King or Governor of Botany Bay*' because he was the biggest man in town. 'We should be apt to conjecture', the paper commented, 'that if Mr. Cooper is considered a king . . . from his size that the worthy captain who escorted the admiral hither, at least must be an *emperor!*' Takai and Langi made their daytime headquarters at Cooper's store; and Dillon made play with the status ascribed to the merchant when he had cards printed for distribution by his protégés to possible well-wishers.

> I, the undersigned, Thaki [Takai], *Fejee Admiral*, beg leave to inform the inhabitants, that I am about to depart from this Colony, and I shall be extremely thankful and grateful for any articles that can be spared me—such as old cutlery, ironmongery, gunpowder, &c. &c. Should any of my friends be kind enough to spare me a few of these articles, I shall thank them to be so good as to leave them with my friend, *Governor Cooper, the King of Botany-Bay*, opposite the old Burial-ground.[40]

In one respect the card was over-optimistic: few vessels visited Fiji; and the *Calder* was not immediately returning to the islands.

Dillon, meanwhile, had business of his own to attend to. He sought to dispose of the cargo he had loaded in South America and the Pacific Islands—mainly to merchant houses, though he advertised a direct sale to the public of 'BOXES of real HAVANNAH SEGARS'.[41] Once again he took up with the government the matter of his rights and obligations in respect of the wreck of the *Phatisalam*.[42] And he engaged two new officers for the *Calder*.

When Dillon arrived in Sydney he intended to continue his return voyage to Calcutta. He offered to accept passengers and freight for that city and for three intermediate ports of call—Batavia, the new British settlement of Singapore, and Penang.[43] But when the *Calder* had been cleared by the authorities he changed his mind. The reasons for his last-minute decision are obscure. He may have been unexpectedly successful in selling the whole of his cargo in Sydney or have failed to obtain an adequate loading for the onward voyage. One factor is perhaps more likely than others, however, to have been uppermost in his mind. John Florence's success at the Thames encouraged him to expedite his own return to South America, both to obtain his share of the prospective profits and to plan further ventures in the timber trade. In any event, when the *Calder* sailed through Sydney Heads at 1 p.m. on 23 March she was bound for Valparaiso.[44]

SEVEN

Dillon in Mid-Passage

1825-26

DILLON kept a journal in these years. Pacing his cabin and dictating to one of his officers or some other suitable person, he recorded the day's events, his impressions of people and places, and his conclusions on matters of public affairs, history or ethnography. He drew on this journal when presenting his experiences in letters and statements to the press or elsewhere; but the only parts of the journal itself which appear to have survived are those that were published in his own lifetime. The factual and imaginative quality of these sections—the short extract describing his visit to the New Hebrides in January 1825 and the long narrative of his voyage in the *Research* during 1828-29 —reveals the loss sustained through the disappearance of the remainder.[1]

The absence of a day-to-day account by Dillon himself of most of his voyages increases the importance of a journal kept by the young man whom he engaged at Sydney as third officer of the *Calder*. The 'Journal of Voyages to various parts of the World written by Geo: Bayly for the amusement of such of his friends as feel themselves disposed to read it' is a fair copy, with the addition of retrospective comment, from the narrative actually recorded at sea. But it was produced not long after the events it describes, when fact was still enmeshed with feeling. Sixty years later, looking back from the tranquillity of old age, George Bayly published a book about his voyages with Dillon. Drawing not only on his journal but also on contemporary letters home he added some further detail; but he excluded a few incidents that reflected, with painful clarity, the anguish sometimes caused to those on board by Dillon's intemperate conduct.[2] George Bayly was an Englishman of good education who had been left stranded in Sydney when the ship in which he was serving his apprenticeship was seized by the navy. He joined the *Calder* understanding that she was bound for Calcutta, whence, he believed, he would have no difficulty in working his passage home to England. He accepted the change of plan, though with a suspicion—almost certainly unjustified—that he had been tricked by Dillon. In later years he became a captain himself and eventually an Elder Brother of Trinity House. He thus interpreted his experience both from the vantage point of a buoyant junior officer and from that of a retired mariner of high professional standing. His journal and his book present complementary portraits of Dillon—against the background of his voyages—not dissimilar in essentials, but the first a sensitive sketch, lively and highly-coloured, the second a more formal likeness such as those hung on the walls of the Royal Academy.

BAYLY's first impression of Dillon was a favourable one.

> When I went on board the *Calder*, the captain was walking the quarter-deck ... He was dressed in spotless white, and wore a very broad-brimmed straw hat. He came forward, and with a pleasant, smiling countenance welcomed me very graciously.[3]

After inquiring about Bayly's attainments, he introduced him to his fellow officers. These were George Ross, the first officer, 'a quaint-spoken American from Boston', and Jack Mossman, the second, who had learnt his seamanship in English colliers. Ross had spent some years in the Marquesas trading for sandalwood on behalf of a merchant in Canton. His life in the islands, Bayly later concluded, had eroded his sense of urgency and his inclination to effort. Mossman, who had served in the *Calder* on her previous voyage, was a fine practical seaman, alert and knowledgeable, but he could neither read nor write.

The crew, apart from the Chinese cook and Bengalee steward, was made up in almost equal numbers of Europeans and Polynesians. The latter were mainly Tahitians, of whom several appeared in the ship's muster under exotic names clearly devised by Dillon—'Governor Macquarie', 'Major Goulburn', 'Buckgarow Riley' and 'Salt Fish'.[4] Bayly noted that Dillon 'always treated [them] with great kindness, and they in turn were devoted to him'.

Bayly had been warned that Dillon's benignity could disappear more suddenly than sunshine before a summer storm; and, shortly before the *Calder* sailed from Sydney, he had his first experience of this alarming transformation. The 'trade' had been brought on deck, to be listed and placed under Bayly's control. 'It consisted of a large quantity of iron tools, fish-hooks, beads and other ornaments, coloured cloth, Jew's harps, and a miscellaneous assortment of articles used in bartering with the natives of the South Sea Islands.' With it had been brought out the collection of island artefacts—'spears, clubs, bows and arrows, paddles, etc.'—that Dillon had acquired, as 'he had been in the habit of purchasing everything the natives would dispose of, for the sake of being on friendly terms with them'. To Bayly's delight, the collection stimulated Dillon into telling him of some of his island experiences. But, while the narration was proceeding, a boy who had been sent ashore 'with 9 or 10 verbal messages to different people' returned on board. On questioning him, Dillon found that one message had not been delivered.

> and Captn D. was so exasperated against him that he seized an axe that laid beside him and hurled it after the boy, who foreseeing what was coming jumped behind the caboose the moment before the axe came flying along the deck after him.

The boy was sent ashore once again; he did not return.

On the voyage to Valparaiso the weather harassed those on board far more than Dillon's stormy temper. A course was set for the South Cape of New Zealand. In February Dillon had brought back from the Bay of Islands a civil engineer, John Busby, who had been in the far south of New Zealand refloating a New South Wales government brig that had gone aground on the island of Ruapuke.[5] Busby had probably spoken favourably of that part of the country, for Dillon intended to put in somewhere on the southern coast. But, from a few days after leaving Sydney, the weather was boisterous; and he did not call. From the South Cape, the *Calder* ran before the westerlies in forty-eight to fifty degrees south latitude. The brig rolled and pitched unceasingly, and often mountainous seas broke over her decks. Working under difficulties, the Bengalee steward continually incurred Dillon's wrath, as he broke the cabin crockery or 'shook silver spoons overboard out of the tablecloth'. Dillon kept a sheet headed 'Crimes' on which he noted these misdeeds. Whenever the number reached twelve, the steward received a dozen lashes with the cat-o'-nine-tails.

The rough weather also made the *Calder* difficult to control. She steered badly when running before the wind. One evening, when the gale was particularly boisterous, she was brought by the lee when a Polynesian assisting the helmsman misunderstood an order that was given to him. While they were trying to bring her round she dived ominously into the trough of the sea and as she rose again shipped a great quantity of water over her bow. Ross seized the wheel and ordered the helmsman to 'get out of the way, quick'. A moment later Dillon appeared, pistol in hand, shouting: 'Where's the villain who was at the wheel?' 'I guess he's just gone forward', Ross replied. 'I sent him out o' this, for fear you'd shoot him.' As the night advanced, the wind rose higher, so that only with great difficulty could the brig be steered. One violent gust that struck her caused a movement of the chain cable and some of the ballast, and she developed a marked list to port.

Several days later, after more damage had been done, the *Calder* turned northward. Better weather was encountered, and she reached the South American coast towards the middle of May without further trouble, forty-eight days out from Sydney.[6] On arrival at Valparaiso the European members of the crew and the steward were paid off. Dillon moved with his family to lodgings on shore. He was occupied with the affairs of the *St Patrick*, as well as those of the *Calder*. The former had arrived early in April;[7] and, according to Bayly, the spars she brought from New Zealand realized 'an immense sum'. From the *Calder*, he had a large quantity of 'military clothing' to dispose of;[8] and he was also busy assembling a cargo for her to carry back to Sydney—'wheat, wine, flour, plums, raisins, almonds, tobacco, &c. &c.'[9] At the beginning of June he was offered a cargo for Callao and agreed to make the voyage. But, within a few days, these plans were destroyed.

On the morning of 11 June a heavy swell entered the exposed bay, accompanied by a rising wind. Dillon was 'in an ill state of health', Bayly writes, 'but came off before breakfast to give his orders'. The brig's stern cable was slipped, so that she could ride head to wind. Mossman, Bayly and the Polynesian seamen remained on duty, and Ross—who had been dismissed for drunkenness—was still aboard. The *Calder* would have ridden out the gale, if the crew of a Chilean brig lying to windward of her had not, in Dillon's words, 'abandoned their vessel to the mercy of old Neptune', letting their ship drive against her and snapping her cables. By this time Ross was lying dead drunk in the cabin. Since he had been the only officer who spoke Tahitian, Mossman and Bayly were severely hampered in their efforts to control the brig. That night she was driven on to the beach, where she rolled alarmingly in the surf, which threatened to stave in her deck.

Dillon was among the crowd that gathered on shore, carrying lanterns, to observe the disaster. Above the roar of the storm, he shouted instructions 'to cut away the masts'. And, when a bridge of sand had formed round the fallen mainmast, Bayly and his companions made a dash for safety. Characteristically, Dillon took the Polynesians, who were 'completely fagged', to lodgings in the town but sent Mossman and Bayly on board again to protect the wreck and her contents from looting.

The bay of Valparaiso, Dillon sourly commented, was 'such as no man but an obstinate Spaniard would think of making the principal port of so fine a country'.

BUT Dillon, despite his illness, set to work at once to repair his fortunes. The hull of the *Calder* was sold at auction for $500 (only £100) though a considerably larger sum was received for her sails and other gear and for Dillon's collection of South Sea Islands weapons. In August he bought his partner's share in the *St Patrick*. Though larger than the *Calder*, she was less stoutly built and a slow sailer, with her best years of service already behind her. But Dillon had been encouraged by the results of her previous voyage and planned to load her again in New Zealand—this time for Calcutta.

Dillon intended to take a direct passage to Calcutta, where he would await the *St Patrick*'s arrival. Meanwhile, he resumed his contacts with the governor, José Ignacio Zenteno, with Christopher Nugent, the British consul-general, and with Thomas Kendall, whom he joined in making a donation towards the upkeep of the foreign burial ground,[10] while he organized the voyage of the *St Patrick*. John Florence remained as master. Mossman and Bayly were appointed first and third mates; and Ross, who was partially forgiven—perhaps because of his useful knowledge of Tahitian—became second mate. The Polynesians who had come in the *Calder* were employed as seamen, along with several others who had found their way to Valparaiso. Twenty British sailors were engaged, most of whom, according to Bayly, had served in the Chilean navy under Lord Cochrane. And Miguel Zenteno, the young son of the governor, joined the ship's company for experience.

Before the *St Patrick* sailed the European members of her company were all entered in the port records as 'naturalized Chileans'. By this time Dillon had changed his mind and assumed command. He was listed as 'Don Pedro Dillon, capitán primero', and Florence as 'Don Juan Florentio, capitán segundo'—a relationship that remained an uneasy one throughout the voyage. On 8 October 1825, with the Chilean colours at the peak and 'an enormous green flag with yellow Irish harp in it' at the main, the ship left for Tahiti.

The first few days at sea were spent fitting out the cabins in a way that Dillon thought appropriate for trading, and if necessary defence, during the *St Patrick*'s passage through the islands.

> Turning aft a few feet from the foot of the companion-ladder, you entered the state-room. This was separated by a strong bulkhead on either hand from a gallery, about four feet broad, between it and the ship's side. It communicated with a smaller cabin next forward, the whole being isolated from the 'tween-deck cabins by another strong bulkhead. These cabins were fitted with lockers and other compartments adapted for stowing away the 'trade', so that every sort of article was ready to hand when required. The galleries were fitted throughout with musket, pistol, bayonet, and cutlass racks, which bristled with these weapons; each musket and pistol had its cartouche-box suspended from it by the shoulder-strap. Against the bulkhead, on the starboard side, stood Captain Dillon's sleeping-berth, and on this bulkhead were racks for a blunderbuss, two pairs of pistols, and some cutlasses, whilst a tough shillelagh, with a spring dagger in the head, lay 'convenient' inside the sideboard of the berth. The gunpowder was stowed in a magazine built in the smaller cabin. Thus, the captain had everything movable belonging to him under his eye, and, having his weapons within reach, was prepared for any emergency at a moment's notice, even when turned in.[11]

These arrangements, Bayly wrote, 'differed . . . entirely from the usual run of cabins in the merchant service'. They did, however, effectively serve the purposes for which they were intended—except on the occasions when Dillon, in a paroxysm of unreason, seized a weapon, too readily at hand, to give expression to his feelings.

Dillon had a high regard for Bayly. He used him as a private secretary—in port, to take down the long and flamboyant letters that he delighted to despatch; at sea, to dictate to him the entries for his journal, which thus differed markedly from the ill-spelt logbook that he wrote up himself, where squally weather always appeared as 'sqrually'. His regard was returned by Bayly. 'Few men were possessed of greater natural ability than Captain Peter Dillon', he declared, 'though I believe he was chiefly self-taught . . . with hands behind his back, he would pace the cabin and dictate an admirable letter on any subject'.[12] Now, as the weather became warmer, they began working together on deck. A large number of old muskets, some barrels of gunpowder and a quantity of lead for bullets had been taken aboard for use as 'trade' in New Zealand and among the islands. The refurbishing of the muskets, to make them look as new, was the work of the armourer. But one day Dillon said to Bayly:

'Mr. Bayly, do you know how to make musket cartridges?'

When Bayly admitted to ignorance, he added:

'Sit down, then, by me, and I'll soon tache ye.'

Day by day, using the logbooks and other manuscripts of a deceased mariner as cartridge paper, they worked together at this task. Sometimes Dillon talked of his experiences in the islands, and sometimes Bayly read aloud from the narratives of the explorers, each adding by his words to the knowledge of the other.

The atoll of Pinaki, in the Tuamotus, was reached on 9 November and those of Vairaatea and Manuhangi on the two succeeding days. At each of these a landing was attempted, unsuccessfully, in the hope of obtaining forage for some horses and donkeys that Dillon was taking to Tahiti.

After a call at Mehetia, the easternmost of the Society Islands, the ship reached Tahiti on 15 November. She remained there for three weeks. To the satisfaction of his crew, Dillon's first concern was the purchase of provisions. Large quantities of fresh fruit, vegetables and pork were obtained from the Tahitians. Goats were bought from Mrs Nott and barrels of salt pork from Captain Samuel Pinder Henry, the trader son of a missionary.

Dillon's associations with individuals were seldom limited, however, to the matter of buying and selling but tended to range as widely as his, or their, interests would carry them. On this occasion he was surprised to hear that Samuel Henry had brought Takai and Langi to Tahiti. He had left them with a friend in Sydney, to await the sailing of a vessel to Fiji or Tonga, and Henry had met them there. They disliked the cold weather, regretted the lack of yams and coconuts, and were nostalgic for the islands. Since their arrival in Tahiti, Dillon learnt, they had become Christians and were now preparing to return home, with Tahitian teachers, to attempt the conversion of their peoples.[13]

It is likely that Dillon also discussed with Henry his discovery of sandalwood in Eromanga. Henry and his brother-in-law, Thomas Ebrill, were already interested in the trade in sandalwood and had been trying to find it in commercial quantities in the Austral Islands. There is evidence that suggests that either one or both of them visited the New Hebrides in the years immediately following Dillon's visit to Tahiti. But the strongest reason for believing that the two men discussed the discovery derives from Henry's actions in 1829, when he organized an expedition of two vessels to Eromanga for sandalwood.

As on his visit, a year earlier, Dillon renewed his contacts with the Tahitian leaders. One day, Bayly records, the Regent, Queen Pomare Vahine, and 'all the Royal Family' were invited on board.

> They were received with a salute of musketry, and escorted down to the state-room. Here I was instructed to exhibit all our treasures. They took a great fancy to the Jew's-harps, and Peter (he was only known by his Christian name amongst these islands) at once presented one to each of them, and showed the way to use them. Their Royal Highnesses all squatted down with their backs to the bulkhead and their harps at their lips, making all manner of faces in their vain attempts to follow the captain's instructions. Peter meanwhile sat on the table with a large Jew's-harp, and twanged away at some lively Irish jig, whilst the queen, princes, and princesses continually burst into roars of laughter at the sight of each other's grimaces, apparently unconscious that they looked just as absurd themselves.[14]

The *St Patrick* left Tahiti on 6 December. She called at Huahine, Raiatea and Taha'a. At the last island, where Fenuapeho and his daughter came aboard and were given presents, Dillon found the people in revolt against the mission because of the harsh punishment that had been meted out to a woman of high rank.

From the Leeward Islands they sailed westward to the Cooks. At Aitutaki, where they hove to outside the reef, 'Several canoes came off to the Ship with shells, coconuts, mats, and various other articles to dispose of'. Among those who came aboard were a Polynesian mission teacher whom Dillon had known in the Society Islands, and who greeted him warmly, and a throng of young men eager to join the crew. The Polynesians, who had been engaged in Valparaiso had left the ship at Tahiti, which was the home of most of them. Another group, including a Marquesan, had joined her there. But, after discussion with the teacher, Dillon agreed to add two Aitutakians. They were the first men from their island, he later noted, to travel beyond the Pacific.[15]

Dillon was an intense man. Though still in his thirties, he was said, on dubious authority, to have already suffered an attack of apoplexy. His creative role in the Pacific and his personal excesses reflected two facets of a consistent character. Retrospectively, Bayly concluded:

> Captn. D. was the most passionate man I ever saw. His wife lived on board and he very frequently gave her a thrashing, sometimes striking her to the deck, and once broke his Telescope to pieces about her head.

On the voyage south from Tahiti, Bayly claimed, Dillon was drunk for eleven days, 'during which time he threatened to blow my brains out because I could not find some receipt which he had mislaid'. The period in New Zealand obtaining *kauri* spars was to prove a trying one; and, during the course of it, the censorious Bayly noted, Dillon 'cursed and swore in such an abominable manner that he was more like an infernal Spirit than a human being'.[16]

The North Cape of New Zealand was sighted on 24 December. As the *St Patrick* was beating down the east coast towards the Firth of Thames, she was prepared for defence against possible Maori boarders. Eighteen-pounders were mounted in each doorway of the roundhouse, and a chest containing muskets and pikes was hoisted into each top. The members of the crew were allocated to particular stations and instructed in their duties. Since nearly all the Europeans had previously fought in the Chilean service and the Polynesians were 'ready to die for Peter', the safety of the ship, Bayly felt, was in good hands. When he mentioned that he was himself without experience, Dillon commented: 'What could yer parrints have been thinking of, that they didn't tache ye how to fire a musket?'

On 31 December the *St Patrick* anchored, according to Bayly, 'off Pârôâ, with West Isles about half a mile to seaward'—apparently in Waiheke Channel.* This was the height of summer, when the coasts of the Hauraki Gulf are made resplendent by the giant *pohutukawa* trees that grow on every rocky headland, their dark green foliage and twisted branches almost hidden by a mass of scarlet blossom. Near the anchorage, some spars that the ship had been unable to carry on her previous voyage lay on the beach ready for loading. But, when

---

* The location of her anchorage presents some difficulties. The name 'West Isles' was applied by Cook to islands on the western side of Hauraki Gulf in his chart entitled 'River Thames and Mercury Bay in New Zealand' (John Hawkesworth, *An Account of the Voyages . . . successively performed by Commodore Byron, Captain Carteret, Captain Wallis, And Captain Cook . . .* (London, 1773), II, facing 323). I have been unable to identify 'Pârôâ' (Paroa).

Cook did not examine the West Isles or therefore delineate them in detail. On the assumption that Bayly applied the name to the whole group of islands on the west of the gulf (including Waiheke, Ponui and Pakihi), I previously placed the *St Patrick*'s anchorage farther south, 'in, or near, Kawakawa Bay' ('Peter Dillon: the Voyages of the *Calder* and *St Patrick*', *Pacific Islands Portraits*, 26). I now think that Bayly applied the name only to the small islands of Rotoroa, Pakatoa and Tarahiki. I am indebted to Mr L. W. Melvin, of Tauranga, for suggesting this interpretation to me. It accords more fully with other evidence in Bayly's Journal than my previous one.

The *St Patrick* had anchored in the same area a year earlier and had been visited there by the Reverend William White. His description is, however, not explicit as to the location (Diary of Reverend William White, 8-10 January 1825—Trinity College, Auckland).

Ross went ashore, he found all the Maori huts deserted, though there were signs that people had recently been there. Next day—1 January 1826—the *St Patrick*'s whale-boat sailed towards the head of the Firth of Thames in search of labourers. Hinaki had been living at Waihihi, on its eastern shore, since his return from Valparaiso;[17] and in the afternoon the boat returned with him and another chief. During her absence, a canoe-load of Maoris had come alongside the ship. From these two parties of visitors Dillon learnt of events since his departure from the Bay of Islands in the preceding February.

The campaign on which Hongi had then been about to embark had ended less decisively than its predecessors. In the battle of Te Ikaaranganui he had lost one of his sons; and, subsequently, his opponents in the campaign—the Ngatiwhatua—had surprised and massacred a section of his own forces. The obligation to avenge these incidents had caused Hongi to prepare for war once again; and, late in the year, he had set out for the Waikato, to which the Ngatiwhatua had fled, on an expedition from which he had not yet returned.[18]

Hinaki explained that most of his people had retreated inland because they lacked sufficient firearms for effective resistance to Hongi's war parties. 'Why', replied Dillon, 'we've come for the very purpose of supplying you'. He offered a musket, or its equivalent in gunpowder, for every twenty spars cut, stripped, and brought out to the ship. Hinaki and his companion accepted the offer on behalf of their people; and, within a few days, a working party began to assemble. About the middle of January—to the alarm of the workers—Hongi's canoe fleet passed by on its return to the Bay of Islands. One of the canoes, loaded with baskets of human flesh and a number of women prisoners, came alongside the *St Patrick*. 'With horrible excess of cruelty', Bayly noted, 'these poor women were compelled to crouch down on the baskets, whilst every time they raised their eyes they looked on the preserved heads of their relatives, which, as trophies, were fixed on short sticks, one on the centre of each thwart, fore and aft'. This unwelcome visit was followed by one from Tokoroa, whom Bayly described as 'the principal Thames chief'.* He persuaded Dillon to

---

* Tokoroa is difficult to identify. I think that he was the chief usually referred to as Te Toko (or, in full, as Te Toko-o-te-rangi), a member of the Uriohau branch of Ngatiwhatua. Marsden wrote in 1820 that Te Toko was 'considered the greatest warrior in the west side of New Zealand'. At the time of the *St Patrick*'s visit many of the Ngatiwhatua and the Ngatipaoa were living at Horotiu. See: S. Percy Smith, *Maori Wars of the Nineteenth Century* . . . (2nd ed., Christchurch, 1910), 32-3, 369-74; John Rawson Elder (ed.), *The Letters and Journals of Samuel Marsden 1765-1838* (Dunedin, 1932), 320-1.

send Mossman with him on a visit to his people, at Horotiu, in the Waikato, to explain that it was now safe for them to come to the coast to cut timber, as Hongi's men had gone home.

The working party consisted of nearly a thousand men, along with many women and children. Work continued till the beginning of April, both near the ship and in the vicinity of the Wairoa River, in Tamaki Strait. Canoes were kept employed bringing food for the Maori workers and the ship's company. Bayly recorded the purchase of 'eight hogs, none less than 130 pounds weight, and about three tons of potatoes—all for one musket'. Since cabbages and other vegetables, as well as peaches, were discovered growing wild on one of the West Isles, the crew lived well.

But Dillon recognized that they were working among men to whom a ship and her stock of arms presented an almost overpowering temptation. Even Hinaki, he learnt, had planned to seize the *St Patrick* during her previous visit, despite the favours that Dillon had conferred on him. Each Saturday therefore the ship's company was drilled and firing practice held. The significance of this routine was not lost on the chiefs. But, when they suggested that it showed lack of confidence in their good will, Dillon simulated an air of injury. He emphasized that his men could easily destroy any hostile fleet of canoes but gave an assurance that he was thinking only of a possible visit by a less friendly party. 'By this treatment'— to quote Bayly—'he kept the natives in good humour, at the same time being always prepared for action'.

During the daytime there was much petty thieving from the ship, and at night a careful watch was kept. But there was no serious trouble until a party led by the chief Pomare, of the Bay of Islands, arrived on a visit. When Pomare came aboard without Dillon's permission, he cut his hand on a cutlass held by a sailor guarding the gangway. Demanding vengeance, he ordered his followers to enlist the support of the working party. The ship's company was ordered to action stations; and, not long afterwards, twelve canoes, each containing seventy to eighty armed men, moved out from the shore. As the canoes approached the ship, Dillon pointed a pistol at Pomare and compelled him to shout to the warriors that he had made friends with Peter. The ruse failed; and the canoes came alongside. 'Don't fire unless they try to board', Dillon shouted. 'If they do, blaze away at 'em.'

The savages stamped all together from side to side of their canoes, rolling them with a tremendous splash either way, till the gunwales were within two or three inches of the water. They uttered diabolical threats; with frantic gestures and the most hideous contortions of countenance, they yelled out their war-cries. They thrust out their tongues like thirsty dogs...[19]

But not a shot was fired. As Bayly wrote, 'every man had caught the spirit of the master'. The canoes returned to the shore. Next day friendly relations were restored, and confirmed by an exchange of presents.

Dillon still had cause for anxiety as to Maori intentions; but he was perhaps more worried by the arrival, towards the end of February, of a naval sloop, the *Larne*, in quest of spars. He was certain to lose the allegiance of his working party when the newcomers offered a higher rate of payment. But he turned the situation to his advantage by supplying the *Larne* from his own stock, at a substantial profit.

During these months Dillon made many trips, often accompanied by Bayly, up both the Firth of Thames and Tamaki Strait, negotiating with the people for the purchase of provisions and the cutting of spars. As Bayly recalled:

> We were all on very friendly terms with them, and Captn D. and myself very frequently went ashore by ourselves unarmed to measure Spars and sometimes up into the woods to see how their work was going on, but we always took care to have nothing about our persons that would make it worth their committing an assault upon us.

These trips left an indelible impression on Dillon's mind of the resources of this part of New Zealand and made him, in the succeeding years, one of the earliest advocates of European settlement in the Tamaki area—where the city of Auckland now stands.

On one trip in early March he found that 166 spars were ready for loading at the Wairoa River; he purchased them for '58!^{b} Gunpowder and 15 Hatchets'. During the following week, the *St Patrick* completed loading at Waiheke and moved to the Wairoa. By the beginning of April she had taken in her full cargo, together with a large supply of potatoes and 'pigsties full of pigs' for the onward voyage.

Before sailing Dillon agreed to give passages to two young men, so that they might see the world and obtain muskets and gunpowder in India. Both, according to Bayly, had 'a profound admiration for "Peter"'. One of them was a son of Tokoroa, the other of a less influential chief. 'It is necessary to remark', Dillon later wrote, 'that the New Zealanders are very fond of being called by European names, as they suppose it ensures them a better reception on board ships'.[20] He considered, also, that Pacific Islanders were seldom treated by Europeans with proper respect unless they were given a rank corresponding to that which they possessed in their own societies. Moreover, he had a personal taste, in suggesting names and titles, for the colourful and even the bizarre. He had introduced Takai to the people of Sydney as a 'Fejee Admiral'. Now, he named his two passengers 'His Royal Highness Prince Brian Boru' and 'His Excellency Morgan McMurragh'.

After leaving the Thames the *St Patrick* remained for three weeks at the Bay of Islands, anchored off Kororareka Bay. For those on board this represented a return towards civilization. A whaler and two other vessels lay at anchor; and, on shore, a few Europeans had established themselves, mainly as artisans who worked for visiting mariners. Dillon arranged to have a new pump and two topmasts made for the ship. But much of his time seems to have been employed in receiving Maori visitors. 'During our stay . . .', Bayly recorded, 'we were visited by a great many chiefs, who were most of them complimented with a small present from Capt.n Dillon'. On the morning of 27 April friends of Brian and Morgan—as they were known to their ship-mates —came aboard to bid them farewell.

> They first rubbed their noses together, then squatted down on their haunches, and howled most piteously, the tears all the time streaming down their cheeks, they then rubbed noses again and again, and departed from the Ship in their canoe.[21]

'In the afternoon', Bayly adds, 'we . . . stood out to sea'.

Dillon planned to call next at Tongatapu, to buy Tongan artefacts for sale in Calcutta and more food for the voyage, and then to visit Fiji. Presumably he intended to collect the bêche-de-mer and tortoise-shell that David Whippy would have acquired and to take Whippy aboard. But two days out from the Bay the *St Patrick* ran into a gale. Old and ill-made as she was, she developed a leak. When the gale had passed, Dillon tried to make for Sydney; but the wind failed him. He then decided to take the Northern Passage to India, round the north of New Guinea. This course brought the ship to Hunter Island on 7 May and six days later to Tikopia, where Martin Buchert and Joe, the Lascar, had been landed thirteen years before. Dillon decided to call, in the hope both of purchasing yams and of hearing news of his former comrades.

Dillon in Mid-Passage 107

Soon after the *St Patrick* hove to, canoes put out from the island. As the first of them drew near the ship, Dillon exclaimed: 'There's the Lascar, standing up in the bow'. The occupants came on board; and, when Joe recognized Dillon, he 'gave a shout, fell on his knees before Peter, and kissed his hands and feet'. A little later Buchert arrived and 'was overjoyed to see Captn D.'. Round his neck Joe was wearing a silver sword-guard. Dillon observed it with excitement. Where had it been obtained? What other European articles were possessed by the Tikopians? From his former companions and the Tikopians, Dillon elicited the story. Characteristically, he instructed Bayly to 'bring up paper, pen, and ink, and note all this down'. Buchert said that, on his arrival at Tikopia, he had seen:

> several chain plates belonging to a ship, also a number of iron bolts, five axes, the handle of a silver fork, a few knives, tea-cups, glass beads and bottles, one silver spoon with a crest and cypher, and a sword, all of French manufacture.[22]

These articles, and others which had been brought to Tikopia more recently, had come from two large ships that had been wrecked on the island of Vanikoro, 'when the old men now in Tucopia were boys'. Joe had been there in a canoe; he had seen large quantities of wreckage; he had talked with two white men.

> He said . . . [they] were very old and told him they had been wrecked there many years ago, and that no vessel had since touched there, that most of their companions were dead but they could not tell how many were alive as they were so scattered about amongst the different tribes of Natives.[23]

Could there be any doubt as to the discovery Dillon had stumbled upon?

As Bayly and Dillon had worked together making musket cartridges, Dillon had talked of the strange and tragic story of La Pérouse; and he had confessed to the desire he had cherished for years to solve the mystery. The skilful surveys that La Pérouse had made during the earlier part of his voyage had long been known to the world, as he had taken every opportunity of sending his journals and charts back to France;[24] but, after he sailed from Botany Bay in March 1788, nothing more had been heard of him or his expedition. The disappearance of this brilliant and much beloved man had grieved his contemporaries and mystified his successors. In 1791 the French Constituent Assembly voted a reward to anyone throwing light on the mystery, and an expedition was despatched under Bruni d'Entrecasteaux to make an organized search. D'Entrecasteaux failed; and for over thirty years the problem of La Pérouse's fate had remained unsolved. Now the Pacific was at last yielding up its long-hidden secret: La Pérouse's ships had been cast away on Vanikoro. The more Dillon racked his brain for alternative explanations of what he had just heard, the more certain he became of the correctness of his first surmise.

A sudden storm forced Dillon to cut short his discussions with the Tikopians. He sailed towards the west, with Buchert as a passenger. For two days the ship lay becalmed in sight of Vanikoro, but without establishing contact with the islanders; she then continued her voyage towards India. During these days Dillon and Bayly minutely examined the sword-guard, which had several groups of letters engraved on it. At last they concluded—erroneously, as later investigation was to show—that one of these groups consisted of the letters 'J.F.G.P.'. Bayly describes the moment: '"Jean François Galaup de la Perouse!" exclaimed Dillon, jumping up in ecstasy. He saw before him an earnest that the dream of his life was about to be realized'. Dillon's inability to reach Fiji may well have changed the course of David Whippy's life; his consequential call at Tikopia was to change, decisively, the course of his own.

THE remainder of the voyage was a trying time for Dillon. To many men of action the discovery of the fate of an explorer who was almost certainly dead—he would now have been well into his eighties, if he had survived the wreck and its aftermath—might have seemed of slight significance; but to Dillon it was far from being so. To him, the explorers were men cast in a heroic mould, their lives and deaths a subject of intense interest; and his discovery at Tikopia identified him with them, and with their world, more closely than before. Moreover, he may already have begun to perceive that it could bring him into touch with those circles in aristocratic and learned Europe where his interests were shared and to which he seems always to have felt he belonged. But before his discovery could even become known he had to sail the slow and damaged *St Patrick* safely to Calcutta. The ship was making between fifteen and twenty inches of water an hour —almost as much as the *Phatisalam* during her last desperate weeks, though in more clement seas.[25] The stock of potatoes had been damaged by moisture from the spars. The pigs had all been eaten; and, when the casks of salt beef from Chile were opened, Bayly notes, 'we found the greater part of the contents completely rotten'. In these circumstances, Dillon's temper became even more uncertain than it had been in New Zealand.

From Vanikoro, the *St Patrick* sailed north-west. This course brought her to Carteret's 'Charlotte Islands', close to Santa Cruz—so named by Mendaña at the end of the sixteenth century but not visited again by Europeans, so far as the records show, till Philip Carteret anchored there in 1767 and lost several of his company from arrow-wounds.[26] Dillon, at this stage, was using Carteret's narrative as a guide and must have been conscious of the latter's misfortune as canoes filled with men all armed with bows and arrows came out to the ship. But contact was amicable: they traded coconuts and some of their arrows for fish-hooks; and, in one of the canoes, a Tikopian who had been caught on board went ashore, intending to make his way back over the more than 200 miles of ocean that separated him from his home. Next, after passing Sikaiana and Ndai, the ship came to Buka Passage, between the islands of Bougainville and Buka. Here, for a week, she lay becalmed; and, as at Santa Cruz, men came out to trade. 'Captⁿ D.', Bayly recorded, 'made signs of peace to them such as are mentioned in Carteret's voyage viz. breaking an arrow over his head pouring water on his head &c all which they seemed to understand and came alongside directly'.[27]

Before proceeding through the Indies, Dillon wished to have the bows caulked and other repairs made to the ship. When the winds permitted, he sailed towards Gower's Harbour—now known as Lambon Harbour—at the southern tip of New Ireland, which had been described and charted by Carteret. He brought the *St Patrick* to anchor there on 9 June. To Bayly's surprise, the people came confidently on board and 'expressed no astonishment at what they saw'—from acquaintance, no doubt, with more recent callers than Carteret, of whom one, indeed, had carved the name 'Le Jeune' on a tree. They exchanged turtle's eggs, breadfruit, coconuts and local artefacts for trade goods. One old man stole a watch from the binnacle.

> Captⁿ D. who was standing by laid hold of the man and ordered the Carpenter to bring his axe, and to raise it over his head and look furious, as if he would cut him in two, at which all the natives jumped overboard, except one who made signs to Captⁿ D. intreating him not to kill the old man & after frightening him for some time, he let him go, but ordered him into his canoe, not to come on board again.[28]

These days at Gower's Harbour were a pleasant interlude for the crew. They went ashore to fill the ship's water casks and cut wood; they enjoyed a change of diet; they watched the skilful diving of Buchert, who 'procured some very large shells of the cockle specie[s] some of them weighing 190!ᵇ and the fish inside 70!ᵇ'. But, in the course of their sojourn, Dillon was guilty of an assault upon his 'second captain'.

One afternoon, as Dillon was dictating his journal to Bayly, Mossman burst into the cabin. Florence had cast off the forestay, he said, without setting up tackle to steady the mast. When the latter was summoned and accused of unseamanlike conduct a quarrel developed. Dillon challenged Florence to a duel with pistols across the cabin table or on the beach, both of which proposals were declined. He then grabbed his shillelagh and whirled it round near his intended opponent's head. The dagger flew out, gashing Florence's forehead so that 'blood flowed in streams from the wound'. Florence left the cabin threatening legal action when they reached Calcutta, while Dillon—calm, as always, after a moment of frenzy—rushed to the medicine chest for dressings and bandages.

On 16 June the *St Patrick* sailed westwards, passing north of New Guinea, for the East Indies. Light winds and calms made her progress exasperatingly slow, as it had been ever since passing Tikopia; and, 'what with the shortness of provisions and the incessant labour at the pumps', Bayly wrote, all hands became impatient for the voyage to end. To relieve the tedium, and dispose of unsold cargo, Dillon began a series of raffles. 'There were always six or eight capital prizes', while those who were unsuccessful received 'a glass of grog and half a pound of tobacco'.

> On these occasions, Peter became a very pattern of urbanity. He had a set of manners to put on when he pleased, which *pro tem.* seemed to put every one round him at ease. He would freely pass his jokes, and his Irish wit produced many a hearty laugh amongst the seamen . . . but no one ever presumed to attempt the least familiarity with him . . . When the list of subscribers was filled up, Peter would take his seat upon one of the hencoops on the quarter-deck, and order an empty hogshead to be up-ended before him. On it were placed the dice and boxes. As the men were coming aft to take their throw, Peter rattled the dice about, and called out, 'Come on, come on, my lads; I'll lead ye to fortune!'[29]

Among the articles offered as prizes was a gold watch; and, on the day on which the ship finally came within sight of the mountains of

New Guinea mainland, its new owner found it had disappeared from a chest in which it had been placed for safe keeping.

This discovery precipitated another explosion of Dillon's temper. The owner of the chest was accused of stealing his companion's watch.

> He was rather impertinent to Captⁿ D. who was in such a rage that he jump'd into the cuddy, seized a cutlass, flew at the man like a tiger, flourished the cutlass over his head, and swore if he did not produce the watch, he would put him ashore on some desert islands which we expected to make in a day or two. He then . . . told him if he saw his head above the fore hatch before the watch was found, he would shoot him.[30]

But again the paroxysm soon passed: he accepted the sailor's protestation of innocence and himself offered a reward of $50 for the uncovering of the thief.

Dillon intended to put in at Kajeli Bay, in the island of Buru. When the ship was to the west of Waigeu, he therefore altered course to sail southward through the Moluccas. Kajeli Bay was reputed to possess ample supplies of buffalo meat, sago and rice and tropical fruits, as well as of wood and water. Moreover, it provided sheltered anchorage and enjoyed a regular off-shore wind at night, which enabled mariners to put to sea without difficulty at any time of year. It had thus become a favourite port of call with whalers.[31] But when the *St Patrick* arrived there on 11 July she was refused permission to enter the inner harbour, since she was flying the flag of the unrecognized Republic of Chile. The Dutch Resident threatened to open fire on her if his ruling were ignored. To this challenge, Dillon had a ready retort. Drawing attention to the *St Patrick*'s guns—in fact, two eighteen-pounders and twenty wooden dummies—he told the Resident he 'would blow his puny fort about his ears'. According to Bayly, 'This threat seemed to intimidate the Governor'.

Once the *St Patrick* had been brought safely to anchor, further work was begun in caulking the bows. But both Dillon and the crew were more interested in trading. The former sold his remaining stock of iron tools to a Chinese storekeeper and bought provisions for the ship and cajaput oil for disposal in Calcutta. The crew were allowed to send representatives ashore to spend their savings on additional food for their mess. The expedition was a disaster. For, as purchases were made, the seamen became increasingly responsive to the storekeeper's hospitality. They despatched one package of food to the ship while they were still sober; but, when they returned themselves, fleeced of the funds entrusted to them, they brought only three brightly coloured parrots.

Dillon's final actions at Kajeli Bay were scarcely less bizarre. On the day before the ship was to sail he dined on shore with the Resident, and the two men cemented their new friendship, in a manner common among Europeans in these latitudes, by heavy drinking. Back on board his fitful sleep was broken into by the beating of drums in a passing canoe. To his confused mind, conditioned by his years in the islands, these sounds had but one meaning: the ship was about to be attacked. He leapt from his berth, picked up his pistols, and fired through the unopened stern windows. Then, with a sheet wound round his waist and his blunderbuss in his hand, he prepared to go on deck. Rather than lose time in unlashing the cabin door, which he had tied with rope owing to a broken lock, he threw his whole weight against it. As he crashed through, the sheet fell off among the debris.

Bayly, who had been wakened by the pistol shots and the sound of breaking glass, was by this time emerging from his own cabin. As he did so, Dillon rushed past him stark naked but still carrying the blunderbuss. He ran to the stern, fired wildly in the direction of the canoe, but caused no injury except to his fingers. Angry and confused, he came towards his officers, who were now gathered on deck, and formally suspended Ross, the mate on watch.

> Captn D. went up to him with a pistol in his hand, struck him violently on the forehead, and told him if he was right served he ought to have the contents of it. The blood streamed from the wound and he retired to his own cabin, telling Captn D. that he should not forget him on our arrival in India . . . [32]

In the morning Ross was reinstated.

Within an hour or two, however, the second mate was again in trouble. When the anchor had been hove up, he was sent out in a boat to take soundings ahead of the ship. He was to hold up one oar to indicate ten fathoms, two for twenty, three for thirty; but, finding no bottom at thirty fathoms, he gave no signals. As the boat returned towards the ship, Dillon 'got on the roundhouse with a musket in his hand, and pointing it at Mr Ross told him it was not his good will, but only the law which prevented him from shooting him'.

Dillon's outbursts of violence were, indeed, reaching a climax; and, several days after leaving Buru, Bayly confronted him on the subject. On this occasion he writes, he had been bullied 'to such an extent that

I entirely forgot some order he gave me, even before I reached the deck'. He said (or so recollected his words when writing his book):

> Captain Dillon, if you continue to act towards me as you have for some months past, I feel that I shall very soon lose my senses . . . When you received me kindly, at the time I joined the *Calder*, I felt grateful to you . . .; but if you go on this way, I shall never live to see Calcutta.[33]

The effect of this statement was surprising: 'He appeared to be quite taken aback . . . He took no offence . . ., but quietly repeated the order he had given me before'. And for the rest of the voyage Dillon retained his self-control.

Life still had its hardships for those on board. The pumps had to be manned without intermission; and the rations remained poor, as supplies at Kajeli Bay had been less plentiful than the guide-books promised. But the *St Patrick*'s onward passage was relatively uneventful. She passed through Ombai Strait, between Timor and Alor, and thence into the Indian Ocean. Reaching Christmas Island on 1 August, she continued westward till, at 82°E., her course was changed to north-west to bring her into the vicinity of Pondicherry, which, ever since the *Calder* had left Valparaiso, had been named in the log-book as her destination, because Dillon believed that a Chilean vessel would be permitted to enter a British port in Bengal only in case of necessity. When the *St Patrick* reached a position east of Pondicherry, he therefore produced a note asserting that the south-west monsoon and the ship's leaky state rendered it impossible for him to take her in, had it counter-signed by his officers, and made sail towards Bengal. On 26 August she approached the mouth of the Hooghly—seventeen weeks after sailing from the Bay of Islands and fifteen after her call at Tikopia. The captain of a pilot vessel which came up with her at first declined to accept the argument that Dillon based on the note in the log-book; but, after 'some altercation', he placed a pilot on board, and she proceeded towards the river.

For Bayly, this first sight of Bengal was full of strangeness, as well as of relief. On 27 August, when the ship was becalmed, he later recalled:

> . . . there was a thick haze for three or four feet above the water, but the atmosphere was perfectly clear above that. I was looking ahead, when a semblance of a dozen black footballs, leaping up above the haze and as suddenly disappearing, came in sight. After this effect had been repeated three or four times, I heard the creaking of coir-bound oars, and men's

voices, and soon discovered that the apparition was occasioned by the disc ends of the oars of a couple of tow-boats ... The tow-boat wallahs had seen the mastheads of the ship, though they could not see the hull, and were soon alongside, and engaged for the passage up the river.[34]

That evening the ship anchored at Saugor Roads, the main sea gateway to Bengal. It was a desolate, forbidding spot, which belied the riches of the interior. To the westward dangerous breakers stretched into the distance. To the east lay Saugor Island, low and jungle-covered, 'the classic region of tigers'.[35] Here, in former times, the devout had gathered each year, crowned with flowers and robed in scarlet, and after their rituals had been completed tried to return, walking and swimming, to the mainland. Those who perished on the way from the attacks of sharks or crocodiles were deemed to be especially beloved of the gods. The ceremonies had now been prohibited; but an air of savagery and gloom still seemed to hang over the island and its vicinity, depressing the spirits of imaginative travellers.

For Dillon, also, this was an exciting time, as he approached the city that had nourished his ambitions, after an absence of more than four years, with news that he believed would bring him fame. On 28 August, leaving the ship in charge of Florence and taking Bayly with him as companion, he set out in one of the tow-boats for Calcutta. The journey was not a comfortable one. At Kedgeree, Dillon ordered a bullock to be sent to the ship; but they had little to eat themselves, as food they had brought became infected with maggots. At night, when they tried to sleep, they were besieged by mosquitoes and cockroaches and disturbed by the wailing of jackals. By day they watched the corpses of animals being devoured by birds of prey. But on the thirtieth they reached Fultah in time to breakfast at 'a house of entertainment'; and by the evening they were at Budge Budge, where they 'proceeded to the house of a Gentleman of Capt.ⁿ D's acquaintance' and were given supper and their first news of the great world since they had sailed from Valparaiso. Setting out again later that night, they reached Calcutta in the early hours of the morning and went aboard a 'country ship' lying at anchor.

In the afternoon Bayly was sent back to the *St Patrick* with supplies of meat and rum for the crew. Dillon remained in Calcutta for a further day. He called on friends and associates; he leased a house— at 38 Doomtollah, near the heart of the city; and he talked to the newspapers about his voyage.[36] Then he hired a boat and had himself rowed down-river to meet the ship. He stayed on board, however, for only a few hours, after which he returned finally to Calcutta accompanied, on this occasion, not only by Bayly but also by 'Prince Brian Boru'. He had much business to attend to and, of even greater importance, a difficult task of advocacy to perform before he would be able to sail again, as he intended, on a voyage that would finally resolve the problem of the fate of La Pérouse.

BAYLY continued in Dillon's service for several weeks after the appointments of his fellow officers were terminated at the beginning of October. His abilities as a private secretary were even more useful in Calcutta than they had been during the preceding eighteen months. He acted as escort and interpreter to Brian and Morgan when Dillon himself was unable to do so; and, no doubt, he took down the many letters that Dillon addressed to the government and the press. But one of his first tasks when the *St Patrick* came up the river was a far less congenial one.

> As soon as she was moored, as a last stroke of Captn D's policy, he, knowing the crew would give any thing almost to get clear of the ship, offered instead of keeping them to discharge the cargo, to pay them off on condition that they would give up a fortnight's wages each towards paying people to work in their room. He knew he could get the Ship discharged for about half the Sum thus obtained . . . However, the men signed the agreement and were paid 3 or 4 days afterwards, but some of them had taken up so many articles of Capt. D. whilst we were among the South Sea Islands, for which about 7 or 800 Pr Cent upon the prime cost was the least that was charged to them, together with the expense of the raffles, that they had not much wages to take, indeed one man was in debt 6 Dollars . . . Captn D. knew they would be exasperated against him. He therefore feigned illness and sent me with his Sercar to pay the men, and I really thought I should never have got clear of them. Some of them threatened to go and pull Captn D. out of bed . . . and they left the house with abundance of execrations against Captn D.[37]

In Bayly's judgement, this incident revealed a streak of meanness in Dillon's character, as well as the ruthlessness which he had never doubted his captain possessed. He recalled, too, during those weeks in Calcutta, the many scenes of violence he had witnessed on board the *Calder* and *St Patrick* and the occasions on which he had himself been Dillon's victim. The final words in his journal about his time with Dillon reflected this facet of his experience: 'I had at last wound up my affairs with this "*humane Captain*" and never was captive bird more pleased to get its liberty, than I was'.

But in his book—of which he signed the preface at Trinity House on 25 July 1885, exactly a hundred years after La Pérouse had been waiting at Brest for a favourable wind to enable him to sail for the Pacific—he gave a fuller account of his state of mind at this time. Dillon asked him to sail on the voyage to Vanikoro and promised him promotion; 'but I had been so long away from home that I was anxious to return, so I declined the offer'.[38] Moreover, a ship of which his father was part-owner was then at Calcutta; and he was able to embark in her for England.

> How I revelled in the contrast between my present and my late circumstances, and in the anticipation of soon seeing old England once more! The captain and officers were kind, my messmates sociable, the crew respectable, and their language free from the horrid blasphemy which continually assailed one's ears in the *St. Patrick*.[39]

George Bayly was a virtuous young man. He had been ill at ease in the rumbustious world of Peter Dillon.

Yet Bayly had learnt that Dillon's ways were well adapted to the circumstances in which he worked. Soon after leaving Valparaiso Dillon gave him 'a lesson which might be useful to many a young fellow just starting as an officer'.

> He had told me to get a couple of hands aft to do something he wanted. I was on my way forward to bring the men, and had reached the gangway, when he called out, 'Mr. Bayly, I want you here!'
> I went aft to him.
> 'Stand by me, sir.'
> I did so.
> 'Now give yer orders, Sir, and make yer voice save yer heels.'[40]

In New Zealand he recognized that Dillon's combination of caution with courtesy was essential to the safety of the ship. When he was sent down the Hooghly on his own, he had difficulty with the Indian boat crew till, like Dillon, he became both dominating in his attitude and liberal in the distribution of baksheesh.

It was, however, the qualities that Dillon possessed beyond the range of professional competence as a mariner and trader that made the strongest impact on Bayly. 'He seemed to have an intuitive perception of the probable results of any course of action', Bayly wrote, 'especially in dealing with the islanders, . . . whose language he spoke as fluently as his own. There were many good traits in his character, but they were marred by his extreme severity toward those under his command.'[41] His portrait of Dillon is of a man whom, though difficult to work with, it was impossible not to respect or ever to forget.

EIGHT

The Search for La Pérouse

PERSUADING BENGAL

IMMORTALITY is conferred by the living on the dead. Most commonly, it is bestowed on men or women who are seen as symbols of some widely shared interest or aspiration; and, among such persons, those whose manner of death has dramatized the purpose of their lives are especially favoured. A prophet crucified, a warrior killed in battle, an explorer lost on his travels—these are more likely than others to live on in the minds of their successors.

Both Cook and Nelson—two of Dillon's heroes—had died in circumstances which became as well known as their achievements and which added poignancy to the story of their lives by providing a terminal note of tragedy. In greater measure, public interest in La Pérouse had been intensified by his mysterious disappearance. The narrative of his voyage as far as Botany Bay had been translated into many European languages; works of fiction and of poetry, and even a comic opera, had been written about him and his men; and, as recently as 1818, a 'serio-pantomimical drama' entitled *La Pérouse* had run for several months in London.[1] La Pérouse had been accorded a place in the European pantheon because he had not only lived as an explorer but, it was believed, had also died in unknown seas in the pursuit of his vocation.

Dillon did not need to justify his contention that an attempt must now be made 'to ascertain the actual fate of la Pérouse's expedition',[2] for his opinion was widely shared by those acquainted with the story of its disappearance. But, if his own ambition were to be fulfilled, he had to obtain acceptance of his views on two far more doubtful issues: that the Government of British India was under an obligation to sponsor the necessary search; and that he was the right man to lead it. His public activities after his arrival in Calcutta—whether consciously planned with this end in view, or, in part, merely a natural expression of his full mind and exuberant personality—constituted a formidable case for sending him back, as he so passionately desired, to Vanikoro.

DILLON allowed the details of his discovery to become known only gradually, over a period of some weeks. The press reports, at the end of August 1826, of the arrival in the Hooghly of the 'Spanish Ship, *St. Patricio*', as she was commonly described, had dwelt on the more routine aspects of her voyage—the places at which she had called, the ships she had spoken, and the damage she had sustained in 'a dreadful gale'.[3] 'The commander', one paper subsequently added, 'a Hibernian as brave and worthy a boy as ever left Erin's soil, is Peter Dillon, well known to us all, transformed into a Spanish noble and now hails to the title of Don Pedro'.[4] The presence was also noted of the two Maori passengers, whose purported status and titles easily eclipsed those now accorded to Dillon: 'His Royal Highness Brian Boru, Prince of New Zealand; Morgan McMurroc, a New Zealand Nobleman and Aide de Camp to the Prince'.[5]

Calcutta responded to Dillon's promotion of Brian and Morgan even more enthusiastically than Sydney had done to his similar introduction of Takai and Langi. The most widely read of the local newspapers, the *Bengal Hurkaru* and the *India Gazette*,[6] found the two young men interesting and entertaining, and they used their supposed opinions and emotions as a means of offering satirical comment on local events. Since each collected stories—mainly from Dillon—and commonly republished those that appeared in its rival, their readers became well acquainted with the exotic visitors.

The first hours in the city of 'Brian Boroimbe' (both papers preferred the Gaelic spelling) were described in detail. He was taken to 'that place of fashionable resort, Mr. Dawson's Hotel', for breakfast, which he ate with 'an edifying degree of relish ... highly complimentary to it and to the much-abused climate of Calcutta'.

> He is rather modest in his demeanour for a Prince, and very guarded in his conversation, as men of rank, birth and station ought to be. In reply to some query about the object of his visit to Calcutta, he merely replied by saying good, good, (pointing to the cold meat); and he parried the pressing questions put to him respecting the political state of New Zealand, by asking for more mustard.[7]

'His Royal Highness's appearance is extremely prepossessing', the *Hurkaru* added; '[he] considers and by his *genealogical* tree can prove himself to be a lineal descendant from his namesake, the celebrated

King of Ireland who died gallantly fighting for his country against the Danes at Clontarf'.

When Morgan was brought from the *St Patrick* a few days later by George Bayly, his arrival provided an even better story. He landed, the *Hurkaru* noted, 'in full uniform'.

> A feathered War-cloak hung from his brawny shoulders, his large circular shield was carried on his left arm, while his right hand grasped three stout lances and his bow and well stored quiver, with two stone *patta-patoos* [*patupatu*], the formidable weapon used in close combat, were suspended in slings of untanned hides from his back.[8]

'His Excellency is as brave as prudent', the paper added, '... the only death he fears is being baked'. And his courage was called upon during his walk from the landing place to Dillon's house. A crowd surged round him, and he was seized by armed police.

> In a strange country, surrounded by hundreds who from this reception he might lawfully look on as fell and ferocious enemies, his Excellency's spirit and courage never failed him for an instant: he lowered his trusty spear, drew his war cloak closer round him, brought his shield to his front, raised his fear-inspiring war-cry, and with one bound, freed himself from his assaillants.

But, through mediation by Bayly, a crisis was averted.

The story, as given to the press by Dillon—'a most exaggerated report', according to Bayly (though, in fact, he confirms its essentials)[9] —was well calculated to amuse the public; but it was given added point by the *Hurkaru*. For two years British India had been at war with Burma. The police, the paper declared, had believed Morgan to be 'a Burman General coming to Calcutta as a spy ... and they thought it not improbable that his army would follow in the night, and storm Fort William'. The incident, it asserted, was 'an extraordinary example of the attachment ... of the native functionaries to the British rule and Government, which must ... stop most effectually, the mouths of those croakers in England, who say that the people of Hindoostan are ill-disposed to their British masters'.

Dillon was well aware of the appeal of the exotic, of the desire of the affluent and influential to meet men from little known parts of the world. Brian had already been entertained at 'the Hospitable Mansion of Edward Brightman'; and, after Morgan's spectacular arrival, the two men 'were invited almost every evening to the different Merchant's houses'.[10] But their visit was also noted at an even higher level:

by the Acting Governor-General, Lord Combermere. On 10 September they were taken by Dillon to the Governor-General's country residence at Barrackpore, where they entertained the company with Maori dances and chants and received presents: Brian, a captain's uniform, a sword and a gold medal carrying a likeness of George IV; Morgan, 'other articles equally pleasing to himself'.[11] And this, it seems, was only the first of several meetings with Combermere.[12]

On his return to Calcutta, Brian was interviewed by the *India Gazette*:

> His Royal Highness appears to be about five feet ten inches in height, robust, and well proportioned. The expression of his countenance ... has more of an European character than we could have anticipated. His hair is glossy black, and rather curly than otherwise. His complexion is dark, but not black. Only a small portion of his face is tattooed, and as the tattooed lines are drawn in a waving direction between the sides of the nose and lip, they have somewhat the appearance of mustachios at the first glance.
>
> The Prince was dressed in the costume of a New Zealand chief, consisting of a kind of kilt or petticoat, and a wide mantle, formed, we believe, of a species of hemp ... He wears no neckcloth, head-dress, or shoes and stockings. Round his neck, suspended by a blue ribbon, the Prince wore a beautiful medal, presented to him by Lord COMBERMERE ...
>
> The object of the Prince's visit appears to be two-fold—a desire of improving himself by travel, and a hope of being able to procure arms for the purpose of securing his people against the incursions of a hostile tribe that dwell near the Bay of Islands.

Brian, the paper declared, was 'himself of a mild temperament' and appreciative of European civilization; if he returned home well armed, he would be likely to use his power to elevate his people and protect Europeans visiting his country.[13]

All the opinions expressed in the article probably originated with Dillon, for he controlled the public appearances of his protégés with a clear eye to his own purposes. But he was also reported in his own person. He told a simple story about Brian's mistaking a man on horseback for a centaur-like creature and a more sophisticated one about his attitude towards British expansion. Why, Brian had asked, did the Indian staff at an inn treat Dillon with such deference? Dillon explained 'that the British had taken this country'. 'Ah', he quoted Brian as saying, 'you will come and take my country too, I have no doubt, as you have taken this'.

And Dillon talked, also—on this occasion, as on others—about the

Maori people and their customs. They were not so barbarous as was commonly supposed and 'were susceptible of high improvement'. Though they still practised cannibalism in times of war, it was 'more as a solemn rite of triumph than a consequence of necessity'. Murder was rarely committed.

> ... an European might travel unmolested from one end of New Zealand to the other, provided he made no such display of his arms, or other property, as to excite the cupidity of these simple Islanders. They not only, he states, would not molest an European thus . . . throwing himself upon their confidence, but they would vie with each other in showing him hospitality and kindness.

These likeable people lived in a fertile well-watered country. If Brian returned equipped to introduce new forms of agriculture and husbandry, the paper suggested, its well being could be largely increased.

During those months when Dillon's mind was largely engaged with his plans for a voyage to Vanikoro, he talked and wrote to the press on many other subjects besides New Zealand. He had already given some account of conditions on Pitcairn. 'An Irish lad', he said, had recently come ashore from an American vessel; 'and by singing his favourite Irish melodies, such as "Paddy O'Rafferty", "Drunk at Night, and Dry in the Morning", "O Whack, Judy O'Flanagan", etc. etc. he made dreadful ravages on the hearts of the Fair Sex, indeed so much so that he was severely reprimanded by Governor John Adams . . .'. The *Hurkaru* stated that Dillon had obtained this story during a visit to the island. In fact, he had almost certainly picked it up in Valparaiso. But it seems to have a basis of truth and to relate to John Evans who had landed in 1823 and married a Pitcairn woman, as had Dillon's 'Irish lad'.[14]

At the beginning of October he returned to the subject of Pitcairn by publishing the account of the early years of the settlement that had been dictated by Teehuteatuaonoa (or Jenny) when he was at Tahiti in the *Calder*.[15] The *Hurkaru* referred to Dillon as 'That very enterprising and skilful navigator . . . to whom we already are indebted for so much valuable and interesting information'; and he himself added a brief introduction.

> All accounts hitherto received respecting His Majesty's Ship *Bounty* after the Mutineers took her from Otaheite, have only been obtained from John Adams. The following statement has been procured from Jenny, an Otaheitan woman ... on the 23rd. day of September 1824. I give it in her own words.

The narrator was the wife of Isaac Martin, one of the mutineers and remained on Pitcairn's Island about 30 years . . . [16]

These sentences are admirably precise; they can only have confirmed the impression that their author was a man of scholarly inclinations.

Three weeks later the *Government Gazette* published a summary of the journal of Máximo Rodríguez, with an explanation of the circumstances in which Dillon had acquired it—the first account in English of the hitherto mysterious Spanish visits to Tahiti in the 1770s.[17]

In the course of discussing La Pérouse's voyage and its apparent fate, Dillon set down his knowledge and opinion on a wide range of related subjects. He described earlier visits to the Solomons, from those of Mendaña onwards, and listed the names given to individual islands by successive explorers and, where he knew them, those used by the islanders. He presented a summary history of the Fiji sandalwood trade—probably the first account to be written—to show that the sword-guard and other relics could not have come from a trading vessel: 'I can assure you the Commanders and Officers of Port Jackson crafts relish their meals much and can do very well without the assistance of Silver Spoons or yet Silver handled forks'. He described his visit in the *Calder* to the New Hebrides. He also provided ethnographic data on Tikopia and other islands.[18]

The *Hurkaru* also published three letters of his, modestly signed 'P.D.'. Two were reprinted from the *Sydney Gazette* and dealt mainly with events on the South American coast.[19] The third was a criticism of claims by a Captain Mitchell to have made discoveries in the Falkland Islands. To set the record straight, he gave a brief history of the Falklands: their discovery by John Davis in 1592; the intermittent interest in them over the succeeding centuries by Britain, Spain and France; the loss there of the French exploring vessel *Uranie*, under Captain Freycinet, 'now Governor of the Isle of Bourbon'; and their current use as a watering-place by vessels bound from Europe to the Pacific coast of America.[20]

Dillon thought of himself as a man with the same passion for knowledge as that which had directed the lives of Dampier, Cook and La Pérouse, or of the travellers of his own day who penetrated to the remoter regions of Asia and returned with notebooks filled with details of their languages, cultures and antiquities. He was indeed now a man of substantial learning and one who had begun himself to contribute to the general stock of knowledge. His demonstration that he possessed these qualities, this cast of mind, was now of great importance to him, for Calcutta, behind its façade of palaces and slums, contained men of influence who were also scholars.

For more than forty years, men of this type had been provided with a focus for their research and speculation by the Asiatic Society, the oldest scientific institution in British Asia, the oldest but one in all Asian countries; it still refused to add the words 'of Bengal' to its title because the Royal Asiatic Society of London was of more recent foundation. Its interests embraced the whole of Asia and, in terms of subject matter, 'whatever is performed by man or produced by nature'. Many important papers had been read at its meetings and published in its journal; much important work in the fields of history, ethnography and linguistics had been carried out by its members. From this research in the human studies, and from practical involvement in the problems of adapting Indian society to the conditions of the modern world—through education and in other ways—intellectual leaders in Calcutta had come to believe that all cultures would be seen to possess certain common characteristics when sufficient was known about them. They were thus keenly interested in Dillon's contributions to the history and ethnography of the Pacific Islands, which they thought of as remote outliers of the Asian world.[21]

Some of the Society's members had been acquainted with Dillon for a number of years. They now came to regard him not only as a merchant and mariner but also as a man of active scholarly interests. Their assessment of him was highly relevant to the fulfilment of his present plans, for the leaders of the Society were men of prominence in many sections of the Calcutta community. In particular, both its president, John Herbert Harrington, and its secretary, Horace Hayman Wilson, were senior government officers, the former a member of the Governor-General's Supreme Council. If they were satisfied that he was the man to resolve the mystery of La Pérouse, his claims were unlikely to be ignored.

ON 7 September the *Bengal Hurkaru* had published a short account of the discovery at Tikopia. Because of Dillon's contacts with the *Hurkaru*, its columns were the natural place for him to launch his story. But they were also the most suitable, for the *Hurkaru* was the paper of the intelligentsia: it supported many of the causes—such as education and a free press—in which its members were interested and maintained a library which they were free to use. At its office, the paper stated, Dillon had deposited the sword-guard for general inspection: 'it certainly bears all the marks of antiquity, and has a stamp on it not very easily decyphered, but a zealous antiquary might readily read J.F.G.P. answering to the initial letters of John Francis Galaup Perouse'.[22]

During the following week other papers repeated the *Hurkaru* story. But Dillon's next action was not taken till 19 September, when he addressed a letter to the Chief Secretary to Government, Charles Lushington.[23] Though he declared, in the course of it, that he had been 'from my Boyhood a rough Son of the Sea' and could therefore 'little . . . grace my tale', he began with an elaboration and formality that somewhat belied his disclaimer.

> Convinced as I am that you partake of the spirit of philanthropy which has always marked the measures of the British Government, I shall require no apology for bringing to your attention the following circumstances, relative to the unfortunate French navigator Count de la Pérouse, whose fate has been involved in uncertainty for nearly half a century . . .
>
> I am further induced to this step by the decree of the National Assembly, made in 1791 (of which I have the honour to enclose a copy), which enjoins 'that all ambassadors, consuls, &c. at the courts of foreign powers, do, in the name of humanity and of the arts and sciences, engage their respective sovereigns to charge all navigators and agents whatsoever, to make every inquiry in their power relative to the fate of the French frigates *Boussole* and *Astrolabe*, under the command of M. de la Pérouse, &c. &c.' In conformity to this injunction, and the impulse of my own feelings, I shall now have the honour to lay before you . . . such intelligence as I possess on the subject . . . I beg to premise, that I shall advance nothing but what I am fully able to substantiate by the most conclusive evidence, oral and collateral.

He expressed the hope that the information would be passed to the French authorities in Bengal and that action would be taken 'to set a question at rest which has so long been agitated, and restore to their native country some of the crew of the French frigates, whom, I have every reason to believe, are still in existence on one of the islands in the South Pacific'.

Dillon related the circumstances that had led him to land Buchert and Joe on Tikopia in 1813 and, consequently, to call there in 1826. He gave a full account of the information he had obtained and a careful analysis of its significance. He recounted his attempt to visit Vanikoro and the causes of his inability to do so. Finally, he offered his services as commander of any expedition that might be sent out. He seemed to think that the French were more likely than the British to take this action. 'But', he added,

> ... I beg distinctly and solemnly to declare, that I am actuated by no hopes of emolument to myself in making this statement; and, let what may occur, I shall, if possible, revisit the islands, and bring off the Europeans if alive, and ascertain more accurate details relative to the wrecked vessels.

Lushington had a discussion with Dillon and suggested that he should visit Vanikoro when returning from his next voyage to South America. Dillon did not at once reject this suggestion, wishing perhaps to sustain the impression created by the *Hurkaru* that the *St Patrick* was 'a noble looking vessel'.[24] In fact, of course, she was nearer to being 'a regular old Tub', as Bayly disenchantedly described her.[25] And several days later Dillon wrote again to Lushington informing him that she could not put to sea till she had been docked and repaired. He proposed that the government should advance him the money for this work, secured by a bottomry on the ship and by insurance, or alternatively that it should give him the use of 'one of the Bengal pilot vessels' for a voyage specifically to Vanikoro.[26] Towards the end of October he received an answer: the government would not agree to finance the repairs to the *St Patrick* but was willing to send him to Vanikoro in one of its own ships.[27]

Meanwhile, interest in the fate of La Pérouse had broadened and intensified. The publication by the press of the substance of Dillon's first letter to Lushington, towards the end of September,[28] led to the writing of a series of well informed and constructive commentaries. On 11 October, for example, the *Hurkaru* published a letter signed 'J.R.O.'—almost certainly John Ralph Ouseley, an army officer and son of a noted orientalist.[29] 'J.R.O.' explained why, in his opinion, d'Entrecasteaux had failed to find any trace of La Pérouse, gave examples of the long survival of shipwrecked mariners on remote islands, and suggested that the public would be willing to contribute to the cost of a voyage to Vanikoro. The following day the *Government Gazette* published a letter from a man described, by the *Hurkaru*, as 'an authority entitled to our implicit deference'.[30]

This was Commodore John Hayes, a ranking officer of the East India Company's navy, the Bombay Marine, who had made a voyage of exploration in the Pacific only a few years after the disappearance of La Pérouse. Sailing from Calcutta in February 1793, he had reached Adventure Bay, in the south-east of Van Diemen's Land, only two months after d'Entrecasteaux had left it. He had discovered and named the River Derwent, which Dillon had since come to know so well. After he left Van Diemen's Land, he had visited New Caledonia, the Louisiade and Bismarck Archipelagos, and the mainland of New Guinea. Hayes had sailed on his Pacific voyage at the age of twenty-five. His subsequent career had been both varied and successful. Since 1809 he had been master-attendant of the port of Calcutta; but his service in the post had been interrupted for lengthy periods when he had been called upon for active service—most recently in the First Burma War, from which he had lately returned on board the East India Company's survey ship *Research*.[31]

In his letter, Hayes set down his own experiences among the Melanesian islands. He then concluded:

> If I may be allowed to add my opinion in favour of the account given by Captain Dillon, of the fate of the lamented Perouse and his companions, I am satisfied that they perished, as stated by him on the Mallicolo [Vanikoro] Islands, to the northward of New Caledonia. Capt. Dillon is justly entitled to the respect and consideration of the Public; and it would be worthy of this great government to send some of their numerous vessels to rescue the surviving followers of the celebrated circumnavigator in question.

Like 'J.R.O.' and others, he recommended that Dillon should be employed in the venture.

Dillon was delighted by the public response; and he commented on some of the points that had been made in an urbane and appreciative letter that revealed his detailed knowledge of the history of Pacific exploration.[32] But he was no less pleased by the interest of the French.

Lushington had sent a copy of Dillon's letter of 19 September to Joseph Cordier, Administrator of Chandernagore, the French settlement farther up the Hooghly. The latter had consequently come to Calcutta, where he met Dillon at a dinner party given by the French consular agent, M. Bonnaffé, and also attended by the French merchant captains then in port. Bonnaffé's guests were impressed by Dillon. They met him again for lunch next day, when he was accompanied by Buchert and by Brian Boru, clad in Maori style. He brought with him the sword-guard, which excited the Frenchmen as they discussed its origin and tried to decipher the inscription. Some doubted that it was French. But Cordier himself was convinced: in his youth, before the Revolution, he said, he had seen naval officers at Brest with sword-guards of the same type. It became his ambition to have Dillon sent to Vanikoro in a French ship.[33]

The recognition that Dillon valued most of all, however, was an invitation to attend a meeting of the Asiatic Society on 1 November. The Society's building, in affluent Chowringhee, reflected its high standing. Its cream stuccoed exterior was distinguished by a massive portico and skilful fenestration. Its interior was dominated by large central halls containing a broad staircase, which gave access, on both floors, to spacious rooms housing the Society's valuable library and museum and providing accommodation for meetings. The secretary, H. H. Wilson, was Dillon's host; the president, J. H. Harrington, was in the chair. During the course of the evening, Dillon was formally thanked for his gift of a collection of articles of ethnographic interest: from New Zealand the 'ornamental Stern of a . . . Canoe', a 'green Marble Battle Axe', and 'basket of Silken Flax', a 'Nobleman's Cloak' and 'Lady's State Dress', and 'One New Zealand Deity'; from Mangaia, stone axes and fans; from Tonga, rolls of tapa and 'pillows'; from Abemama, spears 'set with Shark's Teeth' and a 'Porcupine Fish Cap'; from Vanikoro, 'Beetle Nut Bags', a 'Neck Ornament' and a 'piece of Cloth'; from most of these places, and from Fiji, Rotuma and Tikopia, a wide range of clubs, spears and arrows.[34] Since Dillon was in the habit of selling articles of this kind for a substantial price, his gift was, in a sense, an investment in intellectual respectability. And it was an investment that produced a good return, for he was elected to membership of the Society and listed for some years as one of its principal donors.[35]

Before the meeting concluded, it was moved that a deputation from the Society should wait on the government to urge the sending of an expedition to Vanikoro. Harrington, at this stage, revealed that instructions had already been given; but he allowed the motion to be put and it was carried unanimously.

AT the beginning of November Dillon was confident he would make the voyage that should bring him fame. His hopes of the French had been confirmed by Cordier's enthusiasm, even though the latter could not himself provide a ship but only submit a recommendation to the Administrator-General at Pondicherry.[36] And the response of the British had exceeded his expectations.

In presenting his case for an expedition to ascertain the fate of La Pérouse's ships and rescue possible survivors, he had appealed to men's sense of romance, as well as to their feelings of compassion; and he had been listened to more readily because of his successful stance as a scholar and his skilful exploitation of Brian and Morgan. Not only men of influence, such as Harrington, Hayes and Wilson, had been attracted by his proposal but also Lord Combermere, who, as Acting Governor-General, was the fountain-head of power in Bengal. Combermere discussed it with him several times; and he persuaded himself that a decision to sponsor an expedition would receive the approval of the East India Company's hard-headed Court of Directors in London.[37]

British support of Dillon's plans reduced the significance of Cordier's recommendation to that of a friendly gesture: it was useful, both to Combermere and to Dillon, to have evidence of French interest; but, even if a suitable vessel had been available at Pondicherry, action by the Administrator-General would have come too late to affect the course of events. However, although the Government of British India had decided to send Dillon back to the Pacific in one of its own ships, the arrangements for doing so had not yet been settled. Harrington's reference to the subject at the Asiatic Society had been to the proposal put to Dillon a week earlier. This was a suggestion that he should travel to Rangoon, where the ship *Ternate* would be placed at his disposal. Investigations in the islands would be directed by him; but the ship would remain under the command of her present captain. The proposal was acceptable to Dillon, though not ideal. Subsequently, however, the government had come to doubt its practicability; the *Ternate*'s crew had been engaged for service only in Indian waters; and Rangoon was, in any case, an unsuitable port in which to victual a ship for so long a voyage.[38]

On 11 November an alternative proposition was put to him: he could have command of the survey vessel *Research*, which was already lying at anchor in the Hooghly. He immediately accepted the offer and had a preliminary discussion on the manning of the expedition. On the sixteenth the proposal was formally approved by the government.

Dillon recommended that the *Research* should carry a surgeon, a naturalist and a draughtsman. He suggested that, if his 'new friend and acquaintance, Doctor Tytler' were appointed, the first two roles might be combined. Robert Tytler had introduced himself to Dillon at the Asiatic Society and expressed an interest in accompanying him to Vanikoro. He was a surgeon on the government establishment, with a substantial list of publications on both medical and non-medical subjects. But he was an erratic, self-seeking and vindictive man, as much given to intemperate statement as was Dillon to intemperate action. Three years earlier, for example, he had engaged in an acrimonious controversy with Rammohun Roy, the pioneer in the adoption by Indians of Western learning, in the course of which he had displayed such a violent antipathy to Unitarianism and 'Hindu idolatry' that Rammohun had published a pamphlet defending these beliefs 'Against the Schismatic Attacks of R. Tytler, Esq., M.D.'[39] And Dillon himself later wrote of Tytler, with malice but not without truth: 'He . . . pretended to every kind of knowledge, human and divine . . .'. The nomination of this vain and querulous man as his colleague on a long voyage was a rash act on Dillon's part; but it was accepted with alacrity by the Government.

Dillon also proposed that he should be accompanied by a French observer, a post for which he likewise had a candidate in mind. Late in September he had been visited by Eugene Chaigneau, a young Frenchman who had just arrived in Calcutta from Indo-China. An uncle of Chaigneau's had served for many years in that country, where he had been made a mandarin. Eugène had joined him in 1820 and been left in charge of the consulate at Hue on the elder Chaigneau's retirement. Subsequently, during a visit home, he had been formally appointed as consular agent at Hue; but, when he returned, the French were out of favour with the government, and he was not permitted to present his credentials. He was thus at a loose end. Was it true, he asked, that Dillon intended to make a voyage to resolve the mystery of La Pérouse? 'I intimated', Dillon later recalled, 'that I had it in contemplation'. The two men kept in touch. And, as soon as Dillon received the offer of the *Research*, he advised Chaigneau to seek nomination as French observer. Chaigneau approached Cordier, who readily acted on the request.[40] Unlike Tytler, he proved a congenial colleague.

The men appointed as ship's officers had not previously served with Dillon: J. R. Blake, the first officer; John Dudman, the second; and John Russell, third officer and draughtsman. But some of those who had sailed in the *St Patrick* were employed in humbler capacities: John Mossman as gunner; Martin Buchert as interpreter; the remainder as seamen. The latter group included: George Ross, whose downward slide thus continued; Miguel Zenteno, from Valparaiso; Brian and Morgan; and two Tahitians, two Marquesans, an Aitutakian and a Fijian, all of whom had been living in Dillon's house since their arrival in Calcutta. Some forty other men were also engaged, a mixture of Europeans and Lascars. Monthly pay ranged between 240 rupees

(£30), received by Blake and Russell, and 12 rupees, paid mainly to Lascars and islanders. Dillon was to receive 6,000 rupees (£750) for the voyage, and he was assured by the Administrator-General at Pondicherry that, if his quest were successful, he would be rewarded by the French Government in accordance with the promise of the Constituent Assembly in 1791.[41]

On 22 November Dillon took command of the *Research*. During the following weeks he was both kept busy by a multiplicity of tasks and exposed to considerable strain, since he had not only to satisfy himself that preparations for the voyage were adequate but also to persuade government officers that his requests and recommendations were sound. After the ship had been docked and found to require no major repairs, he directed the crew in fitting her out. He was also occupied in the laying in of provisions and the selection of articles to be used in barter, or as gifts, when the expedition reached the islands. And, of no less importance, he had to advise the officers of the Marine Board on the drafting of his instructions. With regard to the route he should follow, he was faced with initial opposition, when 'some persons, pretending to superior knowledge', recommended that he should enter the Pacific by way of the China Sea and the Philippines. He considered this route impracticable during the season he would be at sea—when the north-east monsoon would be blowing on the western boundaries of the North Pacific—and believed the success of the voyage to be imperilled till he gained agreement that he should sail round the south of Australia. These preparations were made, moreover, against a background of sustained public discussion, with the press producing a steady flow of news and speculation as the *Research*'s departure drew nearer.

On 14 December Dillon became ill. He later declared that the illness was no more than 'a severe cold'. But Tytler, whom he called in, believed he had suffered an apoplectic fit.[42] He bled him, ordered his head to be shaved, and sought the opinion of two other government medical officers. Neither Dillon's testimony nor Tytler's can be implicitly accepted. The former was unhappily conscious that some unexpected misfortune, such as serious illness, might still prevent him from attaining his ambition; the latter, it seems, was becoming less enamoured of the prospect of serving under Dillon.

One of the doctors called in by Tytler was John Adams, the Secretary to the Medical Board. The other was John Savage, a man long known by repute, if not in person, to Dillon. Nearly twenty-five years earlier,

Savage had been appointed an assistant surgeon in New South Wales. But his career in the colony was a controversial one, and he left again for England in 1805. The ship in which he sailed spent two months on the coast of New Zealand, during which time Savage set out to study the country and its people. He befriended a young Maori named Moehanga, took him to England, and had him safely returned in due course to the Bay of Islands. In 1807 he published *Some Account of New Zealand; particularly the Bay of Islands, and Surrounding Country . . .*; it was the earliest book to appear dealing wholly with that country.

Several days after the consultation Savage paid a friendly call on Dillon. He mentioned that both he and Adams had been asked by the authorities whether Dillon was fit enough to command the expedition and had given an assurance that he was. Dillon was disturbed that these doubts had been entertained; but he knew how they had been created, for a friend had already told him that Tytler had recommended his dismissal on grounds of ill health. When he had asked how the man could make such false representations, his friend had replied: 'He . . . wishes to get you out of the way, that a creature of his own may be put into the command of the expedition'. Further inquiries satisfied Dillon that Tytler's ambitions were less circumscribed: with a mariner of his own choice to command the ship, he hoped to obtain over-all control of the expedition for himself. Armed with an affidavit in which he swore he was not subject to apoplectic fits, and with a supporting statement from his regular physician, he therefore called on the Marine Board and the Acting Secretary to Government and successfully scotched Tytler's intrigue.

During those trying weeks, Dillon still had an eye for publicity. And on 22 December the *Hurkaru* came out with a new story about Brian and Morgan. 'The whole of Morgan's mental energies are absorbed in an eager and insatiable desire for knowledge: His Prince on the contrary has the most sublime and prince-like contempt for learning on any subject all he wants are musquets, gun-powder and iron'. Morgan, it was claimed, had even been seen laughing over the jokes in Shakespeare's *Henry IV*.

The anecdote was probably a mere conceit thought up by Dillon. But that evening he accompanied the two men to a performance of *Henry IV* at the Chowinghee Theatre. Like British officers enjoying the nightlife of Brussels on the eve of Waterloo, he maintained a confident front in a time of strain.

The following day he received his instructions, drafted in accordance with his own wishes, and began his final preparations for departure. At the beginning of January 1827 he despatched the sword-guard to France for expert examination and wrote to the Minister of Marine and Colonies. If he succeeded in his quest, he said, he would travel to France as soon as possible after his return. If he should be lost on the voyage, he hoped that the French Government would provide for his children, whose whereabouts in Sydney could be ascertained by writing to 'the Revd Samuel Marsden . . . or to Robert Camel Esqr.' (a characteristic misspelling of 'Campbell').[44] On 7 January the *Research* was towed into mid-stream and, under the control of a pilot, began her slow passage down the Hooghly.

Dillon remained in Calcutta for a few more days, to complete his business and to be farewelled by his friends. And so, unfortunately, did Tytler. After failing to dislodge the commander, the latter had attempted—according to Dillon—to convince people that the ship herself was unsuitable for the voyage. At this stage, he returned to his earlier preoccupation. While Dillon was unconscious on his bed, after returning from a party, Tytler entered his room and was found there by Buchert. What were Dillon's drinking habits, he asked. Did he always sleep in the unusual position in which he was lying? Tytler now seems to have feared that his commander was a victim of alcoholism, as well as of apoplexy; and his anxieties regarding the months ahead were increased.

Dillon joined the ship on 12 January. Several days later he received letters from the city warning him that Tytler, who was to board her farther down the river, was likely to provoke a quarrel that would justify his abandonment of the expedition. The quarrel duly occurred —over the victualling of Tytler's dresser, or 'loblolly boy'—and was patched up only through the intervention of the Marine Board. This was not quite the last of Dillon's worries, for he did not receive the ship's register and authority to complete the passage down river till 19 January. But by the twenty-third all was ready, and the *Research* lay at anchor at the mouth of the Hooghly.

> About six A.M. we got the anchor up, set all sail, and stood down channel towards the floating-light. At half past eight we passed the Reef buoy, and shortly after one of the pilot brigs sent a boat to the *Research* to take out the pilot. We immediately set all sail . . .

Their first port of call was to be Hobart Town.

NINE

The Search for La Pérouse

THE VOYAGE OUT

THE *Research* was a ship of 253 tons, solidly built and, by repute, 'a fine sea boat', though rather slow. Her accommodation was said to be spacious and comfortable. When she sailed from the Hooghly, she carried a company of sixty-eight officers and men, together with several passengers and a number of personal servants. Dillon was accompanied by Mary and apparently by Martha, Tytler by 'his natural son, a youth of about fourteen years of age'; and Captain Samuel Speck, an army officer, was embarked for Van Diemen's Land.[1]

Dillon was more than content to be again at sea, where his nautical talents could be brought to account and his authority was not rightly challengeable. His journal entries reveal both his preoccupation with the particularities of navigation and his interest in the life of the ocean. On 31 January—the ninth day out—he noted:

> We had fine weather throughout this day, and made a rapid progress on our passage. The latitude at noon was 5° 50′N., and longitude 88° 21′E. About seven A.M. there were four tropic birds flying about the ship, of the white tail species: they were the first aquatic birds I observed since we sailed. The current I found setting as yet to the westward; and although we steered south and by east the last twenty-four hours, with the wind free, we did not make better than a south course . . .
>
> At half past nine P.M. the weather became very squally, with rain. Took in the small sails, and reefed the top-sails. Towards midnight the wind shifted to south-east and south, where it is likely to continue for some time.[2]

During the following days the weather remained squally and wet: the crew was kept busy making and shortening sail; and Dillon had difficulty in obtaining noon observations of the sun. But on 4 February he estimated that the ship had passed the Equator, a point that he was able to verify the next day. Till 20 February, when they picked up the south-east trade, the weather remained variable, with some days of sultry calm and others of high winds and seas, which impeded work on board.

But Dillon's problems were with the men under his control, rather than with the elements that determined the *Research*'s progress. On 21 February he wrote:

> At two o'clock we sat down to dinner as usual; but the surgeon was immediately called away to render assistance to a lascar who had fallen from the upper deck into the fore-hold . . . On inquiring the cause of the accident, I was informed that the man had been smoking an intoxicating and poisonous plant called gunja, well known in the east . . .

This incident presented him with only a transient problem: the Lascars' chests were searched and their supplies of the 'deleterious plant'—*Cannabis sativa* (marihuana)—destroyed. Far different, however, was the occurrence of serious illness among those on board.

Four of the eleven South Sea Islanders who reached Calcutta in the *St Patrick*—two Tahitians, a Hawaiian and an Aitutakian—had died there, all, according to Dillon, 'of consumption'. On 29 January he noted in his journal that the other man he had taken on board at Aitutaki and also a Marquesan who had served in both the *Calder* and *St Patrick*—'a very good man, named Wahoey'—were seriously ill and unlikely to recover. About a week later he wrote that Brian Boru was 'ill of the measles, which I fear he caught from a boy, the servant of M. Chaigneau', and that several other islanders were sick. By 12 February six islanders, five Europeans and a Lascar were incapacitated; and the number was still rising.

Most of those who were ill eventually recovered. But on 9 February the ship's company experienced its first death. 'At one o'clock this morning', Dillon wrote, 'Tariou [the Aitutakian] . . ., the first of his countrymen who ever ventured to quit his native island, departed this life'. 'The poor man', he noted, had been 'inconsolable for the loss of his countryman and fellow-traveller'.

> I was extremely sorry for his loss, which deprived me of the pleasure of restoring him safe to his friends and country. He had been rather sickly for a short time at Calcutta, but recovered, and joined the ship in good health . . . At half past seven A.M. we committed his remains to the deep, sewed up in his hammock with two twelve-pound shot attached to it; one of the Otaheitans on board, a christian of the Protestant persuasion, performing the funeral service extempore over the body.

On 16 February Huno, one of the Marquesans, died 'after an illness of eight days'. And ten days later he was joined by Wahoey, whose body had just been cast overboard when a shark appeared. 'I gave directions, however, not to attempt to take it', Dillon noted, 'being apprehensive that the body of our unfortunate shipmate had been devoured by the voracious monster'.

From the first appearance of illness on board, Dillon had been angered by Tytler's neglect of the sick, by his failure to diagnose their ailments or even to put them on an invalid diet. He therefore instructed the surgeon to have them taken off salt provisions and given 'sago, arrow-root, &c.'. He also attended to matters of hygiene. He had the ship thoroughly cleaned and fumigated, and—to Tytler's discomfiture—forbade him to have three Lascar servants sharing his cabin with him and his son.

Dillon's account of his surgeon's delinquencies was probably true, for Tytler was not only erratic and self-seeking but also, by now, thoroughly dispirited. These personal weaknesses—which seem to have been exacerbated by an underlying mental instability—were not, however, the sole cause of the deep antipathy that had developed between the two men. Both were egotists, both could be unscrupulous. On the day Tytler came aboard, Dillon had appealed for his loyalty on the ground that they were both Freemasons; and Tytler had rightly retorted: 'what is freemasonry, sir? you are a public servant and I am another'. But, in the context of their relationship, it was Tytler who was fundamentally in the wrong; and, because his antagonism was directed against his commander, it led him into a line of conduct that was wholly negative or destructive in its effects. The real issue that divided them was not one of professional competence or care; it was that of control of the expedition.

When the *Research* lay at anchor off Saugor Island, at the mouth of the Hooghly, Dillon had written to the French about Tytler: 'A worse selection could not be made, unfortunately for me I recommended him to the Situation before I knew his proper character . . . he is now after doing all in his power to frustrate my plans . . . I fear he will be in some way injurious to the Expedition'.[3] During the first days at sea, Tytler offended Dillon by his claim to be the official recorder of the expedition, by his frivolous attitude—as Dillon saw it—towards his duties as naturalist, and by his attempts to gain the confidence of Buchert, Brian and Morgan. At table, he consistently devoted himself—'in the hearing of officers, servants, and seamen at the wheel'—to denigrating the ship, which, he claimed, would go down before she completed the voyage. Moreover, he told the officers, as Dillon discovered from reading the log-book of John Dudman, that the captain was mad and should be confined to his cabin and bled.

Dillon reacted with vigour. He adopted a hectoring manner in his dealings with Tytler, kept firearms in his cabin (which was next to the surgeon's), and made sure the latter knew of Morgan's threat to have him 'grilled as an entertainment for his numerous wives and friends' when the ship reached New Zealand.[4] He also wrote him several letters. One of them was occasioned by Tytler's refusal to produce documentary evidence that he had been appointed official recorder: 'this conduct of yours', he wrote, 'causes me to suspect ... that such documents as those you allude to never were in your possession, and that you are trying to impose on me, as you have already imposed on the Government with respect to the Science of Botany—Natural History, my Health &c &c'.[5] In the others, Dillon was mainly concerned with warning Tytler that he regarded his conduct as mutinous and would have him confined unless he mended his ways. But, for good measure, he also commented on Tytler's past life, personal as well as professional, in grossly insulting terms.

On Sunday 28 January there was a crisis during dinner. Brian Boru, who was a guest at the captain's table, refused Tytler's offer of wine after Dillon had made a private remark to him. Tytler was upset, believing that the unheard remark had been intended to discredit him. According to Dillon, he then 'introduced his favourite topic of ridiculing the ship, talking in a vociferous tone, so that all the people on board might hear him'.

> He commenced by saying that the *Research* would not steer; ... that she was fit for nothing but a rice hulk; and, though she might get so far on her passage as Van Diemen's Land, that if she proceeded farther, she would certainly be knocked to pieces on the rocks of Tucopia [Tikopia], and, to give more force to what he said, he professed that such was the opinion of the head of the Marine Board at Calcutta. On these remarks being made, I observed, by the altered countenance of some of the individuals within his hearing, that his harangue and gloomy predictions had made a strong impression on their minds.

Dillon became enraged. He rose from the table remarking that 'people talk about ships who know only about gallipots'.[6] He went on deck and asked Mossman for his blunderbuss because, he said, 'there was a person on board trying to bring about a mutiny'. He told Tytler, who had followed him, that, if it became necessary, he would have him taken to the capstan and given five dozen lashes, or put in irons.[7]

Tempers cooled. But, as the weeks passed, Dillon became increasingly anxious about Tytler's insidious influence. He believed that many of the crew would welcome an opportunity of returning to Calcutta, as Tytler wished to do, and might obey an order from him to detain their captain. He knew that the voyage ahead would be onerous for all on board and that it could be completed successfully only if his authority was accepted without question. The dangers that he foresaw were not chimerical; but, because he was a romantic, they assumed unreal proportions in his mind. He saw himself as the successor of Magellan and Mendaña, of Drake and Dampier and Cook—and of lesser men such as Bligh. And he was acutely conscious, as he later wrote, of 'the dangerous spirit of insubordination by which so many Navigators, even the great Columbus himself have been endangered'.[8]

On 27 February Dillon was informed by Dudman, the second officer, that there was 'a mutiny fore and aft the ship'. He was also told by Dudman that Tytler's allegation of his insanity had been made in a letter to Blake, the first officer. When Blake confirmed this story, and admitted that he had resisted Dudman's advice to show him the letter, he saw Blake as a potential Fletcher Christian. He therefore determined to take immediate action to restore his authority. He walked up to Tytler on the quarter-deck, ceremoniously took off 'his Manilla straw hat', and then placed his hand on Tytler's shoulder, saying: 'I arrest you in his Britannic Majesty's name'.[9]

Dillon confined Tytler to his cabin, ordered that his sword and firearms be taken from him, and placed a guard—of Brian and Morgan—between Tytler's cabin and his own. Several hours later he partially relented and informed Tytler by letter that he might walk the deck but was forbidden to speak to any member of the ship's company. At about the same time, he armed 'some old and trusty shipmates' with pistols and told them 'to be ready to use them when called on'.

Tytler now feared for his life and that of his son. Dillon was a powerful man; he carried arms; and he was prone to paroxysms of frenzied anger. Dudman and Mossman, who would loyally carry out any order of Dillon's, he found almost equally frightening. And he regarded Brian and Morgan as 'savages' and 'cannibals'.[10] He declined to avail himself of the permission to go on deck, although, a fortnight after his arrest, he resumed his visits to the sick.

For Dillon, on the contrary, the voyage had now regained a measure of calm, As they moved south he observed with interest their occasional marine visitors. On 2 March he noted:

> Shortly after daylight we were visited by a pair of tropic birds, which bore us company throughout the day . . . Caught a fish of the Boneta species, which weighed ten pound and a-half.

And on the fourteenth:

> At an early hour this morning we were visited by a whale of the black species, which came so close to the ship that the two small orifices or breathing holes in the head could be plainly seen: the animal appeared to be about thirty feet long. We were also favoured with a visit from a few albatrosses and other aquatic birds.

On the morning of 31 March, 'The sea appeared of a light colour, as if we were at no great distance from land'. This impression was confirmed by the reading of the chronometers at noon; the same evening the southern coast of Van Diemen's Land was sighted.

The *Research*'s passage to Hobart Town was not yet quite over. In the early hours of 1 April Dillon wrote, 'very strong gales from the north-westward' blew up, 'accompanied with tremendous squalls of hail and rain'. He went on deck, where, after he had seen that all was in order, he observed: 'how quiet the ship is—all the people are asleep, it is wonderful—except the Doctor, poor man, he looks very ill, I really feel for him'. His remark was overheard by Tytler, who came up from his cabin. 'Captain D', he said, 'if these are your sentiments, here is my hand, and I give it you with all my heart'. In the circumstances, it was a pathetically inadequate gesture of reconciliation. And Dillon replied: 'No, Sir had I known you were there, I would not have said it'.[11] For the time being, however, Dillon's mind was engrossed by the storm.

> Finding it exceedingly dangerous to approach the coast in such violent unsettled weather, I determined to scud away to the S.E. and heave-to. The seas ran mountains high: one of them stove the gig boat on the poop . . . It was extremely cold, and the poor lascars rendered unserviceable by the severity of the weather.

But the storm abated two days later, and on the evening of 5 April the ship cast anchor in the Derwent. At day-break next morning Dillon went ashore to report his arrival.

LIFE in Hobart Town had changed since Dillon's visit in the *Calder* at the end of 1822. Van Diemen's Land had then been ruled by William Sorell, and efficient administration had been combined with a relaxed approach towards questions of law and morality. Customs regulations, and the laws relating to land, were sympathetically interpreted. Informal marital arrangements conferred no stigma: Sorell himself lived with a mistress. And heavy drinking was socially acceptable. Moreover, the Lieutenant-Governor was readily accessible to all who had a problem to discuss with him. Relations between the senior members of the official hierarchy and the settlers were thus easy and generally amicable. In May 1824, however, Sorell's term had ended.

The new Lieutenant-Governor was George Arthur, who had previously held a similar appointment in British Honduras. Arthur had not been popular with the settlers there; but, through his work on behalf of the slaves, he had won support in London—particularly that of Lord Bathurst, the Secretary of State for the Colonies, and of James Stephen, the Colonial Office's influential legal adviser. Arthur held the rank of Lieutenant-Colonel; he was proud, ambitious and hardworking, an authoritarian both by temperament and by experience. He was also a devout Anglican, of deeply Calvinist convictions, obsessed by the weakness and wickedness of most of his fellows. In Van Diemen's Land, he was appalled by the general laxity of moral standards. But he did not seek to raise them by mixing with men whose errors he condemned. Instead, he set out to reform society through the autocratic exercise of his powers.

Round the Lieutenant-Governor there soon existed what the colonists thought of as a 'government party'. Its key member, because of his varied functions, was John Lewes Pedder, the Chief Justice, an Anglican Evangelical and an upright man, though of a peculiarly rigid cast of mind; Alfred Stephen—a youthful cousin of James Stephen—who was appointed Crown Solicitor and Solicitor-General in 1825; and the Reverend William Bedford, a former artisan with an interest in prison reform, who had succeeded the gregarious and self-indulgent Robert Knopwood as senior chaplain in 1823. These men and others formed a little coterie of superior persons, looking down their noses at most of those amongst whom they lived, and devoted to the execution of the Governor's will.

During the three years preceding Dillon's return to Hobart Town, Arthur and his supporters had become involved in a number of *causes célèbres*, particularly concerning the freedom of the press. Arthur believed that in a penal colony the only constructive purpose served by the press was that of publishing official notices, and by very curious measures did his best to extinguish any critical or even independent journals. But in this he was unsuccessful; and, at the time of Dillon's arrival, both Bent and Howe were publishing papers, the *Colonial Times* and *Tasmanian* respectively.

Closely connected with the campaign against the press was that for the removal of Joseph Tice Gellibrand as Attorney-General. Gellibrand had arrived in Van Diemen's Land in the same ship as Pedder; but, unlike the Chief Justice, he had soon formed associations outside the tight little circle of senior officials. A man of independent mind, he favoured the claims of tolerance, rather than those of the predominantly Anglican establishment to make men virtuous by autocratic rule. Arthur intensely disliked him, and, again by highly questionable manoeuvres, was able to suspend and subsequently to dismiss the Attorney-General. Gellibrand remained in Hobart Town; he practised as a barrister and, on the foundation of the *Tasmanian*, he served as its editor.

In March 1827 Arthur became involved in still another controversy. A public meeting was held to urge the introduction of elected representation in the Legislative Council and of civil, instead of military, juries. It was sponsored by Edward Lord, William Angus Bethune, Anthony Fenn Kemp, and other leading colonists, with Gellibrand as their legal adviser. At the meeting a committee was appointed to wait on the Lieutenant-Governor. It was subsequently given a time at which he would receive it. But, when the members arrived at Government House, they were told that he was busy; they therefore withdrew, with a not unnatural feeling of having been slighted. The incident was still being hotly debated at the time of Dillon's arrival.[12]

Within a few days, however, there emerged a new issue for public debate: the treatment of Dillon himself by the colonial authorities. And, as it developed, most of the actors in the continuing Van Diemen's Land drama, including the chorus of citizens, began once again to play their accustomed roles.

When Dillon landed in Hobart Town on the morning of 6 April, he was taken by the Naval Officer, Rollo O'Ferrall, to call on the Lieutenant-Governor. Arthur received him affably. Dillon outlined the objects of his voyage and requested a loan of $4,000 for the purchase of provisions, explaining that he would repay it by drawing bills on the Government of Bengal.[13] Arthur said he would attend to

L

the matter immediately; he invited Dillon to call on him again at 10 o'clock the following morning and to bring Chaigneau and Captain Speck. But, after Dillon had left Government House and was busy placing orders with the merchants, he was hailed by O'Ferrall: the Governor, he said, had received a letter from Dr Tytler seeking permission to come ashore and had directed O'Ferrall to fetch him from the ship.

About a fortnight earlier there had been an exchange of letters between Tytler and Dillon. The former had proposed that he should leave the expedition at Hobart Town. But Dillon had not agreed. He declared that it was his intention to take legal action in respect of Tytler's 'mutinous conduct' on board the *Research*—probably on their return to Calcutta. 'It also comes within your knowledge', he continued, 'that I have been a ship owner and merchant for some years in Calcutta and like all other merchants in business I have had recourse to credit, which credit you have endeavoured to destroy by representing me to be mad and an unfit person for confidence to be placed in'. Only a favourable decision by a 'British jury' could satisfactorily restore his reputation.[14] Dillon's intended course of action made good sense, from his own point of view; but his announcement of it can only have strengthened Tytler's determination to act first. And, in his letter to Arthur, he gave a colourful account of 'the disturbed state of our Commander's intellect' and of the consequences that had, he alleged, flowed from it.[15]

Tytler was received by Arthur and his circle as one of their own. He was a senior government officer, a scholar, and an Anglican. Even his theological interests, whose eccentricity had so troubled Rammohun Roy, were an asset, for they helped to gain him the friendship of William Bedford. Being thus warmly welcomed, he lost no time in denigrating Dillon to his new friends, casting doubt on his good faith, and letting it be understood that it was he himself, rather than Dillon, who was responsible for the sending out of the *Research*.

Dillon was made uncomfortably aware of the changed atmosphere when he called on Arthur on the morning of 7 April. He and his companions, Chaigneau and Speck, were kept waiting outside Government House for more than two hours, though the day was bitterly cold. When they were finally admitted, Arthur told Dillon that he had found it would be inconvenient to grant him a loan, and he remarked that it seemed extraordinary that Dillon had not resolved the problem of La Pérouse's disappearance while he was in the area in the *St Patrick*. At a further meeting between the two men, later in the day, he said that he had had a discussion with Tytler and had advised him to place his complaints before the police magistrates.

On Monday 9 April Dillon was required to attend at the Police Office for a magisterial inquiry into a charge of assault laid against him by Tytler. Several others from the ship appeared as witnesses. Speck, in Dillon's words, 'deposed the truth'. But Blake supported Tytler's allegations, as did Leonard Helmick, the 'loblolly boy', and Richard Munro, Dillon's clerk. The latter two, according to Dillon 'had come in . . . from the ale-house, both more than half seas over, where they seemed to have been primed for the occasion'. 'On this drunken and partial testimony of accomplices'—to quote his own less than impartial assessment of it—Dillon was committed for trial before the Supreme Court.

While he was waiting for the case to be heard, Dillon received much favourable publicity in the local press. Even the pro-government paper, the *Gazette*, carried an article explaining the purpose of the expedition and welcoming, particularly, the visit of Brian Boru, 'a young man about 20 . . . rational, humane and intelligent'.

> If his visit to India was looked upon by the authorities there, as of no small consequence, . . . how much more does it behove us to embrace this favourable opportunity of establishing a good understanding with a neighbour quite as accessible as Sydney, and presenting advantages in a commercial point of view even superior to those which that place affords.

Drawing on information provided by Dillon, the writer emphasized the potential value to Van Diemen's Land of trading in New Zealand for flax and of whaling on the New Zealand coast.[16] But it was Andrew Bent's *Colonial Times* that gave the expedition, and Dillon himself, the fullest coverage. Dillon had known Bent for some years and, following his usual practice, had brought him a parcel of Indian newspapers. On 13 April the *Times* devoted over three columns to an account of his discovery at Tikopia and to his subsequent organization of the voyage to Vanikoro. A week later it republished the narrative of his experiences at Dillon's Rock that had appeared in the Calcutta *Government Gazette* in 1817. These stories provided a firm basis for the paper's judgement of him as a man and a Pacific voyager:

> Captain Dillon's 19 years experience among the Islanders, and his aptitude for acquiring the native language, gives him a decided advantage over every other individual who could be found to conduct the present expedition,

Captain Dillon is a Gentleman well known and respected in this Colony by all classes of the Inhabitants . . .

His reputation, the *Colonial Times* concluded, was 'not likely to be lowered many degrees in the Public estimation' by the case in which he had become involved.[17]

The hearing of the case by the Chief Justice and a jury of six army officers began on Tuesday 24 April and continued till the end of the week. The charge against Dillon was of 'Assault and false imprisonment on the High Seas.[18] Stephen appeared as prosecutor and Gellibrand as counsel for the defence.

In his opening address Stephen appealed to the sympathies of the jurymen by describing Tytler as a military man, since he held a commission in the East India Company's forces, and he asserted that only a verdict of guilty could avenge the insult offered to their profession by Dillon's actions. He belittled Dillon's part in persuading the authorities in Bengal to send out an expedition: not much attention had been paid to Dillon's proposal he contended, till Tytler had privately suggested—though he had not actually moved—the adoption of a resolution at the meeting of the Asiatic Society. He traversed the sorry history of relations between the two men during the voyage, portraying Tytler as a patient man of science and Dillon as a violent and unbalanced boor. He argued that Dillon's action in placing his hand on Tytler's shoulder on 27 February constituted assault and that his subsequent decision that Tytler might walk the deck was subject to such restrictive conditions that it amounted to a continuance of his detention.[19]

Under examination, Tytler firmly supported this interpretation of events. He provided a more vivid account of his arrest than others, including the Chief Justice, were prepared to accept. Dillon he claimed, 'gave me a violent blow on the shoulder, . . . and seizing me very forcibly by the arm, shoved me before him into my cabin, saying go in and consider yourself a prisoner'. But much of his evidence—and that of other witnesses—was concerned with Dillon's state of health and mind, and with his conduct generally, rather than with the substance of the charge against him. He spoke of Dillon's proneness to apoplexy and its consequences. Of Dillon's letter describing his conduct as mutinous, he said 'I considered that it shewed lunacy in every line'. When asked about an allegation he had made that Dillon had been seen eating the carpenter's chips, he informed the court learnedly, if irrelevantly, that such action 'indicated that aberration of mind called by physicians venatio floccorum, a hunting after straws and little particles'. And—for a reason that was clear to Dillon and, no doubt, to others—he developed his fantasy on the origins of the expedition. He claimed he had provided an 'explanation of the cypher on the sword-guard' and said he 'understood' this persuaded the government to act. Gellibrand therefore asked him:

> Then it was through you that this expedition was fitted out—on your representation?

He replied:

> I was expressly told so.

When it was pointed out that he had been in disfavour with the government, he tried to turn even that fact to account!

> The disagreements . . . between the Government and myself were entirely settled at this time . . . I think it was in consideration of the misunderstanding, that this expedition was to give me an opportunity of shining . . .

But he had gone too far: there was 'A loud laugh in the court'.[20]

Dillon was probably more harmed by his use—in conversation and in correspondence with Tytler—of what the *Hobart Town Gazette* described as 'expressions it would be improper to put in print'. He had called Tytler 'one of the vilest hypocrites on Earth', had referred to his 'Judas like' conduct, to 'the various villanous Artifices resorted to by you', to 'the last 14 years of your disorderly and quarrellsome career', and had, without doubt, expressed himself in even more colourful phrases than those that have survived.[21]

On Saturday morning Gellibrand presented the case for the defence. He asked the jury to ignore both Tytler's military rank and Dillon's intemperate language and to concern itself solely with the questions of whether an assault had been committed and, if so, whether it had been justifiable in the circumstances. He discussed the dispute that had occurred at the dinner table.

> If Dr. Tytler did believe that Captain Dillon was mad . . . I would ask you, who is the individual that had driven him into a state bordering on insanity? —if it is true that the ship *Research* was a bad sailer—if it is true that she would not steer well—if it is true that she has been sent out on a most dangerous expedition—if it is true that she is destined to proceed to the rocks of Tucopia, in search of the unfortunate La Pérouse—if it is true that

fear should be banished from the minds of all who are engaged in such dangerous enterprises ... the cuddy table was the *last* place to have introduced such topics, and Dr. Tytler was the *last* man who should have introduced them ... If you had heard conversation like that used by Dr. Tytler, would you not have considered it a duty to put a stop to it? Would you not have gone further?[22]

Dillon had been provoked over a long period by Tytler's 'dastardly conduct'; when he finally arrested Tytler, 'his acts ... were as mild as the circumstances would admit, and were justifiable'.[23]

After Stephen had delivered the closing address for the prosecution, Chief Justice Pedder summed up the case to the jury. Its members must not permit themselves to be influenced, he said, 'by their notions of mutiny or martial law'; the *Research* was 'precisely similar to a merchant vessel', and Dillon's authority was no ampler that that of the master of such a vessel. The only questions the jury had to consider were: had an assault been committed?—and, if so, had a satisfactory justification been made out? He then explained the two alternative sets of circumstances which, he said, might validate a plea of justification: that Tytler had known Dillon was not mad but had stated he was in order to deprive him of his command; or that, although Tytler had made his statement in good faith, Dillon had believed it to be a deliberate falsehood and intended to deprive him of his command. If the jury's interpretation of the facts conformed to either of these patterns Dillon would be entitled to an acquittal, subject to one important proviso: that he had consulted his officers before making the arrest. If the circumstances were other than these he should be found guilty. Thus briefed, the jury brought in a verdict of guilty. But it added a rider: 'The jury are of opinion that Dr. Tytler should have exercised more discretion in introducing observations which he knew were irritating to the feelings of Captain Dillon'.[24]

The Chief Justice then adjourned the court till the following Tuesday. Pedder was a walker, not a runner. Arthur himself once complained that 'he is so tedious and so minute that life is much too short to wait for his opinions and decision'. But Dillon, who was aware of local gossip, accepted a less charitable explanation of the frustrating adjournment. He believed that the Chief Justice was unwilling to act till he had received the advice of the chief executive; and, when Pedder—'whose motions I watched very narrowly'—visited the Governor on the latter's return from a weekend excursion, he regarded his suspicions as being fully confirmed.

On the Tuesday morning Pedder pronounced judgment. He said that the charge had been fully proved. Dillon had acted 'without much violence'; but he had allowed himself to be influenced by an obvious dislike of Tytler. For this impropriety he must pay: 'it is proper, Captain Dillon, that you should be made to feel, that the power given to Masters of ships is one conferred on them for promoting the general interests committed to their case, and *not* one to be exercised by them for the redress of their own wrongs, or the gratification of their own resentments'. He required Dillon to enter into a recognizance to keep the peace towards Tytler, imposed a fine of £50, and sentenced him to two months imprisonment 'in His Majesty's Gaol at Hobart Town'.[25]

Dillon was momentarily crushed by the weight of the sentence. He saw that his plans, which he had cherished with a narcissistic intensity since Tytler had first threatened them in Calcutta, would be finally destroyed if he were required to serve a term of imprisonment. But he also saw—or thought he saw—that he had become a victim of the snobbery of Van Diemen's Land officials. The existence of a prejudice against him had been implicit in Stephen's appeal to the professional pride of the military jurymen. It had been made explicit by the terms of the judgment.

Dillon lived in an age when force was commonly used by those in authority—by officers against their men, by husbands against their wives, by teachers against their pupils. He was more prone to acts of violence than most; but his behaviour on board the *Research* had been no stormier than that during the voyages of the *Calder* and the *St Patrick*. Moreover, his procedure during the arrest of Tytler—the raising of his hat, followed by the recitation of a brief, formal sentence—had been consciously framed to accord with his new status as a master in the service of the East India Company and an explorer. Yet neither his instinct for propriety—a quality that lay behind his easy acceptance by men of widely differing classes and cultures—nor his position as the commander of an important expedition had gained him any consideration, because the man he had laid his hand upon was regarded by Arthur and his cronies as his social superior.

The outcome of the case was widely discussed in Hobart Town. Many influential colonists condemned Pedder's imposition of a term of imprisonment.[26] They recalled two other instances of assault on the high seas where no criminal charges at all had been laid. Alfred Stephen had been horsewhipped by a local physician who was a fellow passenger, and the latter had subsequently been assaulted by the captain, who broke two of his antagonist's ribs. In civil actions, Stephen had been awarded damages of £50, the physician of £2—'Twenty shillings a joint', as Dillon wryly commented. Dillon's supporters considered that he had been victimized by the authorities; but, like him, they were even more concerned with the likely practical consequences of the sentence. Some government officers, on the other hand, reacted very differently. They took the view—apparently suggested by Tytler (not without inconsistency)—that Dillon himself might have engraved the cypher on the sword-guard and that the whole expedition was a fraud.[27] But a greater number seem to have shared the opinion that Pedder had erred and that Dillon should be released.

Meanwhile, from his new quarters in the gaol, where he had been given rooms in the gaoler's own apartment, Dillon continued to attend to his personal affairs and those of the expedition. On Wednesday 2 May—the day following his imprisonment—he was visited by Edward Lord, who brought a petition seeking his release. It boldly declared that 'the Eyes of the whole European World are turned with anxious expectation towards the result of the *Research*'s present voyage'. It bore the signature not only of Lord, Bethune and Kemp, who had organized it, but also of others who had earlier been their associates in the campaign for civil juries and an elected legislature, and of many who had not. The signatories—thirty-two in all—represented a broad cross-section of the Hobart Town *élite*, apart from those who belonged to the aristocracy of office. Next morning Dillon forwarded it to the Lieutenant-Governor, together with a memorial of his own, drafted for him by Gellibrand, in which he solicited a suspension of his term of imprisonment and offered to enter into an undertaking to return after the voyage to complete it.[28] On 4 May he dealt with another problem. He arranged lodgings on shore for Buchert and sent George Ross, with the ship's papers, to Sydney. Since these were the only men, apart from himself, who could act as interpreters in the islands or who knew the precise location of Vanikoro, which he had always been careful not to disclose, he now felt confident that the expedition could not proceed without him.

Arthur's intention was to attempt a reconciliation between Dillon and Tytler.[29] If he were successful, he would remit the remainder of Dillon's sentence. If he were not, he would try to reorganize the expedition, with the ship under Blake's command and Tytler in overall control. The second alternative was favoured by Tytler, whose evidence in court had been calculated to show his suitability for this elevated role. But, since he could attain it only through Arthur's good will, he wrote a letter—probably at the latter's suggestion—recommending the release of Dillon.[30] Provided with testimony to Tytler's apparent magnanimity, Arthur sent Stephen as his emissary to the gaol.

Dillon gave an account of the ensuing interview. He reported Stephen as saying:

> 'Captain Dillon, . . . I can assure you that you will not be released unless you make matters up with Doctor Tytler, and give your officers as bondsmen . . . , that you will keep the peace towards the Doctor during the remainder of the voyage'.

He replied:

> 'Sir, do you suppose I am going to sea with my hands manacled? . . . Doctor Tytler can rejoin the ship and continue his duty. I will not molest him, unless his conduct merits it.'

Stephen then remarked that, if those were his sentiments, the Governor would send the *Research* to sea under Blake. And Dillon retorted that such an action would constitute piracy.

The interview took place on 4 May. During the next few days events moved swiftly. On 5 May Dillon learnt that Tytler had informed the government that he wished to leave the expedition, rather than continue serving under him, and that Blake had declined a suggestion that he should assume the command. On the seventh he was handed a further petition seeking his release—signed by a group of civil and military officers, including Stephen and four of the six jurymen at his trial. On the eighth he wrote again to Arthur. Since he thought it necessary to counter personal prejudice against him, he began with a reference to his background.

> I am the son of the late Peter Dillon Esquire, of Meath Ireland, Nephew of the late Sir William Dillon of the same place, and related in the next degree of affinity to the Countess Bertrand.

He went on to explain the seasonal changes in the winds in the Solomons area, as far as he understood them, in order to demonstrate that any further delay in the ship's departure from Hobart Town would involve the abandonment of the expedition. On 9 May the question of remitting the remainder of his term of imprisonment was on the agenda for the Executive Council.[31]

When Alfred Stephen was leaving London for Van Diemen's Land, his cousin James had written to Arthur about him.

> He is a pleasant, lively, talkative youth, who has neither thought nor read deeply upon any subject. He is just that sort of man who would have made a most agreeable, if not a brilliant, inmate of London Drawing Rooms, if he had been born to a great inheritance.[32]

Arthur had not been disappointed: he had found him a congenial colleague, not given to contradicting him. Stephen's signature on the petition almost certainly indicated that the Lieutenant-Governor had decided, as early as 7 May, to accept the logic of events. But after the Executive Council had considered the question of Dillon's release he was able to report that he had acted in accordance with its advice. Pedder opposed remission, since it was sought on grounds of interest, not of mercy, and he was supported by the Colonial Secretary. The two other members, who were men in closer contact with the local community, however, recommended immediate release, and Arthur, as chairman, agreed with their recommendation.[33]

Next morning Pedder 'looked out of the back window of his apartment, and observing a ship under weigh', he turned to Dillon's solicitor, who had called on him, and remarked: 'I suppose Dr. Tytler is gone'. He then gave instructions that Dillon should enter into sureties to be of good behaviour and pay his fine: 'that is all that will be necessary to obtain his liberation'.

> I left the prison with Mr. Lord under one arm and Mr. Bethune under the other, and thus escorted, met the Lieutenant-governor in the street. If the countenance be the index of the mind, there was sufficient pourtrayed in his at that moment to warrant a surmise that these gentlemen would be remembered on a future day, for the testimony of esteem thus paid to one who, they knew, enjoyed so small a portion of his Excellency's good graces.

He was again a free man: but—as he never forgot—he was £521 poorer when he had met all the expenses attendant upon his trial.[34]

Dillon had many matters of business to settle before he could sail. The most important was that of obtaining funds to pay for the supplies he had ordered for the ship. This issue had been resolved, in principle, well before the trial. After considerable discussion, the government had agreed to lend up to $4,000, provided it was repayable in London, not Bengal; and Dillon, with reluctance, because the proviso forced him to act beyond his instructions, had drawn bills on the head office of the East India Company. But the government had not yet carried

The Search for La Pérouse

out its part of the agreement. When he asked for the money, he was told he must give a bottomry on the *Research*, an even more embarrassing condition that was not withdrawn till Stephen had given a legal opinion that it was inappropriate. Finally, however, on 14 May, he received a cheque.[35]

There was also the need to seek men to fill the places of those who had left, or intended to leave, the ship. Tytler was replaced, as surgeon, by John Griffiths, a government medical officer, and Blake—who had tendered his resignation and then unsuccessfully sought to withdraw it—by W. Deane, the chief officer of a ship then in port. Dudman also left, and Munro, Dillon's clerk, deserted; but no replacements for them were found at Hobart Town.

On the morning of 20 May Dillon was ready to sail for Sydney. Shortly after he had ordered the anchor to be weighed, five European seamen deserted. The remainder, he wrote, were 'all nearly drunk, their faces dreadfully mangled, with black eyes, broken noses, and scratched jaws'. During his absence discipline had collapsed. And the ship herself had been allowed to become so dirty and untidy that she had been dubbed by the facetious the 'Lascar man-o'-war'.

Dillon—so careful of his own appearance and that of his ship, so unbending in his notions of discipline—thus left Van Diemen's Land under conditions that could bring him no pride. But he was overwhelmingly relieved to be leaving. And as the *Research* moved out of the Derwent into the open sea he indulged himself, or so he later claimed, in this improbable soliloquy:

> Van Diemen's Land I bid you adieu! Land of corruption and injustice, farewell! Adieu to the place where the crackbrained antiquarian and noisy polemic of India, the redoubtable and learned naturalist, botanist, historiographer, geographer, and doctor of all arts and sciences (if we believe his own account of his literary acquirements), Robert Tytler, so easily succeeded in impressing a belief of his worth and excellencies on the minds of a governor, secretary, preacher, acting attorney-general and judge, who looked up to this visionary pedant as a second admirable Crichton.

'CROWDED all sail for Port Jackson', Dillon noted in his journal on 21 May. The wind was fair; and, although it later fell away, the sense of exhilaration reflected by his words stayed with him. As in 1821—after the wreck of the *Phatisalam*—he felt that he was approaching the shores of a colony where things were done more justly. Had he gone first to Sydney, he mused, his trial would have been before a civil jury impervious to 'whining cant' and without 'fear of offending a military governor'; the ship could have been refitted while the case was being heard; 'and in all human probability, the expedition would have been rendered more satisfactory'.

On 31 May the *Research* reached Port Jackson and was brought to anchor in Watson's Bay, just inside the Heads. Because of the time that had been lost in Van Diemen's Land, Dillon did not intend to remain for long. He believed—correctly—that in the Solomons, as in the Banda Sea, strong monsoonal winds from the north-west would begin to blow by December and make further investigation of Vanikoro impossible.[36] Moreover, if he finished his work there early enough, he would be able to return to Calcutta by way of New Ireland and Buru, as he had done in the *St Patrick*, instead of being forced to take the longer route through the China Sea. Before he sailed, however, he had important matters of business to attend to in Sydney, and on the day following his arrival he moved from the ship to lodgings in town.[37]

Colonial editors were little interested in the distinction between news and comment. But in Hobart Town only the anti-government papers had given much space to Dillon's defence, while the pro-government *Gazette* had emphasized the case for the prosecution. In Sydney, on the contrary, all four papers were sympathetic towards Dillon. News of his trial and conviction had, of course, preceded him. On 17 May *The Gleaner* had expressed 'much concern . . . that our old, and respected friend, Captain P. Dillon . . . has been sentenced' to a term of imprisonment; somewhat earlier it had described him as 'a well-known Naval Commander'[38]—an error that must have pleased him. On 1 June Robert Howe, of the *Sydney Gazette*, republished an article on the trial from the *Tasmanian*, the paper owned by his brother George and edited by Gellibrand; and over the following week, briefed by Dillon himself, he provided his readers with a full account of the origins and purpose of the expedition. 'To set on foot so praiseworthy an endeavour', the *Gazette* declared, '. . . is highly praiseworthy'. It believed that the public would be 'all expectation' for Dillon's return.[39]

The cultivation of a favourable press was merely an incidental gain; it formed no part of Dillon's object in calling at Port Jackson. He had been particularly anxious that his own account of events in Van Diemen's Land should reach the government in Bengal before those it was bound to receive from Tytler and Arthur had badly damaged his reputation. And, when he learnt that Tytler had been able to embark for Calcutta only a day after his arrival in Sydney, his anxiety was intensified.⁴⁰ To ensure the safe delivery of his despatches he arranged with the Colonial Secretary for their transmission as official mail.⁴¹ He was also concerned with filling vacancies in the ship's company. He found replacements for Dudman and Munro and engaged additional seamen. But his search for a naturalist—made necessary by Dr Griffith's inability to perform that side of Tytler's duties—was unsuccessful. One further change was made in the crew: Dillon agreed to allow Mossman, who had now been his colleague for some five years, to remain in Sydney, where he had a wife and family. After a supply of vegetables and some sheep and poultry—obtained through his old friend Robert Campbell—had been taken aboard, Dillon was ready to put to sea.

On 4 June the *Research* sailed for Tonga. Dillon intended to refill the water-casks there, as he was uncertain whether sufficient water would be obtainable at Tikopia and was reluctant to have men ashore unnecessarily at Vanikoro, where the inhabitants might be hostile. He also intended to re-stow the ship, for some of her handling deficiencies —which Tytler had dwelt on so unconscionably—appeared to be caused by excessive stowage of heavy articles, such as spare anchors, in the bow.

At this season, Dillon thought, the westerlies of the southern ocean should reach as far north as the latitude of Sydney. By sailing directly eastward till he reached the longitude of Tonga, he expected to make a fast passage. But, when the ship was two days out, the wind shifted to the east, where it obstinately remained, merely veering between north-east and south-east. On 13 June it rose to gale force and split the main-topsail. On the seventeenth a lunar observation showed their position to be 167°29′30″E., or still nearly eighteen degrees west of Tongatapu. After several more days of unfavourable weather, Dillon thought of calling, instead, at Tana, in the New Hebrides, which lay more directly to the north. Before finally deciding to change course, he checked the ship's supply of water, which Blake had been instructed to replenish at Hobart Town. To his distress, he found that the assignment had not been completed and that many of the casks which had not since been broached were empty. In the circumstances he concluded that he had no alternative to putting in at the Bay of Islands.

On 25 June, when land was sighted, he noted in his journal:

> Shortly after daylight observed that the sea assumed a light colour, and indication that we were not far from the coast of New Zealand ... At half past one P.M. land in sight bearing N.N.E. per compass, distance ten leagues, which proved to be the Three Kings, off the north coast of New Zealand.
>
> The wind blowing directly from the shore, we could not approach it. Carried as much sail during the night as the ship could conveniently bear, beating to windward.

Because of the unsettled weather, he decided to sail round the north of the islands, rather than risk a passage between them and the mainland. Four days later the *Research* was still in sight of the Three Kings, though by then to their north-east. During the afternoon of 29 June she finally got to windward of them. And on 1 July she entered the Bay of Islands and came to anchor in Kororareka Bay.

Dillon was again anxious about his ability to fulfil his quest. At this season, he wrote, ships from Sydney usually reached the Three Kings 'in eight or ten days at most'; but, because of contrary winds, the *Research* had been at sea for twenty-five before she passed them. Moreover, the need to call at the Bay imposed a further delay. And he had an additional cause for anxiety in the conduct of some of the men under his command.

In his *Narrative*, he wrote: 'The European part of my crew were without exception the most abandoned set I ever met with; they were all deserters from other ships, not one of them going by his proper name'. He claimed they had been encouraged in their insubordination by the slackness of Blake and—maliciously transferring the epithet from the colony to the man—'by the Van Diemen's Land convict judge, who had given them to understand that I had no more authority ... over my men than the master of a merchant vessel trading between London and Botany Bay'.

> If an officer now requested them to do their duty, he was treated with the grossest insolence; as they fancied that they ought to be permitted to act in the same manner as formerly, and that the lascars should clean the ship, leaving these mutinous unprincipled rascals nothing more to do than steer the vessel, eat, drink, and sleep.

At Port Jackson some of them had smuggled spirits on board and became 'intoxicated and riotous'; at the Bay of Islands, despite his threats of punishment, they repeated the performance.

Nor was he happy with his new second officer, whom he had found asleep on deck during his watch:

Being on a voyage fraught with danger, not only from the seas, but from surprise while at anchor in the ports, on shores which are inhabited by barbarians relentless and treacherous, or by cannibals, who besides their naturally savage disposition, are further impelled to seek our destruction by their horrible propensity to devour us,—I deemed it more imperatively necessary that the officer on watch should at all times and in all places be on the alert.

He therefore posted a notice on the log-board.

'Received information that one of the officers has been in the habit of sleeping on deck in his watch: found it to be the case. Looked over the offence this time . . . I am determined, should such an occurrence take place again, to disrate the officer and send him off the quarter-deck. An officer who sleeps on his watch, exposes himself to the sarcasms of the common sailors, and can never command with authority, having placed himself in the power of his inferiors.'

But, as with the seamen, his warning was ineffective.

Dillon did not rank the Maoris with the 'barbarians' he expected to meet at Vanikoro; but he knew that some of them would be sorely tempted to seize the *Research* for the sake of the weapons that she carried. For this reason, he called a meeting of the officers on arrival at the Bay and told them 'not to suffer their vigilance to be lulled by the friendly appearance of the natives'. Several nights later, however, he wakened to a wholly somnolent ship.

At 2.1/2 A.M. the moon shone with peculiar brilliancy. All was hushed in the most solemn silence on deck: not a foot in motion throughout the ship, although there ought at that time to have been fifteen men on the alert . . .

He went up to the quarter-deck, where he saw 'the second officer sound asleep upon a small cask, loudly snoring as he sat'. He remained watching him, to see when he would wake. Eventually a seaman appeared and, 'feigning to look out of the port near to which the officer was still sitting asleep, he had the audacity to stand upon his foot . . .'.

Towards the end of his stay at the Bay of Islands, still depressed by the failings of his men and the inhospitality of the seasons, Dillon wrote a letter to Gellibrand. It might be necessary, he said, for him to return direct to Calcutta, without visiting Vanikoro.[42]

Despite his anxieties Dillon enjoyed the three weeks he was delayed at the Bay. As the *Research* approached the anchorage, he had stood on deck shouting a greeting in Maori to the men and women who approached in canoes.

> At length one of the young ladies called out most lustily, notwithstanding her delicate sex, 'Rangatheera no Patareeckee,' it is the captain of the *St. Patrick* . . . This recognition was re-echoed in every New Zealand throat, and nothing for sometime was audible but the word 'Peter,' the name by which I am known by the South Sea Islanders.

And from that moment till his departure he was almost constantly in the company of one group or another of the local people.

As soon as the anchor had been let go and the sails furled, they received their first visitors.

> Several young ladies condescended to come on board, and the decks were shortly crowded with females, some of whom made a very genteel appearance, being dressed in English gowns, shirts, and petticoats: others were in their native costume. Without solicitation, they proceeded voluntarily to amuse us with songs, dances, war whoops, and comic performances, in which they succeeded inimitably.
>
> Many of them were so kind as to remain all night on board, and indeed did not depart during the ship's stay.

Dillon himself, it might be thought, had less need of kindness than others, since Mary, who was still no more than thirty, was travelling with him. But this does not seem to have been his own opinion, for during their visit—or perhaps a little later, on his return from Vanikoro —a local girl became pregnant by him and in due course gave birth to a daughter.[43]

Maori hospitality was, of course, returned. Dillon made sure that the men's paramours were rewarded with small presents and gave muskets and powder to the chiefs who encouraged them to live on board. He entertained chiefs and women of rank at his table in European fashion. And, through a fortunate accident, he provided them with entertainment even less susceptible of imitation than the performance by the women when they first came aboard.

One day he had a visit from a woman whom he described as 'a priestess'.

> She appeared to be of middle age; her complexion brunette, with sparkling black eyes; and her jet black hair . . . gently flowed in ringlets over her shoulders, waving gracefully in the air as she walked. She . . . conveyed to the mind a forcible idea of savage royalty.

After she had drunk a tumbler of rum and lit a cigar, she began to show interest in the surgeon's assistant—'an elderly gentleman named Richardson'—and asked him to salute her in Maori style by touching noses. Her request was accepted; but its execution terrified her, for as he bent forward his wig fell off. 'She screamed most dreadfully', Dillon related, 'having for the first time seen a real proof of that skill in the black art, which she pretended that she was possessed of'. Could Richardson take off his head, she asked. How many evil spirits did he control? 'I replied, that with regard to the number of evil spirits . . ., it was out of my power to inform her truly; but as regarded his hair I assured her he could dismember himself from head to foot with the greatest facility.'

On the following day Dillon received a further visit from the priestess. This time a retinue of unbelievers had accompanied her, and the ship's officers had persuaded Richardson to improve his act.

> With this view they prevailed on him to submit the bald part of his head to the draftsman's art, who in a short time metamorphosed it in such a way, that had he been in ancient Greece or Rome during the sway of Pagan superstition, he might have obtained worshippers as the god Janus, who had in pity to men condescended to pay them a visit. His head presented the perfect appearance of an additional phiz, most hideously pourtrayed on the bald part of the cranium.

Dillon observed subsequent proceedings with delight. 'Infidelity itself', he wrote, became convinced of Richardson's magical powers; and only his explanation of the mechanics of European vanity eventually restored tranquillity.

Another of Dillon's visitors was Jemmy, the English-speaking Tahitian whom he had met on his first visit to the Bay of Islands in 1809. Jemmy had then been about to take a Maori wife and settle among her people; now he was accompanied by a son, 'a lad of about twelve years old'. Yet another was a Lascar who had lived contentedly with the Maoris equally long. The experience of these two, like that of the Europeans living at Kororareka, confirmed Dillon in his belief that New Zealand had become a country ready to absorb foreign residents and to accord them security.

A darker side of the changing social pattern was exemplified, however, in the tales he heard from his most constant visitors, the leading chiefs of the Bay area. He learnt that the wars between their people and those of the Thames and Waikato had not ended and that he himself bore some responsibility for their continuance. He had asked the chief Pomare to bring a working party from the Bay of Islands to cut timber for the *St Patrick*, but had sailed before it arrived. Disappointed in their expectation of acquiring additional muskets and powder, Pomare and his men had decided to make war on the southern tribes. In the ensuing fighting Pomare himself, his eldest son, and many others had been killed, and the war party broken up into small groups of fugitives. Early in 1827 a new force had gone south to exact vengeance but had also been defeated, as a result of which the chiefs were once again organizing for war.[44]

Dillon realized that this story had an urgent significance for him because of the presence on board the *Research* of Brian and Morgan. He was first told it by Pomare's nephew, Whetoi, whose attitude towards the two young men from the Thames starkly emphasized the dichotomy in Maori thinking between public obligations and private good will. Whetoi said to him: 'You must deliver them up, that we may kill and eat them directly'.

> He was clothed in a war mat, with a mantle of dog-skins thrown loosely over his shoulders; his countenance at this moment assumed an aspect of the most savage ferocity, his eyes starting from their sockets with the intenseness of desire to seize on the innocent relatives of a people with whom he happened to be at war.

But, when Brian and Morgan came on deck, he talked with them amicably and warmly praised Brian's father. The latter, he said, had saved two of Pomare's sons and some others who had been captured and sold into slavery. He had ordered their release, provided them with a canoe and a supply of food, and sent them home.

At the time of Dillon's arrival, the most influential personages on the Kororareka side of the Bay—Te Whareumu (also known as King George), his mother Te Ruru, and his uncle Moehanga (or King Charley)—were away from home, as were the sons of Pomare. On their return they all visited him. The older people were warmly affectionate towards Brian; and the two youths explained that Brian's father had implored them to remember his kindness if his son should pass through the Bay of Islands. But, on the public issue involved, their attitude was essentially similar to Whetoi's: the two defeats inflicted on their people must be avenged.

The subject of warfare also dominated Dillon's first conversation with Titore, a brother-in-law of Hongi Hika. Titore explained that Hongi had recently made war on the people of Whangaroa, 'one half of whom he slew, and drove the other half from that part of the country'; but he added that in the course of the battle Hongi had himself been shot through the chest. He was now living on the captured lands, sick but unsubdued.

The Search for La Pérouse

Dillon saw this tragic record of almost incessant fighting, which was gradually destroying his Maori friends, as, in part, a result of European contact. He recognized that the obligation to avenge past defeats derived from custom; but he also knew that the impulse towards aggression had been powerfully stimulated by the coming of the white man. He apparently regarded the process as largely inevitable and experienced no sense of guilt from trading in firearms. But he was concerned—as, indeed, he had been since he first learnt of the *Boyd* massacre in 1810—with the consequences of acts of inhumanity by visiting mariners and of their failure to comprehend the intricacies of Maori culture. He therefore encouraged the elderly Te Ruru and her brother Moehanga to talk to him about past conflicts between Maoris and Europeans.

He found Moehanga, 'a man with a small shrewd eye', particularly informative on the subject of the *Boyd*. He already knew that a young Maori of chiefly rank had been returning in her to Whangaroa deeply embittered by the treatment he had received as a seaman. He was told by Moehanga of the basis of the young man's bitterness, which included not only lack of payment for work he had done but also denial of his personal status, a grievance that was appropriately redressed by the massacre. He was given a detailed account of the killing and eating of most of the ship's company and—perhaps of greatest interest to him—an explanation of the role of the Bay of Islands chief, Te Pahi. He had been distressed by the story that Te Pahi, the friend of Marsden, had turned against Europeans because of the raid on his potato grounds by men from the *Mercury* and by the news of the chief's death at the hands of whalers, who regarded him as the instigator of the affair. Now it emerged, if Moehanga was correct, that Te Pahi had visited the *Boyd* in an attempt to rescue those who, at the time, were still alive. To Dillon this explanation carried the stamp of truth, as did the whole of Moehanga's narrative. When he published it, he added a comment on its authenticity.

> Various accounts of this horrid affair have appeared, all more or less incorrect. The present may be depended upon as the most accurate yet published, having been obtained from information communicated to me by a native, who visited the scene of action a few days after it had happened. The interpreter employed for this purpose had been living there for four or five years, and, from my own knowledge of the language, could not, had he been so inclined, impose on me.

Dillon's account of the massacre was not definitive; but his claim that it was superior to earlier ones was justified. Moreover, his reference to the assessment of oral evidence and the use of interpreters was significant—since it helps to place him among the more competent traveller-ethnographers of his time.

Dillon collected other stories of past conflicts that have similarly been drawn on by later historians—most notably, one from Te Ruru about the killing at the Bay of Islands in 1772 of the French explorer Marion du Fresne. But the conduct of historical inquiries necessarily took second place to the attainment of the purpose for which he had come to New Zealand.

At the northern end of Kororareka Bay a clear stream descended through a rocky bed punctuated by small waterfalls, overhung by tree-ferns and berry-bearing trees attractive to birds, till most of its water flowed under a shingle beach at its mouth. The stream was a magnet drawing ships to that part of the Bay of Islands, where they could rely on being able to refill their water-casks. At the time of the *Research*'s visit, it was unusually low, for, although the weather was 'damp and dismal', the winter rains had not yet fully set in. 'The whole force of the stream', Dillon wrote, 'was not greater than if it ran through a pistol barrel'. This disappointing trickle unavoidably delayed his sailing, even though he kept a watering party at work both night and day.

While waiting for the casks to be filled, he had other business to attend to. He had the ship re-stowed, obtained new yards and blocks to replace ones that had been damaged during the passage from Sydney, and replenished the ship's supply of firewood. He also dealt with requests from some of his Maori friends for passages to India. After considerable discussion with the suppliants, he agreed to take five of them: Moehanga (who was anxious to see his old benefactor Dr Savage), along with one of his sons, named by Dillon 'Murtoch O'Brien'; 'a New Zealand doctor', unflatteringly called 'Robert Tytler'; and Titore, who was to be accompanied by one of his 'confidential friends'. The last of these became 'Phelim O'Rourke'. But upon Titore, whom Dillon considered, 'without exception, one of the finest made men I ever met with', he bestowed a more dignified title. As Titore held 'a rank similar to that of a marquis in Europe', in his opinion, and lived at the village of Waimate, he named him 'Fingal, Marquis of Wyemattee'.

Dillon also decided to take some of the women who were living on board as far as Vanikoro. One was the companion of Buchert, who expected her to remain with him at Tikopia. The others would be returned to the Bay of Islands—in the *Research* or possibly in a whaler bound for New Zealand—before Dillon sailed for India. He later justified his decision by asserting, not wholly untruthfully but somewhat disingenuously, that the presence of women on board was intended to satisfy the Vanikorans that his intentions were not aggressive. But, in conformity with the practice followed by whalers, he made presents to the women to confirm his understanding with them. It was an action that laid him open to the far less favourable interpretation of his motives which the Reverend William Williams, of the Church Missionary Society, recorded in his journal on the day the ship sailed.

> It was reported to us last night that a number of native females had been purchased the day before for muskets by Dillon and different persons in his vessel . . . In the course of the night six escaped to the shore, but the rest are reported to be thus violently carried away. We shall hear more of this abominable act in a few days . . .[45]

To William Williams and his colleagues, Dillon was not a latter-day Dampier or Cook but, as Henry Williams wrote, a former master of the brig *Active* 'now commanding *pro tempore* one of the Company's cruisers'.[46]

Dillon sailed on 24 July. He was bound for the River Thames, where he intended to land Brian and Morgan and to obtain spars and fresh provisions, both of which had been scarce at the Bay of Islands. But he sailed into stormy weather.

> As the wind was now, I considered that entering the Thames would be attended with much loss of time, and communicated this my opinion to Prince Brian Boroo, who implored me most piteously to land him . . . He stated that, should he delay his return two or three years, he would, in all probability, find his father, brothers, sisters, and friends had been murdered or carried off by the enemy; and he therefore wished to land and share their fate, whatever it might be, as he had no desire whatever to survive them. He further observed, that his presence would encourage his friends, and the arms which he had procured in India would be of the greatest service in repelling the enemy.

Faced with this plea Dillon relented; but, because of the direction of the wind, he found it impossible to get close in to the coast. He therefore laid a course—once again—for Tongatapu.

Shortly before Dillon sailed from Bengal, he had been informed of the despatch from France of the corvette *L'Astrolabe* 'for the purpose of exploring the coast of New Guinea and those of New Zealand with a view to discover the spot where the Count De La Perouse perished'. If he fell in with her, he was to explain his reasons for thinking La Pérouse had been wrecked at Vanikoro.[47] He had welcomed neither the information nor the instruction. But he had inquired about the *Astrolabe* at each of his ports of call, and at the Bay of Islands he had received definite news of her: she was under the command of Captain Dumont d'Urville, had been at the Bay in March and, when she sailed, had been bound for Tonga.

On 12 August Dillon sighted the high island of 'Eua, which lies some ten miles south-east of Tongatapu.

> At 7 P.M. light variable airs from the eastward. Not wishing to approach the land before daylight, I ordered the small sails to be handed, and the ship to be hauled to the wind on the starboard tack, and thus we spent the night beating to windward.

Because the winds remained light next day, he did not make contact with the people till the morning of 14 August, when canoes put out from the shore 'loaded with yams, potatoes, sugar-cane, cocoa-nuts, seashells, clubs, spears &c. for barter'. In one of them was an American who was living on the island, as he informed Dillon, with a chief's daughter. He also told him that several months previously he had heard the report of cannon fire at Tongatapu and that soon afterwards news was received of fighting between Tongans and the crew of a ship flying 'a white flag', in which three islanders and a foreigner had been killed. Dillon concluded that the ship involved must have been the *Astrolabe*.

On the following day, when he brought the *Research* to anchor at Tongatapu, he received a fuller account of his rival's misfortunes. Dumont d'Urville had run the corvette on to the reef while entering the lagoon and, fearing she would sink, had prepared to move her company ashore. 'Fortunately, however, he was dissuaded from this premature step . . .', Dillon wrote, with a touch of condescension, 'and ultimately succeeded . . . in rescuing her from her perilous situation'. But, meanwhile, members of the crew had formed associations with Tongans, and some had decided to desert. When two succeeded in doing so, a boat-crew sent to apprehend them had been captured. Subsequent reprisals by the French—burning of villages and destruc-

The Search for La Pérouse

tion of canoes—had led to armed resistance by the Tongans, in the course of which a corporal of marines was bayoneted and, in Dillon's words, 'instantly expired'. Dumont d'Urville had then moved the *Astrolabe* near to the village of Ma'ofanga, the seat of an important deity and a sanctuary, and had bombarded it over a period of several days. Eventually he had secured the return of the men who were on shore, apart from the two deserters, and sailed—it was understood—for Fiji.

Dillon had been given no new reason for fearing the future achievements of Dumont d'Urville. But he did not himself underrate the difficulty of dealing with the people of the Friendly Islands, as the group was still commonly known. According to the Wesleyan missionary, John Thomas, 'He says there is not a more treacherous or designing people than the Tonga people'.[48] At 'Eua he had declined an invitation to go ashore, 'not feeling inclined to be bound to a cocoa-nut tree for an indefinite period, or till an enormous ransom was exacted for me'. At Tongatapu he gave a talk to members of the crew, 'to keep their vigilance alive', in which he told them of all the vessels that had been 'cut off' by the Tongans. Moreover, he was acutely conscious of a further danger: he knew, as Dumont d'Urville had discovered, that the chiefs would encourage sailors to desert, in order to have their assistance in the waging of war.

Because of the risks involved, he did not permit his men to land; but he welcomed many Tongans—particularly chiefs and women—on board. On several evenings, when a chief was visiting him, the crew provided an entertainment.

> The European seamen capered in reels and jigs to the sound of the fife and drum, which were then varied by the New Zealanders coming on the stage with their warlike and animating dances . . .
>
> The lascars also performed their dance, according to the Asiatic custom, rapping their toes and heels against the deck in symphony with the squeaking of a wretched old fiddle, without even its proper complement of strings. Nevertheless the Tonga chief seemed to consider this discord as verifying the line of Pope:
>
> 'All discord's harmony, not understood,'
>
> and commended that as pleasing kind harmony which the Europeans could not comprehend.

Dillon's Tongan visitors included some of great interest to him: his old friend Langi; Mafi Hape, once the adoptive mother of William Mariner, whose book, *An Account of the Natives of the Tonga Islands* he valued highly; Tupou (or Aleamotu'a), the Tu'i Kanokupolu, whose titular eminence was recognized throughout Tonga; and Fakafanua, the chief of Ma'ofanga.

Since Dillon had last met Langi—in Tahiti in 1825—the latter had returned home with Tahitian teachers to attempt the conversion of his people to Christianity. He now told Dillon that the Tu'i Kanokupolu and many of his 'subjects' had adopted the new religion—it was a claim that over-simplified a complex situation. He also told him that John Williams's boat, which was blown off the Society Islands and found at Atiu by Dillon in 1824, had finally been wrecked at Tongatapu; and he brought two survivors of the wreck to see him. The men were Aitutakians. They explained that the boat had been towed to Aitutaki from Atiu by a trading schooner and from there it had been sent, with a crew of ten, on a voyage to Rarotonga. But it had been driven by a gale farther south than its destination and had then drifted westward before the trades, with the crew 'undergoing all the pains and miseries that human nature could support for the want of food'. Five men had died from starvation, but the others had survived —on sharks and sea-birds and a little rainwater—till, after five months and a drift of some nine hundred miles, they had been cast up on the reef of Tongatapu.

The visit by Mafi Hape interested Dillon because of her earlier role as the informant and protector of Mariner after the seizure, in 1806, of the privateer *Port-au-Prince*. According to John Martin, who recorded Mariner's account of Tonga, she had taken 'the greatest pains' to perfect her adoptive son's knowledge of the Tongan language and of Tongan custom. 'In all respects, and on every occasion', Martin wrote, 'she conducted herself towards him with the greatest maternal affection, modesty, and propriety: she was a woman of great understanding, personal beauty, and amiable manners'.[49] She still possessed 'a most graceful appearance', in Dillon's opinion; and, when he showed her the engraving in Mariner's *Account of the Natives of the Tonga Islands*, he claimed, 'She immediately recognized the likeness, and exclaiming "it is Tokey," she wept bitterly'.

Dillon invited Mafi Hape to breakfast and presented her with articles useful to a lady of quality, such as chintz, beads and scissors. He received Tupou with a salute of three guns and, in the evening, had the crew provide entertainment. Next morning he received from Tupou 'one of the largest hogs I ever saw, and a hundred yams, which would each average seven pounds': it was the gift of one high chief to another.

A visitor of a very different background was the Reverend John Thomas. A former blacksmith with a rigidly evangelical conception of his role, Thomas was a missionary of the type that Dillon found least congenial; but he was received with no less courtesy than the Tongans. 'I was made welcome on board by Cap. Dillon', he recorded in his journal, 'the conversation of civilized people, though not of the same religion is gratifying to us'. He was pleased by Dillon's suggestion that the mission should be abandoned, apparently interpreting it as recognition of the hardships he was forced to endure, and by his gift of ten gallons of spirits, which promised some intermittent alleviation of them. But, when conversation turned to the voyage of the *Research*, he was soon out of his depth, for he gained the impression that Dillon was looking for men 'formerly belonging to the French ship La Perouse, which was lost about 38 years ago, and has not been heard of since' and that evidence of their whereabouts had been found during a call at the island of 'Toopia'.[50]

Dillon's most valued visitor, however, was Fakafanua, who came out to the ship almost every day. As the chief of Ma'ofanga district and the most important priest in Tongatapu, Fakafanua was a man of power. He was also a man of advanced years, with an excellent memory, who was able to give an account, in considerable detail, of the European visits to Tonga following those of Cook, which satisfied Dillon that La Pérouse had called there, as he intended, on his voyage from Botany Bay towards the Solomons. But most of his assistance was of an immediately practical kind. He organized parties of Tongans to procure water and firewood, thus saving Dillon from the need to send his men ashore. He encouraged his people to bring hogs and yams for sale to the ship. And, being a kindly man, he brought on board 'a numerous retinue of Tonga ladies'. He was rewarded for his services with muskets and powder, cutlery and ironmongery; and, when the ship was ready to sail, he obtained Dillon's agreement—according to the latter's account—to the embarkation of two members of his family, a son and a daughter, in order that they might visit the island of Rotuma.

By a combination of friendship and caution—his usual formula for dealings with islanders—Dillon maintained good relations with the Tongans. But he was less successful with two of the ship's company. He found that the second officer was again sleeping while on duty and, after failing to cure him of the habit by coming on deck himself during the night watch, suspended him. He accepted the man's request for a discharge in Tonga but later reinstated him, after intercession by Chaigneau. He lost another member of the crew, however, apparently by desertion. This was John Elliott, a man not referred to by Dillon but said by John Thomas's wife to have been the purser.[51]

Before Dillon sailed from Tongatapu, on 26 August, Thomas had revised his opinion of him. Two days earlier he had noted: 'The conduct of the Captain and others on board the *Research* is very bad. they buy the native women for their beastly purposes'.[52] His disapproval increased after Dillon's departure, when he met Elliott and learnt of the embarkation of the young Tongan woman (whom he believed to be one of Fakafanua's wives, not his daughter). He was told that Elliott had left the ship because of ill-treatment. He wrote angrily of Dillon's action in regard to the woman.

> He as taken with him . . . one young woman, that is wife to a Chief at Mafanga, this woman the Captain as bought—and takes her for his base purposes. This is an abominable thing . . . the captain gave him two Muskets for this woman.[53]

Thomas's interpretation of events appears to contain an element of truth, as does Dillon's account of his agreement with Fakafanua. But his understanding was defective, and Dillon's statement incomplete. The brief encounter between the two men was thus filled with ambiguities, and it was deeply coloured by mutual antipathy. The encounter was to be remembered and brooded upon by both Dillon and Thomas and, when they met again ten years later, to provide the basis for a public controversy of extreme bitterness.

DILLON described the harbour at Tongatapu with considerable care. 'Being at the mast-head myself', he wrote on the day of his arrival, 'I observed the channel to be strewed with sunken dangers, such as coral banks, which certainly must have grown there since the harbour was surveyed by Captain Cook'. He later recorded detailed sailing directions for the guidance of future mariners.

Dillon took seriously his obligations as a hydrographer and surveyor; and, when he set out on the last stage of his voyage to Vanikoro, his mind was much occupied with these aspects of his elected role as an explorer. As he sailed north-westward, he carefully noted the position and appearance of each island that was sighted. On 27 August, for example, he recorded that the peak of Ogea, in the Lau group of Fiji, was visible and added: 'I am of opinion that in clear weather this island might be seen eighty miles at sea'. He also watched out for islands reported by his predecessors and noted the accuracy, or inaccuracy, of the references to them in the books and charts he had with him: James Burney's *A Chronological History of the Discoveries in the South Sea or Pacific Ocean*; 'Norie's Nautical Tables for the year 1810'; 'Malham's Naval Gazetteer'; Bowditch's 'Epitome'; 'Lynn's Tables for 1825'; and 'Arrowsmith's chart'. On 28 August he searched for Niufo'ou—'Onooafow, or Probey Island of the *Pandora*'—and on the twenty-ninth for Futuna (Hoorn Islands)—' "Foodoonattoo," or "Island Perdio" of Bougainville', 'the Forlorn Hope of Norie'. But, although he had clear weather and sailed many miles off his course in the hope of sighting them, he was unsuccessful in both quests, and the positions given for the islands in his sources were incorrect.

He later wrote in highly critical terms of the errors he discovered in books and charts during this part of his voyage.

> It is really surprising how so many mistakes could have originated in the taking of latitudes and longitudes, at the close of the enlightened eighteenth century.
>   Not one of the latitudes and longitudes said to have been ascertained on board the *Pandora*, in 1791, with which I have fallen in as yet, is correct... But these errors are not, in my opinion, to be imputed to the naval officers of that ship, who no doubt were fully competent in this as well as every part of their duty; and I therefore rather suppose that they originated with the printers and chart-sellers, who, to obtain a ready sale for works, put a late date to them, with a seeming correction in the situations of islands and places from former works of a similar kind, thereby removing them really from truth or error.

This homily was provoked by the sighting of the island of Fatutaka, north-east of Tikopia. But his aspersions on the land-lubbers seem to have been as unjustified as was his confidence in the navigators.[54]

Dillon's preoccupation with the problems of hydrography was interrupted by a brief call at Rotuma on 1 September. Since he knew that the island was sometimes visited by whalers, he hoped to be able to take on a final stock of fresh provisions for the difficult period that lay ahead; but, to his disappointment, he found that the people were short of food. His Tongan passengers, too, were disappointed. They had made their journey to obtain tribute for Fakafanua, to whom the priests of Rotuma were considered to owe allegiance; but, faced with the prospect of a lengthy sojourn in 'a hungry land', they decided—as Dillon put it—'that they had rather die on board of sea-sickness than go ashore to be starved'.

Despite his inability to purchase supplies, Dillon found much to engage his interest at Rotuma. He was delighted by the landscape itself, 'which had a beautiful verdant appearance, with plantations and houses from the sea-side to the summit of the highest hills'. But he spent his time, in the main, seeking knowledge of the life of the islanders. What were the forms of their social organization? With what other islands were they in contact? How often were they visited by Europeans? He asked his questions as a man with clearly formulated opinions about the general character of Polynesian society and with some knowledge, acquired elsewhere, of conditions in Rotuma. On board the *Research*, for example, he had a Rotuman passenger. This man had been a member of a boat crew that had set out some eight years earlier on a voyage to Vaitupu, in the Ellice Islands, 'to procure shells'. The canoe had been blown off course and had eventually made a landfall in Samoa, whence Dillon's informant had travelled to Tonga.[55] Moreover, as an interrogator he was unusually well placed, for apart from the rejoicing engendered by his bringing home a man long believed lost at sea, he found that he could converse with many Rotumans in the language of Fiji. He was thus able to record much information about Rotuman society, which he later published in his *Narrative*. It was equally characteristic of him, however, that he also inquired about the fate of a former companion. In the crew of the *Active*, in 1814, he had had 'a very old Sandwich Islander, well known at Port Jackson by the name of Babahey, who had been for many years employed out of Sydney as an interpreter to the north-west coast of America, the Sandwich Islands, Otaheita, and the Feejees'. He had later heard that Babahey, 'finding his end approaching fast', had been put ashore at Rotuma. 'I . . . was sorry to learn', he wrote, 'that he had died about eight years ago of a decline, leaving a daughter behind him on the island, who is now twelve years old'.

Since leaving Tongatapu, the *Research* had sailed before the south-east trades, which remained strong and steady. On the day after his call at Rotuma, Dillon therefore began to prepare for his work at Vanikoro.

> Being now at no great distance from the place where all my hopes of success lay, and wishing to preserve a perfect good understanding with the natives, who are unaccustomed to see Europeans, I issued orders to the crew

and passengers on no account to trade, barter, or traffic for the smallest article with the islanders whom we might visit for the future. I had their articles of agreement rehearsed, and reminded them of their engagements with me, and how imperatively necessary it was that the tenour of them should be adhered to now, at the crisis of the expedition, when all our hopes of ultimate success depended so much on an unanimous cordial co-operation in the accomplishment of the one grand object. I also read them some extracts from my instructions relative to restraining trading and the use of fire-arms, and endeavoured forcibly to impress upon their minds how much good conduct would recommend them to the favourable consideration of the Government on our return to Calcutta.

On 4 September the *Research* passed Fatutaka. On the fifth Dillon wrote: 'At half-past seven this morning the island of Tucopia was seen from the poop bearing W.S.W. twenty-one miles. Hauled up S.W. by S. to pass round to the southward of it'. That afternoon he was visited by Tikopians and by Joe, the Lascar. And Martin Buchert made a trip ashore. The main work of the expedition was about to begin.

TEN

Vanikoro

DILLON knew that he would soon be living as an explorer. It was not the search for evidence of La Pérouse that would, in itself, give his life this quality but the particular circumstances in which he would pursue it. He had previously approached, but never quite attained, this level of experience. Even at Tana and Eromanga, where few Europeans had preceded him, he had had the guidance of Cook's narrative; and at Ono Levu, which he had believed to be a new discovery, he had not anchored. Now, at Vanikoro he, and all those for whose safety he was responsible, would be for many weeks at the mercy of the previously unknown. In 1813 and again in 1826 he had looked from a distance upon Vanikoro's shores and its central mountains capped in cloud. But, among Europeans, only La Pérouse and his companions had penetrated its coastal waters and made contact with its inhabitants. Their fate, like the misfortunes suffered by Mendaña and Carteret at the neighbouring island of Santa Cruz, emphasized the dangers that lay ahead of him. Uncharted reefs, winds and currents of unknown strength, the uncertain attitudes of the islanders—these would provide the background to his work. Upon his own skill and vigilance, and his ability to maintain high standards of conduct among his crew, the safety of the expedition would be largely dependent. It was a formidable responsibility but one that he looked forward to with eagerness, if not without apprehension.

Meanwhile, at Tikopia, Dillon was still within a world that was familiar to him, not only because of his previous calls at the island but also because the Tikopians, unlike their neighbours of Vanikoro, were Polynesians and possessed a language and a culture akin to those of Rotuma and Tonga. Moreover, on the day of his arrival, he was visited by a European and was told by his chief officer of three others whom he had met when near the shore in one of the ship's boats. He was disturbed by the presence of these beachcombers. Their stories of how they had reached Tikopia were inconsistent and obviously untrue, and they were in conflict with what he learnt from Joe, the Lascar. He had no doubt that the men were convicts who had escaped in a stolen boat from New South Wales. None the less, he decided to accept their request to be taken on board, as he could employ them usefully at Vanikoro.

Like a mountaineer at his final base-camp before attempting the summit, Dillon was preoccupied with the task ahead. He made presents to the chiefs to ensure their continuing friendship. He sent a boat ashore for fresh water, though unsuccessfully 'as the water-run was not above the size of a stream from a goose-quill'. He bought all the relics of the La Pérouse voyage that could be obtained: pieces of iron, copper and brass; bells, some 'such as are used by the Muleteers in Spain', others 'after the fashion of those used in christian churches'; and a silver sword-handle with cyphers on both sides.[1] He was most interested in the last of these.

> The moment the silver handle of the sword was produced, both M. Chaigneau and I recognized it as belonging to the sword-guard taken by me to Calcutta in the *St Patrick*; the cyphers exactly corresponding.

He also questioned his Tikopian visitors on the loss of the two ships and the fate of those who had been on board. His most useful informant was Ratia—or, in Dillon's spelling, 'Rathea'—a man of about fifty, who had spent five years at Vanikoro and was said to speak the language fluently. When Ratia suggested he should join the expedition as pilot and interpreter, Dillon immediately accepted his offer.

On the afternoon of 6 September—Dillon's second day at Tikopia —Ratia urged that they should sail immediately. The coast of Vanikoro, he said, was 'abounding with reefs' and they should take full advantage of the present moonlight nights. Dillon had not intended to leave so soon: only one of the five Europeans had then come on board, and Joe had not made up his mind as to whether he would leave Tikopia. But he was convinced by Ratia's argument.

> I considered the loss of one night's moon of more importance than the services of the four Europeans and the lascar, and therefore at half past seven . . . I bore up W. and by N.1/2N., and set all sail toward the long-wished-for Mannicolo.

His spelling of the name itself emphasized his uncertainties. At Tikopia he had heard it pronounced as 'Malicolo'. Soon he was to decide that the island was 'more correctly called Mannicolo or Vannicolo'. And, after he had been in contact with its people for several weeks, he was to conclude that they had, in fact, no name at all for the whole island; they used 'Vanikoro' (or one of its variant forms) to refer collectively to the villages on its windward side and 'Vanau' (or Whannow', as he spelt it) for the remainder.[2]

At ten o'clock on the morning of 7 September Dillon sighted Vanikoro in the north-west. As the *Research* came nearer to the island's eastern coast, he saw a bay towards the north-east point where it might be possible, he thought, to find anchorage. His decision to send out boats to explore it caused the first of many arguments with Ratia. The people in that part were hostile, Ratia said, and 'fought with large bows and poisoned arrows'. His friends lived to the southward, at a place called Tanema, which the ship could reach, he admitted, only by passing through dangerous reefs. This difficulty he discounted, however, for he thought their contacts with the shore should be limited because of the prevalence of fever on the island; they should buy the relics his friends would bring out to the ship and then, within three days, return to Tikopia. For Dillon, the talk of fever and poisoned arrows was evidence of the need for extreme caution, not for a change of plans; and, after persuading Ratia of his inflexibility in regard to the latter, he completed his preparations for despatching the boats.

Shortly before dawn next morning two whale-boats left the *Research*. Each carried an officer, five oarsmen and a 'sitter'. Ratia and Buchert, who were the 'sitters', were provided with gifts for distribution among the Vanikorans—'Ten pairs of scissors, ten clasp-knives, ten chisels, fifty large and small fish-hooks, ten strings of beads, two dozen gilt buttons, four American axes'. The officers and oarsmen were forbidden to land and instructed to return as soon as they had explored the bay. They were strictly enjoined to keep out of range of arrows fired from the shore and to avoid the use of firearms 'unless their lives were in real danger'.

Dillon anxiously awaited the boats' return. Meanwhile, he studied the island from his position some miles to its north-east. In most places, steep hills covered by dense rain-forest rose almost immediately behind the coral beaches, with their fringe of coconut palms, while only a few areas of flattish land, where small clusters of huts could be seen, appeared suitable for settlement. Several miles out from the shore, along the north coast, breaking waves betokened a reef system through which it might be difficult to take the ship. But he made one discovery that he thought would prove important to him: a bay that 'appeared five miles deep and two broad at its entrance' ran southward from the north coast. He surmised that this joined the bay on the east which he had sent the boats to explore, so that the north-east quarter of Vanikoro—as he had supposed it to be—was apparently an off-lying island, behind which he might expect to find deep, sheltered water where he could anchor.

As the hours passed, Dillon's anxiety increased. The boats failed to return by noon, as he had instructed them to do, or to respond to shots fired to bring them back, when he feared a change in the weather. But shortly before dusk they hove in sight; and, when they reached the ship, they had an encouraging story to tell him. The two bays were, in fact, connected, though by a channel only about two hundred yards in width, on either side of which good anchorage was available. Moreover, the boat-crews had established friendly relations with the people of two villages on the off-lying island. As they approached the first of these, named Tevai, the inhabitants had shown signs of terror; but, after Ratia had spoken to them in their own language, they 'brought peace offerings of green boughs and threw them into the water, inviting Rathea to land, which he instantly did'. At the second, they were received at once with friendliness, as their proceedings at Tevai were already known. At both places, Ratia explained that Dillon was a 'great king' who was visiting the islands to bestow presents such as the tools and beads that he and Martin were distributing. 'With such an explanation they were mightily delighted', Dillon recorded, 'and promised by no means to molest my boats, but to assist me to the utmost of their power with yams, cocoa-nuts, and whatever else their island afforded'. From Buchert he received four adzes said to have been made out of iron obtained from the wrecked ships.

Dillon now possessed some of the knowledge he needed for planning his campaign. His first concern was to bring the *Research* to anchor. He knew that there was a navigable passage from the east into the protected waters behind the off-lying island; but he was loath to use it, as both the passage and the anchorage immediately beyond it were directly exposed to the south-east trades. He therefore sent the boats out again to look for a passage through the reef off the north coast. Meanwhile, he named the physical features that had already been seen and sought to build up his knowledge of the island and its people. His first selection of place-names was intended to honour 'the noblemen and gentlemen' in India who had made his voyage possible. He named the large off-lying island 'Lord Combermere's Island' and a smaller one after Lord Amherst, the Governor-General, for whom Combermere had been deputizing during Dillon's five months in Bengal.* The broad bay to the west of Lord Combermere's Island was called 'Charles Lushington's Bay' and that to the south 'W. B. Bayley's Bay', in honour of another senior government officer. Two headlands on the north coast were designated 'Cape Hayes' and 'Cape Harington'. As the weeks passed, a great number of physical features were to be identified by the names of Dillon's benefactors, officers and friends, until, towards the end of his stay, he bestowed his ultimate honour and named Vanikoro itself 'La Pérouse's Island'.

Dillon was particularly sensitive to the honorific: in the islands 'Pita' was almost a title; elsewhere he was 'Captain Dillon'. He attached importance to the apposite naming of places, for by this means a man's name, and perhaps something of his fame, could be kept alive in the minds of later generations. He therefore approached this activity at Vanikoro without frivolity: it was more than an agreeable conceit; but it was merely incidental to those that were directly related to the pursuit of his main objective. And on 9 September he received his first visit from Vanikorans.

> At 11 A.M. I espied a canoe coming out of Charles Lushington's Bay, which at noon reached the ship, rowed by one middle-aged man and two youths. They approached with less fear than I anticipated, one of them standing up occasionally and holding up a cocoa-nut. I made a sign to them with a white flag to approach, and gave the end of a rope from the stern to them, which they held on by . . .
>
> This being, I considered, the first Mannicolan who ever ventured out to a ship at sea, I was determined to encourage him; I therefore handed to him in the canoe two pieces of Tongataboo cloth, each six yards long and two wide, six pieces, each about one yard square, two yards of blue gurrah, one adze, twenty fish-hooks large and small, with two strings of red beads . . .

Later, he offered them some more cloth, which they declined, indicating that they had no coconuts to give in return.

Whether this behaviour originated in innate honesty (a failing with which the generality of South Sea islanders cannot be justly charged), or that they

---

* These two names have been reversed on the map of Vanikoro in Dillon's *Narrative* (I, facing p. 1)—see Plate 6 in this book.

had already sufficient of the article on board, or whether they dreaded some design on my part, cloaked under the specious shew of generosity, I could not decide.

But during the afternoon four other canoes came out, bringing coconuts and taro and 'four small fish'. In one of them was an old man who seemed willing to come on board.

Dillon did not then encourage his would-be visitor, as Ratia was away with the boats. Next day, however, when he kept both the Tikopian interpreter and Buchert with him, he allowed four Vanikorans to climb on deck. One of them, he wrote, 'was a man whom I supposed to be about sixty or sixty-five years of age, from whom I expected to obtain most important information'. But he found that interrogation was unexpectedly difficult. Though he could understand Tikopian, he could not speak it, so that he was compelled to communicate with Ratia through Buchert—a German-speaker by birth—whose knowledge of Tikopian, he discovered, was no more adequate than his limited English. Moreover, he had repeatedly to attempt to stop Ratia answering the questions himself, instead of putting them to the elderly Vanikoran. The experience was frustrating and he later commented: 'as Swift justly observed, every thing suffers by *translation* except a bishop'.

Dillon had already questioned Ratia on the subject of the wrecks; and, although Ratia's answers contained inconsistencies, he had been able to form a general picture of what had occurred. One ship had struck the reef off Vanau, in the north-west of the island, the other that off Peu, in the south. The former had subsequently sunk in deep water, where many of the men on board her were known to have drowned, for their bodies had been washed ashore. Those who had succeeded in reaching the land had been killed and their skulls preserved in a 'spirit house'. The latter had been blown off the reef into deep water, and most of her company had come ashore in good order. Under the direction of their officers, the men had erected a palisade, within which they had built a two-masted vessel out of material salvaged from the wreck. Eventually all but two of them had sailed away. The visitors had been thought to be spirits, Ratia said, because they had projections 'from their foreheads or noses a foot long' and did not eat in the same way as ordinary men.

Despite the difficulties of interpretation, Dillon was able to put some questions to the Vanikoran and obtain general confirmation of Ratia's account.

> Q. 'How were the ships lost?' — A. '... They got on the rocks at night, and one ship grounded near Wannow, and immediately went to the bottom.'
> ... Q. 'How was the ship lost near Paiow?' — A. 'She got on the reef at night, and afterwards drifted over it into a good place ... the people had time to remove things from her, with which they built a two-masted ship.'
> Q. 'How many moons were they in building it?'— A. 'Plenty of moons.'
> Q. 'How did they procure any thing to eat?'— A. 'They used to go into the *tara* fields, and pull up the roots, and then plant the tops for a new crop. After they sailed away, the people put their fields in order again.'
> Q. 'Had these people no friends among the natives?'— A. 'No. They were ship spirits ... Their chief used always to be looking at the sun and stars, and beckoning to them. There was one of them who stood as a watch at their fence, with a bar of iron in his hand, which he used to turn round his head. This man stood only upon one leg.'

A picture began to take shape in Dillon's mind: the Frenchmen had lived on the island for a long time; the officers had worn cocked-hats and continued to make astronomical observations; the sentinel had been armed with a musket. But a number of tantalizing questions remained. Had La Pérouse himself been among those who had survived the wrecks? Only the men who had remained behind could give him the answer. And what had been the fate of those who put to sea in the vessel built out of wreckage? Probably they had been engulfed by the ocean or cast ashore on some remote island; but no one was ever likely to know for certain.

On the morning of 11 September Dillon nearly gained a participant's understanding of the subject he was studying, for, as he tacked towards the north-east of the island, he saw that detached coral patches extended some distance out from the reef: 'had I stood on to the westward fifteen minutes longer, the *Research* would have shared a similar fate to that of La Pérouse's ships on those dangers just described'. On that day and the next he noted that the weather was stormy; 'I was very uneasy'. But on the thirteenth, when conditions improved, he decided it would be safe to anchor. He had now learnt that there was a passage from the north into Charles Lushington's Bay; but, as it was narrow and the wind from the north-east, he could not use it to reach the protected waters that were his destination. He therefore stood in from the east for Bayley's Bay.

> In consequence of keeping to the southward of the course steered out by the boats, we met with a number of coral banks and patches with three, four, five and six fathoms water on them ... We were sailing over one of

them for ten minutes, but by keeping to the northward we soon got into deep water.

When they had rounded the south head of the bay—which he named 'Research Head'—he ordered that the anchor be let go. His sense of relief was, however, short-lived, as he soon found that the ship was dangerously close to coral patches—he called them 'Treacherous or Tytler's Shoals'—and unnecessarily exposed to the trade winds. He was unable to bring her to anchor farther into the bay till the period of intense darkness between sunset and the full rising of the moon.

Once the *Research* was safely in Bayley's Bay, Dillon was in a position to begin his systematic investigations. He had been visited by fifty or more Vanikorans as the ship entered the bay, and he remained in friendly contact with the islanders throughout his visit. Like the eighteenth-century explorers whom he sought to emulate, he set out to describe them and their culture. They were similar, he wrote, to the people of Santa Cruz, 'jet black with woolly hair, which is combed backward and tied behind'; their lips and teeth were stained red from the chewing of betel nut. They pierced their nostrils and ears, adorning the former with 'white feathers of the domestic cock or hen' and the latter with 'generally from ten to twenty rings of tortoise-shell'. They wore necklaces of white shells, bracelets on the upper arm, and round the waist a girdle to which a small piece of cloth was attached in front and passed between the legs.

> They want but one appendage more, *viz.* a pair of horns, to complete the appearance of his infernal majesty, as represented in the picture shops of London, for they are already furnished with a tail in the Fan-palm, which they thrust into their belts behind, and which tends not a little to heighten the resemblance.

He added this comment later, when he was turning his journal into a publishable narrative. It was a mere literary conceit, not an indication that the Vanikorans were, by disposition, diabolical. In fact, he found them 'to be tractable, generous, and grateful; and so independent in their principles, as not to receive a single article without making what they consider an equivalent return . . . a people not comprehending in themselves even such a thing as the breach of a friendly compact, and unsuspicious of such baseness in others'.

Dillon's most valued companion while the ship lay at anchor was an elderly man to whom he gave the name 'his majesty, king Nero'.

Nero was the principal personage of Tevai, and he seems to have acted towards the visitors with a combination of dignity and courtesy similar to that which they had experienced from influential chiefs in New Zealand and Tonga. He brought Dillon gifts of fish and coco-nuts and 'some pudding made with arrow-root and cocoa-nut, and some of another sort made of cocoa-nut and *tara*'. He expressed an interest in accompanying the ship's officers on their visits to other parts of the island and did his best to procure relics of the kind Dillon was seeking.

Now that members of the ship's company were in constant contact with the islanders articles from the wrecks began to be brought to them in considerable quantity and variety. Dillon therefore established a procedure for dealing with everything they had received.

> First, the trading officer purchased the articles in presence of Monsieur Chaigneau, the French agent, and all the other officers and persons on board; and then I obtained a certificate from those gentlemen, specifying the time and place, and from whom the articles therein enumerated were bought . . .

He deposited relics of particular significance and suitable size in tin boxes, which were immediately sealed.[3] In this way he hoped to avoid imputations of later tampering with the evidence of the kind that Tytler had maliciously alleged in respect of the sword-guard.

Dillon's primary objective was to visit Peu, where the survivors of the shipwreck had built the two-masted vessel, 'as it could not be supposed that the one or two hundred Europeans who built her . . . would have departed without leaving some memorial of their mishap, and ultimate departure . . .'.

> There appeared a great probability of meeting with some such memorial among the trees, rocks, stones, or on some leaden or copper plates, descriptive of who and what they were, whence they came, whither bound at their departure, how the accident happened, the nature of it, and many other particulars, which their peculiar circumstances rendered it probable they would record, during so long and lonesome a seclusion from the civilized world, when their only pleasure could have been derived from erecting such memorials of the disaster which separated them from society, and consigned them to a savage land.

But he did not think it prudent to visit a district inhabited by antagonists of his Vanikoran friends till he had had the long-boat fitted out and equipped with a carronade.

On 16 September, while he was supervising this work, he despatched three whale-boats to Tanema, where a piece of iron much larger than the bolts and other articles he had so far acquired was said to be lying. They returned in the evening with valuable, though disappointing, information and a substantial collection of relics. The officer in charge had gone ashore, together with Ratia and Buchert, Chaigneau and Brian Boru, and been well received by the villagers. The latter told them that they had been in the habit of diving to the wreck off Peu but had not done so recently, 'as it has become rotten and been drifted away by the sea'. They also talked of the two men who had remained behind: one was a chief and had died about three years previously; the other, a commoner, had subsequently left the island with his Vanikoran host. But, although two lines of inquiry seemed thus to be ruled out, the articles that the landing party bought from the villagers made a useful contribution to Dillon's growing body of evidence. The large piece of iron was a ship's tiller; and the other things brought back included not only a variety of bolts and sheaves, a 'small brass mortar' and copper cooking pots but also a 'silver vessel . . . somewhat resembling a sauce-boat, with the *fleur de lis* stamped upon it in two different places, besides other ornamental flowers'.

Dillon found that work on the long-boat would take longer to complete than he had expected; but he decided it would be unwise to postpone further investigations. He feared an outbreak of fever amongst the ship's company. He was worried by the equivocal attitude of Ratia, who seemed to alternate between a determination to return immediately to Tikopia and an inclination to desert at Vanikoro. He was constantly aware of the problem of maintaining discipline. While the landing party was on shore at Tanema, the boat-crews had raided the supply of rum that had been put on board. And the second officer had still not overcome his tendency to fall asleep on watch. On 19 September he therefore sent the whale-boats on a voyage round the island.

He again decided not to go himself, as he feared a gale from the north-east to which the ship would be dangerously exposed, and placed Russell in charge of the expedition. He provided him with detailed written instructions. The boats were to sail first to Tanema, where presents were to be given to the chiefs and an attempt made to persuade one of them to embark as a guide. They were then to proceed to Peu and Vanau. At Peu they were to search not only for inscriptions left by the visitors but also 'for the remains of any stone or wood fortification' and 'for any trench or channel that might have been dug out for the purpose of launching the vessel'. At Vanau they were to inquire about the skulls said to have been preserved in the 'spirit house' and, there and elsewhere, to seek further information about the circumstances in which the ships had been wrecked. On all occasions Russell was to ensure that their friendship towards the people was made clear by the interpreters and by the distribution of gifts and that articles from the wrecks were obtained only on terms acceptable to those who offered them. Dillon's remarks regarding interrogation were equally explicit.

> At no time place confidence in the Tucopian, who answers in a way that he thinks will please us. With respect to Martin, he understands our language indifferently; you will, therefore, make him understand your questions clearly before he puts them to the islanders through Rathea.

If they observed these precautions, and were 'particular in not putting any leading questions', it should be possible to draw firm conclusions from the evidence they acquired. His instructions were an excellent statement of sound fieldwork methods.

Towards dusk on 20 September Dillon sighted the boats returning. It was a moment of high excitement for him; but Russell's report, though valuable, proved to be less decisive in its contents than he had hoped. At Peu they had found no inscriptions, fortifications or launching channel; and at Vanau they had been unable to persuade the people to talk about the killing of white men or the preservation of their skulls. But the circumstantial evidence they had obtained was impressive. At Peu they had been shown a spot on the river bank where the vessel was said to have been built and another farther up from which the timber had been cut and rafted down; the cleared space at the building site and the axe-hewn stumps up-river appeared to confirm the Vanikoran story. Furthermore, the articles that they brought back included many which Dillon was sure would help to identify the wrecked ships with La Pérouse's expedition. Two, in particular, were of quite special interest to him: a ship's bell and a large brace for a stern-post. The bell which was of brass and 12 1/2 inches in diameter, carried upon one side 'the holy cross erect, between the Virgin Mother and the image of a holy man bearing a small cross upon his shoulders' and upon the other 'three images . . ., with the sun shining over them, who seem to be the Virgin Mother, the Saviour, and St. John'. More significantly, it bore a statement about its maker:

'*Bazin m'a fait*'. The stern brace was 'curiously cased with a composition of brass, lead, &c.', which indicated to Dillon that it pre-dated the general adoption of brass for these fittings. And the answers to questions the party had asked added substance to his understanding of the catastrophe: that the storm on the fatal night had been fierce enough to destroy many houses and trees; that survivors from the ship which grounded off Peu had been washed ashore clinging to wreckage along nearly ten miles of coast, between Tanema, in the south-east, and Nama, in the west.

Meanwhile, on board the *Research*, Dillon continued to receive daily visits from the people of the neighbouring villages, who brought him fruit and vegetables and fish, and further articles salvaged from the French ships. When Buchert and Ratia were available, he continued to interrogate them—about their way of life, as well as about their former French visitors. He obtained a poisoned arrow for testing on a pig, which was affected, though not fatally, by the wound, and samples of the nuts from which the poison was derived, so that these might be examined in Bengal. He noted the diseases from which the islanders suffered. On 27 September he wrote:

> A poor islander came alongside to-day grievously afflicted with a disease in the testicles . . . Without exaggeration, this wretched man's parts were swollen to the size of an English half-barrel of gunpowder. The islanders on board made the poor fellow's infirmities a subject of merriment . . .

He showed his own feelings towards the man—recognition of lost pleasures, perhaps, and regard for European proprieties—by giving him 'two or three yards of blue gurrah'.

But after the return of the boats Dillon also began to make preparations for sailing. With the co-operation of his friend Nero, he arranged for a supply of yams and other fresh provisions and of coconut-leaf baskets for their storage. He similarly obtained Nero's permission for the cutting of firewood by a party 'under the command of the Marquis of Wyemattee and Morgan McMurragh'. And he observed with interest the easy association that developed between Maoris and Vanikorans while these tasks were being performed. On one occasion Morgan accompanied Nero and two of his men in a whale-boat:

> and although they could not understand each other's language, with the instinct of savages, they managed by signs to communicate their skill in handling their respective war instruments; the Mannicolans describing with what unerring aim they could at a great distance implant a poisoned arrow

in their enemy's eye, while the New Zealander mimicked the style in which he could cut off an enemy's head.

On another occasion the ebullient Morgan amused a party of Vanikorans by letting them see their reflections in a looking-glass.

Dillon's main concern, however, was with the course he should follow in taking the *Research* to sea. It might be possible, he thought, to sail out to the east, though on a more northerly course than that by which he had come in; and he therefore had his officers examine the passage that would be available for him for width and depth and the strength and direction of currents. On the other hand, if the southeast trades should continue to blow, it might be necessary to take the ship through the narrow passage between Tevai and the main island and sail out to the north. Because of the delicate handling this would require of him, he undertook the investigation himself.

The passage—which he named 'Dillon's Passage'—had an overall width of about 600 feet; but a ledge of coral rock ran down the middle of it. To the north of the ledge there was a channel with a width of ninety feet and a minimum depth of about three fathoms at low water. This, he considered, would be navigable under favourable conditions; and, as he saw no sign that the wind was likely to shift from the southeast for some time, he proceeded to buoy it. For several days he was prevented by high winds from putting his judgement to the test; but on the morning of 29 September he considered it safe to begin unmooring the ship. Before moving her, however, he thought it prudent to consult Deane and Russell and found that the two were divided as to the wisdom of his proposal. Since Russell believed it would be less dangerous to sail out to the east, he delayed the attempt to take the ship through the channel till the coming of spring tides.

By this time Dillon had resolved not to leave Vanikoro without himself examining the reefs off Peu and Vanau for evidence of the wrecks. He therefore had the ship re-anchored closer to the shore and four whale-boats prepared for sailing next day. As a gale was blowing in from the south-east and the seas were running high when they left, he set their course through Dillon's Passage and Charles Lushington's Bay, to the north coast. This course brought them first to Vanau, where they landed.

For Dillon the visit was an occasion of intense interest. He was welcomed by the villagers as he stepped ashore and, with Russell and Chaigneau, escorted to the 'spirit house', where they were provided with mats on which to sit and coconuts and baked turtle to eat.

[The villagers] said that they had good success yesterday in fishing, having caught a turtle with a new net. They shewed me an oven in which they had baked the turtle, and expatiated on its excellence in a strain that would do credit to the most turtle-loving alderman in London . . . They then pointed to four large bundles of bananas hanging up, and a quantity of *tara* ready scraped for pudding, and invited us to remain and partake of the feast to be given to the gods by the owner of the turtle net, for the success they had bestowed upon the new net.

Dillon declined the 'hospitable invitation', explaining that they had to travel farther before nightfall.

He was no less interested in the design of their dwelling houses.

In the centre of all the houses I entered there was a fire-place about eight feet square, and a post at each corner supporting a bamboo hurdle, which served as a repository for their cooking utensils, and as a drying-place for their fishing-lines. Here also they place their bags or haversacks, with which they are invariably provided when travelling, and which will contain a bushel of grain.

By one fireside he saw, to his excitement, 'a thick sheet of copper, measuring 3 feet 4.1/2 inches, by 3 feet 4.7/10 inches, in excellent preservation'; he acquired it in exchange for an axe, in the face of strong opposition by a woman of the household. And other relics were brought to him in the 'spirit house'; they included 'the bottom of a silver or plated candlestick with a coat of arms engraved on it, which some of us think are those of the Count de la Pérouse'.

From Vanau the boats sailed south-west to Nama. By now the whole party shared Dillon's enthusiasm for the search. A sailor discovered 'a decayed piece of fir or pine plank, with a fleur-de-lis and other ornamental work' barricading the doorway of a house, and an officer 'a small mill-stone, such as is used for grinding grain in the north of Ireland and the highlands of Scotland'. The latter interested Dillon particularly.

The account . . . [of] the expedition fitted out under la Pérouse, states that his dry provisions were shipped in kiln-dried grain, with several pairs of grinding-stones to prepare the same as wanted; which description of stones seem to correspond so exactly with the one above-mentioned as to form a strong link in the chain of circumstances that go to fix the identity of the ships lost at Mannicolo.

But these, and the large collection of bolts and nails and pieces of broken pottery that were found here, as elsewhere, did not exhaust their discoveries, for as Dillon was about to wade out to the boats he 'espied a man at some distance on the beach sweating under a bulky load, which on his nearer approach I discovered to be a copper boiler capable of containing fifteen or twenty gallons'. All these articles, he was told, had been recovered from the reefs where the ships had been wrecked.

Shortly after five o'clock Dillon reached the river at Peu—he named it 'Russell River'—on the banks of which the stranded mariners were said to have built their vessel. As he sailed along the coast from Nama, he had studied the fringing reef, without a single break, backed by 'uninterrupted forest and impervious underwood'. But here there was a bay deep enough to float a small ship and, on the west bank of the river, a clearing some seven acres in extent, with a hollow running down to the water from which, according to some old men with whom he spoke, the vessel had been launched. The evidence convinced him: this was the scene of the Frenchmen's sojourn at Vanikoro.

'The tea-kettle was boiled', Dillon noted, 'we supped at dusk, and anchored in the middle of the river'. Buchert and Ratia went on shore to sleep; their companions remained in the boats, because Dillon thought it safer, and passed a night troubled by torrential rain and myriads of mosquitoes. They arose to a wet and windy dawn.

Dillon's plan for the day—1 October—involved a division of the party. Russell, with two of the boats, was to examine the reef between Peu and Vanau before returning to the ship by way of the north coast. He was to land men on the reef, 'where he found it dry or with little water', so they could search for relics and for inscriptions cut on elevated rocks; he was also to look for passages through which the vessel built at Peu might have put to sea. Dillon, with the other boats, would search the reef between Peu and Tanema and return by the east coast.

The plan was made difficult of execution by the bad weather—particularly for Dillon and those accompanying him, who were sailing into the teeth of the storm. Dillon's arms and ammunition were soon 'quite drenched with rain and spray off the sea, which ran very high'; but, despite this disability, he decided to land when hailed by men of a village east of Peu. He found the villagers assembled in one of the houses round 'a lively fire of dry wood, . . . on account of the chilliness occasioned by the wind and rain'. After he had bought a few relics, the boat-crews boiled their kettle and had breakfast. When they left the protection of the house the weather was no better.

The rain still poured down in floods, and the land was sometimes imperceptible at the distance of a quarter of a mile from the boats, being enveloped in thick clouds. It was during such weather as this, I suppose, that the unfortunate French navigator got on the reefs of this island.

To add to Dillon's worries his boat was leaking badly. He abandoned investigations and, keeping where the water was smoothest, set out for the ship.

Early in the afternoon they came abreast of Tanema, where the people were out to welcome them. 'I would certainly have landed to refresh my people', Dillon wrote, 'but the surf ran so high on the coral reef fronting the shore, as to render it dangerous to make such an attempt'. Later, when they neared the entrance to Bayley's Bay, conditions worsened.

> Here our danger was increased, as there were no reefs on the weather side to break the violence of the sea, which rolled mountains high through Birch's Passage, and frequently broke into the boats, and threatened every moment to sink us. It was a short sea, and ran so high as to prevent us from seeing our consort-boat, although not fifty fathoms distant; and notwithstanding we were not more than a mile from the land, it was invisible for intervals of a quarter and half an hour at a time, from the thick weather... I expected every moment to see the boat filled with the waves, which... seemed to mock our exertions to keep the boat afloat. I cheered up my men, and kept the boat's head to the sea until we got Research's Head to bear west, when I kept her before the sea, and managed to steer her tolerably well with a whale-boat steer-oar twenty-four feet long.

But danger was by no means past; and, after Dillon had nearly been thrown into the sea by the long oar, he ordered the men to strip, so that they could swim in case of need. 'Providence, however, intervened', he relates, and at five o'clock he and his crew, naked and weary, rejoined the ship, together with those in the other boat.

An hour later Russell returned. His boats had not been exposed to the wind but had been impeded by rain, which had greatly reduced visibility on the reef. They had, however, collected an interesting range of articles, including a 'leaden cistern belonging to a ship's head' (delicately described as being 'used for certain purposes') and, of more value for identification, four brass guns, each bearing a number.

Dillon was still not satisfied that he had obtained all the evidence that the reefs could reveal; and, as the storm had passed by the following morning, he sent Russell on a third circumnavigation of the island. But he now devoted most of his own energies to the essential preliminaries of departure. He checked the buoys he had previously placed in Dillon's Passage and examined Charles Lushington's Bay and the pass through the barrier reef to its north. By 5 October he was awaiting only the right combination of weather and tide before moving the ship.

> At 1 P.M. I got under sail and stood for the passage, through which I threaded the needle. I had top-sails, top-gallant sails, and jibs set. I sent two boats to lie one on each side of the narrowest part of the channel, and the ship passed between them so close, that she might be touched with the oars of each; and in five minutes we were clear of all danger into Charles Lushington's Bay, where I anchored at 2 P.M., in thirty-three fathoms water, over a bottom of fine soft mud, with the water as smooth as in a mill-pond.

He was now free to sail from Vanikoro without waiting for a change in the winds.

During the next two days he made his farewells. To Nero and several others he gave presents of axes and Tongan tapa cloth and small pieces of parchment that they were asked to preserve and show to any ships that might call:

> This is to certify that the honourable East India Company's Ship Research anchored at Mannicola on the 13th of September last and has procured five Brass Cannon, one Brass Mortar and some plate belonging to the Frigates Bussole and Astrolabe Commanded by Count De La Perouse. The Research is to sail for the Islands to Leeward tomorrow in search of a Frenchman belonging to the above Ships, and from there to land her Interpreter at Tucopia.
>
> The bearer* . . . behaved well to our crew while at anchor of his village, we entered his port from the East and sailed out West
>
> October 6th   Peter Dillon
>
>   1827   Captain of the Research

Dillon thought this document would serve two purposes: gaining the friendship of Dumont d'Urville or others for its bearer; and conveying knowledge of his own movements, in the event that some misfortune might befall him.

On 7 October he gave an order to the crew to heave up the anchor; but, when clouds and rain closed in on the ship, he countermanded it. The following morning he recorded in his journal: 'Strong trades, approaching to a gale, with fine clear weather'. And soon after ten

---

* A copy of this document survives (ATL MSS ALS 129), of which the bearer was 'Tongarooa' [Tangaroa], a man of Polynesian descent from 'Mame' (Tinakula?) then living on Vanikoro. Dillon published a précis of it (*Narrative*, II, 267).

o'clock he sailed out through the reef, into the open sea. 'During the twenty-five days we anchored off Mannicolo', he added with satisfaction, 'an uninterrupted harmony subsisted between us and the natives, who regretted our departure with unfeigned sorrow; and, much to their credit, no instance of dishonesty occurred, though frequent opportunities were not wanting to tempt them'.

DILLON was now confident that he possessed sufficient evidence to convince France, and the world, that La Pérouse had been wrecked at Vanikoro. But he was also sure that this fell short of what was obtainable. He had been hampered by the necessary brevity of his visit and by dependence on imperfect interpreters. He believed that an intelligent European with a knowledge of the language would be able to pick up much more, not so much by asking questions—which tended to arouse an attitude of caution or defensiveness—as through participation in the conversations of old men. He had discussed this opinion with Charles Stewart, the beachcomber who had joined the ship at Tikopia. Stewart, he wrote, was 'a shrewd young man, about twenty-five years of age, with a good understanding, improved by a tolerable plain education'; and he had responded favourably to the suggestion that he should remain on the island for several years, for the purpose not only of learning more about the fate of La Pérouse but also of collecting information on 'the religion, manners, and customs' of the Vanikorans. He was willing, according to Dillon, to endure the attendant privations if this could 'be the means of bringing himself forward'. But when the *Research* sailed he remained on board, for her search was not yet quite ended.

Dillon had been told that the sailor who had left Vanikoro several years previously had accompanied the chief with whom he lived on a voyage to one of the islands to leeward. He had pored over the published references to these islands—in Burney's narrative of the voyages of Mendaña and Quiros: in Hawkesworth's of that of Carteret; in Labillardière's of Bruni d'Entrecasteaux's 'voyage in search of La Pérouse' in the 1790s—and he had talked at Vanikoro with a Polynesian from an island to the northward who had 'made a chart on the deck with charcoal' of the islands that he knew. Dillon recognized that the geographical data available to him formed a mixture of fact and fantasy, and had many gaps; he realized that the old sailor might well have died, at sea or in his unknown refuge; but he knew that he must look for him.

A few hours after sailing, he was off the coast of Utupua, a high island some twenty miles north-west of Vanikoro. Here he had cause to remember the parchments he had left with Nero and his other friends, for the man at the masthead failed to notice the ship's approach to shoal water and the main bowline came adrift during a belated attempt to put her about: '. . . I expected to see the ship strike, but fortunately she stayed'. Next morning he sent boats ashore to inquire for the Frenchman and his companion. They returned without news of them, though with confirmation of his impression that no islands lay between them and Ndeni, or Santa Cruz, despite Carteret's contrary report.

On 10 October he sailed for Ndeni, where he remained for four days, repeating his inquiries (with no great success), refilling the water-casks, and noting down the characteristics of the island and its people. He anchored near the head of Graciosa Bay, so named by Alvaro de Mendaña in 1595, and pondered the tragic, bloody history of the settlement Mendaña had made there and where he had died. On his final day he met a man whose words seemed to carry an echo from that distant past.

> A native this evening pointed to his village, north-east from the ship, and inquired if I would not go to Pueblo, which was the name he mentioned. Now as *pueblo* is the Spanish for a 'town', perhaps it was here that Mendana built his town, which has still retained the name.

On the same day he gave Stewart permission to leave the ship, in company with two Tikopians taken on board at Utupua, to make his way back by canoe with them to Vanikoro and thus become perhaps the first European since Mendaña to live, by his own decision, in this part of Melanesia.

Earlier in the day Dillon had called a meeting of the senior officers of the expedition. It had been his intention to proceed from Ndeni to other islands in the vicinity, but while the ship was off Utupua Russell and several seamen had retired to their berths with 'fever and ague'. Now Chaigneau and half the European seamen were down, and many others were ailing. Would it be wise, he asked, to continue the search? The officers were in agreement that it would not. And what of his promise to Ratia to take him back to Tikopia? He had offered Ratia the alternatives of remaining in Ndeni with a stock of goods that would make him an influential man or of accepting a gift of the long-boat, so that he could sail himself home; but both offers had been

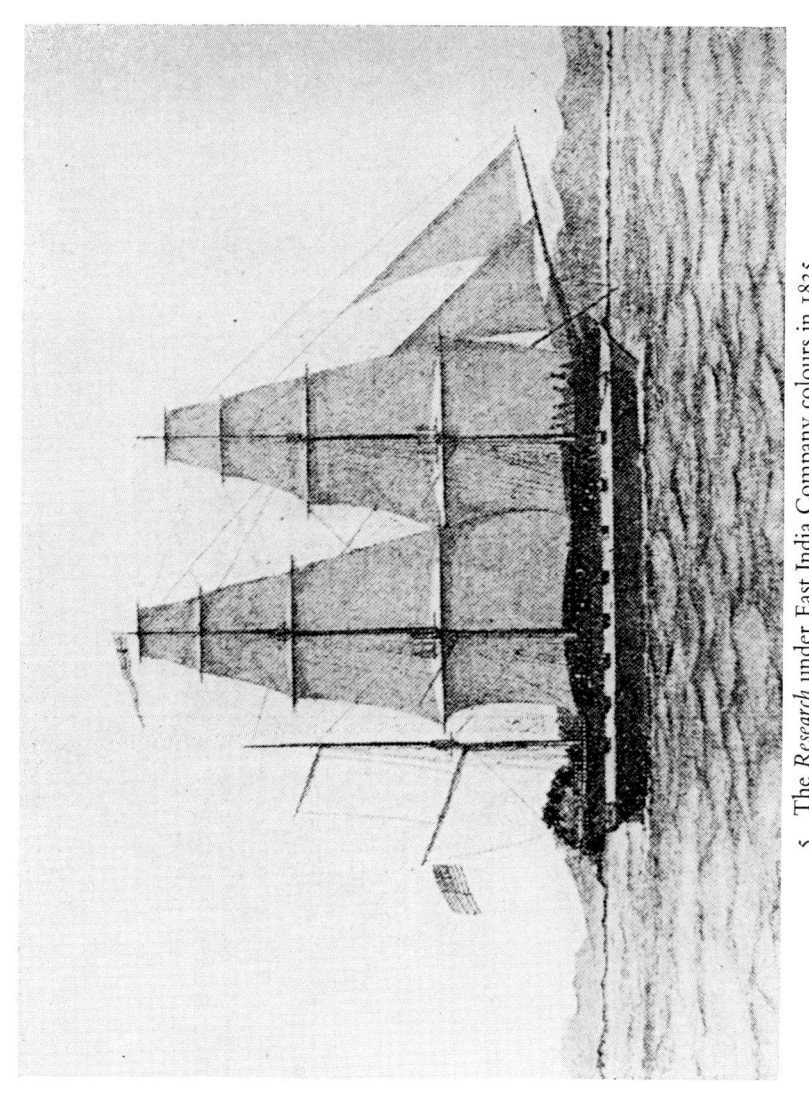

5 The *Research* under East India Company colours in 1825

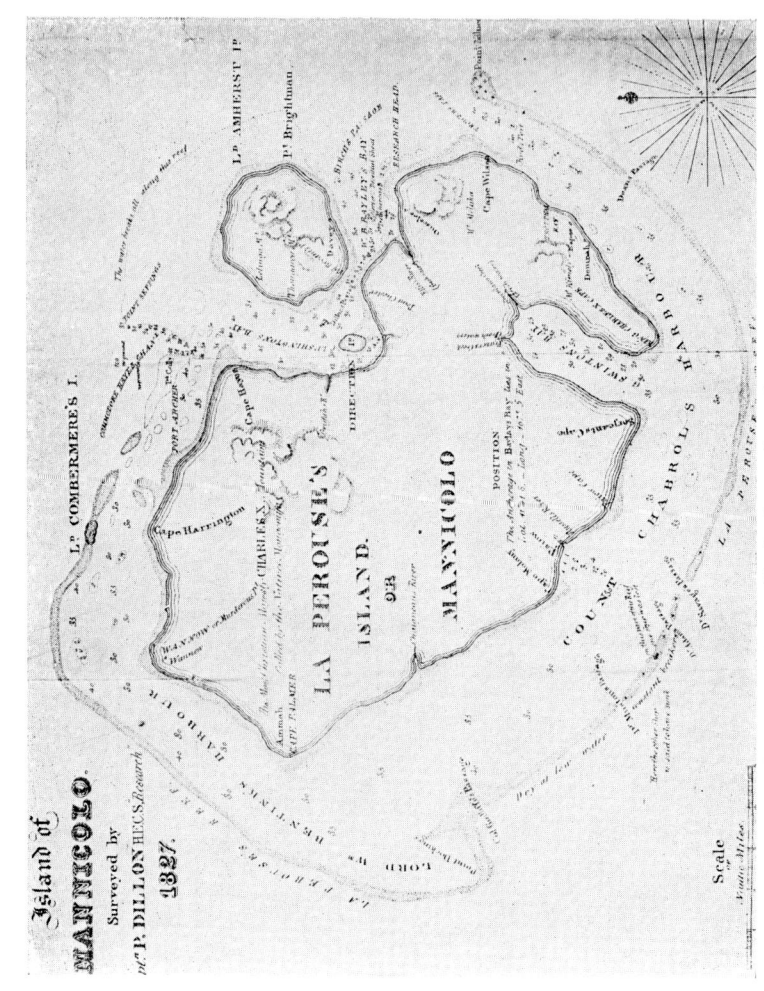

6 Dillon's chart of Vanikoro

declined. The meeting decided that the original promise remained binding. Since Tikopia lay to the south-east, however, it considered that the ship should stand to the southward till she passed out of the trade-wind zone, then steer to the eastward and finally approach the island from the south, with the help of the trades.

Dillon had gained time in which to restore the health of his crew; and next morning he issued orders for sailing.

> Having anchored in forty-two fathoms with a chain anchor and chain, I began to heave up at 4 A.M., but did not succeed in getting it to the bows till 8; and such was the reduced state of my crew by fever and ague, that had I remained among those islands a week longer, I think I should not have had sufficient strength to weigh anchor in ten fathoms water.

During the preceding weeks, facing dangers similar to those that had confronted his illustrious predecessors, he had shown himself a highly competent commander: he had avoided the disasters that had overtaken Mendaña and La Pérouse, the armed attack by Melanesians experienced by Carteret; he had followed the example of Cook in keeping his ship clean and well aired, his men supplied with fresh fruit and vegetables. But now—perhaps as a consequence of his men's exposure to fever-carrying mosquitoes when sleeping in the boats[4] —he began to fear that he would suffer another of the misfortunes that had commonly befallen the explorers: the loss of men through tropical disease. He was driven to save their lives, if he could, not only by a sense of duty but also by affection for some of those who were sick—particularly John Russell and Eugène Chaigneau. Moreover, now that he was so near to being able to tell the world of his success, he did not wish to tarnish his record.

By noon of 20 October—six days after leaving Ndeni—he was to the westward of New Caledonia, in 20°51′S., 159°12′E., and still sailing south. Ten days later, as the number down with fever was still growing, he asked the surgeon for a written opinion as to the action he should take. A return to the tropics could not be made, Dr Griffiths wrote, 'without running the risk of losing several lives, and by that means endangering the safety of the ship'. He should, instead, 'proceed immediately to a port in New South Wales, or New Zealand, for the purpose of procuring refreshments for the sick now on board, as well as to give them an opportunity of recovering from the disease under which they now labour'. It was the answer he expected and, no doubt desired. He set a course for the Bay of Islands.

O

ELEVEN

Return from Vanikoro

On the morning of 5 November the *Research* entered the Bay of Islands. For three weeks Dillon had largely ignored his own ill health; but now that he had brought the ship back to a familiar port he was forced by sickness 'to quit the deck'. Since none of his officers shared his local knowledge, he ordered that a gun should be fired at intervals as a signal for a pilot. Late in the afternoon the call was answered, and by 7 p.m. the *Research* lay safely at anchor off Kororareka.

Over the next few weeks Dillon remained unwell, though his bouts of fever came and went. The Reverend Henry Williams, who visited him during one of his bad spells, wrote in his journal:

> We called on board . . . when I saw Capn. Dillon: he was very ill and could scarcely move. I thought a word would be seasonable and spoke accordingly but he was on the rack in an instant and changed the subject.[1]

John Marmon, a young man from Sydney who had been living among the Maoris for some years, also found him ill. In his memoirs Marmon claimed to have been with Dillon at the Thames—during the voyage of the *St Patrick*—and to have been summoned on board the *Research* and employed as interpreter at '10s. a day and lots of grog'.[2] As Marmon's story illustrates, Dillon did not permit his illness to disrupt the business of the expedition.

His most pressing concern was with the sick, for twenty-two persons, including all but one of the officers, were now incapacitated and many others far from well. He needed fresh food for them and wine, as a stimulant. Robert Duke, a sea-captain then living near Kororareka, sent him 'two fat wethers, six fowls, and a dozen of wine', and the missionaries provided milk and vegetables and all the wine they felt they could spare. But the fact that the latter failed to comply with his further requests—particularly for 'a daily supply of fresh meat'—weighed upon his fevered mind and caused him to criticize them bitterly when he wrote his *Narrative*.³ Moreover, he was disappointed that most of his Maori friends, from whom he also expected to obtain supplies, were away working in their food gardens when he arrived. He thought, however, that the most debilitated members of the crew needed not only good food but also an opportunity to rest in more spacious quarters than those on board. On his first day therefore he went ashore, despite his continuing fever, and arranged with a settler at Kororareka for the use of his house, to which the sickest men were duly removed.

Another problem that began to trouble Dillon soon after his arrival was that of repatriating Ratia and the Tongan passengers. They were 'much affected', he wrote, 'at losing their New Zealand shipmates'— who, apart from Brian and Morgan, immediately disembarked—and asked him when they would be taken home. As soon, he told them, as the crew had recovered. But this did not satisfy them. 'The sick will die', he reported them as saying, '. . . we shall then be left here, and if the New Zealanders do not eat us, we shall at least be compelled to remain in a land where there are no cocoa-nuts, yams, bananas, or sugar-canes'. Influenced less by this objection than by considerations of time and cost, he then suggested that they might be placed on board a whaler bound for the tropical South Pacific. But this alternative pleased them even less: they would not be well treated by the crew, they said, and might be put ashore on a strange island. Dillon accepted the validity of the islanders' fears. He was now anxious, however, to save the three months that would be taken up in returning to Tonga and Tikopia and decided to write to Henry Williams asking for a charter of the mission schooner *Herald*.

He did not have to wait long for an answer. The missionaries, who had condemned him for taking Maori women from the Bay of Islands, were not disposed to help him face the consequences of what they suspected to be similar actions elsewhere. Moreover, the *Herald* was needed for the work of the mission. Williams's letter refusing the request was formal and polite; and it drew his attention to the fact that there were two other vessels in New Zealand waters which might be available. Dillon described the letter as 'laconic' and claimed that it 'surprised and vexed' him. But he acted on the suggestion it contained and wrote to Captain Kent, the master of the brig *Governor Macquarie*, which was then lying at Hokianga, on the west coast. On 14 November he received a letter from Kent, who had travelled overland to see him, offering to charter the brig at £600 for the voyage. He considered the proposed charge excessive; but, when Kent came on board next day to negotiate with him, he 'was suddenly seized with a cold fit of ague, and compelled to retire to bed'. Three days later, however, the two men agreed on a charter with the fee fixed at £500.

When Dillon told Ratia and the Tongans of his intention to send them home in the *Governor Macquarie*, he was faced with a demand that they should be accompanied by him or by his 'brother' to protect them against the possible unscrupulousness of strangers. His supposed brother was John Russell, who, to Dillon's satisfaction, said he would go.

This assumption that the two men were brothers reflected the close association that had developed between them. Like George Bayly, Russell was a young man of talent, with a good education. Like him, too, he had been engaged as the most junior of the ship's three officers, a formal rank that he still retained. But, during the course of the voyage, he had become Dillon's most trusted subordinate. His ability as a draughtsman and surveyor, and his tact during the trouble with Tytler, had first gained him Dillon's respect. His reliability over the difficult months that had seen the departure of Blake and Dudman at Hobart Town and the final suspension of the latter's successor at Vanikoro had further enhanced his standing. But it was his capacity for imaginative involvement in the voyage's objective that had eventually made him more influential even than Deane, the new first officer, a good practical seaman about whom Dillon wrote no word of criticism. In his *Narrative* Dillon included accounts of the successive boat journeys round the coast of Vanikoro written by 'the officer in charge': all were by Russell.[4] And, when he was preparing to move the ship through Dillon's Passage, he had noted in his journal: 'I took the opinion of the draughtsman, who was now second in command in case of accident'.[5] When he had subsequently been faced by major problems —whether to abandon the search for the missing Frenchman; whether to charter the *Governor Macquarie*—Russell and Chaigneau had been the two men whose advice he had sought.

But Dillon's regard for his third officer was also affected by the latter's possession of distinguished and influential family connections. One of Russell's uncles was Sir William Betham, the Ulster King of Arms, a genealogist and historian, with a special knowledge—of no little interest to Dillon—in the claims of Irishmen to their family lands.

At Vanikoro Dillon had shown his deference for Sir William by naming a river in his honour. Now, from the Bay of Islands, Russell wrote to his uncle describing the coat of arms on the candlestick they had found at Vanau and asking for his help in its identification.[6]

Russell forwarded his letter to Sydney by the schooner *Herald*, which sailed on 19 November. She also carried an account by Dillon himself of his visit to Vanikoro.[7] This was his first opportunity of informing a wider circle than that of the Bay of Islands of his success; and he waited impatiently for the day when his companions should be sufficiently recovered for him to be able to sail himself and receive from the leaders of New South Wales a first instalment of the public acclaim that he knew was due to him.

Meanwhile he attended to the work of the ship and the welfare of his sick companions and, as always, received a steady flow of visitors. Henry Williams, or his brother William, came on board to hold a service every Sunday and to make a collection for the Bethel Union Society.[8] Robert Duke talked about his life at the Bay and portrayed the effects of Christian teaching in less roseate terms than the Williams', since it had caused the missionaries to condemn him for living with a daughter of Te Whareumu: 'The daughter . . .', Dillon noted approvingly, 'undertakes the management of this gentleman's household affairs, her father affording him protection for his property . . .'. It was, however, the visits of Maori chiefs that brought him most satisfaction.

On the morning of 13 November he received a visit from Titore, who had left the ship a week earlier suffering severely from fever. He had not, however, forgotten the needs of his former companions and brought with him a gift of 'five large hogs . . . and nearly a thousand pounds of potatoes'. 'Contrast, reader, the generous, sympathizing, and disinterested conduct of this heathen', Dillon wrote, 'with the unfeeling selfishness of the saintly preachers who undertake to convert him from the errors of his ways!'

And on the same morning the great warrior Hongi Hika also arrived, 'accompanied by his chiefs and family in two splendid war canoes'. At the time of Dillon's visit in July, Hongi had been living quietly at Whangaroa, recovering from an injury suffered in battle. Now he was organizing yet another campaign.

> Though labouring under the effects of a wound that is fast sinking him to his grave, his frame being already reduced almost to a skeleton, his manner

is still commanding. Ferocity and cunning twinkle in his piercing eyes, while his curling lip and short teeth proclaim him a genuine savage, but one in whom traits of intellect are manifested.

His wound is singular, a bullet having passed through his lungs, whence a hole appears upon his breast and back, through which latter the wind issues with a noise resembling in some degree that from the safety-valve of a steam engine; which, however, he himself makes a subject of merriment. Although he does not experience much pain, it is evident he cannot last long, and of this he seems fully aware, by the haste with which he is preparing to take the field in a few weeks, as generalissimo, to a general gathering of the chiefs of the north, the object of which is an attack on the river Thames.

Dillon presented Hongi with 'a stand of arms' and was pressed by the chief to take his daughter as a wife. She was, he wrote, 'an interesting girl about thirteen, who was sitting upon the hammock rail with a cloth in her hand, staying the issue in her father's back'; but he declined the offer.

He was acutely conscious of the toll that warfare and introduced disease were taking of his Maori friends. Tuai, who had accompanied Hongi to Sydney in the *Active* in 1814 and later visited England with Titore, had died several years earlier.[9] Pomare and many others he had known had fallen in battle. And, when he examined his current experience, he found more to remind him of man's uncertain hold on life than the sickness on board and the approaching death of Hongi, with its probably disastrous consequences for those dependent on his prowess. For Ratia had become 'ill and very low-spirited'; and during a boat trip up the Kawakawa River on which he had taken the Tikopian in an attempt to 'divert his melancholy', he had discovered that many Maoris were suffering from a complaint they believed they had caught from the *Research*'s men.[10]

In Ratia's case, his efforts were unavailing. When the *Governor Macquarie* arrived from Hokianga on 3 December, Dillon pointed to her as the vessel that would soon take him home. But Ratia replied that it was already too late: 'Had I cocoa-nuts, bread-fruit, bananas, &c which I have been accustomed to, I might once again see Tucopia; but as it is, I cannot live'. And on 7 December, he died, 'chiefly of a broken heart'. Dillon recognized the extent to which his own success had been dependent on Ratia's assistance; and, as the corpse left the ship for burial on shore, he fired a salute of three guns.

He was also uneasy about local attitudes towards Brian and Morgan. Hongi had told Brian he intended to make war on the latter's father, but he had embraced the young man 'in the most tender manner'. Te Whareumu, on the contrary, was showing an interest in both men that became openly hostile. After Dillon contemptuously rejected his suggestion that they should be left with him when the ship sailed, he expressed his anger at their returning home with the arms they had acquired in Calcutta. Subsequently he tried to persuade Captain Kent to abandon his voyage, became 'very insolent' during a meeting with Dr Griffiths, and threatened to kill any of Dillon's crew who might remain at the Bay of Islands, if his forces were defeated in the forthcoming war. Dillon decided that Te Whareumu's attitude made the previously friendly settlement of Kororareka, where he lived, a potentially unsafe place not only for Brian and Morgan but also for others from the *Research*; and he brought the men who were convalescing there back on board.

Though the first part of December was a troubled time for Dillon, it was also one in which he was hopefully engaged in planning for the future. He prepared instructions for Russell and Kent and supervised the transfer of Brian and Morgan, Buchert and the Tongans to the *Governor Macquarie*. On the morning of 11 December he went on board the brig to accompany his friends as far as the mouth of the harbour.

> On taking leave of these affectionate people, they evinced genuine grief at our separation. Brian Boroo and Morgan McMurragh in particular, lamented with tears that they were about to leave me probably for ever...
>
> Poor Martin Bushart also was much affected at leaving me, though he was determined on returning to Tucopia, there to end his days in retirement from worldly affairs.

Before Dillon returned to the *Research*, he learnt from Buchert the true story of Charles Stewart and the other Europeans they had found on Tikopia: Stewart was a former ship's officer who had been transported to Van Diemen's Land after conviction of forgery; there, he and ten others had seized a small sloop, in which they intended to sail to Hawaii; but, after landing some of their number at Futuna, in the New Hebrides, at Walpole Island and at Nomuka, the remainder had reached Tikopia and decided to sail no farther. Dillon was interested in the story: he had been told of the act of piracy by the sloop's owner at Hobart Town but had failed to associate with it the young beachcomber in whom he had aroused so keen an interest in history and ethnography. Buchert's reason for relating it, however, was a strictly practical one: would Dillon, he asked, instruct Kent to remove the men still on the island? He had no power to order their removal by force, Dillon replied; but, if persuasion were sufficient—and with this Kent agreed—Buchert's request would be carried out.

When Dillon again boarded the *Research*, he found two of Te Whareumu's kinsmen, Whetoi and his brother, waiting for him. Whetoi complained that the young woman who had been living with Brian—known by Dillon as 'Madam Shelagh Boroo'—had sailed in the *Governor Macquarie*. She had been brought to Kororareka from the Thames as a slave and sent to Brian in the hope that she would decoy him ashore. As she was the property of Whetoi's brother, she had been expected, at least, to return when Brian left; but 'canoe after canoe arrived from the brig, till at length the last boat put off without her, when expectation gave way to despair, and they set up a howl like wolves bereft of their prey'. Whetoi argued that Dillon owed his brother reparation.

> I asked why they cried so bitterly for the loss of one slave, when they had so many to replace her: they replied, 'Would you not cry if you lost the handsomest woman in your country?' I said, perhaps I might; but added, addressing myself to Ethaey [Whetoi], 'Why do you cry? you have lost no woman.'—'Oh,' rejoined he, 'I cry to keep my brother company . . . , for it is shameful to see a man lamenting alone.'

They demanded Dillon's double-barrelled gun. When he refused it, they accepted his invitation to breakfast. Before they left, however, they declared that they would seize the *Governor Macquarie* and kill all on board her, if she returned to the Bay of Islands.

Dillon did not regard the threat as an idle one; and, as the weather had by now become boisterous, he feared that the brig might be forced to put back. He decided to delay his own sailing for two more days, so that he could provide protection. During the afternoon his anxieties were partially set at rest, after he had rescued Titore from the harbour, where his canoe had been swamped by the waves. Titore had braved the storm to bring a farewell gift of new potatoes. But he responded nobly to the fresh emergency: he and Hongi, he assured Dillon, would prevent Te Whareumu's followers from carrying out their desperate plan.

On the morning of 13 December Dillon weighed anchor. It was the right time to sail. The brig, it could now be assumed, had got safely away. The sick were improving, though many, including Dillon, had not yet fully recovered. The day was fine and warm, with a gentle breeze; and, on the rocky headlands and islands of the harbour, the scarlet blossom of the *pohutukawa* was beginning to appear.

TOWARDS noon on 29 December Dillon sighted the lighthouse on the South Head of Port Jackson, and by late evening the ship lay at anchor in Watson's Bay. Her passage from New Zealand had not been a fast one; but the fine days with light breezes, which had endured since she sailed, had been in tune with the needs of her company. In Sydney Dillon intended to deposit an account of his discoveries (in case 'any casualty . . . might occur to the *Research*'), to take on supplies, and to rest his crew before setting out on the long voyage back to Bengal.

Next morning he went into town. His most important business was to arrange finance for his purchases. When he called on the Colonial Secretary, he was asked to attempt to deal directly with the merchants, who, he was told, were usually willing to accept bills drawn on the British authorities in London. As he had found at Hobart Town eight months earlier, however, bills on Bengal were much less popular because of the limited trade between the colonies and India. He was consequently given an undertaking by the New South Wales Government that it would assist him; but only after three weeks of negotiations, interrupted on his side by a further bout of fever, did he receive the sum that he needed.[11]

On his second visit to town he was confronted by another unwelcome complication: a request from the harbour master that he 'bring the ship up into the port'. He had anchored in Watson's Bay, just inside the Heads, to avoid port dues and—no doubt remembering his troubles at Sydney with some of the sailors in the *Calder*—to avoid exposing the crew to 'the priests of Bacchus, hundreds of whom infest the ordinary landing-places in town, prowling for the purses of simple mariners'. With an apology for 'introducing a sprinkling of that *fashionable dialect*, which is better understood here perhaps than any other language', he described the evil such men could do.

> These fellows, after a libation or two, in which they bear the sailors company, begin to inquire into the particulars of the voyage, what treatment Jack met from his captain, &c., and listen till some instance of punishment for neglect or disorderly conduct is related by the simple tar, when away they drag the simple son of Neptune to a neighbouring pettifogger, who on the merits of this pot-house narrative, determines whether the *cove's* case is a 'prime' or 'flat move'. He is then plentifully provided (if his case be hopeful)

with the 'oh be joyful' by the kind assertor of his wrongs, who instructs him in the manner he is to proceed to obtain redress and 'cast the captain', and how to train his witnesses for the purpose. Should Jack succeed in recovering damages, or his pay and clothing (for by this time the fool has been induced to desert), then the affair is regarded as 'a regular flash move' and nothing remains to be done on the part of the minister of Bacchus and his friend the sea-lawyer, but to gull the misguided seaman out of his money and wearing apparel.

Despite these horrid possibilities, however, he decided to do as the harbour master wished, for—fearful as he always was of official persecution—he was anxious 'to prevent . . . his representing things to my prejudice'. He therefore moved the *Research* closer to town, though not close enough to please the public, keen to gaze upon her and hopeful of inspecting her romantic cargo.[12]

Dillon's success at Vanikoro had, of course, become known in Sydney before his own arrival. On 5 December the *Sydney Gazette* had published part of his letter from the Bay of Islands. Two days later it had carried an erroneous, but well-meant, note on the Solomon Islands and a flattering reference to Dillon himself.

> The enterprising commander of the . . . *Recherche* (PETER DILLON, Esq.) will be munificently rewarded by the French Government; and there is little doubt, in the event of his visiting France, that Captain DILLON's compensation will be something beyond mere pecuniary consideration. He is an eccentric character—has accomplished a most singular undertaking—and will meet with unprecedented applause. By a lucky hit of Fortune, the name of DILLON will be handed down to posterity with that of LA PEYROUSE.[13]

And in January, with Dillon and his colleagues in Sydney talking about their experiences, the flow of news and comment greatly increased.

After Dillon had brought the *Research* into the port, he arranged a display of his discoveries in one of the cabins. And during the following weeks the ship was 'daily thronged with visitors'. They included not only senior civil and military officers and leaders of the business community, but also men such as the Reverend Samuel Marsden and his Presbyterian *confrère*, the Reverend John Dunmore Lang. The relics, according to the *Sydney Gazette*, 'the moment they are seen, strike conviction into the mind of the most sceptical'; '[we] are as satisfied of their identity as if we had seen the immortal LA PEROUSE taking soup with the spoon out of the Roman Catholic silver dish that formed part of the relics adverted to!' The most interesting of all the articles on display, in the opinion of the *Gazette*, was the plank ornamented with the fleur-de-lis from the stern of one of the ships; 'had it all been cut up into small splinters', Dillon commented, 'they would all have been carried off, so great was the avidity to obtain a portion'. And Dr Lang added: 'I could not help thinking they possessed an additional interest from the circumstance of their being thus brought back, in the first instance, to the very country from which the unfortunate navigator had last sailed . . .'.[14]

In the evenings Dillon was less scholarly, more convivial. 'He entertains his guests in a most princely manner', the *Gazette* reported, 'and we should have been inclined to foster the idea, from what we have personally witnessed, as well as heard, that Captain Dillon had, in his life-time, trodden upon the renowned and hospitable land of Old Ireland'. One evening, when guests 'had promiscuously assembled' and been invited to dine on board, a long series of toasts had been proposed, some solemn, some polemical—'The Governor', 'The Colonial Secretary', 'An independent Magistracy and Trial by Jury',—and each had been drunk to the firing of a gun.[15]

At noon on 26 January, however, he used the ship's guns for a purpose more compatible with official protocol: the firing of a royal salute on Anniversary Day.[16] It was exactly forty years since the men of the First Fleet had landed at Sydney Cove—and, perhaps of more importance to Dillon, since La Pérouse had first sighted Botany Bay.

In Hobart Town, as well as in Sydney, men were discussing the fate of La Pérouse's expedition. On the night of his arrival in Watson's Bay, Dillon had learnt from one of the Sydney pilots that Dumont d'Urville's ship, the *Astrolabe*, was then lying at anchor in the Derwent. Over the preceding months, he had acted towards his rival with great propriety, encouraged by his confidence that the latter stood no chance of reaching Vanikoro before him. At Rotuma and Tikopia he had left letters for him explaining his own intended movements.[17] At Tongatapu he had refused to see one of the deserters from the *Astrolabe*, 'on account of his conduct to his former commander'; and, in talking with John Thomas, he had said that only concern for the safety of the missionaries had prevented him from giving the recalcitrant Frenchmen's Tongan protector 'five hundred lashes'.[18] Now, he hoped that Dumont d'Urville would come to Sydney to meet him.

But the meeting did not take place. Dillon had made some bitter enemies in Hobart Town, less perhaps by his supposed ill-treatment of Tytler than by the sarcasms he had directed at the government and its senior officers—not only in speech but even in print.[19] When Dumont d'Urville had asked what manner of man he was, Gellibrand and Kelly, the harbour master, had spoken well of him; but others—in Governor Arthur's entourage—had sniggered at the mention of his name, and called him a 'madman' and an 'adventurer'. Late in December Dillon's letter to Gellibrand from the Bay of Islands in July, suggesting the possible necessity of abandoning the expedition, finally reached its destination. When its contents became known, Dillon's antagonists eagerly accepted his transient fear as fact. A few days later, however, the *Sydney Gazette* of 5 December, with a report of his success at Vanikoro, arrived in Hobart Town. Those who wished Dillon ill refused to accept the report's veracity. Why had Dillon provided so little detail? asked James Ross in the pro-government paper. Why had the missionaries at the Bay of Islands not mentioned his presence there? 'But the most ridiculous thing of all is the inconsistency of Captain Dillon having made such a discovery, and not proceeding direct to Calcutta instead of returning back to New Zealand.'[20] Dumont d'Urville's attitude was more realistic: he sailed, within a few days, in search of Vanikoro.[21]

In Sydney the news of these hostile comments in Hobart Town brought the press to Dillon's defence. Edward Smith Hall, of the *Monitor*, printed an account of Dillon's trial eight months earlier, which he ended with the words:

> On the whole, we shall learn no more to feel surprised at the decisions of the Supreme Court of V.D. Land, so long at least as Judge Pedder presides there and Col. Arthur continues Lieut. Governor.[22]

And Robert Howe, of the *Gazette*, referred to Ross as an 'empty scribe' intent on depriving Dillon of 'that reward, and those honors to which he is so justly entitled'.

> For his present elevation in life, Captain Dillon is indebted to industry, perseverance, and strong natural talents. We acknowledge that there is a species of manly daring about the discoverer of LA PEROUSE, which is not a feature in the composition of many of his order; but he seems to us to have been cut out for the work in which he has been engaged, and we only hope he may live to be crowned with . . . French laurels . . . [23]

Both writers had known Dillon for many years and were, in some degree, his friends; but their support was no less encouraging on that account.

On 1 February 1828 Dillon noted in his journal:

> At daylight began to heave up the anchor. At 10 A.M. a strong breeze set into the harbour from the north-eastward: we had to make several tacks, and at noon got clear to sea. Having determined to return to India by the passage through Bass's Straits, I shaped my course for Cape Howe.

During the month Dillon had spent at Sydney, one seaman had died of the illness he had contracted at Vanikoro; another, whom the surgeon considered insufficiently recovered to continue, had received his discharge; and the surgeon himself left the ship before she sailed because of poor health. Dillon was sorry to lose Dr Griffiths: 'Your gentlemanly and becoming conduct during an eight months' voyage, in the midst of perils and dangers', he wrote, 'has endeared you to all on board'.[24] But, in the main, after the period of rest and warm summer days, the crew was fit to return to sea; and Dillon himself, who was suffering from a partial paralysis of the right hand (perhaps nervous in origin, though he seems to have attributed it to the fever),[25] was buoyed up by his memories of the reception in Sydney and his expectations of acclaim by the wider world.

The voyage, though long, was uneventful. On 22 March the *Research* crossed the Equator. On the twenty-seventh she spoke the *Nandey*, homeward bound from Calcutta; and Dillon sent an officer on board to receive the news of Bengal and to transmit that of his own discovery to Europe.

> On the officer's return, he informed me that one of the *Nandey*'s passengers stated that the people in Calcutta doubted the safety of the *Research*, and that their fears were increased by the malicious reports of Dr. Tytler . . . Captain Ramsey sent me a Bengal news paper, containing an account of the late glorious battle of Navarino.

On 5 April a pilot came on board off the mouth of the Hooghly. And two days later, sixty-six days after sailing from Sydney, Dillon landed at Calcutta.

THE following weeks were for Dillon a time both of public success and of private misfortune, a brief and sharply defined period of his life that, in retrospect, possessed a flavour that was both sweet and sour. For, though he received the public recognition he so avidly craved, he also learnt, as soon as he entered the city, that Joseph Barretto and Sons, who acted as his agents, had become insolvent while he was away.

Like the cholera that was again ravaging Bengal,[26] picking off affluent and well protected Europeans, as well as large numbers of less fortunate Indians, a financial malaise was destroying both prominent agency houses and many smaller enterprises.[27] Several years earlier the government had helped the agency houses to raise additional capital by lowering the rate of interest on its own loans; but after the outbreak of the costly Burma War in 1824 it had been forced to reverse its policy. The change had coincided with a fall in export earnings and with a period of stagnation in the 'country trade'. A great deal of the new investment had thus become, at least temporarily, unproductive; and the agency houses had experienced difficulty in servicing their recent borrowings. When English-based houses took fright and began repatriating such liquid capital as they still possessed, a financial panic had ensued. The insolvency of Barrettos seems to have been brought about primarily by these circumstances that affected the business community as a whole. But there was probably a further contributing cause: Joseph Barretto himself had died in 1824, and his personal affairs were still incompletely settled when the firm was forced to close its doors three years later.[28] By the time of Dillon's return, the surviving partners—except perhaps Brightman—had fled to the neighbouring Danish settlement of Serampore to escape their commitments.[29]

Dillon variously estimated his loss from the failure of Barrettos at '£20,000' and 'nearly £30,000'. And, though it may have been somewhat less than either of these figures, it certainly represented the whole of his capital. He had left the *St Patrick* with Barrettos to be sold on his behalf. They had also held the proceeds from the disposal of her cargo and any money that may have been due to him from his insurance policies in respect of the *Calder*. Now, all these assets were gone. Moreover, almost the whole of his salary as master of the *Research* had been absorbed in the payment of his legal costs at Hobart Town and other expenses during the course of the voyage. He therefore found himself almost penniless.[30]

Dillon was deeply affected by the irony of his fate: his voyage to Vanikoro would bring him celebrity, but it had already cost him the personal security he had so strenuously won for himself and his family during his years as a merchant mariner. Now that he was as poor again as he had been in his youth, he began to look to his public standing as the only firm foundation upon which to rebuild his private fortunes. And, to begin the superstructure, he determined to extract every form of recompense that he could out of his discovery of the fate of La Pérouse.

Meanwhile, during his first days in Calcutta, he had much business connected with the expedition to attend to. Immediately on his arrival he despatched a report to the Secretary of the Marine Board giving an account of the voyage since his departure from Sydney in June 1827.[31] He had dealt with earlier events—including his trouble with Tytler and his trial—in a previous report. But he was still concerned about the damage that might have been done to his reputation by Tytler himself and by the Government of Van Diemen's Land; and, before Chaigneau left the ship to visit the French Administrator at Chandernagore, he obtained a letter from him that he could use in support of his own interpretation of events.[32] The precaution was probably unnecessary.

On 9 April he received an invitation to breakfast with the Acting Governor-General on the following morning and to arrange a display of the relics at Government House. He was received by his host 'with much affability and kindness' and congratulated on his success by the 'numerous train of civil and military officers' who were his fellow-guests. After he withdrew, the Governor-General held a meeting of his Council, at which the correspondence and other evidence relating to the expedition was examined—in the words of the Council's resolution—'with the interest and attention which it is naturally calculated to excite'. After endorsing and commending Dillon's achievement, the resolution continued:

> It appears therefore, in the judgment of the Governor-General in Council, to be highly desirable that the whole of the relics brought by Captain Dillon should be transmitted to Europe by an early opportunity, and a sense of the enterprizing conduct of Captain Dillon, as well as his ability to afford the French government such further information as they may require, naturally indicate him as the most proper person to be entrusted with the charge of them, should he (as is understood) be desirous of accompanying them.

There remained only the task of finally settling the accounts of the expedition.[33]

A day or two later Dillon received a warm invitation from Cordier, the French Administrator, to be his guest at Chandernagore.[34] Before he had an opportunity of accepting it, however, the two men met at the Governor-General's country residence at Barrackpore, where once again Dillon was flattered and delighted by the attention shown to him by the senior British representative in India. But, when he came to write his *Narrative*, he nowhere named his hospitable host. The omission was obviously intentional. Dillon was both a snob and a man who regarded name-dropping as a technique of self-advancement. He mentioned that he received the invitation to Barrackpore in 'a letter from Sir James Colquhoun, one of the Governor-General's aide-de-camps'; he adorned his published writings and private letters with references to 'Lord Amherst', the former Governor-General, and 'Lord Combermere', his deputy in 1826. But at this time the high office was temporarily occupied by a man without title—Mr William Butterworth Bayley, after whom Dillon had named the bay in which the *Research* first anchored at Vanikoro. It was therefore more advantageous, in his estimation, to refer simply to 'His Excellency' or 'the Governor-General'.

He also resumed his satisfying contacts with the Asiatic Society, to which, he learnt, he had been elected during his absence. 'I am highly gratified', he informed the secretary, 'to be admitted a Member of so respectable an Institution'.[35] He placed the relics on public display in the Society's museum and made another major donation of articles from the South Seas—broadly similar in character to his earlier gift but containing some novelties, such as '2 stuffed Zebra Wolves' from Van Diemen's Land and a whalebone axe ominously described as 'Morgan McMurrag's carving knife'. At a meeting on 7 May he was thanked for his generosity and praised for his achievement.[36]

Nor was Dillon's name on the lips only of men of affairs and men of science, or of those who drove out to Chowringhee to see the relics. For the press had never lost interest in him since his arrival in the Hooghly with the sword-guard from Tikopia. In July 1827 it had reported the dismal news of his trial and conviction in Hobart Town and lamented the likely termination of his voyage.[37] After his triumphal return it continued for many weeks to publish information and comment on his discoveries. As in the past, it received Dillon's enthusiastic co-operation. He presented his friends of the press with copies of the certified lists of relics, of his report to the Marine Board, and of the articles about him and the voyage that had appeared in the Sydney newspapers, all of which were duly printed.[38] He made lively and controversial statements on a variety of subjects—such as his claim that in Tongatapu he had 'found the Missionary establishment exercising an inquisitorial rigour, that compels many of the natives to fly the island, and has materially thinned the population';[39] or his letter to the *Bengal Hurkaru* on 'The Jury at Van Diemen's Land', in which he

7 The village of Manevai, Vanikoro

8 The inauguration of the monument to La Pérouse at Vanikoro by Dumont d'Urville in 1828

attacked, at considerable length, the judicial procedures operating in the Australian colonies.

> In August 1819, I visited Pinang at which time there were only 53 British subjects upon that Island. From among these and the shipping in harbour grand and petit Juries were chosen four times a year to determine all matters whether of a civil or criminal nature: and yet, from the SIXTY THOUSAND ENGLISHMEN in Australia, has the British Parliament deemed it advisable to withhold this privilege which is their birth right and only protection from that worst of all oppression, legal oppression—and which has nevertheless been conceded to the barbarous Malay and to every petty West India Island.[40]

And, beyond Dillon's own contributions to the projection of a public image, the men of the press found references to his voyage and that of Dumont d'Urville in European journals and republished them.[41] During April and May newspaper readers in Bengal were kept as aware of Dillon, of his achievements and opinions, as even he could have wished.

Yet, during these weeks when he enjoyed the applause of the Europeans of Bengal, he was unable to forget the problem of his penury. Though the government approved of his travelling to France, it declined to meet the expenses of his visit. And, in common prudence, it could not have decided otherwise, for the Court of Directors of the East India Company was severely critical of the deterioration in the Bengal finances brought about by the Burma War and the decline in trade. The Court was critical, too, of Combermere's decision to sponsor a search for La Pérouse—the encouragement, as it were, of a romance in the wings, while the body politic lay sick and ill-attended in the centre of the stage. But, for Dillon, the government's refusal of help introduced a further complication: he needed money not only to enable him to travel but also to pay his expenses in Calcutta and to provide himself with support in Europe till France should give substance to her gratitude. In these circumstances, he was forced to borrow £1,200 from 'a relation' in Calcutta.[42]

With his financial difficulties thus temporarily resolved, Dillon booked passages to London for himself, Mary and Martha—at a cost of £400—on board the *Mary Ann*, a 'superior Teak Ship' of 600 tons. He remained busy till he sailed—working on his papers and those of the *Research*; employing an artist to make finished drawings from Russell's sketches and plans; and re-packing the relics.[43] But he was now able to relax. According to the owner of the *Mary Ann*:

P

> The splendid scale of this Vessel's accommodations, and the celebrity she has acquired as a *passenger Ship* are too well known to require the aid of comment.

And, in reporting Dillon's intention of travelling in her, the *Hurkaru* wrote:

> It only remains for us to congratulate Captain Dillon on the success which has attended his researches and to express our hope that he will be rewarded for them in a spirit worthy of a great and enlightened nation like France.[44]

He was returning home from the East in a style befitting a man who had responded, with success, to the spur of opportunity.

On the evening of 15 May the Dillons embarked in the *Fire-fly* to join the *Mary Ann* at Fultah. Their passage down river was swift and uncomplicated by the tedious tacking to which Dillon was accustomed. For the *Fire-fly* as her name suggested, was a steam vessel, the first of her kind in which he had travelled. She belonged to an age far removed in spirit from that of La Pérouse and of Vanikoro. And Dillon himself was young enough to adapt to the new era and to his new status as a public figure, to launch out on a new career: he still had a month to go before reaching his fortieth birthday.

TWELVE

In Quest of Recognition

LONDON AND PARIS 1828-29

THE voyage home began inauspiciously. The south-west monsoon was sweeping the Bay of Bengal; and, as the *Mary Ann* followed the Indian coast, beating to windward, she ran into mountainous seas. Off the coast of Coromandel she was held up for ten days, 'some days gaining a few miles, and other days losing'.[1] She took forty days to reach the line, as Dillon noted with interest—and probably with irritation—since he favoured a more easterly course from the mouth of the Hooghly at this time of year. Even then, when the south-east trade was expected, the winds remained variable. 'Under these circumstances', he commented, 'I fear little can be said as to the steadiness of the trades in the Indian Ocean, between the equator and the 10° south latitude, at any season of the year'. On 22 July they sighted the island of Rodriguez, east of Mauritius, on 7 August the coast of Natal; a week later they were off the Cape of Good Hope. On 31 August the *Mary Ann* anchored at James Town, in St Helena—nearly three and a half months after leaving the Hooghly.

Dillon had not been idle during the tedious passage. He had, of course, observed the ship's progress with the eyes of a mariner and, no doubt, used his gifts as a raconteur to enliven the days of his fellow passengers—a varied group including civil and military officers from Bengal, as well as his former colleague Eugène Chaigneau.[2] But, like many travellers in the days of sail, he had also been working on a book, converting his journal of the *Research*'s voyage into a narrative that he was confident would find a publisher because of the widespread interest in La Pérouse.[3] And he had, in addition, prepared an account of his discoveries for the French authorities.

This was an impressive statement, in which Dillon displayed a capacity for the systematic exposition and documentation of an argument that would have done credit to a professional administrator or a scientist. Apart from describing his visit to Vanikoro and explaining the significance of some of the more important relics, he touched on a number of other matters. He expressed the opinion that La Pérouse had sailed north-eastward from Botany Bay, by way of New Caledonia and Tonga, as the explorer had stated his intention of doing in a letter sent home from New South Wales. For in Tonga he had himself been told of a call at the island of Nomuka by two large ships subsequent to the visits of Cook and prior to that of d'Entrecasteaux. Their commander had been referred to as 'Lowagee', which he compared with the Tongan pronunciation of 'Cook' as 'Tootee'. Two men were said to have joined the ships at Nomuka, so that it was possible, he wrote, that those who remained behind at Vanikoro were not Frenchmen after all, or even Chinese (of whom there were some on board), but Tongans. It was a shrewd suggestion—and one which he later developed. He also referred to errors in the statements in European journals about the organization of his own voyage—particularly regarding the appointment of Chaigneau, which he had recommended in order to have with him a completely independent observer.[4]

Dillon and Chaigneau had worked closely together during the course of the voyage, trusting and confiding in one another. At first they had been faced by a problem of communication, for Chaigneau 'could not speak one word of English, nor I, a particle of the French Language'; but they had found that they both possessed some knowledge of Spanish,[5] and Chaigneau had learnt English. When the *Research* was at Sydney in January, Chaigneau had paid an impressive tribute to Dillon:

> the utmost praise is due to Captain Dillon for the coolness, intrepidity, and skill, which he displayed at the island of Manicolo . . . Captain Dillon's attention to his crew, too, at the time when sickness and death began to stare them in the face, was more like that of a *paterfamilias*, than that of a tyrannical and imperious commander.[6]

But on board the *Mary Ann* relations between the two men deteriorated. And, a week after Dillon finished his report to the French, he wrote to the Minister for the Navy about Chaigneau. Looking back on the recent past with a jaundiced eye, he declared: 'On my return to Bengal everything I had done for Mr Chaigneau was forgot. Gratitude, friendship, every tie vanished; all [he] sought for at the end of the voyage was self interest and aggrandisement':

> I am informed that he intends to publish an account of my Voyage on his arrival in France.
> To prevent that publication I must beg Your Excellency's timely interference from a sense of justice to all concerned . . . [7]

After three months confinement on board a small ship Dillon was becoming unduly sensitive to gossip, a victim of over-developed, though not wholly unreal, anxieties.

The call at St Helena—a usual one for ships returning from India—was welcome to Dillon as relief from the tedium and the tension of shipboard life and, even more so, because it was here that Napoleon—in whose honour he had named his younger son—had lived out his final years. On first sight the island appalled him.

> I have travelled a great deal, but never met with any thing half so sterile in appearance as the external view which St. Helena presents to the eye . . . Its bleak and dismal aspect conveys something awful to the feelings of the spectators . . .

But, once he had landed, he knew he was treading in the footsteps of the great. 'The bed-chamber assigned to me [at the lodging-house] was that in which the Duke of Wellington had slept on his return from India, and the one in which the ex-Emperor Napoleon reposed the first night he landed on the isle of his captivity.' And next morning he and others set out on a pilgrimage to the places that recalled his hero's sojourn. They went first to Napoleon's grave, where they were given 'a few branches of the willow trees growing near to the small iron pallisading which surrounds the plain blocks of stone that cover his ashes'. Then they visited 'Hutsgate', 'the former residence of the Count Bertrand and his family'—a house of intimate interest to Dillon, since the Countess Bertrand had been born Fanny Dillon, of Martinique. Finally they reached 'Longwood', where Napoleon himself had lived. Dillon entered the house 'by a back door'. He found it was now used as a barn: the living rooms contained 'a large quantity of oat straw, with numerous rats crossing to and fro'; the former Emperor's bedroom housed a threshing machine. 'In this dreary abode', he wrote, 'ended the life of confessedly one of the greatest men Europe ever produced'.

After St Helena, the voyage remained relatively uneventful, punctuated by little but the fear of attack by pirates, when they saw a brig painted black cause another to heave to—both privateers from Buenos Aires, they discovered, bound for the Caribbean. On 20 October they made their first contact with Europe, for a woodlark, a screech-owl and seven starlings landed on the ship and 'fed heartily on grains of rice, dead cock-roaches, and crumbs of bread'. Six days later the *Mary Ann* put into Plymouth, and the Dillons disembarked to make their way to London.

DILLON had been absent from Europe for nearly twenty-three years. He had left, as a youth, only two years after Napoleon had become Emperor of the French and before he had embarked upon his campaigns of continental conquest. He had returned, as a man of forty, to a Europe that could look back upon thirteen years of relative peace. In England people were experiencing the excitements of technological advance—the introduction of steamships, the building of the first railways—and the strains of industrial and political unrest. Yet for Dillon, who interpreted history in terms of the achievements of great men, the thread of continuity remained unbroken; for the Duke of Wellington, who had been not only Napoleon's predecessor (and his own) in the bedroom at St Helena but also one of the principal architects of Napoleon's final defeat at Waterloo, now held office as Prime Minister.

He had returned to an England where educated men and women possessed a taste for the romantic. They were commissioning buildings —such as the gatehouse and screen at King's College, Cambridge, and the new court at St John's—in a style that echoed fifteenth-century Perpendicular; admiring the highly dramatized paintings of John Martin and Benjamin Robert Haydon; reading the novels of Sir Walter Scott and the exuberant early works of Bulwer Lytton and Benjamin Disraeli. They shared the enthusiasm of those who had reached manhood about the time of Dillon's birth for the narratives of the eighteenth-century explorers, which continued to be republished in 'collections' of voyages, and were avid readers of new books describing life and travel in exotic parts.

He had returned with a story that accorded with the tastes of the age. Already his name was familiar to men of greater prominence than such humble companions of his youth as James McCabe, of Bermondsey, the employee of 'Mr Frinch . . . ho kept a Rope Walk'.[8] Since the first half of 1827 London journals—and some in Paris—had been carrying reports of his voyage in search of La Pérouse; one had also published an account of his exploits at 'Dillon's Rock'.[9] And after his success at Vanikoro news had first trickled in from the Bay of

Islands and Sydney and later arrived in larger volume from Calcutta. Newspapers in several cities, as well as the *Literary Gazette*, had published Sir William Betham's identification of the coat of arms described to him by his nephew as that of Jean-Nicolas Collignon, a member of the company of the *Boussole*. Most fully informed of all, however, were the readers of the *Asiatic Journal*, which had regularly reported his movements over the last two years and, on the eve of his arrival in London, had reproduced from the Calcutta newspapers an account of his voyage and the lists of relics.[10]

Dillon reached London on the morning of 29 October. One of his first calls was at the Jerusalem Coffee House, in Fleece Passage, Cornhill, a common meeting place for mariners and merchants concerned with the East. This was a 'subscription house', where the members— who paid only £1 a year, if they were seafaring men—could learn of the movements of shipping (and of their friends home from the East), read the newspapers from the British settlements in Asia and Australia, and deal with their correspondence.[11] Dillon became a subscriber and made frequent use of the house's facilities whenever he was in London. During this initial visit he wrote a letter to the Secretary of the East India Company, James Dart, announcing his arrival in England.[12]

From the Jerusalem Coffee House he walked to the East India House, in Leadenhall Street, to deliver his letter and the despatches he had brought from Calcutta. He saw Dart, whose reception of him was, in some respects, not discouraging. The British and French authorities would be informed of his arrival, he was told, and the Company— whose officers were renowned for their fondness for feasting—would give a dinner party at which the relics would be displayed.[13] But on this occasion, and on two subsequent calls, he was unable to meet the Chairman of the Court of Directors, William Astell, M.P., or to obtain any assurance as to when he might be able to do so.[14] He learnt that the Directors had been displeased at money being spent on his voyage and that their displeasure had been intensified by his action of drawing bills on London while he was at Hobart Town. Moreover, his position had been further worsened by events that remained unknown to him. For Lieutenant-Governor Arthur had sent a despatch regarding his trial to the Secretary of State for the Colonies, and in replying to it the latter had written:

> I have not failed to bring the circumstances of the case under the notice of the Court of Directors ... in order that Captain Dillon may be deprived,

as a just punishment for his misconduct, of any advantages which might have been held out to him by the Government of India, on the successful Terminating of the Expedition.[15]

After his talk with Dart he was no longer able to assume that the Company would help him financially—for example, by continuing his salary during the period of his visit to Europe, as he believed it was under a moral obligation to do. Indeed, he was told that it might ask the French for repayment of the costs of his voyage to Vanikoro.[16] This last suggestion particularly upset him, since, if it were acted upon, it would undermine his own claim to the reward promised to the discoverer of the fate of La Pérouse.

Dillon's next official call was on the French Ambassador, Prince Jules de Polignac, an accomplished courtier and diplomat, who immediately put him at his ease. He encouraged Polignac to believe that his association with the East India Company was close and friendly, telling him he expected to be given command of a ship in which to complete the search for traces of La Pérouse; but he also emphasized his connections with France—his birth in Martinique; his possession of relatives (or so he said) living in Paris. Polignac was impressed and gave him a letter of introduction to the Minister for the Navy, Baron Hyde de Neuville, in which he asked that Dillon should be received with the goodwill 'qu'à tout d'égards, il a droit d'espérer de vous'.[17]

On Saturday 1 November—only three days after reaching London—Dillon left for Paris to see the Minister. Like the French Dillons, Hyde de Neuville was of English descent on his father's side. Moreover, he had spent a substantial part of his life in England and the United States, so that he was able to talk with his visitor in the English language. From Dillon's point of view, their meeting was a great success. Hyde told Dillon that 'he had no doubt his most Christian Majesty [Charles X] would do what was proper' towards him; and he promised to have a study made of the records of La Pérouse's expedition to facilitate the identification of the relics. Dillon's main reason for visiting Paris so soon, however, was to seek protection of his right to publish the sole narrative of his voyage—a right that now seemed as essential to his continued solvency as to his future fame. In his letter criticizing Chaigneau's supposed intentions, he had suggested French 'patronage' of his own book. Now, he asked specifically that Chaigneau should be forbidden to publish 'a surreptitious account'. In this matter, too, as in regard to his suggestion that he should be permitted to make homage of the relics to Charles X, he was given assurances of Hyde's support.[18]

On his return to London he found that, at least to those interested in the East, he was a man of some note. In the *Asiatic Journal* he read further news of his voyage and praise of the skill with which he had conducted it. At a meeting of the Royal Asiatic Society, when he presented a collection of South Sea artefacts and introduced three Maoris—'Two of them . . . in their native dresses'—to the members, he was himself the central figure.[19] And, of most direct importance to him, he was granted an interview by the Chairman of the East India Company on the day after he arrived back from Paris.

In one respect Dillon's meeting with Astell was reassuring, for he was told that the relics would be transferred to the Foreign Office for presentation to France. But he found the Chairman insensitive to his own judgement of the voyage—as one undertaken from motives of humanity and in the interests of science, and one which, by its success, had significantly contributed to Anglo-French friendship. He saw that the latter shared the unimaginative views—as they seemed to him—that he had heard from Dart. He therefore set out his case in a long, formal letter to the Chairman and Deputy Chairman of the Court of Directors. On this occasion he played up his Irish origins and his gentility. Although he 'happened to be born in a French colony', he was 'of Irish parentage', was 'educated from infancy' in Ireland, and served in the Royal Navy. Government officers in Bengal, he wrote, were 'aware of the respectability of my connections' and of his standing as a merchant and shipowner. He was thus well qualified for the command of an expedition sponsored by the Government of British India and supported by the Asiatic Society, a body of which—as he pointed out—he was himself a member and that was still 'inspired by the same spirit of scientific research which was infused into it by its great Founder Sir William Jones'. But the expedition had reduced him to a state of penury which, he implied, the Company should alleviate. He asked, in particular, for its patronage of his forthcoming book.

> In the case of other similar expeditions as that of Capt. Cook or Capt. Parry it has [been] considered the just prerogative of the Commander to narrate his own efforts and discoveries, and should the Hon. East India Company or the British Government grant their countenance and patronage to the publication of my Voyage to the South Sea Islands I hope to be able to show that few portions of the globe are more worthy of attention in a moral, commercial and geographical sense.

Finally, he suggested that he should himself take the relics to France.[20]

Dillon's letter produced a prompt, but disconcerting, response: it had been laid before the Court of Directors, the Secretary informed him, and forwarded to the French Government, 'to whose consideration the Court conceive that any claims which you may have . . . should be submitted'.[21] By this time little remained of the £1,200 Dillon had borrowed. Before he left India he had spent more than two-thirds of it—on living expenses in Calcutta for himself and his family, on their passages to England, and on warm clothing and other comforts for the voyage. And since his arrival in London his expenditure had been heavy, for—as his past practice showed—he believed that immaculate dress and lavish entertainment were marks of a man of quality, and he was determined to impress those whom he met. His most urgent need was for ready money.[22]

For some weeks Dillon could not obtain the return of his journal from the East India Company and was consequently unable to resume work on his book. For a longer period he was left without information as to whether plans were being made in London for the despatch of the relics or in Paris for the recognition of his achievement. At Christmas his mind was in tune with the bleak winter weather, rather than with the spirit of festivity that engrossed those around him. Yet, in fact, he had not been forgotten. And early in January 1829 he was informed that he was to travel to Paris and present the relics to the French authorities; on 12 January he was invited to the French Embassy to discuss the form that his reward should take. The King, he was then told, would probably wish to confer an honour upon him, and the government would be willing to assist him in the publication of a French edition of his book.[23]

Dillon was warmed by this evidence of regard for him. But he could not ignore his straitened financial circumstances. He therefore wrote, rather apologetically, to the Embassy.

> I beg to say that though any mark of approbation from one of the greatest and most enlightened Nations of Europe, I should esteem as the highest honor, yet however gratifying this might be to my feelings as a man, and as a Navigator, I feel bound in the first place to bear in mind that I am a husband and Father of a Family, and how much those who depend on me for support have already suffered by this Expedition.

He asked for 'a small pension' and for the payment of his expenses in travelling home from India. The prospect of recognition was sufficient, however, to bring out his sense of grandeur. He had to educate his sons, he declared, 'so as to qualify them for either a Military, or Naval, life'. For himself he promised that, if he became the recipient of a French pension, 'my services should for the remainder of my life, be at the disposal of your Nation'. In the near future he could usefully be sent back to Vanikoro, as in one of the neighbouring islands he had left a young man 'for the purpose of learning the language and making himself acquainted with the whole account of the disaster'. And over the years that lay farther ahead he could continue to serve France among the peoples of the South Seas, for—he declared—'My knowledge of these Sons of Nature, their manners, Customs, Countries, Produce and Manufactures; has I flatter myself never been either equalled or surpassed by any navigator'.[24] After his summons to the Embassy, he began to dream of a life for himself and his descendants scarcely less ample than that of the Dillons who had left Ireland in the retinue of James II.

But, on the day that these modest requests and immodest aspirations were communicated to the French, the *Morning Chronicle* published an account of Dumont d'Urville's visit to Vanikoro that Dillon saw as yet another threat to their realization. It gave Dumont d'Urville credit for having discovered where La Pérouse was lost, described his erection of a monument on the island, and lavishly praised his 'glorious toils'. Dillon believed, correctly, that his rival had heard ill of him at Hobart Town and, erroneously, that he had now returned to France and was responsible for the story. He retorted angrily in a letter which the *Chronicle* printed several days later.[25]

He gave an account of the means by which Dumont d'Urville had been helped to find his way to the scene of the disaster. At Hobart Town, the Sydney press report of his own visit to Vanikoro 'was read to him by some gentlemen holding high offices at that place, viz.: the Honduras Hero, Colonel Arthur; his learned friend the Political Judge Pedder, and the pious and ranting Dr Bedford'; 'these cavaliers, with an empty scribe named Ross [the editor of the *Hobart-Town Gazette*]' also described to him Dillon's earlier discoveries at Tikopia. At the latter place, 'the enterprising Navigator of the 19th century' received the letter Dillon had left there and talked with Martin Buchert.

> With the aid of such instructions, . . . he must have found it almost as easy to find relics of the wrecks at the Island, as it would be to collect bullets and bones on the field of Waterloo six months after the battle was fought.

He was no less bitter in his comments on the reported monument.

> Without making the slightest mention of my previous discovery, the writer of the paragraph (probably Captain D. d'Urville himself) goes on to state, that he had caused a monument to be erected to the memory of La Perouse and his companions . . . Instead of setting up a post or pillar, with an inscription, among a race of savages, where letters are not known, and where such a thing would soon be pulled down for the sake of the materials, I deemed it a more suitable memorial to La Perouse to affix his name to the island which it has immortalized, and to the reef on which he perished . . .
>
> This is the monument which has been erected to the much lamented and celebrated French Navigator by the English; who, through my exertions, have been the first to ascertain the fate of his expedition.

With this piece of invective before the eyes of the British public, he felt that his reputation was secure and prepared to leave for France.

Dillon reached Paris on 6 February and established himself at the fashionable Hôtel Meurice, in the Rue St Honoré.[26] Although he had previously visited Paris for only a few days, he had, in a way, come home, for the city which had long drawn to itself so many men of talent or authority from all over Europe had already begun to cast its spell upon him. Its spirit—a brilliant amalgam of absorption in the present and consciousness of the past—was, indeed, peculiarly congenial to him, as a man who combined an innate sensuality with a highly developed capacity for nostalgia. But it now possessed for him a particular splendour, because he had come to receive recognition of his achievement. During his more than twenty years abroad, he had responded with the whole force of his being to the life of the South Sea islands, had enjoyed the exotic affluence of Asian cities and the untidy vigour of South American seaports; but he had always thought of himself as having his roots in Europe. Even when he was living with Fijians and Society Islanders as a young man, or when ten years later he was struggling to fit out his first ship, he had retained a sense of his quality that was essentially European and aristocratic in character. Now, in Paris, his private conviction was to be transformed into public fact: he was to be acknowledged by those whom he had always regarded as his equals as one of their own.

During the following weeks Dillon spent much time in the company of public men, of men of letters, and of officers of the French navy, all of whom were keen to hear his story and to inspect the relics. One of his new acquaintances with whom his meeting was unexpectedly fruitful was Jean-Baptiste Hapdé: twenty years earlier Hapdé had written the words for a pantomime dealing with the voyage of La Pérouse; he now determined to write a book paying tribute both to the explorer and to the discoverer of his fate, and he published it later in the year.²⁷ Another with whom he was especially glad to talk was Admiral Rossel, who had served with d'Entrecasteaux during his unsuccessful search for La Pérouse and had later written the official narrative of the expedition. But by far the most exciting of his contacts was that with Barthélemy de Lesseps, the only man to have sailed with La Pérouse and returned to Europe.

As a young officer in the consular service, de Lesseps had joined La Pérouse in the capacity of interpreter. In September 1787 he had been put ashore at Petropavlovsk, in Siberia, to make his way overland to Paris carrying a record of the expedition's proceedings up to that time. Now, as a man in his sixties, he minutely examined the relics, in company with Dillon, reviving his memories of the distant past.

> The piece of board with the *fleur de lis* on it, he observed, had most probably once formed a part of the ornamental work of the *Boussole*'s stern . . . The silver sword-handle . . . he also examined, and said that such swords were worn by the officers of the expedition . . . With regard to the brass guns, having looked at them attentively, he observed that the four largest were such as stood on the quarter-deck of both ships, and that the smallest gun was such as they had mounted in the long-boats when going on shore among the savages.

But the item that interested him most was the small mill-stone. 'This', he exclaimed, 'is the best thing you have got: we had some of them mounted on the quarter-deck to grind our grain'.

Meanwhile, Dillon was also in touch with Hyde de Neuville and officers of his Ministry. He was told that the relics would be placed on display in the new Musée Charles X et Dauphin, 'with an inscription describing their loss and recovery'. He was again encouraged to publish a French edition of his book. And, of greatest concern to him, he was informed of the character of his reward: a pension of 4,000 francs (£160) a year, of which half would continue to be payable to his wife, should she survive him, together with a grant of 10,000 francs towards his expenses in travelling from India; and, in ad the conferring on him of a knighthood, as a 'Chevalier de l'Ordre royal de la Légion-d'Honneur'.²⁸ When he learnt of the King's generosity—he noted in his *Narrative*—'I returned my most grateful thanks to this illustrious prince, for his generous condescension in thus noticing and approving of my services'.

On 2 March Dillon was presented to Charles X. The King spoke to him in English.

> He appeared to be perfectly well acquainted with the history of la Pérouse's expedition, and addressed several very judicious questions to me regarding the circumstances attending the loss of that celebrated navigator. With an anxiety creditable to his feelings, he inquired what was my opinion as to the probability of any of the crew being yet alive on the Solomon Islands? After an interview of half an hour I was allowed to retire, at which time this most amiable monarch made use of the following obliging expression, 'Good bye, Captain Dillon: I thank you.'

He felt that he had joined the elect.

THE Chevalier Dillon—as he would in future be known—had become a public figure, though he had not yet become aware of all the consequences of his changed status. For not only had his voyage and his presence in Paris been noticed by the daily press but his intemperate letter to the *Morning Chronicle* had also been republished in the *Annales Maritimes*.[29] Like other professional men, naval officers are quick to resent the denigration of a colleague by an outsider; and, since Dillon's aspersions on Dumont d'Urville were baseless, they reacted to them angrily and with justification. The Directeur des Invalides at the Ministry for the Navy, who had to arrange for the payment of Dillon's pension, was embarrassed by his responsibility. In May his office noted that he wished the matter to be handled discreetly, in order to avoid public criticism. Not until July did Dillon begin to receive it.[30]

Soon after his presentation to Charles X, Dillon left Paris. At the end of March he wrote from London to Hyde de Neuville taking up the King's question about possible survivors. The two men left on Vanikoro, he had now decided, were almost certainly Tongans. But he thought it possible that some of those who embarked in the vessel built at Peu—particularly Chinese, 'who would be likely to live many years in a Tropical climate'—might be found in the neighbouring islands. If an expedition were sent out, it could also make a survey of the Solomon Islands and a study of the winds in that part of the Pacific; these were tasks, he explained, that might reveal the feasibility of following more direct routes than those currently used between India and South America, between China and New South Wales. He offered his services as the expedition's commander.[31]

But after his return to London his energies were largely concentrated upon the writing of his book.

THIRTEEN

Dillon's Narrative

DR JOHNSON—a writer with whose work Dillon was acquainted—once remarked: 'No man but a blockhead ever wrote except for money'.[1] Dillon would have understood the aphorism; but he would not have felt that it conveyed the whole truth. For, though he was desperately anxious that his book should make money, he also hoped that it would bring him increased celebrity. Moreover, as his contributions to the press of Sydney and Calcutta had already shown, he felt a compulsion to communicate through the medium of the printed word—to make known to the public his hopes and his grievances, his knowledge of history and of the ways of life of Pacific peoples; to offer comment on the foibles and inconsistencies of the Western world. His ambitions as a writer, in the more formal sense, were not confined to the publication of a narrative of his voyage in search of La Pérouse. He intended also to write 'a complete history of the Beetee [i.e., Viti, or Fiji] Islands, from its first discovery to A.D. 1825, which will describe the manners, customs, &c. of these peoples . . .', and 'a full description' of the 'civil and religious customs' of the Maoris of New Zealand.[2] But neither of these later books ever appeared, probably for the reason encapsulated in another of Dr Johnson's epigrams—one with which Dillon might reluctantly have agreed: 'I allow you may have pleasure from writing, after it is over, if you have written well; but you don't go willingly to it again'.[3]

Dillon knew the value of the observations of travellers in far countries. For not only had he pored over the narratives of early travellers in Asia and the Pacific, but at the Asiatic Society, in Calcutta, he had met men who, like Marco Polo long before them, had written accounts of courts and peoples seldom visited by Europeans. Among more recent writings on the Pacific he had studied William Mariner's account of the people of Tonga with particular care, because Mariner 'having arrived among them in early youth, and become perfectly acquainted with their language, manners, customs, and modes of thinking, had better opportunities of observation than any one who either went before or came after him'.[4] He believed that he could himself, whilst recounting the course of his voyage, also communicate to his readers some of the realities of the island world.

As soon as he had found suitable lodgings, engaged an amanuensis, and obtained the return of his papers from the East India Company, he settled down to work. He chose a title for the book that, through its very verbosity, provided a clear description of both its contents and its organization: *Narrative and Successful Result of a Voyage in the South Seas, performed by order of the Government of British India, to ascertain the actual fate of La Pérouse's Expedition, interspersed with accounts of the religion, manners, customs, and cannibal practices of the South Sea Islanders.* After an introduction describing La Pérouse and his voyage, and French efforts to find him, Dillon began the main text with a chapter on the *Hunter*'s visit to Fiji in 1813, since in the conflict at Wailea lay the origins of his own discovery. In the remainder of the narrative he was concerned with his experiences between his finding of the swordguard in May 1826 and his presentation to Charles X in March 1829. Only in passing does the book refer to other episodes in his life; but on almost every page, and more particularly in the digressions, it is revealing of its author's mind—his knowledge, his opinions and his style.

The Introduction—which runs to some sixty pages—is mainly drawn from an English translation of the *Voyage autour du monde . . . de la Pérouse*—one of several, that which was first issued by the Robinsons and their co-publishers in 1799[5]—and from the English edition of Labillardière's account of the voyage of d'Entrecasteaux. These sources are summarized with care and intelligence; and, where they are quoted directly, the transcription is reasonably accurate by the standards of the time. In matters such as punctuation, however, the original forms are not strictly adhered to. Moreover, the omission from these quoted passages of phrases or whole sentences is not noted, and several purported quotations are, in fact, mere summaries. The introduction is somewhat more, however, than a digest of the literature, for it contains comments on the work of La Pérouse and d'Entrecasteaux that only a mariner with Dillon's knowledge of the Pacific could have made and touches of the orotund style that was peculiarly his—'the immortal Cook'; an odd description of Java as 'that deleterious island'; a reference to 'a very distinguished officer [with La Pérouse], who incautiously deviated most unfortunately from the strict injunctions laid on him by his very experienced commander'.⁶

Dillon revealed the less likeable side of his character most clearly in his treatment of his relations with Tytler. At the end of the book he added an appendix of documents which related mainly to this episode. All but one of the items that he included were accurately transcribed from a stated source. The exception was an account of his trial and conviction at Hobart Town. He appears to have taken this from the *Colonial Times* of 11 May 1827; but, if he did so, he made small, but important, alterations in that journal's report. References to Tytler's defaults were subtly intensified, those to his own violence in speech and action were softened or deleted. Most significantly, perhaps, he altered the words referring to the medical report on his illness at Calcutta from 'the malady was temporary' to 'it was only a temporary illness caused by severe cold'.

In the text of the book he denounced, with a tedious perseverance, 'the outrageous person' who had said he was insane, and added in a footnote:

> It is proper to notice here, that the person who invented this calumny, has long since been placed under restraint for the very malady which he wickedly imputed to me: so awful and speedy, sometimes, are the dispensations of retributive justice!

He ridiculed Tytler for his eccentric publications and chided the people of Van Diemen's Land for accepting their author as a man of learning.*
Referring to Tytler's claim to have been responsible for the voyage in search of La Pérouse, he wrote:

> ... he pretends that the Government of British India was so sorry for having had a difference (or rather a thousand differences) with the great Doctor Tytler, that to make it up to him they fitted out an expedition to the South Seas, at the expense of 150,000 rupees, to give him an opportunity of exploring the tract of the Queen of Sheba, the golden coasts of Ophir, and the course of the aerolite, which he says (in 1823) travelled through the air from the island of Java to Allahabad, where the Doctor then resided, to give him warning of his approaching voyage to the part of the world whence it came—and thus end his life with the practical confirmation of

---

* Tytler's publications included 'Budaic Sabism, 1817; Remarks on Morbus Oryzeus, 1820; Illustrations of Ancient Geography and History, 1826' (D. G. Crawford (compiler), *Roll of the Indian Medical Service 1615-1930* (London, 1930).

these and other such visionary dreams, in which he had wasted so many years, thereby insulting the understanding of the public.

And again:

> In short, the good people of Van Diemen's Land seem to have been imposed on by the wild rhapsodies entitled 'Tytler's Illustrations of Ancient Geography and History,' which were apparently regarded there as the *ne plus ultra* of human ingenuity. They seem to have believed, on his authority, that he was at least one of the sons of the prophets, and I his persecutor; that, as he pretends, Sumatra was the Ophir of the Scriptures, and Java the isle of Sheba: and had he continued the voyage with me, he would no doubt have treated the world with a learned treatise, proving that the island of Mannicolo was the Laputa of Gulliver, which, yielding to the universal force of gravitation, had at last ceased to float over its dependent isles, and sousing like a water-fowl into the Pacific Ocean, had taken root, swallowing in the vortex thus created the ships under the command of la Pérouse. Surely no punishment could be too severe for the person who cut short the prophetic career of so great a man in the eyes of his wise disciples!

Dillon's style always became florid when he wrote in anger; and he had been embittered by Tytler's attempts to ruin him more deeply than by any other experience.[7]

Dillon gave expression to his disenchantment with other men in the course of the book; usually it was disenchantment with fellow Europeans who, he believed, had acted wrongly, or unwisely, towards Pacific islanders or towards him and his men. But more commonly he wrote with sympathy and euphoric gusto. As in his letters to the press, he displayed an extraordinarily detailed and accurate knowledge of European penetration of the Pacific. For the age of exploration, this was mainly extracted from his well-thumbed copies of Burney's *Chronological History* and of the narratives of the eighteenth-century navigators.[8] For the history of his own times, it was derived from newspapers, and from innumerable conversations with mariners, missionaries, traders, beachcombers and islanders. His memory for what he had read or heard about events in the islands was unusually reliable, because he attempted to relate each piece of information that he gleaned to a broad picture of the changing Pacific; like a man set on solving a jigsaw puzzle, he knew that each piece had its special place. Not unnaturally, his interest in history was strongest where it impinged most closely on his own experience. He wrote, for example, about the discovery of new passages, such as that by 'the celebrated Dampier' of the strait between New Britain and the north coast of New Guinea, and about the knowledge possessed by the Rotumans and the Vanikorans of islands as yet unvisited by Europeans. He touched on the history of trade and of whaling and gave accounts of the conflicts between men engaged in these enterprises and the people of Tongatapu and of northern New Zealand. But he did not confine himself to subjects that were closely related to his own experience, nor did he ignore recent developments. In the chapters covering the *Research*'s two visits to the Bay of Islands, for example, he described the work of sawmillers from New South Wales and the abortive attempt at colonization by a London company shortly before his arrival. He looked to the future, as well as to the past: he was already convinced that New Zealand was destined to become a country of white settlement.[9]

Yet, as Dillon himself recognized, it was not his references to the Pacific's Western invaders that were the most valuable of his digressions, for these were the product of an interest in history that he shared with others, but his 'accounts of the religion, manners, customs, and cannibal practices of the South Sea Islanders'. In the Preface he made this point, emphatically.

> ... the reader is requested to observe, that this work has many claims to notice quite peculiar to itself. It is not an account of nations which resemble ourselves in manners and civilization, or of countries which had been a hundred times before visited and described; on the contrary, in this voyage the reader is conducted amid the savage tribes of the South Seas, through tracts never before fully explored, and made acquainted with human nature under a new aspect, described from the personal observation of a living witness, who has had ample opportunities of studying their characters both in peace and war, and who had nearly fallen a victim to their cannibal propensities.

The boldness of this claim was nicely balanced by evidence, perhaps unconsciously provided, of its author's genuine humility; his most prolonged excursion into ethnography was almost wholly a *précis* of parts of Mariner's *Tonga*.[10]

Dillon based his long chapter entitled 'Manners and customs of the Friendly Islanders' on the earlier work not only because Mariner had enjoyed exceptional opportunities of observation but also because he was able to vouch for its 'general accuracy'. Following a procedure similar to that which he had used in writing the Introduction, he reduced the relevant chapters in Mariner's book to between a third and a half of their original length by combining rigorous condensation with some direct transcription. He added a few points of his own—for example, correcting Mariner on the Fijian term for 'kava' and telling his readers how kava was used in Tahiti: 'At Otaheite the people drink it in the morning while fasting, but eat along with it, saying that food improves the effect'.[11] But he repeatedly made it clear that Mariner, not he, was the authority on Tongan society.

Dillon's own contributions to Pacific ethnography were, however, substantial and valuable: they have continued to be drawn on by scholars equipped with a professional training that he wholly lacked, but envious of his experience among island peoples before their ways of life had been much changed through contact with the West. His descriptions of material culture, as well as of the diverse forms of social control, were the product of a mind little tainted by assumptions of its own superiority. His accounts of cannibalism and torture in Fiji, of chieftainship in Rotuma, of the weapons and canoes and houses in use in many islands—all these added to European knowledge. But, above all, his statements about life in Tikopia and Vanikoro possessed lasting value, for his was the first report on these islands.

He included a passage of about 1,250 words on the culture of Tikopia.[12] 'The Tucopians', he began, 'are an extremely mild and inoffensive race, hospitable and generous, as their reception of Bushart and the lascar sufficiently proves'. He described their diet:

> They lived chiefly on vegetable food, having neither hogs nor poultry . . . They at one time had both, but they were voted common nuisances and exterminated by general consent. The hogs destroyed their plantations of yams, sweet potatoes, tara, and bananas. These, and the breadfruit and cocoa-nuts, with fish, are what they subsist on; but, owing to the deep water round the island, fish is by no means plentiful.

And their system of government:

> The island is governed by one principal chief, with several petty ones, who act as magistrates. They live very peaceably, and never have any war amongst themselves or with their neighbours. This probably may be attributed to their Pythagorean diet. But it does not restrain an intuitive propensity for thieving; and though the punishment in case of detection is very severe, the lower classes often rob each other's gardens and plantations. If the thief is caught, he is carried before one of the chiefs, and if convicted, his property and ground are forfeited to the individual he has robbed.

He described the acceptance of polygyny and the form of the marriage ceremony.

A plurality of wives is allowed. The wives are exceedingly jealous of each other, and if the husband bestows his caresses more freely on one than another, the despised one takes it to heart so much, that she puts an end to her life . . . The marriage ceremony is curious. When a man wishes to take a wife, he first politely consults the lady he had placed his affections on, and if she consents and her parents agree, he sends three or four of his male friends at night, to take her away by force as it were. He then sends presents of mats and provisions to the relations of the bride, and invites them to a feast at his house, which usually lasts for two days.

As at all the islands he had visited, he had sought information on the work of the gods.

> In each village on Tucopia there is a large building, called in their language the 'spirit house', set apart for the use of disembodied spirits, which are supposed to reside in this building. On the approach of bad weather and thunder and lightning, which alarm the islanders extremely, they flock to the spirit house, and remain there while the storm continues, making offerings of cocoa-nuts, cava root, and other eatables. They imagine the storm is caused by the presiding spirit, who when he is displeased goes to the top of the highest land in the island, and manifests his wrath by raising a tempest. When he is appeased by the offerings, he returns to the 'hall of ghosts.'

His account of Tikopia was not free from inaccuracy;[13] but, since it was based on no more than one visit ashore, in 1813, and on the questioning of Buchert and Ratia and of islanders who had come on board, it was a meritorious attempt at ethnographic description.

No less valuable was the material Dillon presented on voyaging by islanders: his story of the boat that had disappeared from the Society Islands and eventually been wrecked in Tonga; that of the Rotumans who had set out for the Ellice Islands and were blown to Samoa; his references to inter-island travel in the southern Solomons.[14] But most revealing of his own cast of mind were the passages in which he discussed relations between Europeans and islanders.

He drew conclusions relating to this latter subject from many aspects of his experience in the South Seas. For example, he wrote:

> I have often conversed with savages, who informed me that when they first beheld Europeans, they supposed them to have descended from the clouds; nor could they imagine what our business was in their country, unless to carry off their provisions, wives, and children, as slaves: this idea being grounded on the universal practice in those islands of men carrying off the women and children of their enemies in their war expeditions;

whilst, on the contrary, when they pay a friendly visit to a neighbouring island, or to a strange country, their wives and children usually accompanied them.[15]

For this reason—as well as for the more obvious ones—he encouraged local women to remain on board when he was anchored in an island port and liked to have women visible on deck whenever he approached a strange shore.[16]

He believed that it was equally important for a European to show his respect for islanders and for their manner of life.

> Savages are characterized by a peculiar susceptibility of indignity, while they are equally susceptible of gratitude. In fact, the extreme to which these opposite passions predominate in their breasts, forms one of the principal traits in the uncivilized mind.[17]

And by recognizing these personal sensibilities, and by acting in accordance with custom, a European gained much more than mere physical security, for

> a strict regard to this line of conduct toward these islanders is the most effectual mode of conciliating their esteem: It serves this end more powerfully than bestowing the most costly presents. The one excites their cupidity, and ensures their friendship only in proportion to the amount of your gifts, and their expectation of more; while the other insensibly gains their affections, and at a cheap and easy rate secures a place in their best regards.[18]

The acts required of the European varied, of course, from place to place. 'It is the custom in New Zealand', he wrote, 'when friends or relations meet after long absence, for both parties to touch noses and shed tears'.

> With this ceremony I have frequently complied out of courtesy; for my failure in this respect would have been considered a breach of friendship, and I should have been regarded as little better than a barbarian, according to the rules of New Zealand politeness. Unfortunately, however, my hard heart could not upon all occasions readily produce a tear, not being made of such melting stuff as those of the New Zealanders; but the application of a pocket handkerchief to my eyes for some time, accompanied with an occasional howl in the native language, answered all the purposes of real grief.[19]

For similar reasons, he exchanged names with friends in Vanikoro and Ndeni.[20]

When he wrote about indigenous priests, about witchcraft, or about the supernatural generally, he often set his story in a cross-cultural context. At Tikopia, remembering—or so he implied—the alleged influence of the Reverend William Bedford with Governor Arthur, he had 'sent on shore five axes as presents: one for the principal chief, and one for each of his three subordinates; the fifth being for the high priest, as I had lately learned how necessary it is to be on good terms with these reverend gentlemen'.

> By means of these presents to his holiness, I thought he might be induced to prevail on the temporal chiefs to interest themselves in my favour. Nor let anyone sneer at this precaution: for I have found it good policy to acquire the favour of the clergy in barbarous, as well as in more polished society: these interpreters of the will of heaven having in general as much direct and immediate influence over the councils of the rulers here, as the clergy have in certain British colonies.[21]

At Ndeni he had been visited 'by an old man who had two most singular teeth in his lower jaw'.

> I learnt that this person was a priest, and of course a magician, such as are on most of the islands of the Pacific... I ordered him some yam and pork, but before it came up he pretended to be seized with violent fits, during which he sung, cried, laughed, and appeared to converse with a spirit who inspired him. Our people on board stared with amazement: and the Serang told me that this was a bad man who would bewitch the ship. He said he once saw a fellow of the kind at Muscat, who used to create living goats out of wood and sell them... The seamen, who are ever ready to make merry at the expense of their betters, christened him Parson Bedford (from his resemblance, as they said, to a clergyman at Van Diemen's Land, particularly about the lips).[22]

Dillon wrote like a committed anti-clerical.

He was always ready, however, to use the belief of others in the supernatural, and their trust in its human interpreters, for his own purposes. When he was asked by Te Tinana, of the Bay of Islands, for a passage to India in the *Research*, for example, he had not simply refused the old man's request.

> I told him that I would give him an answer in the morning, as I should most likely dream on the subject in the night: a course the most likely to please him, as these people place implicit reliance on dreams, and I had resolved, too, by that means to rid myself of his importunities.

Next day he informed Te Tinana of the truth that had been vouchsafed him:

'I dreamt last night that we were at Calcutta, and that both you and I died there. Now, should I die, which of course I shall since I dreamt so, what will become of you? no person there knows you, and it will be out of your power to return to New Zealand.'

For confirmation of his interpretation of the dream, an appeal was made to a Maori 'priestess', who, 'true to the practice of her profession, observing that I did not wish to take him, gave an appropriate explanation of the fatal consequences likely to result from a contumacious neglect of divine warning'. And thus, Dillon added, he disposed of the request without arousing the ire of the man who had made it.[23]

In his comments on marriage Dillon entered an even more sensitive area of cross-cultural relations. He wrote approvingly of Brian Boru's liaison with Shelagh at the Bay of Islands.

> They lived together until the ship was on the point of sailing, when Brian ransomed her by presents to her lords, which they accepted, and she then became his lawful wife according to the customs of the country, which regard the dilatory process of calling in church, applying for and taking out licences, &c. as impolitic and unnecessary, since even Malthus himself would not have any apprehension of the principle of increase, where such an outlet exists for surplus population in the *army* and the *oven*.[24]

And he was caustically critical both of the missionaries' condemnation of cohabitation between European men and Maori women and of their refusal to regularize these relationships through Christian marriage. Of the former he wrote: 'Now at New Zealand this sort of intercourse is not only lawful, but considered by their friends as highly honourable, and tantamount to marriage with us'; it was therefore 'unnecessary and absurd', he declared, to insist on a formal ceremony 'among people, who consider the mutual consent of parties as sufficiently valid and binding'. Of the missionary refusal to wed a Christian to a 'heathen', he commented: 'This seems to spring from the doctrine, that marriage is a religious sacrament and not a civil contract'.[25]

And from this secular and relativist position he criticized the private lives of the missionaries themselves.

> I consider it highly impolitic in the missionaries who are bachelors not to chuse wives from among the native females: as many advantages, both personal and as regards their conversion, would result from such marriages. The offspring of these men being instructed in the various trades of their fathers, would become good tailors, shoemakers, carpenters, curriers, &c., and these again intermarrying among the aborigines, would gradually

spread, not only the doctrines of christianity which they received from
their parents, but also civilized habits and useful handicrafts. The creoles
inheriting their ancestral estates on the mother's side, would also succeed to
their country's honours, which in due succession would devolve on them,
and thus, in course of time, would a civilized nobility spring up, who
could not fail of giving a tone to the habits of thinking and acting among
their dependants, while the missionaries should aid, by precept and example,
to establish civilization and christianity at one and the same time: for let
theorists advance what absurd propositions they may, arts and civilization
must precede, and not follow the establishment of christianity.[26]

This was an argument of substance and subtlety; but, at least in its
advocacy of inter-racial marriage by missionaries, it was incompatible
with the doctrines of Protestant Evangelicals—or with those of the
church of which Dillon was a nominal member.

In a footnote to his plea for the teaching of the practical arts, Dillon
added a comment on the attitudes of the missionaries at the Bay of
Islands:

> The mission sends out mechanics to instruct the natives in handicrafts; but at
> present the persons sent out for this purpose assume the title of the Reverend
> Mr. So and So, and consider it quite derogatory to their cloth to condescend
> actually to handle the sledge-hammer, the awl, the needle, the rope-winch,
> &c. Thus is the public imposed on by these sanctified mechanics, whom it
> intended not to act as clergy, but to use their hands as St. Paul did before
> them, and actually work as blacksmiths, carpenters, shoemakers, tailors,
> rope-makers, or even tent makers, like the holy apostle above named of
> whom they pretend to be the followers.

His sarcasm became even more explicit in his references to Henry
Williams, who had formerly held a commission in the Royal Navy, as
'the reverend lieutenant'.[27]

He also attacked Williams and his colleagues for their social ex-
clusiveness and lack of charity towards Europeans. They were, he
wrote, 'too deeply immersed in the theoretical parts of christianity, to
emerge into the ordinary practice of its most essential dictates, to
succour the helpless and visit the sick'. He cited their failure to help a
mentally deranged seaman who had been callously put ashore from an
American whaler and their refusal to kill a sheep or a bullock for the
invalids on board the *Research*, when they had been 'gasping for a
little fresh meat or a bowl of nutritive broth'. He contrasted 'the
conduct of these enlightened professors of the reformed doctrines of

christianity with the really christian conduct of the benighted ministers of the catholic religion at Lima'.

> As soon as the news reaches these venerable padres of the arrival of a vessel, they repair on board, and with the benignity of habitual charity, inquire after the health of those on board. If any are sick, they immediately remove them to the hospitals..., and the utmost care and attention is paid till health be restored to the patient; or, should death be approaching to terminate his sufferings, his bed is watched with paternal anxiety, and spiritual consolation is administered to his departing soul. They will not accept any remuneration for their disinterested care, feeling themselves amply compensated by an approving conscience; nor do they inquire of what country or religion the invalid is, or whether he be a saint or a sinner: it is sufficient for them that he stands in need of aid, and therefore do they administer it.

He strengthened his condemnation of the New Zealand mission by this eloquent tribute to the priests in Peru. But he did not make the comparison in a sectarian spirit, for he was equally ready to bestow praise on Protestants where he thought it was merited. He referred to his old friend Samuel Marsden, as a 'truly pious and venerable man', who had 'for many years laboured so zealously in the cause of Christianity as to be justly considered the apostle of the South Seas'. Had Marsden been present, he declared, affairs at the Bay of Islands would have been conducted far differently.[28]

Dillon's mind was his own. He judged men by their quality as human beings, as he showed in his warm regard for many Pacific islanders. And he did not spare the European world, or its most eminent personages, from his criticism or the exercise of his wit. He related Moehanga's account of his presentation to George III and his queen.

> 'After I arrived in London, a friend of Dr. Savage (Earl Fitzwilliam) took me to King George's house: I was dressed in my New Zealand mats. We entered a large room, and shortly after King George and Queen Charlotte came in. I was much disappointed: I expected to see a great warrior; but he was an old man that could neither throw a spear nor fire a musket. Queen Charlotte was very old too: she was bent with age. They behaved very kind, and asked me what I liked best in England to take home with me. I told them *tokees* [axes]. Queen Charlotte put her hand under her mat into a little bag that was there, and took out of it some red money (meaning guineas) and gave it to me. Queen Charlotte asked me to give the war-dance of New Zealand. When I did so she appeared frightened: but King George laughed, saying, ha! ha! ha!...
>
> 'Shortly after this I got a wife with some of Queen Charlotte's red money; her name was Nancy. She was very fond of me, and proved pregnant.'[29]

To Dillon, the manners and customs of the Europeans could bear looking at through the eyes of a South Sea islander.

Dillon's book provided a convincing portrait of its author. It also revealed him as a writer of talent, with an unusual gift for narrative and an ability to convey not only the outward form but also the inner feeling of life in exotic communities. It showed his gift for polemic, as a man who could communicate his strong and unconventional opinions through the hammer-blows of invective or the gentler thrusts of wit. Yet, when he had finished it, he was still uneasily aware that he was a sailor, not a writer.

The most famous of his precursors, 'the immortal Cook', had confessed to his own sense of inadequacy in the General Introduction to his *Voyage towards the South Pole, and round the World*.[30] He had asked the reader of his narrative 'to excuse the inaccuracies of style, which doubtless he will frequently meet with' and to 'recollect that it is the production of a man, who has not had the advantage of much school education, but who has been constantly at sea from his youth'. 'After this account of myself', Cook had continued, 'the Public must not expect from me the elegance of a fine writer, or the plausibility of a professed book-maker; but will, I hope, consider me as a plain man, zealously exerting himself in the service of his Country, and determined to give the best account he is able of his proceedings'.

Modelling his apologia on that of his master, Dillon wrote of himself in his Preface:

> As his professional education, studies, and habits of life, have however been hitherto directed to action rather than to the description of the acts of himself or others, he has entered with diffidence on the task of authorship, only when thus imperatively called on to do so, in order that the world may be put in possession of a correct account of the important transactions and extraordinary scenes in which he has had the honour to take part. He does not, therefore, attempt to engage attention by an eloquent style or flowery description, but rests his claim to notice on a simple statement of facts, set forth without ostentation in the unadorned language of a plain seaman. He trusts, therefore, that the reader will not expect from him the niceties of diction which may be justly required of a professed author, but will treat the work with indulgence, as the first essay of an unpractised pen.

If his modest disclaimer was, in part, contradicted by the sophistication —and Irish exuberance—with which it was expressed, he was probably not displeased.

DILLON completed his manuscript towards the end of July.[31] While he was still working on it, he had taken up the matter of its printing and publication. He had read Cook's remark in *A Voyage towards the South Pole*: 'some friends . . . are pleased to think, that what I have here to relate is better to be given in my own words, than in the words of another person'. And he knew that Cook's narrative of his first voyage to the Pacific had been altered when it passed into the editorial hands of John Hawkesworth. For his part, he was determined to retain full control of his work, so as to avoid placing himself 'at the mercy of speculating Booksellers, who would convert the Book into whatever form might suit their own interests'.[32]

He was able to meet his expenses during the period of writing from the 10,000 francs he had received from the French; but he lacked the money with which to finance the book's production. On 23 May he therefore wrote to the Court of Directors of the East India Company suggesting that the Company's printer, J. L. Cox, should be ordered to print it and to receive payment through a first charge on sales.[33] An arrangement on these lines was probably made, for the book was printed by Cox and dedicated 'To the Chairman, Deputy Chairman, and Court of Directors of the Honourable East-India Company . . . by their most obedient, and very humble servant, Peter Dillon'.

He arranged for publication by Hurst, Chance & Company. This was a relatively new firm but one with influential connections. Its senior partner, Thomas Hurst, had formerly been a partner in Longmans and in Hurst, Robinson & Company, of which the latter, in addition to its own publishing activities, had acted as agent for Archibald Constable, of Edinburgh, the founder of the *Edinburgh Review* and owner of the copyright of the *Encyclopaedia Britannica* and Scott's *Waverley Novels*. In the financial crisis of 1825-26, however, both Constable and Hurst, Robinson had become bankrupt. The circumstances of their respective failures had aroused the active sympathy of their literary and business associates. And, when Hurst re-entered publishing in 1827, he was soon able to build up a distinguished list.[34]

By the end of 1829 Hurst, Chance had published over a hundred titles, mainly in the fields of scholarship, travel and *belles lettres*. They included books such as Lockhart's *Life of Robert Burns* and a new edition of Gilbert White's *Natural History of Selborne*. They also included the volumes in 'Constable's Miscellany', the inexpensive series launched by Archibald Constable in the short period between his bankruptcy and death. Although the firm had published a book on Christian missions and was about to publish one on Australia, and had a new edition of Mariner's *Tonga* in the Miscellany, it had shown no special preference for books on the South Seas.[35] But Thomas Hurst, who was—in Constable's words—'beyond all question one of the best men of business in the book trade', was also an enthusiastic patron of aspiring writers and artists of talent: he was presumably impressed by the quality and interest of Dillon's manuscript and, not improbably, by the vivid personality of its author.[36]

During the months preceding the book's appearance, Dillon's name was brought before the interested public on a number of occasions. The *United Service Journal*, in its June number, published an article entitled 'Discovery of the fate of La Pérouse', in which it related Dillon's achievement and made unfavourable reference to 'a Capt. D'Urville' who, it said, had tried to 'wrest from him the merit of the discovery'. 'Our readers', the editor added, 'may depend on the accuracy of this statement, the materials having been kindly furnished by Capt. Dillon'. In November the same journal carried Jenny's narrative of the early years of the settlement at Pitcairn, with which the editor had 'been favoured by Capt. Dillon'. The latter, the editor stated, had 'acquired perhaps a more intimate acquaintance with the manners and customs of the South-Sea Islanders, than any other person living'.[37] And on 17 December the *Times*, in referring to a paper read by Dumont d'Urville on his own findings at Vanikoro, added the comment: 'It is a pity that the gallant captain should have forgotten, in alluding to this subject, all mention of our countryman, Captain Dillon, who had preceded him in this voyage, and had ascertained facts which he did little else but confirm'.

The book itself had been mentioned by the *Asiatic Journal*, in September, as being in the press;[38] and on 15 December 1829 it was published—'In 2 vols. 8vo, price 24s. with Plates'. Dillon was not then in London: he had left for Paris soon after his completion of the manuscript; and he remained there for a year, making arrangements for the French edition and trying to launch himself upon a new career. It was thus from Paris that he despatched copies to his friends and to the eminent whom he wished to honour or to thank. And it was in Paris that he read the first notices of the work by which he set such store.

The book was well received. In February 1830 the *Edinburgh Journal of Natural and Geographical Science* devoted two and a half pages to it.

The profession of Captain Dillon bespeaks indulgence on the score of literary acquirements, though even in that point of view we have little to find fault with in the work, and the energy with which he conducted himself in the enterprize, the difficulties with which he had to battle, render the progress of his expedition a source of pride and interest, and the success which has attended his efforts, have fully entitled him to those rewards and to that credit which he has obtained from European courts, and the suffrage which will be unanimously given him by a British public.

The reviewer made only one criticism: that there was little point in reprinting material from Mariner's *Tonga* 'after its appearance in Constable's cheap Miscellany'.[39]

In March the *Asiatic Journal* carried a review that ran to eight pages. It opened with the sentence: 'The discovery made by Captain or, as we must now designate him, the Chevalier Dillon, ranks amongst the most interesting of modern times'. And it concluded with a comparison between the paper by Dumont d'Urville to which the *Times* had earlier referred and Dillon's book: 'Rhetorical flourishes, and passages written in a style to produce a *sensation*, abound in the former'; it was 'very unlike the simple seaman-like composition of Capt. Dillon'.[40]

The *Narrative and Successful Result of a Voyage in the South Seas* attracted less attention than several other books describing life in distant parts that were published at about the same time. It attracted less, for example, than Lady Raffles's memoir of her late husband, or than M. Caillié's book on Central Africa, or than a book by a former missionary in the Society Islands—William Ellis's *Polynesian Researches*. But it brought Dillon recogniton as a writer, and enhanced his reputation as a navigator.

FOURTEEN

A Chart for Catholicism

1829-30

DILLON returned to Paris with a new plan to enhance his fame and restore his fortunes. Since his arrival in Europe he had been hoping that either the East India Company or the French Government would offer him an appointment in the East; but he had not yet been approached with any such proposal. Now, he had thought out a scheme for the establishment of Roman Catholic missions in the South Seas, under French sponsorship and his own expert guidance and direction.

Before he could devote himself fully to this project, however, he had a more urgent task to attend to: the completion of arrangements for the French edition of his book. In London he had been told that two alternatives were open to him. He could have the book printed, free of charge to himself, by the Imprimerie Royale or, if he chose to have it produced elsewhere, he could be given an undertaking that the government would purchase a sufficient number of copies to reimburse him for his outlay. In Paris, though only after a discouraging delay, he obtained confirmation of the offer and began to examine the alternatives. At the royal press he was informed that the setting of the type could not begin till the translated text had been officially approved and that production of the book would take at least a further three months. He therefore decided to have the work done commercially, since he was afraid that 'Galignani or any of the other Publishers' might buy a copy of the English edition and quickly issue a French translation. When he informed the government of his decision, he was offered a subscription for six hundred copies at a price of fourteen francs, provided he submitted the manuscript or proof-sheets for approval. It was an arrangement, he later wrote, that would cover 'the exact amount of my expense for translating, plates, paper, printing &c &c'.[1]

While he was seeking support for his book, he also launched his campaign for Roman Catholic missions by outlining his ideas to the

Reverend Patrick McSweeny, who, as Rector of the Irish College—a seminary that trained young Irishmen for service as priests in their own country[2]—was well acquainted with the ecclesiastical world of Paris. McSweeny told Dillon that the foundation of a mission to the South Seas was already the overriding ambition of a priest then in Paris, the Reverend Henri de Solages. And he brought the two men together.

For Dillon, Solages was the ideal collaborator. Henri-Gabriel-Jérôme de Solages, a man then in his early forties, was the son of a royalist aristocrat, the Marquis de Solages, and of an English mother. He was both influential and wealthy. Moreover, like other Frenchmen of similar background, he was bilingual and had spent his youth in exile in England. His early interest in the Pacific had been stimulated by the fact that he had been born in the same region of southern France as La Pérouse, and he had been influenced in his decision to enter the priesthood, he later claimed, by a desire 'to work among the savages of the South Sea Islands'. In May 1829 he had taken action towards realizing this desire by seeking the support of the Association for the Propagation of the Faith. During the following month he received a generally favourable response to his proposal for a South Seas mission from the Association. But in July he was offered and, after some hesitation, accepted appointment as Prefect Apostolic of the island of Bourbon (now Réunion) in the Indian Ocean; he hoped that in his new position he would be better placed for the attainment of his larger ambition.[3]

About the end of August Dillon had several discussions with Solages. Sensitive, as always, to the convictions of a listener whose good will he wished to obtain, he talked of his long-established interest in seeing their common religion brought to the islanders, of his own birth in Martinique and consequent desire to promote the political and commercial interests of France in the Pacific: their meeting, he said, made it seem 'as if Divine Providence itself was at work'.[4] His enthusiasm was at least as much simulated as real; but it convinced Solages, who later described him—in words that echoed his own—as a man 'procuré par la Providence' for the propagation of 'notre sainte religion' in the South Seas.[5] On 7 September, at the request of Solages, he committed his ideas to writing.

Dillon's memoir, though addressed to Solages, was also intended for the eyes of others—particularly in government circles.[6] For this reason he began and ended it with references to matters of state. The South Sea Islands, he declared, could soon become as important to the Powers as were those of the Caribbean. They lay athwart the routes from the

American coast to China, India and New South Wales; they possessed valuable resources; they were at the centre of the southern whale fishery. A French colony in the area would be a significant national asset. And, after he had set out his own knowledge of the islands and explained the nature of his influence with many of their rulers, he concluded with a claim that he could now gain for France, with ease, what she would be able to win later only through war and at great expense. The time was ripe, he wrote, for the foundation of French colonies and of French missions. In regard to the latter, he expressed the conviction that the devout Catholicism of Charles X and his most influential minister, the Prince de Polignac—who had recently been recalled from the Embassy in London—ensured official backing.

One of the problems that Dillon and Solages had discussed was that of financing the voyage of the first missionaries to the islands. Dillon's solution of it formed the core of his memoir. Every year, he wrote, a ship was despatched from France with supplies for the French naval vessels based on Rio de Janeiro, Valparaiso and Lima. Ordinarily, she sailed home by the same route in ballast. This programme could be varied, he suggested, so that the ship would also carry a party of missionaries on her outward voyage and, after unloading her cargo, land them in the Pacific before finally returning to France by way of the island of Bourbon and the Cape of Good Hope.

If this plan were adopted, the ship's first port of call after leaving the American coast would be Pitcairn, whose pious inhabitants, he said, lacked a missionary and would therefore welcome a Catholic priest. Next she might visit the Marquesas—where George Ross, his loyal but erratic subordinate in the *Calder*, the *St Patrick* and the *Research*, had once lived as a sandalwood trader. From the Marquesas, she would sail south-west to the Society Islands. This group was almost home to him, he declared: he was the adoptive son of an ancestor of the present queen of Tahiti and owned land in one of the neighbouring islands, on which he would establish the missionaries. He would have no difficulty in persuading the people to accept the Catholics and expel the 'Methodists', as he called the men of the London Missionary Society.

Continuing westward the ship should visit Tonga—where the chief of Ma'ofanga was his special friend—and, after that, Samoa ('the Navigators'). Thence she should proceed to Fiji, 'the most beautiful and fertile of these countries', a land with large rivers that gave access to the interior. Naulivou, 'the king of the largest of these islands', was his friend and had given him the island of Makogai. He could be persuaded to cede his realm to France: it would provide a base for French commerce in time of peace and for the French navy if war should break out between France and England.

After leaving Fiji, he suggested, the ship might perhaps make a deviation—to fulfil the purposes of the voyage he had suggested to the Minister for the Navy six months earlier. In the Santa Cruz Islands a search could be made for possible survivors of La Pérouse's expedition; in the Solomons the work of geographical and ethnographic observation and description could be carried on and an attempt be made to verify the belief of Mendaña and his men that the islands contained deposits of gold and copper. But, in relation to the evangelical and political purposes of the expedition, her next—and final—place of call should be New Zealand. A course should be set for the Hauraki Gulf ('the Schoracai River'). Here, there was ample land for a French colony or factory. New Zealand flax was already in demand in New South Wales and would, in time, become the basis of a substantial trade. Fine timber was plentiful—he could, indeed, readily obtain a cargo of spars to offset the costs of the voyage. And the soil was well suited to the development of viticulture. Moreover, the region had not yet been entered by the Protestants, so that it would be an excellent place at which to land French missionaries, for whom he could obtain the support of Brian Boru and his powerful father.

Solages saw Dillon's memoir as adding material substance to his vision. He translated and printed it, as *Mémoire adressé a M. le Préfet d'Île Bourbon par le Capitaine Dillon*. He sent copies of it to church authorities in Paris and Rome and to the Minister for the Navy.[7] He used it as the basis upon which to build the next stage of his campaign.

Much to his satisfaction, Dillon himself became directly involved in Solages's politicking. In addition to their visits to church authorities, the two men were granted an interview by the Minister for the Navy, Baron d'Haussez, during which they emphasized the military value to France of accepting Dillon's plan. They referred to the existing tension between France and Britain and suggested that, in the event of this leading to war, New South Wales could be attacked from the proposed settlements in Fiji and New Zealand. In a subsequent letter to the Minister, Solages declared:

> The greater part of the population of this colony is composed of Catholics of Irish origin, who long for the moment when they will be able to throw off the English yoke.

It was a mischievous and erroneous claim that seems certain to have been inspired by Dillon.

The two men were remarkably successful in their advocacy. Although their arguments were, in part, specious or disingenous, they were presented to a government anxious to strengthen its hand against England and deeply sensitive to the claims of the Church. As a result, Solages received from Polignac in mid-October the offer of a ship. She would not be the annual storeship to South America but a naval vessel placed wholly at his disposal for the duration of the voyage. Moreover, a little later—after Dillon had written a second letter enlarging on the commercial advantages of French settlements in the Pacific—the government offered to provide free passages for the missionaries, to purchase land for them in the islands, and to supply them with tools and other equipment they would need.[9]

Before the end of October Dillon returned to London to prepare for the expedition that he was confident would sail from France early in the new year. Prior to his departure he had also completed arrangements for the publication of his book by a reputable Paris firm, Chez Pillet Aîné, and for the forwarding of the proof-sheets to the Ministry of Justice for approval as they came off the press.[10] The French edition, when it emerged from the hands of the author and the translator, differed in some respects from the English. It bore a slightly different title—*Voyage aux îles de la Mer du Sud en 1827 et 1828, et relation de la découverte du sort de La Pérouse* . . . —and a new dedication—'A Sa Majesté Très-Chrétienne, Charles X, Roi de France et de Navarre'. Dillon also made changes in the text. He omitted the long chapter on the 'Manners and Customs of the Friendly Islanders' and condensed the appendix of documents relating to the confrontation between him and Tytler—probably in both cases to reduce cost. Elsewhere, he added a few short passages to clarify the narrative and made a number of small corrections—for example, in his references to d'Entrecasteaux who, he had recently discovered from reading Rossel's narrative, had actually sighted Vanikoro and named it Île de la Recherche after one of his ships. And, probably with an eye to his new association with Roman Catholic dignitaries, he deleted a tribute to Samuel Marsden.[11]

Back in London, he ordered his life to accord with his expectations. While awaiting the arrival of further news from France, he fitted himself out for the forthcoming voyage 'at great expense'. In addition to clothes and books, he bought a new set of nautical instruments,[12] more adequate symbols, no doubt, of his present status as a navigator than those he had used to win it. And the news, as it gradually trickled through to him, seemed to justify his extravagance. He learnt that the ship *Dordogne* was assigned to the expedition, that Solages's approaches to the ecclesiastical authorities were being favourably received. At about the same time as his *Narrative and Successful Result of a Voyage in the South Seas* was published, he received a letter from Polignac informing him that he had been appointed 'vice-consul *honoraire* dans les îles qui composent l'archipel de l'Océan Pacifique'. His Majesty, Polignac wrote, wished to send missionaries to the islands and also to establish commercial and shipping connections with them.

> You have shown yourself more suitable than anyone, sir, to carry out this mission with some chance of success, since you combine with an already proven zeal a knowledge of the customs and language of the islanders.
>
> I have no doubt that your efforts will fully justify the honourable selection of which you are today the object.[13]

Dillon also received word that he would be granted a sum of 3,000 francs for his expenses.[14]

In this moment of triumph, when he had become known in London not only as an explorer but also as an author, a French consul and the prospective leader of an important French expedition to the South Seas, Dillon had only one cause for worry and regret: except for his small pension, he was entirely without funds. He remembered the unpaid claim for his expenses in chartering the *Little Mary* after the wreck of the *Phatisalam*. On 23 December he therefore wrote to the Secretary of State for the Colonies, Sir George Murray, explaining the circumstances and seeking repayment of £245, together with 'Colonial Interest at the rate of 8 p. cent' per annum.[15] But, as the letter failed to elicit a quick response, his only source of ready money was from the sale of his 'furniture and plate at a considerable sacrifice'.[16]

Precariously solvent but confident about his future, Dillon despatched his outfit for the Pacific voyage to France; and early in January 1830—'in the midst of a tempestuous winter'—he set out for Paris, accompanied by Mary and Martha.[17]

FIFTEEN

In the Wake of Success

1830-34

IN AUGUST 1830 Dillon returned to London by himself. He was still short of money;[1] the July Revolution in France must have brought with it immediate uncertainty, and in the upshot brought with it a reduction of his French pension—apparently his main source of fixed income—to 3,750 francs or at that time about £145 a year. He had therefore to leave Mary and his daughter Martha in Paris, and what provision, if any, he was able to make for his children in Australia is obscure.[2] But he had high hopes that he would soon be able to return to them, his claims vindicated, and with money for the style of life he considered their due as well as his own. Poor as he was, he may have felt himself relatively fortunate among the doleful retinue of refugees —former officials of Charles X—who were crossing the Channel on the morrow of revolution. For example, his old acquaintance the Baron d'Haussez, formerly the Minister for the Navy, arrived in London *incognito* under the name of Mercher.[3] Ironically, it was Charles X's Prime Minister, Polignac, from whose patronage Dillon must have entertained high but reasonable anticipations, who by his ill-judged decrees had brought on *Les Trois Glorieuses* and the downfall of the legitimist dynasty.

Dillon was returning to a London where his name should now be more widely known: his book had been out for eight months, and while it had not been so extensively reviewed as some others in similar fields, notices had been favourable and even flattering; perhaps most gratifying in a more than implied preference for his narrative to that of Dumont d'Urville. Despite the upheaval of the Revolution, things must have seemed set fair.

In London Dillon settled at 2 South Crescent, Bedford Square, a pleasant tree-shaded spot just off Tottenham Court Road, in the house where Sandford Arnot and Duncan Forbes conducted the London

Oriental Institution, teaching Hindustani, Persian, and Bengali to young men about to serve in the East.[4] Forbes had been a master at the Calcutta Academy, and in 1837 was to become Professor of Oriental Languages at King's College, London; Dillon had probably known both men in Calcutta. During the next few years, when he was in London, Dillon seems to have used a clerk or student of theirs as his amanuensis,[5] and probably some of his contacts with scholars and scientists were made through them. The Institute was also useful as a good accommodation and forwarding address.

Other friends from the Pacific were in England: Edward Lord, who had supported him in Hobart, and Peter Bays, who was writing his *Wreck of the Minerva Whaler*. There were also more eminent acquaintances from the Calcutta days, for instance Earl Amherst and Lord Combermere, to whom, amongst others, he presented copies of his book.[6] Among scientists he knew Aylmer Bourke Lambert, F.R.S., Vice-President of the Linnean Society, who had been a friend of Sir Joseph Banks. Such a connection with the associate of Cook was a sure title to Dillon's interest, and Lambert came to possess, by gift or purchase, one of the medals distributed by Cook in the Pacific and picked up by Dillon in the New Hebrides, and the Rodríguez manuscript which he had acquired at Lima. Dillon seems also to have had a number of friends among the Irish aristocracy.

DURING Dillon's last months in France, when it seemed likely that the missionary project would either fail or else succeed without his own participation in it, he had begun to think of other ways of returning to the Pacific or India. He tried to interest a group of 'friends and relations of mine in France, Frenchmen bred and born'[7] in emigration to New South Wales or Van Diemen's Land. The scheme was for them to invest their capital of about £30,000 in a ship and a cargo of French goods for sale in the colonies, in the manner he himself had found profitable on his voyages from Calcutta. On arrival the migrants would apply for grants of land to develop as vineyards, use the ship as a whaler, and establish a business house. His friends, he declared, were willing to embark on this venture if he could provide them with satisfactory answers to certain questions, which he put to the Secretary of State for the Colonies in April 1830.[8] Would Frenchmen be given land grants proportionate to the capital they introduced into the colony, 'as is the case with British subjects'? Would they receive the same whaling privilege as 'was formerly held out to foreigners who were allowed to settle at Milford Haven, for the purposes of carrying on the whale fishery in the South Seas'? Would a French ship, with a cargo of French goods, 'be permitted to enter at the Custom House', and what duty would be payable? He gave, in some detail, his own interpretation of the relevant legislation, and declared that if the rate of duty levied should be (as seemed likely) not higher than 'fifteen per cent ad valorem on the invoice price of the goods in France', his friends would think this reasonable. He himself, apparently, would have been the leader of this expedition.

The Colonial Office boggled at this demand for answers to such highly technical questions and referred the matter to the Board of Trade.[9] After a delay which Dillon found most exasperating, he was informed, in May, of what was being done in the matter.[10] Finally, towards the end of June, he got his answer: 'I am directed to inform you that their Lordships [of the Board of Trade] have informed the Secretary of State that it is not the function of the Board to return answers to Queries on the effect of Acts of Parliament, proposed to them by persons engaged in commercial operations . . .'.[11] With this bland piece of bureaucratic unhelpfulness, the project was effectively killed. To Dillon it was one of many such acts from which he suffered and which drove him increasingly to seek his objectives, where officials were concerned, by fair means or foul.

Meantime, however, he had not been placing all his hopes on this one venture. In the middle of May he told Lord Stuart that he hoped shortly to return to India: 'If a rupture should take place with the Chinese', he wrote optimistically,' . . . it will give me an opportunity of once more advancing my fortune, being an experienced pilot for the China Seas. I would . . . most likely be again employed to command one of the cruisers or armed steam vessels.'[12] But that prospect, as he cannot have been wholly unaware, was not much more than an opium dream.

Now, in London, during August and the following months, he turned his energies towards much nearer objectives. Behind the exuberant façade he presented to the world there lurked, never far from the surface, a nagging fear of destitution. He remembered the hungry days of the past winter, the present poverty of his wife in Paris, the angry faces of his creditors. He had returned to London seeking the money he believed was due to him.

He was certain he had a clear case against the Colonial Office in respect of the money he had been forced to pay in 1821 for saving the ship's company, passengers and mails from the wrecked *Phatisalam*. He had protested to Governor Macquarie at the time and then to his successor Sir Thomas Brisbane, but in vain. He had left the matter standing until his return to England because, he said, of advice from his lawyers that a legal action against the Governor would be fruitless. In December 1829 he had written to the Secretary of State for the Colonies, Sir George Murray. His argument was straightforward.[13]

The schooner *Little Mary* had been chartered at a cost of £200 by the commandant at George Town to rescue the shipwrecked people and the mails. But if the passengers and crew were British subjects, as they were, the government had an obligation to assist them, clearly defined by the Act 32 George III, c. 33; as for the mails, Dillon was carrying them without remuneration, and the East India Company was liable for the cost of salvage. But, in fact, before he left Port Dalrymple he had been required to accept liability for the costs by bond, and eventually he was obliged to pay it. Moreover, since he could get no promise that his Lascars would be fed and housed at George Town, he had been forced to spend another £45 for their passages to Sydney. These two sums had been wrongfully demanded by the New South Wales Government, and he therefore asked the Colonial Office to repay him the £245, plus interest for eight years. The ultimate responsibility as between New South Wales and the East India Company could then be settled at an official level—it was no concern of his.

The Colonial Office felt that Dillon's argument had considerable substance, but all he was told before he returned to Paris in the New Year (1831) was that the matter had been referred to the Commissioners for the Affairs of India.[14] A month later he was told that the Commissioners had in turn forwarded the correspondence to the East India Company's Court of Directors, which had decided that it had no obligation to pay for the rescuing of the convicts, since Dillon had already been paid for transporting them from Calcutta to Sydney.[15] Not a word was said about the saving of the passengers and crew or of the mails. Dillon concluded, as did the Colonial Office after a further exchange of letters, that the full correspondence had not been forwarded to the Company. In July the Commissioners were asked to refer the matter again to the Directors, and Dillon was told that he would hear the result from the Company direct.[16]

But the Colonial Office was not to be allowed to escape so lightly. Back in London, and in urgent need of funds, Dillon bombarded the office with more letters. He began with a note to Hay in October:

> Captain Dillon's compliments to Mr Hay and begs Mr H. will pardon the liberty Captain D. takes in trepassing on his time, which he certainly would not do was it not that he is at present in great distress for the want of money, being now completely pennyless; having lost of late several hundred pounds sterling by the evil proceedings of the Prince de Polignac...[17]

On 1 November he wrote again to Hay, whom he regarded throughout these proceedings as his friend.

> I have been reduced from oppulence to poverty and distress... The above sum of £245 to me at the approach of a tempestuous winter may save myself and family from ruin, it would be more to me at the present moment of distress than £2000 at any other period of my life.

And he added—thinking of what he had bought or been given in the Society Islands and Fiji—'I have a considerable property left from the wreck of my fortune, but it is situated at the remotest parts of the Globe from which I cannot derive immediate relief'.[18] Two days later he set out the facts, once again, to Sir George Murray. Was it lawful for the government to take steps, regardless of cost, to rescue the victims of shipwreck, and then force the captain to pay? If so, then surely the fact should be made public so that 'shipwrecked and ruined commanders may know the dreadful fate that awaits them in British Ports'.[19]

On the following day, 4 November, Hay wrote to Dillon on his earlier letters: 'I am directed by Secretary Sir G. Murray to express his regret that your case, altho' a very unfortunate one, does not admit any relief being offered to you by H.M. Government'. This of course led to a further exchange. Dillon claimed to have important new evidence and asked for an immediate interview with Hay and James Stephen, the Legal Adviser; he was told to submit his evidence in writing, and did so. He explained that in 1821 he had received an advance from the New South Wales Government for victualling the Lascars while they were in the colony, undertaking to repay this if the expenditure were disallowed in England. In fact, his bond had been cancelled, but he had since found that the Colonial Office had obtained reimbursement from the East India Company. This was an admission by the Directors of the Company's responsibility for shipwrecked Indian seamen, and a claim made at the same time by the Colonial Office for the expenses of the schooner would also have been met.

Dillon had put forward this view in discussion with the Chairman of the Court, William Astell, M.P., and believed that the Company would now meet the claim; he therefore asked the Colonial Office to resubmit the matter to the Company. Alternatively, he wished to petition the King-in-Council. If neither course were adopted, he threatened to bring an action against Sir Thomas Brisbane personally.[20]

After further prodding, the Colonial Office did ask the Company to reconsider the matter.[21] But Dillon, financially distressed as he was, thought that he should receive reimbursement at once. In December he wrote to the new Secretary of State, Lord Goderich, asking for an interview, backing this up with a letter of introduction from Lord Amherst and the gift of a copy of his *Narrative*. Murray, he said, had left the matter to Stephen, whose legal opinion differed from that of much more distinguished lawyers; but as to Goderich, 'the generality of men in England gives Your Lordship the credit of being a Nobleman perfectly conversant with business'.[22] Goderich saw him, and apparently his petition was presented; but still he got no money.

By January 1831 his position was really desperate. His pension, his only steady source of income, was paid into his account with the banking house of Lafitte. Jacques Lafitte, the head of the firm, had been one of the principal organizers of Louis Philippe's accession to the throne and became the first Premier of the July Monarchy. By the end of 1830 his bank was in serious difficulties: Lafitte had placed its resources at the disposal of the new régime and, absorbed in politics, had lost touch with its affairs. At this time it had temporarily closed its doors.[23] Dillon wrote again to Goderich: '. . . I am without a Shilling occasioned by the late interruption of business in Lafitte and Co's Banking house at Paris . . .'.[24] In his anguish, he came out openly with a suspicion that had long been in his mind. All his life he believed that nepotism was one of the strongest motives in the actions of public men; he did not disapprove of it, but he bitterly resented the fact that he had no relatives able or willing to pull strings for *him*. Now he suggested to Goderich that Sir George Murray had been unhelpful because of family connections with Brisbane. He himself, a gentleman born and bred, had rendered important service 'to humanity' and had 'Capacity and Experience sufficient to benefit the commerce of his country': but lacking influence, he was left to starve.

This imputation of improper motives did him no good. Even if—or even more if—his charge had had some basis, this attack by an outsider was bound to be resented; Lord Howick, the new Parliamentary

Under-Secretary, simply refuted it, and a chastened Dillon had to declare 'I have to regret my credulity'. For the time being, his onslaught on the Office was dropped.[25]

DURING these same months Dillon had been pursuing his claims against the French Government. While he was in Paris the Ambassador, Lord Stuart de Rothesay, had helped him privately, but explained that he could not take up his case officially without instructions from the Foreign Office. On legal advice, Dillon made a deposition of the facts to the Lord Mayor, transmitted a copy to the Foreign Secretary, and asked that it should be passed to the Ambassador for action.[26] He explained that his pension—reduced like other French pensions by three per cent—was 'now all that is left to us'. He argued that it must be regarded not as an indemnity for expenditure but as a reward for achievement, otherwise 'a great Nation . . . was repaying by instalments, which I could not expect to live long enough to receive'. This request was dealt with as he requested, and the papers forwarded to the Ambassador.

Meanwhile, Dillon wrote also to the Duc d'Orléans, eldest son of Louis Philippe, and to Talleyrand, then Ambassador in London, and had received sympathetic replies from both Princes.[27] Talleyrand in his second letter averred 'I wish it was in my power to put an end to the embarrassment in which you find yourself'; he had written twice to the Minister of Foreign Affairs insisting 'in the most pressing manner, on the necessity of repairing by a prompt decision the fatal results of your voyage to Europe'.[28]

When Lord Granville replaced Lord Stuart as British Ambassador in Paris, Dillon feared that his case might be forgotten—a groundless fear, as Granville soon exerted himself on behalf of his claims.[29] Late in February 1831, however, Dillon returned to Paris, partly to press his claims on the spot, partly to rejoin his wife and daughter. Within a few weeks, he was busy lobbying the French Government.

He began in March by interviewing several Ministers to force the agreed quota of his books on Ministries which had not taken them, while canvassing his general claims more widely. He wrote, for example, to a courtier, Comte Laborde, whose brother had sailed with La Pérouse, recounting not only his loss of fortune but the petty indignities to which his poverty exposed him: 'My plate is in the hands of a pawnbroker at Paris, my baggage . . . is now detained at the custom house at Southampton . . . My chronometers and instruments, are detained by MMrs Barraud in London, as a pledge; and my watch is in the hands of an English pawnbroker'. He asked Laborde to use his influence and, in particular, to try to obtain permission for his daughter Martha to enter one of the schools for the daughters of French 'knights' at St Germain or St Denis.[30]

Dillon's position at this time was an alternation of hope and despair. On 13 April, on the request of Lord Granville, he was granted an audience by King Louis Philippe—his second meeting with a French monarch. To the King he presented a memorial of his claims, but six weeks later, having received no answer, he declared that he was returning to England to 'throw myself on the mercy of the British Public'.[31] But he did not go: instead he settled down to prepare an Address to the Cabinet, with a selection of letters and accounts to prove his case *A Son Excellence M. le Président du Conseil des Ministres, Et aux Membres composant le Conseil de S.M. le Roi de France*,[32]—an elaborate document of over twenty pages, well printed on heavy quarto paper. There are both French and English versions of this Address and its accompanying *pièces justificatives*.

In the Address Dillon repeats that he had been 'so unfortunate' as to discover the fate of La Pérouse, and was subsequently dealt with 'in a cruel and unchristian-like manner' by the former government. At Tikopia he had learnt that survivors of the expedition were said to be still alive; 'overwhelmed with grief at this melancholy intelligence, I considered it a duty which I owed to God, to humanity, to science, to relieve the victims of scientific research from bondage . . .' He described the voyage of the *Research*, his losses in Calcutta during his absence through the Barretto failure, and his return to Europe. Of the promises made to him in 1829 by the Polignac Government several had still not been honoured: he had not received pay and allowances, at the rate granted him by the East India Company, during the voyage of the *Research*, for the subsequent period in which he claimed to have been serving France; he had not been given a return passage to India; the agreement to purchase copies of his book had been kept only in part. During 1830 he had incurred further heavy expenditure in preparing to go out to the Pacific, as French consul . . . The total result of his relations with the French Government was that he was reduced to destitution and was heavily in debt.[33] He asked that 'the present enlightened Monarch and Ministers' should see that justice was done.

For the rest of July he followed up the Address by calling on Ministers and writing to them. He suggested that his claims could most easily be met by an order on the French Resident at Chandernagore; if this were given quickly, he could leave at once for India and collect from the Resident when the receipts from salt and opium sales were received in October. But the government doubted the validity of his claim: it could find no written authority in the files. This of course greatly angered Dillon: 'I have throughout life bore the character of an honest man and gentleman, doubt was never thrown on my word until unfortunately, unfortunately I say I had something to do with the French Government'.[34]

During August two interludes, one a private affair and the other an affair of state, occupied some of Dillon's time. Earlier in the year the trial and conviction for rape of a young namesake, Luke Dillon, had aroused widespread controversy in Ireland. Luke Dillon was a personable young man of good family, a Dillon of Mount Dillon, County Roscommon; he had been a gay and self-assured defendant, and many people thought he had been wrongfully convicted. When the original sentence of death was commuted to transportation for life to New South Wales, his family and friends took steps to ensure him a sympathetic reception in the colony. One of those upon whom they called for help was Peter Dillon; he wrote letters for the young man to take with him—one to Alexander Macleay, the Colonial Secretary, another to Father Therry.[35] Dillon showed an intimate awareness of the background and circumstances of the 'unfortunate youth' who had fallen 'a victim to one of the darkest female conspiracies ever formed against man', and declared that any help that could be given him would be 'a great favor' to himself. We shall meet Luke again.

At about the same time, he tried to promote yet another scheme which would enable him to return to the South Seas. As a result of the Belgian rising of 1830 against the Dutch, the Powers had drawn up a protocol in January 1831, establishing the boundaries of an independent state, and in April had given Belgium the first King Leopold. What did a new nation want, thought Dillon, so much as a few rich colonies? In discussion with the Belgian envoy in Paris, he suggested the acquisition of Fiji and offered to command the expedition to be sent to annex the islands. The envoy sent an account of the talks to his government, but no action followed—it took eight years and some hard fighting before the Dutch recognized Belgium's independence.[36] Once again Dillon was denied the opportunity of becoming an Empire Builder.

From these digressions he returned to the business of trying to extract money from the French Government. He printed his long letter of 17 September to Sebastiani, which was in large part a commentary on a letter from the Minister to Granville, of which he had received a copy.[37] It was reprehensible of Sebastiani to cast doubt on the motives of Lord Stuart in supporting Dillon's claims so strongly; the Ambassador had simply maintained what he believed to be right. Sebastiani had referred to the decline of interest in La Pérouse since the reward had been offered in 1791[38]; but the lapse of time had not made Dillon's own voyage less costly, either in terms of the East India Company's money or the hardships of himself and his family. Sebastiani had accused him of a wearisome persistence in regard to both his claims and the proposed expedition of 1830; but what other course could he have taken in the face of disingenuousness and intrigue? His initial mistake had been to believe that the word of a Frenchman was as sacred as that of a British Minister... Again, Sebastiani had listed the honours and rewards that Dillon had received: but the 10,000 francs for his expenses in coming to Europe had fallen short of his actual expenditure; his pension had been reduced from 4,000 to 3,750 francs (proportionate to cuts in other pensions); and the years of enforced unemployment had reduced him to 'frightful poverty'. As to the honour bestowed upon him, he had not asked for it and would have refused it had he thought that acceptance would debar him from receiving financial justice.

What could now be done? Dillon suggested that he and Sebastiani should each appoint an arbitrator as the quickest way to reach a settlement;[39] he would bind himself to accept the decision. But he added a more limited request—one he had made before, but in vain. Would the government pay him his pension for three years in advance? This would at least enable him to satisfy his creditors and to return to his children in India.[40]

As autumn turned to winter Dillon was still in Paris waiting, vainly, for some sign of a decision. Early in the New Year he probably received the remaining sum due to him for the copies of his book.[41] He decided to return to London, leaving Lafitte to present to the Chamber of Deputies a petition for which he had received promises of support from 'several members from the centre and opposition benches of the house'.[42] To wind up this part of the story, on 24 May 1832 the East India Company asked the Secretary of State for Foreign Affairs to secure from the French reimbursement of the cost of the La Pérouse expedition; on 26 May the Foreign Office replied that no claim could be made.[43]

DILLON was back at South Crescent, or at least using the address, by 14 March 1832, when he wrote to Lord Stuart de Rothesay of his new plans: 'I am now thinking of going out to India or to one of the New Settlements about to be formed on the South Coast of New Holland or New Zealand'. To some extent this was anticipating the facts, but against the background of his need for a job, his optimism is not surprising, for there were indeed groups of people in England concerned with founding settlements in both southern Australia and New Zealand. In the latter case, the interest was a fairly narrow commercial one: a group was interested in exploiting a process sponsored by one J. J. Donlan to render *Phormium tenax* (New Zealand flax) a satisfactory substitute for hemp, and the time seemed ripe for its large-scale commercial exploitation.[44] The position as regards southern Australia was different. Charles Sturt's descent of the Murray, known in England by the end of 1830, had revealed a great area of well-watered land accessible from the southern coast, and a group of men interested in Edward Gibbon Wakefield's principles of colonization, as well as in making their own fortunes, were planning the settlement of South Australia.

Dillon heard of this project while still in Paris, and wrote to one of the promoters telling him of his own visit to the area in 1815.[45] On his return to London he was asked if he would give evidence as to the suitability for settlement of Kangaroo Island and Port Lincoln. This he did, and his answers were included in a promotional pamphlet.[46] His answers were straightforward: he told of his experiences in catching seals and collecting salt, referred to the difficulty in obtaining fresh water on Kangaroo Island, and spoke of 'the verdant plains without trees' that he had seen on the mainland. It seems likely that he hoped to obtain the command of the colonizers' ship *Nereid*, but the post went to a Captain Sutherland, who had shown less scruple in speaking of the desirability of South Australia.

Whether for this reason or more public-spirited ones, Dillon now became an avowed enemy of the South Australian colonizers, although his evidence continued to be quoted. When he read the pamphlet, he wrote to R. W. Hay at the Colonial Office, saying that he had answered specific questions put to him; but had he known that his statements were to be used to justify to the public the whole scheme, he would have felt compelled to mention also less favourable aspects.[47] As the months passed, he observed with apparent satisfaction the increasing confusion of the project, writing again to Hay to congratulate him on his successful opposition and adding caustic comments on the originators.⁴⁸ Major Anthony Bacon and Mr Robert Gouger he dismissed as needy adventurers: Bacon had ordered the purchase of the *Nereid* though funds had not been available to pay for her, had misappropriated £700 of the proceeds of the forced re-sale, and then 'like a brave patriot set out to espouse the cause of Don Pedro at Oporto'; the respectable persons cited by Gouger as supporting the project 'knew no more of its origins than the Grand Mogul'.

Dillon was more positive on New Zealand: it was after all a country he knew well and for whose people he had a warm regard. If he could have his choice, it would be one of the two or three places in the Pacific where he would most happily settle. He urged the settlement of New Zealand upon all he met, especially business men who might be induced to put up the capital for a pioneering venture, and even claimed to have persuaded Sir Augustus d'Este, the illegitimate son of the Duke of Sussex, to consider the possibility of becoming Governor of New Zealand should it become a British colony.⁴⁹

In May he published a pamphlet, *Extract of a letter from the Chevalier Dillon, to an influential character here, on the advantages to be derived from the establishment of well conducted Commercial Settlements in New Zealand,* in which he set out his views, based on 'deliberations and experience'. New Zealand was 'one of the finest countries under the sun', with a 'fine agreeable climate' and 'as well watered as any in the world', endowed with excellent harbours and many navigable rivers—so many indeed that in the northern part of North Island 'So great are the facilities afforded by water carriage . . . that there will not be any necessity for roads or bridges for many years to come'. Above all it possessed a variety of products for an immediately valuable export trade. In other colonies, such as those in Australia, a major difficulty had been the lack of an export staple in the early years; in New Zealand this difficulty would not exist.

As for 'the sons of nature' who inhabited New Zealand, Dillon had 'always found them to be a generous, kind hearted, and grateful people'. Objection was often made to their cannibalism, but they were by no means unique in this: the Caribs, the people of interior Brazil . . . It must needs be said, also, that the Maoris neither tortured their victims nor killed a man just 'for the sake of eating him':

> It is, therefore, more a religious rite to which superstition compels them to submit, than any natural propensity to cruelty. And if we consider the female sacrifices of India, so recently abolished, and the sanguinary rites of the Druids in our country in former times, we will rather be inclined to look

with pity on the ignorance of the New Zealanders, who are so many ages behind us in civilization, than to regard them as naturally more inhumane than other tribes of men.

Indeed, when once the Maoris had benefited from intercourse with more civilized people, 'there is no reason why New Zealand should not improve as this country has done, which was itself in a similar state in the time of the Romans'.

Already it had been proved that Europeans could live happily among the Maoris. Those few who had suffered at Maori hands had brought their fate on themselves by the injury they had done; for the rest, missionaries and traders lived in peace, and among the latter many had 'married into the most respectable native families'.

The British population of New Zealand already numbered 'upwards of five hundred', who had built up a substantial trade. They bought flax and potatoes from the Maoris, produced salt pork, made planks, oars and rafters from New Zealand timber, built vessels—'and all these works are carried on without the smallest support from the government of this country'. If English capital and business organization were applied to New Zealand, this commerce could be rapidly expanded, and moreover the country could be used as a base for the development of trade with the Pacific Islands.

At this point Dillon inserts a prospectus, in the best manner of an eighteenth century projector, of the trade of a well-organized company, amounts and returns duly itemized. After twelve months, 'or say in the course of the second year after their arrival in the Country', they could export 1,500 tons of flax, 1,000 of cocoanut oil, 500 of sperm oil, 50 of arrowroot (demand for these four items increasing yearly); 400 tons of potatoes, in great demand at Sydney; 6,000 lbs of tortoiseshell, in demand all over the world; say three cargoes of spars, sawed timber, and oars, needed in China, South America, New South Wales, and even Europe. These items alone, at current rates, added up to £13,900 a year. Moreover there were pearls, mother of pearl; salt fish 'To be had in ship-loads'; seal skins; 'Various beautiful Sea Shells Some selling, now in London, as high as 15 guineas each'; shark fins for China; ambergris ('scarce, but it can be procured at some of the Islands'); bêche-de-mer or trepang—'The real Black kind' worth £110 12s a ton at Canton; barilla [an inferior alkali from kelp]; potash, and tan bark, all 'in abundance'; rope from coir and hemp, both 'In great demand all over the world'; rattans or canes 'in Ship-loads'; nutmegs 'in great abundance, will pay well, though not of the first quality'; rosin in plenty from the pines; green marble, 'A very rare commodity in Europe, and will no doubt, pay well'; and finally sandalwood, 'Very abundant on certain islands', especially 'the Fegee Islands', which has sold in Canton at £50-60 per ton, though now worth only £33.

On 9 May 1832 Dillon sent a copy of the pamphlet to the Secretary of State for the Colonies, Lord Goderich, saying that 'As my friends intend to proceed as proposed in my letter, I beg the kind protection of your Lordships department for so laudable an undertaking'.[50] Clearly, if a company were to be formed he hoped to be one of its principal officers; but the acknowledgement of his letter opened up a new and almost startling possibility:

> His Lordship desires me to acquaint you, that H.M. Govt. have not overlooked the importance of the commercial intercourse which at present exists between this Country and those Islands, and that it is in their contemplation to place a Resident at the Bay of Islands or other suitable Station in New Zealand for the better protection of the persons who may be engaged in it.[51]

No whisper of this intention had previously reached Dillon or his friends. He had been working for a commercial settlement, with the expectation that there would be some political intervention in support of it later; but now it seemed that the government was already prepared to act. This required a change in his own tactics: for who could be so well qualified for the post of British Resident as he?

In fact, however, Hay had given him only half the story. For some time the Colonial Office had been hearing of the lawless behaviour of British subjects on the shores of New Zealand and of the consequent deterioration of relations between Maoris and Europeans; it had been realized that some action would have to be taken soon. While Dillon was still in Paris, the Secretary of State had become acquainted with the merits of a young man who was home from Sydney looking for a job. This was James Busby, whose father had fled from the Bay of Islands—with Dillon—in 1825; he had held an official post in New South Wales and appeared well-informed and intelligent. In March 1832 Goderich had decided to instruct the Governor of New South Wales to appoint Busby as Resident in New Zealand.

Knowing nothing of this decision, Dillon at once prepared a Memorial setting out his claims to the position. He referred to his visits to New Zealand, his friendship with Maori chiefs, and his practice of taking 'Chiefs and superior Men with him to various parts of the

World to shew them the manners and customs of Christian and Civilised Nations, that they might introduce improvements into their own country'; he had spent money on these travellers, 'education, victualling, clothing and dispensing Medecine amongst them and in having them vaccinated &c.'. Because of the knowledge of their language and customs thus gained, and of his sympathetic contact with the Maori people, he averred that he would be a better Resident than someone who lacked these advantages and was 'unacquainted with the management of savage tribes of Men'.[52]

He did not immediately forward this document to the Secretary of State. Experience had made him wary of relying simply on his own arguments; government posts went to those who had influential backers. He therefore sought assistance from powerful acquaintances. The six signatories to a note supporting his Memorial indicate the circles in which he moved; they were Aylmer Lambert and his brother-in-law John Benett, M.P.; Dominick Browne, M.P., who had served in China and was Vice-President of the Royal Asiatic Society; Sir Francis Vincent, M.P.; and Mr T. Bracken, partner in Alexander and Company of Calcutta. All the M.P.s are described as 'Liberal'.[53]

Before actually presenting his Memorial, Dillon called on R. W. Hay at the Colonial Office.[54] At this interview he received the unwelcome news that the New Zealand Residency was already promised to someone else. That avenue closed, he at first turned his mind once more to fostering commercial promotion, but received little response. By the end of July he felt so dispirited that he decided to try again for an official post. He sent in the Memorial as a proof of his merits and deserts, and asked that he might be considered for 'any other situation which may be vacant in that quarter of the globe'; Hay's reply was discouraging.[55] Dillon did not yet give up, and at the beginning of October Hay offered to talk to him again about the matter, while making it clear that any offer was very unlikely.[56] By this time Dillon was once more hopeful of interesting his business friends in commercial schemes: he had been talking with 'commercial men, Bankers, Merchants, Ship Owners' and others, and giving them copies of his pamphlet.[57]

He found them ready enough to accept his opinion of the economic possibilities of New Zealand, but loath to risk their capital until there was some form of British administration. The picture that had been built up in England of the Maoris as warlike cannibals, inclined at any moment to turn upon unoffending and defenceless settlers, was hard to break down; Dillon's vivid accounts of his Maori friends roused no answering sympathy in the minds of his hearers. He therefore submitted to Hay that if the government would support the Resident with a small force of troops, investors would be ready to venture their capital.[58]

But time passed, with no visible result for Dillon's labours. He talked of his plans; he kept in touch with his friends; he followed the news day by day in the vain hope that circumstance would present him with an opportunity. His past achievements were not quite forgotten; a writer in the *Nautical Magazine* wrote of 'the indefatigable research of Captain Dillon'; Edward Gibbon Wakefield referred to 'Captain Dillon, the well-known discoverer of the remains of La Pérouse'.[59] But at forty-five, when he still hoped that the most distinguished part of his career lay ahead of him, he was rendered helpless by his lack of funds. No capitalists would found a Pacific colonizing company of whose operations he could take charge; no government would give him an appointment; the French would not pay him the money he believed was his due.

WEARILY, he turned back to the East India Company to press again the old *Phatisalam* claims. He received sympathy, but no money. In June 1833 he wrote once more to Hay: 'I beg that you will pardon the liberty I take in informing you that I have been transferred back again to the Colonial Department with my claim'.[60] On the previous day he had left a long petition with the Rt Hon. E. G. S. Stanley, the Secretary of State, traversing yet again the whole history of the wreck and arguing with some force the legal points involved.[61] 'On an examination of these Papers', Stanley minuted a few days later, 'I am inclined to think the claim well founded. I should be glad to be informed on what grounds it is resisted, not as between one Department and another, but as between the Govt. and the individual.' Hay, too, was inclined to favour Dillon, though he thought there was 'something very equivocal' in parts of his argument. Only James Stephen, the Legal Adviser, rejected the claim out of hand. Dillon, in conversation with officials, came to know of this difference of opinion within the Office; in October he drew Stanley's attention to the effect of Stephen's antagonism, and again the Secretary of State minuted his belief that the claim was justified.[62] In November Dillon asked Stanley's private secretary, Earl, to try to expedite a settlement, as he expected to sail for India shortly. In January 1834 he called on Earl to discuss the matter further, writing next day that the justice of his claim had never been disputed; but he had received no money because of the dispute as to whether the liability was the government's or the Company's.[63]

Through all his arguments with the Colonial Office, Dillon had justifiably regarded R. W. Hay as his supporter. It was for this reason that he had written to Hay so often, sending him information (on the misdeeds of Major Bacon and Mr Gouger, for example) and congratulating him when he believed sound decisions had been based on his advice: it was wise to miss no chance of cultivating the good will of well-disposed officials. It was therefore a bitter blow to realize that on his visit to Earl he had actually passed Hay without recognizing him. He wrote the next day: 'I regret extremely that I had not the pleasure of recognizing you yesterday until after you passed me on the stairs. I did not know who it was until I enquired of the Porter'.[64] But he was not subdued by the mishap. He suggested that the Colonial Office should accept his claim and give him an order on the Colonial Treasury at Sydney, as the easiest way out of an embarrassing situation. He added a sneering reference to the new South Australian scheme: 'I find that Mr. Gouger has taken the field once more . . .'.

A month later Dillon wrote to Hay again, still pursuing his claim —'I rely on your kindness for support'—but abruptly introducing an entirely new topic. He expressed regret that 'the few men left in charge of the British Flag on the Falkland Islands have been murdered by the people of Buenos Ayres'.

> If a chart of these Islands is required at the Colonial Office I will be happy to supply one. I have been there several years back, and went all round the Island during which time I sketched out a Chart of it which will be found very correct. I also know something of its produce &c. &c.

From a minute on the letter it seems that Stanley himself was anxious to see the chart.[65]

But this interest was never pursued, for his long years of poverty in Europe were almost over: Dillon had at last found backers for a commercial venture in the Pacific, a project at least in part based on his pamphlet. It was not a scheme on the grand scale he had hoped for; it would not bring him fame and probably would not make his fortune; but at least it would restore his solvency and take him back to the part of the world he loved. He would once more be among people who revered him and whom he understood. He was to settle in New Zealand as a trader buying flax from the Maoris and processing it for export on machines which he would take with him, going out initially for three years on a salary of £300 a year and provided with a clerk, Charles Stewart, to help in the management.[66] It also seems likely that the development of trade in the tropical islands, on the lines indicated in his pamphlet, was a less immediate objective.

THIS restoration of his fortunes quite renewed Dillon's old exuberance. Once again he was a man who could command the attention of the influential and successful, instead of having to plead for it. He paid a short visit to Paris to settle his affairs there; Martha Dillon was probably at school there (she later spoke and wrote fluent French), and it seems fairly certain that he left her and his wife in Paris, presumably with the pension. When he returned to London he wrote to his old companion Eugène Chaigneau, now in the Ministry of the Navy, regretting that the brevity of his stay had prevented him from inviting Chaigneau to dinner, but promising to write about subjects of mutual benefit and offering to render any possible service with Talleyrand, still Ambassador in London. He enclosed two letters to French officials, which he asked Chaigneau to deliver.[67] They contained a request for copies of the published narratives and charts of d'Urville's and Laplace's expeditions, which as he told Chaigneau, 'would be very acceptable to me in my present undertaking'.

He also tried to finalize his negotiations with the Colonial Office and believed that he had got a promise from J. S. Lefevre, the new Parliamentary Under-Secretary, for the order on the New South Wales Treasury. But when he wrote to Lefevre on 10 June asking for the document as he was sailing 'on Sunday or Monday next', he was put off.[68] He called at the Office to collect the order on 16 June, to be told that Stanley had left office and that the new Secretary, Spring Rice, would have to sign it. The claim was thus held over, but not forgotten, being left in the hands of an agent. In mid-June Dillon entered on a new phase of his career, setting out on the long voyage to New South Wales.

SIXTEEN

Interlude in New Zealand

1834-36

DILLON sailed from Gravesend in the *Prince Regent* in June 1834.[1] His fellow-passengers included one of Samuel Marsden's daughters, and a Church Missionary Society party—the printer William Colenso, W. R. Wade (both with their wives), and John Flatt. Though Wade described the voyage as uneventful, there was enough of interest for the passengers to issue a weekly news-sheet called *The Main-sheet.*

The *Prince Regent* reached Sydney on Sunday 26 October. Dillon was now back in old haunts, among friends of his youth, his sons and his relatives by marriage; but he came back from his European poverty with at least a modest competence, and as a famous man. The *Sydney Gazette* wrote 'Among the arrivals by the Prince Regent we notice the name of Captain—now the Chevalier Dillon—the celebrated navigator and successful enquirer after the relics of the ill-fated La Pérouse. We cordially welcome the return of our distinguished countryman to the shores of Australia.'[2] According to the *Australian* he was 'Consul for the King of the French for the Pacific'.[3] Sydney was larger, more diversified, more sophisticated than it had been a decade ago; then Dillon had known some of the leaders of colonial affairs, but he could now move in society with more assurance.

In January 1835 Dillon visited Government House, where Sir Richard Bourke had invited him to meet the Quaker missionaries Daniel Wheeler and James Backhouse, and brief them for their proposed visit to Fiji. Roger Therry was the Governor's guest at the same time, and found Dillon 'like Yorick . . . "a fellow of infinite jest and merriment" ' with a boisterous and somewhat malicious humour.[4] He recalled Dillon's advice to Wheeler, to go ashore with his ample waist girdled by a leather belt with a brace of loaded pistols, a double-barrelled gun over his shoulder, and a sword by his side; with half-a-dozen similarly armed backers, he might have a chance of his life.

'Oh!' replied Wheeler, 'that is impossible, as all my ways are "ways of peace." I am determined to land unarmed, placing my trust in Providence.' 'I have a great respect for Providence, too,' replied Dillon, 'but if a set of black devils were approaching me with a design to kill and eat me, I should place my confidence in a double-barrelled gun and a brace of pistols.'

Therry also recounts another of the Chevalier's tales, that after 'a Mr. T—— [Terry], then a well-known opulent merchant in Sydney', had baulked him of a debt of £350 by pleading the statute of limitations, Dillon warned Mr T—— that, if he did not direct his executor to pay the sum within twelve months after death (when paying up would 'give you *no very particular pain*'), then

> mark my words! as those of an earnest religious man, an article of whose creed it is to believe in the transmigration of souls . . . your soul, after your death, will be transmigrated into the body of one of your own bullocks, and you will be dragging your own wool under one of your own teams over the Blue Mountains of Bathurst.

At a rather less exalted level than Government House, but still a very respectable one, Dillon attended the St Patrick's Day dinner (17 March) at the Pulteney Hotel, with Alexander Mcleay, Mr Justice Burton, and leading Roman Catholic clergy.[5]

Two of his European preoccupations remained with him: La Pérouse and the *Phatisalam*. Early in 1835, apparently, he met a Captain Bond, of the whaler *Anastasia*, who had found some relics, presumably of La Pérouse; these Dillon sent to some unknown person in the French Ministry of Marine. In the same letter he asked again for copies of the narratives of D'Urville and Laplace (and also Duperrey), an indication that he did not intend to confine himself to New Zealand.[6]

The *Phatisalam* affair must have dragged on in London, or perhaps Dillon lost confidence in his agent, for in February 1835 he resurrected the case by yet another letter to the Secretary of State, still claiming the £245:

> This sum was forcibly torn from me through an error of judgment . . . My case is a just one; it was admitted to be so by that ablest of lawyers, Sir J. McIntosh, Lord Ellenborough, Lord Ashley, the Marquis of Graham, Sir John McDonald, and the Honble C. Grant, Member of the Board of Control, who all concurred in my opinion that my claim was a just one and a fit subject for the humane consideration of His Majesty's Government, and that it lay with the Secretary of State for the Colonies to decide on it. From this opinion in all England there was but one dissenting voice, *viz.*

Interlude in New Zealand 261

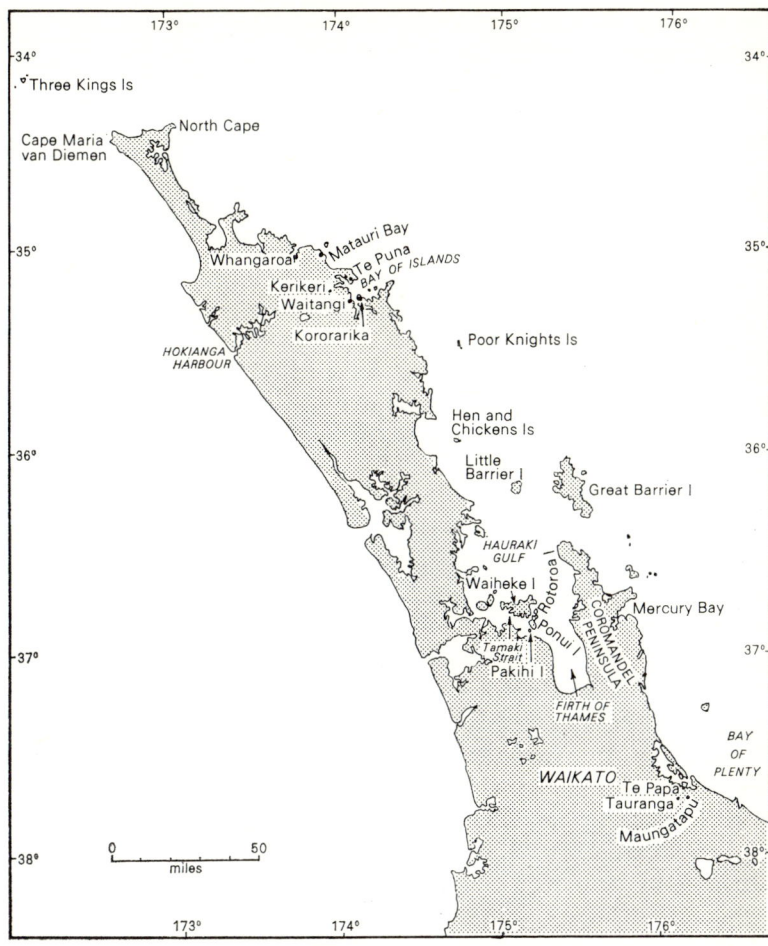

3 Northern New Zealand in Dillon's time

that of Mr. Stephen, the legal Adviser of the Colonial Office, who never took the trouble of reading my Documents, at a time when he received the affair to be sent to the Board of Control, as it was unconnected with the Colonial Office. This young man's opinion, compared with that of the great Sir J. McIntosh, ought to have had no weight, however, it had; and I have been kept out of my Money through it for more than seven years.

Dillon further claimed that before he left London he had been informed that the Secretary of State would give instructions for the claim to be met; but the Colonial Office denied that there had been any such commitment.[7]

BUT BEFORE the reply to his complaint could have reached Sydney, Dillon had embarked on the main enterprise which had brought him back to the Pacific: he had sailed for New Zealand, presumably in his 'handsome and trim little clipper sloop' or cutter *Robulla*.

He acquired (or had earlier acquired) land at Maungatapu, on Tauranga Harbour, at the eastern end of the Bay of Plenty. Here he settled, certainly by mid-July and probably earlier, since towards the end of that month the Reverend A. N. Brown was lamenting the loss of one of two houses built by the local Maoris of the great bullrush (*raupo*) for the CMS mission station at Te Papa, which had been moved a couple of miles to Maungatapu: 'It now forms the residence of the Chevalier at Maungatapu. I could not take any steps in the matter myself, being ignorant of the intentions of my Brother below with respect to Tauranga. I am sorry that the natives have acted as they have, but I feel that we have not much cause for complaint.' He added, wryly, 'Brother Preece I hear has volunteered for Tauranga, with his knowledge of the world, fancy Mr. Preece as Missionary at such a place, with the renowned P. Dillon as neighbour'.[8]

The long narrow northern peninsula of North Island, indented by many fine harbours and rich in timber and flax, had indeed changed since Dillon had last visited it, eight years before: colonization had already set in. Little groups of traders and missionaries were scattered around the coasts, from Hokianga past the Bay of Islands—'the Bay' *par excellence*—Hauraki Gulf, Dillon's old haunts on the Firth of Thames, to the Bay of Plenty. Some of the mission stations had fairly substantial buildings, with churches, and contained good furniture and china, which were possessed also by the local 'Kings'. There were also grog shops . . . Maori farming had begun around Waimate, and Mission farming was perhaps at its peak. James Busby was established as Resident, no sinecure position on a coast alive with trading activities, some carried on by distinctly raffish men and measures, and still serving as a base for whalers.

Dillon came into this busy little world with a reputation at once European and local, and although information as to his actual commercial operations is scrappy, there is plenty to show that his arrival was an event of importance, to the Maoris as well as to the missionaries. Brown wrote in his Journal, 'Waharoa called, but he seems unable to talk on any other subject than the great riches of Peter Dillon who has arrived at Tauranga. Peter styles himself French Consul, but is occupied in the rather unconsullike work of purchasing flax, pigs and potatoes for muskets and powder.' A few days later he had another visit from Te Waharoa: 'He said that the Natives of Maunga Tatari were on their way to Tauranga with flax for Peter Dillon who had engaged to place a "white man" with them . . .'.[9]

Among Dillon's visitors was his fellow-passenger on the *Prince Regent*, W. R. Wade, who gives us a glimpse of the settling-down period. On a visit to the Te Papa mission

> . . . we proceeded to Mangatapu about 2 miles to the southward of Te Papa. This Pa is computed to contain about 300 natives and is one main division of our field of labour. . . Two Europeans reside here, a Mr. Jones a flax agent, and Peter now Chevalier Dillon who has just taken up his quarters here with machines for dressing flax. It was not my intention to claim old acquaintance with Dillon; but he sent for me and I could not refuse to go. Poor Charles Stewart opened the gate of his enclosure looking like a native of the lowest order. The Chevalier was very polite chiefly enquiring about the news of the Bay [of Islands].[10]

Dillon's new life, like its setting, was a world away from his European experience. There, despite his genteel penury and his painful haunting of the Colonial Office bureaucracy, he had mingled on fair terms with the intellectuals of the Royal Asiatic Society, with publicists and promoters and the Irish nobility; he had met a King of France and a King of the French. Now he was struggling to keep his footing in the rampantly competitive world of the Bay traders. He seems always to have cut a dash: 'the Chevalier', and on occasion more: 'Count Dillon is on the coast (Bay of Plenty) flax gathering, and surveying, he says, for a French colony'.[11]

He had of course his salary, doubtless commissions and trading on the side, and profits from the *Robulla*, which in his absence was managed for him by Gilbert Mair and William Powditch, the leading chandlers and general merchants at 'the Bay', the commercial centre of northern New Zealand. The struggle was severe: there is a note from Gordon Browne to Mair asking him to collect £3 6s 1d from Dillon, 'the amount of my account against him thro' Captain Stewart', and a letter from Dacre and Wilks, Sydney merchants, regarding another debt—'Dillon's bill is not paid—we are astonished at your risking so much'.[12]

Only one material incident is recorded from this period, and that ended inconclusively. On 18 November 1835 Mair and Powditch appeared before Busby at Waitangi to make a deposition. It appeared that in August the *Robulla*, sailing from Hokianga to the Bay of Islands, had put into 'a small Bay at a place called Matauri', some twenty-five miles north of the Bay. Here she was boarded by a man named Phillips, who was building a small vessel near by, and a companion. They brought rum aboard, and the master of the *Robulla*, Jones, joined in an evening's drinking. Next morning it was discovered that the cutter's anchor had gone. When she arrived at the Bay of Islands, Jones reported merely that 'the cable had parted from the Anchor'. Later evidence clearly indicated to Mair and Powditch that Phillips had secured the anchor for his new vessel, and they suspected Jones of connivance. On the morning on which they went to Waitangi, Phillips's completed craft had arrived at the Bay, and the agents wished to go aboard her, with a witness to the theft, to identify the anchor and lay a charge.[13] But it does not appear that any legal action followed.

Dillon's stay in New Zealand was to be short. The interlude was probably happier than the long waiting on the insolence of office (as it appeared to him) in London and Paris; but all is obscure. There are a couple of hints of a search for acceptance and reassurance: when at the Bay, Dillon often called on the Mairs, and was long remembered by the children: 'The Chevalier was a huge man with a fierce expression, which rather repelled us children when he visited at our house. About this time a French whaler, the Jean Bart, came to the Bay.'[14] This last sentence, and Gordon Browne's note about surveying for a French colony, bear witness to a natural association of ideas between the Chevalier and anything French, and rumour about the schemes of Baron de Thierry was going the rounds of the Bay.

The obscurity of these years suggests that, happier or no, they were years of failure. Instead of the 'three years certain' he spent only nine or ten months actually in New Zealand trading in flax. Flax prices were falling, and he was unable to raise the capital for entry into the timber trade; but it would seem that he regarded this New Zealand venture as merely a stepping-stone to the larger schemes of Islands commerce implied in his 1832 *Extract from a Letter*; in the 1839 edition of this he simply says *inter alia* that he 'was head of an establishment' in New Zealand from 1835 to 1838. He retained his business interests at Maungatapu; but on 16 March 1836 he sailed from the Bay for Sydney on the American brig *Chalcedony*.[15]

SEVENTEEN

Finale in the South Seas

1836-38

IMMEDIATELY after his arrival, Dillon gave the Sydney press news from the Bay of Islands—mainly on shipping and trade movements, but including the news that Baron de Thierry was 'daily expected' in New Zealand:

> From Chevalier Dillon we learn that this Baron Thierry is a son of a Baron Thierry, who was a French refugee in England during the reign of Napoleon, and that it is on the faith of some bargain with some stray New Zealand Chief in England that he now approaches with his sovereign aims.[1]

The *Sydney Gazette* reported:

> 'His Most Christian Majesty's' South Sea representative, the indefatigable Chevalier Peter Dillon, we perceive, has honoured Sydney again with a visit from his Consulate in the Pacific.

It wished the Chevalier, 'an indomitably enterprising, a keen, and a clever man', every success in his projected cruise of discovery among the Islands.[2]

In fact, it took Dillon nearly a year to realize his intentions. The reasons for this delay can only be surmised. Did he have difficulty in finding a suitable ship, or in raising the money to buy one? Was he involved in negotiations with the London interests which had financed the Maungatapu venture? No evidence on these points seems to survive. He had some anxiety over the *Robulla*, which was badly battered on a voyage from the Bay of Islands to Sydney and indeed was given up for lost until she eventually arrived, probably early in May.[3] Early in 1837 he gave witness in favour of the Reverend John Adair, who was charged with forging and uttering a bill of exchange, but acquitted when Dillon and others testified that they believed him to be harmless but 'of unsound intellect'. In the trial proceedings Dillon appears as

'Chevalier De Dillon'.[4] At this time he seems to have been stressing his French connections, and he may himself have been using 'De Dillon'. Throughout his later life, he was very sensitive to the dignity of names and titles: Don Pedro Dillon, Count Dillon, the Chevalier Pierre Dillon, Chevalier Sir Peter Dillon, all appear at one time or another; and it seems unlikely that he was without some responsibility for these dignified forms of address. It is also clear that he was disappointed at not receiving a British knighthood for the discovery of the fate of La Pérouse.

The link with La Pérouse, and Dillon's friendly interest in the wreck of *L'Aimable Josephine*, were responsible for an indirect approach from the French Government. The Prince d'Eckmühl was about to make a voyage round the world and was asked to report on European trade and navigation in the Pacific; Comte Molé, the Foreign Minister, recommended Dillon to the Prince in these terms:

> You will find at Sydney an officer of the English marine, Captain Dillon, an interesting man, to whom we owe the discovery of the relics of the unfortunate La Pérouse, and who has recently taken upon himself to make up for the lack of a French agent at Sydney, by collecting and forwarding to my Department the papers of a French captain murdered in these regions.

The Ministry was apparently considering, very likely at Dillon's request, appointing him consular agent at Sydney; but d'Eckmühl did not arrive there for another two years, by which time Dillon was in London.[5]

EARLY IN 1837 Dillon bought the schooner *Jess* for £800.[6] She was a small vessel, 'British-built, coppered and copper-fastened', and almost at once Dillon advertised for passengers or freight to 'the Bay of Islands, Society and Friendly Isles'.[7] Dacre and Wilks, who acted as agents for several New Zealand traders, shipped a variety of goods to Gilbert Mair at the Bay of Islands.[8] They also wrote to Mair asking him to persuade Dillon to take a consignment on the *Jess* to Gordon Browne at Mahurangi: 'If possible persuade the Chevalier to call there shipping the blankets on her as we have discussed them—they charged us 30 Guineas . . . in the Jess and I am sure we have not much more than 10 tons—Dillon ought to consider this—Mercury Bay is not the least out of his way'.[9] This statement clearly implies that Dillon had not given up his interests at Maungatapu, but intended to call there on his way to the Islands. He also secured freight for the Wesleyan Mission in Tonga.

The list of seven passengers does not include the most interesting of them—Luke Dillon. He may have been signed on as one of the crew, but it is highly unlikely that he was expected to do any menial work. Whether there was any family connection between the two Dillons is unknown; but Peter had shown a friendly interest in his young fellow-countryman at least since the rape case of 1831. Then he had written to Father Therry on his behalf: an account 'in the public prints . . . is nearly unfounded on truth. He is an injured man . . . If you can do anything to aleviate his misfortunes . . . you will confer a great favor on me.'[10]

In 1831 Luke Dillon was twenty-three or twenty-four years old, an Ensign in an infantry regiment, the son of a well-to-do woollen merchant. A lively and attractive young man, he rather casually proposed marriage to a young acquaintance, Anna Frizell, and after an evening's drinking at a hotel they went to bed. Next day Dillon apparently had second thoughts, but the girl was overcome with fear or remorse. She told friends that they were already married, and wrote appealingly: '. . . If you value my life, my honor; everything depends on you . . . Really, I am about dead with grief. Indeed, my dearest Dillon, on you depends my future happiness in life.'[11]

Dillon did not marry her, and in April was charged with rape. His family spared no money over the defence, and witnesses from the hotel deposed that Miss Frizell had been a consenting party; but he was convicted and sentenced to death. His gaiety and assurance had evoked wide sympathy, and even Anna's friends now pleaded for him. His sentence was commuted to transportation for life, and in December 1831 he arrived in Sydney by the convict ship *Bussorah Merchant*.

He had of course other introductions; Roger Therry received one from a friend at the Dublin Bar giving serious reasons to doubt the justice of the verdict, and Dillon was warmly received by people who had known his family in Ireland, though James Mudie reserved some of his best abuse for 'this caitiff' who 'plays the part of a regular Bond Street lounger, or Australian exquisite,' and 'was even noticed as a friend and a gentleman by some of his countrymen holding high rank in the colony'.[12]

Although Luke Dillon had received a conditional pardon in 1834, this depended on 'his remaining in the Australian Colonies'.[13] But he was impatient for the free pardon that would enable him to leave the colony, and the arrival of his namesake and old supporter, with his own ship, seemed to provide an opportunity to circumvent the law's delays.

The *Jess* sailed on 18 March 1837, but heavy weather forced her back to Sydney three days later, leaking and with damage to her pumps.[14] In the days just before the schooner's original departure and in those between her return and final sailing on 30 March,[15] there was much discussion and correspondence concerning Luke Dillon's intention of leaving the colony. Peter Dillon apparently consulted the Attorney-General on the proposal, and the latter set down his understanding of the position in writing, for the Chevalier's guidance and protection. He noted that 'the Pardon of Mr. Luke Dillon is not to be found in the office of the Colonial Secretary or any of the public offices', but did not hesitate to state that there need be no fear whatever of breaching the law if Luke were allowed to go on the *Jess* 'to any of these Islands'—there would be no offence unless Luke were taken to Europe. The Attorney-General took this view 'as I am informed that he has now his outfit and other articles of some value actually on board'.[16] The whole tone of the letter—its reference to 'Mr.' Dillon, its concern with the expense of the 'outfit', its convenient forgetfulness of the actual terms of the conditional pardon—shows the friendly feelings with which Luke Dillon was regarded.

Friendly feelings were not enough, however, to overcome the scruples of the customs authorities; when the *Jess* was ready to sail again, Luke Dillon had to tell the Colonial Secretary that these officials required a formal authority to permit him to leave.[17] This requirement seems to have been obligingly met, since the Colonial Secretary's papers include a draft order for the Governor's signature: 'The said Luke Dillon . . . shall have full permission to depart from the said Colony of New South Wales, and to [travel?] to any other part of His said Majesty's Australian Colonies or to any of the Islands in the Pacific Ocean thereto adjacent'.[18]

The sequel was probably not unexpected. At some convenient point, the Bay or Tahiti, Luke Dillon simply disappeared from the *Jess* and made his way back to Europe. His free pardon was received in Sydney in 1840, but by that time he was sinking back into the obscurity from which the one night in a low Dublin hotel had snatched him.[19]

This was far in the future. When the *Jess* sailed from Sydney, her immediate destination was the Bay of Islands, which she entered on 27 April.[20] How long Dillon spent on the New Zealand coast is unknown, but there are several references in the Mair papers to

Finale in the South Seas

transactions with him up to 18 May. Trade was increasing, so were taverns; tribal war was also rife, affecting his own domain at Maungatapu: 'In April, 1836, the tribe where my establishment was fixed' made war on a near-by group, killing (and eating) seventy of them in a month, after which 'the Town Point [Makata] tribe surprised my friends at night, and killed, roasted, eat and carried off as slaves upwards of four hundred of them'.[21] From this unpromising scene Dillon sailed to Tahiti, perhaps not directly; but the *Jess* was at Borabora by 10 October. The Society Islands were scarcely less agitated.

Much had happened in the ten years or more since Dillon had been in Tahiti. The first flush of success for both the monarchy and the mission was over; there had been years of trouble, civil and ecclesiastical. More traders had set up on shore; more whalers were using Papeete as a port of refreshment. Most significantly of all, French Catholic missionaries—working to a plan very similar to that which Dillon had drawn up for Solages—had attempted to establish themselves. For most of his career, the Chevalier, a one-time servant of the Honourable East India Company, seems to have switched his enthusiasm between British and French interests, according to the main chance of the moment, with engaging freedom; or perhaps it was merely what we now call ambivalence—after all, he was born in Martinique, and the Dillon connection itself was divided between Ireland and the Irish emigration. At all events, Dillon seems to have engaged in the Tahitian intrigues, on the Catholic and hence French side; though whether this had any practical effect may well be doubtful, since his letters seem to have arrived in France years after the events.

On 10 October 1837, Tapoa II, *arii no Porapora*, wrote a letter to Dillon, obviously inspired by the latter. Tapoa II was a considerable figure, who had regained complete control of Borabora from a rival of his father's, and married Pomare IV in 1822, to become 'King Tapoa II of Porapora and Tahu'a'. The marriage had been dissolved three years before Dillon's arrival.[22] The letter stated 'I have already informed you how myself and your other friends have been disposesed of our Birth Right the Sovereignty of the Island of Otaha by the King of Uleitea and his allies', and went on to ask Dillon for military aid— possibly from France. Tapoa also wrote a letter to forward to Louis Philippe, asking for French missionaries; no reply was received.[23]

Dillon did not stay long enough in the Society Islands to take an effective part in the tangled politics of the group. Probably towards

T

the end of October he sailed westwards towards Niue, Tonga, and Fiji, where he was to involve himself in incidents which were to fuel controversies for years to come.

THE *JESS* made her first landfall in the Tongan group on the island of Tongatapu, whither she was carrying stores for the Wesleyan Mission. Dillon knew the island well; in 1827 he had been particularly friendly with the chief of Ma'ofanga district and had taken several younger members of the chief's family with him to see the world.[24]

In 1827 life on the island had been peaceful and prosperous; the Wesleyan missionaries had only recently arrived. Now the people were torn by dissensions between Christians and 'pagans'. Ma'ofanga was apparently one of the principal centres of the pagan faction—still a majority in the island—and the two parties had been on the verge of war since 1835. The ambitious George Tupou (Taufa'ahau), ruler of Vava'u and Ha'apai, was expected in Tongatapu in support of the Christian faction and his own ambitions.[25] The stories that Dillon heard from Tongan friends and European residents were strongly biased against the missionaries; it seemed to him that the blame for the disruption of peaceful conditions must be laid at their door.

The stay at Tongatapu was brief: the *Jess* was anchored near Nuku'alofa, the Christian stronghold, and a dispute arose over Sabbath observance. According to David Cargill, an attempt was made by 'the police' to arrest Dillon himself. As a result, the *Jess* sailed for Vava'u without even unloading the mission stores.[26]

At Vava'u, which was reached on 11 November,[27] conditions seemed even less happy. The resident missionary, the Reverend John Thomas, was a sombre, harsh and arrogant man, devoted to his calling but lacking in human sympathy. Worse, he was the adviser of Taufa'ahau. From Europeans like Joseph Meyrick, former surgeon on the whaler *Thetis* and a resident on the island since early 1835,[28] Dillon heard stories of floggings and other brutalities carried out at Taufa'ahau's orders, with Thomas's support. He heard also of the recent attempt by Bishop Pompallier to establish a Roman Catholic mission.

Pompallier and a party of missionaries had arrived at Vava'u from Tahiti, on Jacques-Antoine Moerenhout's schooner *Raiatea*, on 22 October, intending to leave some of the party to found a mission station. Their first impressions were favourable. A French resident—Charles Simmonet, a deserter from the *Astrolabe*—was able to advise them on local conditions, and it seemed that Taufa'ahau was agreeable to the establishment of a Catholic mission. But soon his attitude began to change; when he came on board to dine, he spoke non-committally. Pompallier and his party did not doubt that Thomas was responsible for this change, and a meeting between the rival parties confirmed this belief. Thomas declared that Vava'u was too small to stand two rival missions, and suggested that the Catholics should turn their attention to Wallis Island (Uvea), a convenient four hundred miles to the north. Taufa'ahau supported him, and refused to permit the party to stay. Pompallier had no alternative to accepting this 'advice'.[29]

Some of the European residents had sided with the Catholics, no doubt hoping that Catholic influence would save them from the puritanical laws made by Taufa'ahau at Thomas's behest. But their advocacy was not needed to make Dillon see this incident as yet another example of Thomas's evil influence. Pompallier was a Frenchman, the representative of a French missionary order, charged with carrying out part of the programme of Catholic expansion which Dillon himself had first suggested in 1829; and was not Dillon in turn honourably associated with the French cause?

All in all, he felt ample reason to be disgusted with the Wesleyans in Tonga, and in particular with Thomas—the mission's most influential figure, who stood out as the prime exemplar of this ignorant, uncouth, evangelical group. He determined to frighten Thomas into stopping the war and later, when he returned to England, to expose him. To these ends he wrote Thomas a long letter, dated from Port Refuge, Vava'u, on 20 November, and sent him a copy as he was about to sail.[30]

He began in a tone of dignified remonstrance:

Sir,
    I beg that you will excuse the liberty I take in addressing you . . . a sence of Christian justice, of honour, and humanity, my feelings as a man, a parent, and a Christian, cause me to do so, and to shudder at the communications made to me by my countrymen, and the Natives of Tongataboo a few days past.

Dillon then proceeded to outline the stories he had been told. It was alleged that at Tongatapu Thomas had sought out the descendants of the former kings of that island, whose family had been deposed over fifty years previously, and had claimed to be a friend of George IV 'who was himself a Missionary'. If they would become Wesleyans, George IV would help them to regain the throne in Tongatapu. The bait was taken and they became converts—externally—and then 'threatened all the Noblemen of Tonga with death and destruction' unless they too conformed to Wesleyanism and acknowledged one of the old ruling family as absolute king. These threats were treated with contempt by the Tongan chiefs, and Thomas, accused of 'being a Public disturber of the peace' thought it best to 'seek safety by flying from Tonga' to Vava'u 'where there was a Chief more pliant than those at Tonga' (this was Finau Ulukalala, who died in 1833).[31] On the death of Finau, Thomas was accused of helping 'a blood thirsty usurping assasin' to seize power, excluding the rightful heirs.*

The usurper's only claim was that, in Thomas's hands, 'he was an humble instrument of torture, death, and destruction . . . by whose means and bloody assistance you undertook to propagate the mild doctrine of our Lord and Saviour Jesus Christ'. By 'religious cunning and Jesuitical intrigues' Thomas had made 'this monster' a 'complete despot' and introduced barbarities hitherto unknown in these 'once happy Isles'—tortures such as cropping of hair, branding of unbelievers, 'flogging of innocent females of noble birth with tared English ropes knotted at the ends such as an English bullock drover would be imprisoned for if he was known to use the like on a bullock'.[32]

Dillon went on to say that it had been stated to him that Thomas prevailed on his 'pliant and bloody friend' to invade Tonga, assuring these *soi-disant* Christians that they were fighting in God's cause, 'who marched in their ranks although invisible'.† In Tonga these savages committed revolting atrocities, ripping open pregnant women and mutilating little children.[33]††

---

* [Taufa'ahau 'is now named King George—he continues a steady friend to our cause. Though it is clear he has no hereditary right to Vavou. The rightful successor being then alive— . . . though considered inefficient. In this matter the Missionaries I learn were called to give their opinion; which was done in favour of George.' Joseph Orton, 'Memoranda regarding the Friendly Islands', Methodist Missionary Society, London, 'Personal Papers' (in Biographical series), South Seas, Box 6.]

† [George 'was sent for by Tubo . . . a Xtn. king who considered himself in danger from the rebellion of the heathen chiefs . . . it is certain that whatever had caused this state of affairs and had Xty. had nothing to do in the matter Tubo would have called for the assistance of George or any other chief likely to be of service to him, and that the consequence might have been more woeful'. *ibid.*, replies to questions 19 and 20.]

†† ['Did George in this attack behave cruelly, slaughtering men women and children . . . ? This is partially true. George having been greatly aggravated during the contest, in the heat of feeling gave directions in storming the place "*not to leave a grasshopper*" . . . implying indiscriminate carnage which was lamentably fulfilled to the letter at least for a time when women and children who came in their way were slain. When this came to the knowledge of the Missionaries [they told George] of the impropriety of such a procedure, and advised to avoid anything of the kind in future . . .'. *ibid.* question 23 and reply.]

Finale in the South Seas

It was said that only a few weeks before the writing of the letter Thomas and his colleagues from Tongatapu and Ha'apai had held a congress at 'Lafuga' (Lifuka) to plan another bloody campaign against the Tongans

> whose only crime was that they would not embrace the creed of Dr. Wesley and submit their property, liberty, and lives to the will of a usurping despot who has already committed the most barbarous outrages on their innocent wives and children and that at the very time when you assured the monster that the true God marched in the ranks with the bloodthirsty Banditti.

Dillon implores Thomas in the name of God, humanity, and the honour of Britain to prevent the effusion of more innocent blood by the fleet which had sailed 'on Monday last' for Ha'apai.

From this point Dillon enters on a denunciation to which only extended quotation can do justice:

> I have also learned that a few weeks past the daughter of the Duie Tonga was striped tied to a Post in the usurper's yard where this unfortunate Princess was flogged with the above described piece of Rope until the Royal and noble blood flowed freely from her lovely shoulders and breast her only offence was that of endeavouring to join her beloved and lawful husband at Tongataboo which in your opinion was a heinous crime as he is what you term a heathen and did not instantly fall down and embrace your creed . . . *
>
> Oh Mr Thomas, what will the noble minded and respectable families of England think when they learn that the daughter of so great a Prince's blood was shed by a public executioner — the antiquity of whose family far surpasses the pedigree of any family in Europe.
>
> I say, Mr Thomas, God forgive you for the offences you have committed in brutalizing and debasing the higher order of People on those Islands. What did our Saviour say when the woman caught in adultery was brought before him for sinning. Let him who is guiltless throw the first stone. I presume, Sir, you are not clear of Sin how could you direct this respectable individual to be scourged within the hearing of your Wife and family whose shrieks and screams were heard by them. Mrs T. I am sorry to say is a cold blooded English woman otherwise she would have sallied forth with true born British spirit and say to the usurper spare the Princess on my account.†

* ['The person whom Dillon styles a Princess is represented by Hobbs to be an extremely vulgar woman of Masculine appearance and habits though a person of some rank . . . Her crime appears to have been the joining other Natives in stealing a boat from an American whaler . . . .' *ibid.*, reply to question 25.]

† ['Mrs. Thomas must have known of the occurrence and may have been within hearing, but she had nothing to do with the affair. Nor could she have interposed as it was a political offence and punishment . . . '. *ibid.*, reply to question 25.]

What will the charitable British people think, who contribute their mite to your Society and on whose bounty you live in luxury in these Islands when they learn that you are propagating the Sacred Scriptures by destroying man, woman and child on Tonga as above described. What will the English Nation think of the caricatures in the Print Shops of a Wesleyan Missionary propagating his doctrine by causing the assassination of innocent females, the ripping open of their bowels, the mutilation of their tender offspring &c. &c. Such outrages were never committed in Algiers or the other Barbary States.

Mr Thomas, it is my duty, as a British subject and a gentleman to bring these barbarous outrages before the British government and House of Commons and give them publicity in every part of the Globe. It is also my duty to lay a statement of those outrages before the King of France whose commission I have the honour to hold.

As originally drafted, the letter ended here; but before he delivered it to Thomas, Dillon received fresh news of the war fleet which had sailed for Tongatapu.[34] His informant had reported that 'the usurper' had invited all the chiefs of Tongatapu to a feast; as was customary, the guests would come unarmed, but the Vava'u warriors would have butchers' knives hidden beneath their clothes, to slaughter the guests to the last man:[35]

With this bloods thirsty design I understand you are well acquainted thus for the love of God and the propagation of his sacred scriptures several hundred more of the human race are to be exterminated on the bloody alters of Tonga.

If you are not acquainted with this treacherous design I now apprize you of it and beg of you to avert the blow . . . should wind and weather permit I shall steer directly for Tonga and apprise the People of that I[slan]d of their danger.

With respect to the Nav[igators'] Is[lands, i.e. Samoa] I am perfectly well aware of your design & desire of extending the usurpers power to them Islands in fact you wish to estab. an Empire and place your tool at the head of it . . . Pray bear in mind Mr Thomas that there is a God and such places as old baily and execution dock.

To Dillon the Friendly Islands had been devastated by a sour and ruthless bigotry; but at least, when he sailed from Vava'u, he had uttered a protest, and a threat, which might re-echo beyond the Islands.[36] Yet, paradoxically, in the next stage of his voyage we find Dillon co-operating, if grudgingly, with Wesleyan expansion in Fiji.

FROM VAVA'U, the *Jess* sailed for Fiji, where she had stores to land for the Wesleyan mission at Lakeba. She arrived there on the afternoon of 28 November and was at once boarded by the missionaries, William Cross and David Cargill. They learnt that there were letters and periodicals for them, as well as trade goods; but that night, before the mail and freight had been unstowed, the *Jess* bore out to sea again, as the anchorage was poor and 'the wind was strong and the aspect of the weather terrific'. The schooner remained some distance off-shore for the next two days; on 29 November Dillon sent ashore a note expressing surprise that no boat had been sent for the stores and saying that he would be sailing shortly. Cross and Cargill could not persuade the Fijians to go out, 'lest their canoes should be broken by the rolling of the vessel', but on the next day they came out themselves in a whale-boat and took a few light cases ashore.[37]

They were received amicably by the 'Chevalier de Dillon' (as Cargill styles him) and discussed the possibility of transporting Cross and his family to Bau: since their arrival in 1835, they had worked in Lakeba and neighbouring Lau islands, but now wished to start a new station in the heart of Fiji. The navigation was difficult and hazardous from the great number of reefs; such charts as were available were very inadequate indeed. 'The unwillingness of owners and Captains of vessels to visit the FeeJee Islands is greatly increased by the lamentable number of accidents which occur in Feejee', and hence Dillon's visit was very fortunate, for 'than he no person is better acquainted with the Feejee Islands . . .'.[38]

This admission of Dillon's usefulness was wrung from them by their need of him; though they were unaware of his letter to John Thomas, they were under no illusions as to his general attitude. A year earlier, indeed, Cargill had found occasion to denigrate Dillon's book—though at that time his own knowledge of Fiji was scarcely such as to warrant him to pass judgement. 'Peter Dillon, the discoverer of the fate of La Perouse', he wrote, 'has published a work, in two volumes, in which he tells many tales about the Feejeeans; but no dependance can be placed on his statements, as they are principally made up of bombast and inaccuracy'.[39] Now their pleasure at being able to establish themselves at Bau, albeit with Dillon's help, was tempered by several considerations. Not least of these was the story told them by some Fijians, that 'a person on board the *Jess* assured them that the religion which we teach is not true, and that the author of that religion is a false God'. Whether Cargill believed Dillon to be the author of this statement is not made clear in his letter, though it is by no means unlikely that he did so believe; but he commented only that the person concerned 'dishonours his Christian name, and ... forfeits all right to the apelation [sic] of a gentleman'.[40]

While they were aboard, Dillon told Cross and Cargill that he was sailing next day to the island of Moce, where lay the wreck of the London whaler *Harriett*; some of her crew were at Lakeba and reported that some salvage was still possible. After this visit Dillon moved on to Oneata, where his old friend Takai (or Thaki) was living; here, according to Cargill, Dillon 'was then known to the natives of this part of Feejee, as 'Tuta',—the name by which the distinguished navigator Captain Cook is known to these Islanders'.[41] The missionaries were much annoyed to receive a message from Oneata requesting them to send canoes at once to collect their freight from the *Jess*; they complained that the payment for this trip much reduced their limited supplies of trade goods.

Later in December Dillon returned to Lakeba, where his actions further compromised him with the missionaries. According to Cargill, he gave tobacco pipes to the 'King of Lakemba' in return for 'what I am reluctant to mention'.[42] He also met there a Tongan chief, Lualala, who had apparently been a leader in the war against the Christians in Tongatapu earlier in the year. Lualala, who seems to have become a supporter of the mission at about this time, allegedly informed Cargill that Dillon 'told me that he would give me ten kegs of powder and ten muskets, and take me and my people to Tongatabu, in his vessel if I would again raise war, and destroy the praying people'.[43]

For all that, if they were to get to Bau Cargill and Cross were in no position to be squeamish about Dillon's principles. Accordingly, on Christmas Day they went aboard the *Jess* to negotiate 'for the passage of Brother Cross and family to Bau,—and for conveying thither his goods,—including such articles of Mission property as are necessary for commencing a new station'. Dillon asked £150 but agreed to accept £125, which the missionaries thought still too much.[44]

On 28 December, in pouring rain, the Crosses went on board; 'The Chevalier', they noted, 'received us with kindness'. Two days later the *Jess* sailed via Moala to Kiuva, between Kaba Point and Rewa, whence Cross travelled the few miles to Bau by land. He was anxious to establish his station at Bau because of its importance in Fiji in terms both of rank and influence. To this end he interviewed Seru (later known as King Cakobau), the son of the ruling chief Tanoa, who was away from Bau. Seru, who had led his father's supporters during prolonged civil strife within Bau, was in virtual control of affairs. Cross asked him whether he would permit a mission station to be established on the tiny island. Seru replied 'It will be most agreeable to me if you think well, but I will not hide it from you, that I am now engaged in war, and cannot attend to your instructions, or even assure your safety.[45]

In these circumstances, Cross decided to seek the protection of Tanoa's ally, Tuidreketi, at Rewa. He arrived there on 8 January 1838 and was well received; he began at once to move his goods from the *Jess*, and on 14 January, 'our first Sabbath in Rewa', he preached both in Fijian ('the dialect of Lakemba') and in English—the latter for the benefit of any European residents—deserters from ships—who might be attracted. Only two attended. Dillon's action on this day disappointed Cross: 'The Chevalier sent his boat to Rewa to trade, notwithstanding that it was the Sabbath'.[46]

With the mission party safely landed, the *Jess* sailed for New Zealand, calling at Levuka, in Ovalau, where a number of Europeans and Americans lived, more or less on the beach and acting as interpreters for vessels in the bêche-de-mer trade. The timing and purpose of Dillon's visit are not clear; it is possible that the *Jess* carried a message from Cross, who had fallen ill towards the end of January, asking for a member of the Levuka community to come to the aid of his family, but Dillon probably left Fiji before this.[47] The best-known and most reputable of these white men was the American, David Whippy, who had lived there since the mid-1820s and had been adopted into the local tribe with the title Mata-ki-Bau.[48] Dillon met Whippy, who probably performed some service for him; in any case, he was a useful man, and Dillon drafted a recommendation for him as a man who understood the Fijian language and customs, knew the islands well, and was a competent pilot. He signed this in his capacity as French Consul to Fiji, and sealed it with a rough seal.

Dumont d'Urville saw this curious document, and with the contempt of a professional for an amateur explorer, and a commissioned officer for an apparently self-appointed one, commented 'Je souris en lisant cette pièce de l'invention du Capitaine Dillon, et des titres qu'elle confère et à son possesseur et à son donateur . . .'.[49] As we have seen, Dillon had given useful information on Pacific happenings to the French Government since the fall of Charles X; and it was doubtless in reliance on these links, and still more on the absence of any formal

French authorities in the South Seas, that he seems to have 'let it be known', if he did not formally claim, that he still held a status to which his title is obscure. The nearest approach to a formal recognition at this time seems to have come from Bishop Pompallier. According to Dillon himself, soon after his arrival at the Bay of Islands in February 1838, the Bishop wrote to him from Hokianga, and then in March visited him at the Bay, accompanied by a sympathetic chief. Dillon says that he introduced Pompallier to the most powerful local chiefs and to the leading British and American residents; while Pompallier gave him a letter to Mme Adelaïde, Princesse d'Orléans, in which he recommended Dillon as Consul in New Zealand.[50] Whatever the true position, Dillon did not long stay to exercise any functions.

Early in February the *Jess* anchored in Tauranga Harbour.[51] Dillon brought with him a number of Tongans and Fijians; at Lakeba he had responded—as so often in the old days—to the requests of a Tongan chief, Tupou Toutai, to see the world. On the voyage from Fiji, the *Jess* had picked up a Fijian canoe with eight men and a small boy, driven far out to sea by the weather. These were given aid and comfort —they were in most need of blankets to face the New Zealand weather —by the missionaries; and Dillon's old fellow-passenger on the *Prince Regent*, W. R. Wade, who was visiting the CMS mission, was most interested to meet Tupou Toutai—Will Mariner had lived with his father.

From Tauranga, the *Jess* sailed to the Bay of Islands, where she remained some weeks. Here Dillon was amongst a host of friends and former associates, and new ones included Bishop Pompallier. The schooner cleared from the Bay on 27 March and entered Sydney Harbour on 12 April: there was to be one more visit, a very brief one, to the Bay of Islands, but in effect Dillon's Pacific days were over.

[At this point there is a hiatus in Professor Davidson's drafts. In his earlier synopsis there was to be a Chapter XXVII, 'Preparing for Retirement'; in the final one, this was to be Chapter 18, 'Home from the Sea, 1838-39'. All that we have to cover this period, from Dillon's arrival in Sydney on the *Jess* in April 1838 till his visit to the Bay of Islands on H.M.S. *Buffalo* in June, consists of two short handwritten notes. One refers to a letter from Joseph Meyrick (see above, p. 270) which probably reached Dillon in Sydney: 'M. says the *Conway*, visiting Vava'u shortly after D., investigated but whitewashed Thomas'. The other suggests reasons for Dillon's return: his contract with his London backers had obviously expired by 1838, and the venture had not been financially successful—the flax trade was in the doldrums, Dillon had not been able to get spars, and so on.

The circumstances in which Dillon joined H.M.S. *Buffalo* are therefore unknown, though detailed research in colonial archives might still give hints. As for motive, he had no obvious financial basis in the Pacific—he could hardly rely on French consulships!—and at the age of fifty he may have felt tired; his wife and daughter were on the other side of the world; and there may also have been some disillusionment with the South Seas. If, as Davidson suggests (above, p. 264) the Maungatapu spell was probably happier than the spell of waiting on the great and the bureaucrats in London and Paris, the disruption, at missionary hands, of the Islands life he had known must surely have depressed him: after Tahiti and Tonga, it must have seemed that the old freedom and informality, in which he could indulge his extrovert personality without inhibition, was gone forever. It may be also that he harboured a genuine zeal to return to Europe to carry the Tongan war into the enemy's headquarters; some of his actions support this view. Yet, as we shall see, he was soon casting longing eyes towards New Zealand once more. One may suspect a deeper and unconscious motivation: an almost manic-depressive ambivalence, in Europe yearning for the vigorous freedom of the South Seas, in the South Seas for the social and intellectual sophistication of Europe . . . O.H.K.S.]

EIGHTEEN

An Uneasy Londoner

PETITIONS AND POLEMICS 1839-47

AFTER leaving Sydney in mid-May 1838, H.M.S. *Buffalo* called at the Bay of Islands in June.[1] For a few days Dillon looked again, for the last time, on one of the principal scenes of his happy and tempestuous years in the South Seas. Here as elsewhere, the reactions to his personality had been most diverse: he had gained the affection of many Maori leaders, the respect of some of the white settlers and the dislike of others, and the angry scorn of the Protestant missionaries. There were new developments—the formation of the settlers' association to maintain law and order in the Kororareka township, the beginnings of Catholic activity under Pompallier—and old associations to recall or forget. In a village on the Kawakawa River his half-caste daughter, now a handsome child of about eleven, was living with her mother's family.[2]

There is a blank of four months between Dillon's leaving the *Buffalo* in Rio and his arrival in London on 10 January 1839: possibly he went to England by way of France. Ten years earlier he had arrived in Europe eagerly anticipating fame and fortune from his achievement in Vanikoro; now he was older, many of his cherished hopes had been disappointed, his wife was ill; and people were no longer interested in the story of La Pérouse. One thing remained unchanged: he was still short of money. His difficulties only made him fight harder to attract attention to himself and his deserts. He sought to re-establish his contacts with the politically important, the rich, and the socially eminent, both for the satisfaction such contacts gave him and for the use to which he might put them; he sought also to strengthen his links with influential circles in France. His activities included attempts to secure government appointments, British or French, in New Zealand or Tahiti; publicity for commercial schemes in the Pacific; attacks on Protestant missionaries and Wakefield's New Zealand Company; a

280

leading role in the Aborigines Protection Society; assistance—not entirely disinterested—in the organization of French Catholic missions. All these might be expected, but we also find him producing a potboiler on Russian history. Several of these activities were carried on simultaneously. They involved many letters to public men and to the press, seldom dated, from the succession of lodgings, mostly in shabby-genteel streets, where he and Mary lived, but generally from more dignified addresses—the Jerusalem Coffee House (the favourite), the Colonial Club House, even on occasion East India House.

WITHIN a fortnight of his arrival in London he began to bombard the Government, writing to Palmerston, then Foreign Secretary. He opened in standard form— '. . . the Chevalier Dillon, late of the Honble. E. India Company's Service, who a few years past discovered the fate . . .', and went on:

> I have, within the last 15 days, returned from a voyage to New Zealand and the South Sea Islands, and was surprised to learn that some designing persons in this country from interested motives, have tried to impose upon Your Lordship by stating that it is the intention of the French Government to establish a Colony at New Zealand.—This I can assure Your Lordship is not the case; and what has afforded ground for this report is that two French missionaries have been sent to New Zealand to propagate the Christine Doctrine, by a religious Society in France which has for the last two hundred years been in the habit of sending out Missionaries to China, Cochin-China, Siam, Thibet and Tartary, and with which Society the Government has no connection whatever.
>
> Should Your Lordship require any further information on this subject, I shall be happy to give it whenever you think proper.[3]

The Foreign Office sent a copy of this letter to the Colonial Office for the information of the Secretary of State, Lord Glenelg. Three days later Dillon wrote directly to Glenelg, repeating the points in his letter to Palmerston but adding a new one:

> Your Lordship may perhaps recollect that when Mr. Thomas Peel projected the establishment at Swan River a similar report was raised here viz. that a French Expedition for that place had actually sailed from France and had arrived at the Brazils on its way out. This Report was set in circulation with a view of stimulating the then Ministry to forward Mr. Peel's views which had the desired effect.
>
> The sooner that fine country is colonized by the British the better as no part of the globe at the present day offers such advantages both in a Commercial and Political view to this country as New Zealand.[4]

Dillon's argument is sensible—colonization, but not by a company (unless, doubtless, one of his own). The link between the propaganda of the New Zealand Company and that of the Swan River promoters is a shrewd one, and marks the beginning of an attack on the Wakefield group which he was to develop more strongly over the next two years; but only after he had tried, and failed, to join forces with it.

Already, however, he was trying to find a way of returning once more to the Pacific; the growing interest in New Zealand as a country to settle him gave him one lead. He had his pamphlet of 1832 reprinted with some interesting amendments,[5] and in April he formally offered his services to the New Zealand Company:

> I beg that you will excuse the liberty I take in addressing you on the following subject the person who has that honour is the Chevalier Dillon, lately returned from an expedition to New Zealand after being in intercourse at different periods with the Inhabitants of that country for thirty years.
>
> Enclosed I beg leave to send a prospectus which I published in A D 1832 at which time I endeavoured to form a Company for colonizing New Zealand, from the tenure of the enclosure you will plainly perceive the great advantages to be derived from a British settlement at New Zealand (if properly formed and conducted) in which Country I have some land, a dwelling house, stores and outoffices, on the shore of a very good small harbour.
>
> From the enclosure you will perceive how I have been employed my qualifications for an undertaking in New Zealand etc etc where your party will have innumerable difficulties to contend with from the English Missionaries, their adherents, and other foreigners established in that country, I had great difficulties to contend with from that class which I overcome by being determined and could no doubt do the same in your case.

Dillon then goes on to say, truly enough, that he was an experienced trader and could be useful in selecting cargo and crew, the latter being very important in a new undertaking. He then says that he understands the Company is about to appoint a Commissioner to New Zealand, and asks to be excused for remarking that 'on so great and difficult an undertaking' the Commission should consist of at least two persons, preferably three, since should a single Commissioner 'loose his life by sickness, the upsetting of a boat, or by the hands of the Natives, all would be lost'.

This is sensible, but designed to lead to the offer of his services as one of the Commissioners, on the terms on which he went out in 1834—£300 a year for three years certain, five per cent on all purchases, passage out and home for himself and clerk—and should

> this arraingement answer the views of the Company I shall with great pleasure take one share in the concern and be enabled most likely to prevail on some friends to follow my example in fact they have promised to do so already.
>
> My house, stores, and garden, can be made use of for surplus stores and the company's servants, until a proper establishment is formed.[6]

This offer met with no response; in fact it would have been almost impossible for the Company to have accepted it. The preliminary expedition was nearly ready to sail, and Colonel Wakefield left for New Zealand a fortnight after the date of the letter. From this time Dillon never wavered in his antagonism to the Company and all it stood for.

The problem of making a living remained, however, and the growing interest in New Zealand offered other opportunities besides employment with the Company. In August he issued the following handbill:

NEW ZEALAND.

CAPTAIN DILLON

Offers for Sale

Twelve Hundred Head

of

HORNED CATTLE

To those about to Emigrate
to New Zealand,

In Lots to Suit the Purchasers.

The Colonists will find this a good opportunity to supply themselves, as these Cattle are at Ulieta [Raiatea], one of the Society, or Otaheite Islands, about ten or twelve days sail from New Zealand.

For further Particulars apply to Captain Dillon, 92, Charlotte Street, Rathbone Place.

London, August 24th, 1839.

Meanwhile Dillon was brooding on a more ambitious scheme than mere cattle-dealing: he would himself go into competition with the Company. In the London *Morning Chronicle* of 15 October he announced his proposal to open a 'New Zealand House of agency in Broad Street, City, where the best information could be obtained by persons desirous to emigrate to that island'. His own qualifications were set out—his past positions as 'French Consul at New Zealand', his long period 'in constant intercourse' with New Zealand and the Islands. 'It was he who first established the church missionaries in the Bay of Islands. He speaks the native languages, and has great influence over the various islanders, and possesses extensive tracts of land, and numerous herds of black cattle, horses etc. etc. on some of the islands'.[7] He proposed to 'lay on three ships for freight and passage' and would himself go out by the first of them; emigrants who should join him 'will have a fair opportunity of choosing such land as they require in the country, and of making their own bargains with the native chiefs, under the sanction of Lieutenant-Governor Hobson, lately sent by the British Government'; or they could buy from Dillon himself at from 2s 6d to 5s an acre, as against the Wakefieldian New Zealand Company's price of £1 at Wellington. Labourers could be obtained from New South Wales by paying £5 passage money, or from adjacent islands for half that sum. Dillon would supply the settlers with horses, cows, bullocks and merinos on very moderate terms. Finally, if any of them did not like New Zealand, they could move on to New South Wales, where there were ample opportunities for new settlers.[8]

When news of this move reached Sydney, the *Australian* described it as a 'land-sharking advertisement'. It was, of course, that and a good deal more: in his references to Hobson, Dillon had quite irresponsibly drawn conclusions about future land policy. Few of his promises could have been honoured. But he lacked the means to launch the scheme, which is chiefly interesting as an indication of his desperate resolve to return again to the Pacific in search of a fortune.

EARLY in 1840 Dillon began once more to assail the government with his views, in a series of letters to Lord John Russell, then the Secretary of State for the Colonies. The main objects of these letters seem to have been to attack the New Zealand Company and the Church Missionary Society, and to obtain employment in New Zealand; they are dated from 9 Great College Street, North, Camden Town, where Peter and Mary Dillon were now living.

In the first of three letters,[9] he opens his attack on the missionaries, particularly in regard to their acquisition of land—and the resulting inter-tribal war. Dillon says that in 1825 the chief Hongi told him that he had sold his own and his tribe's land to the Church Missionaries for a few trifles, and that 'they gave him to understand that he must move off it'—which he did by attacking the Wangaroa tribe and seizing their land. Again, in 1830 Hongi's brother-in-law 'Tetorey' and his tribe sold the Waimate, the finest tract in New Zealand,

> ... to the said Missionaries, who gave him to understand that his absence would be good company, as they wanted the land for their children and the Society in London. This warlike powerful tribe took the hint ... they fixed their eyes on the Corararicca district, inhabited by the chief Bomarey and his followers; this was the place most frequented by shipping ... a bloody battle followed ... Bomarey was obliged to abandon his paternal inheritance: the Waimate party took possession of Corararicca, where they now remain.

Then follows his conclusion: paid by the charitable people of England to convert the savages, these missionaries were the first to cheat them of their land, thus occasioning 'more war, bloodshed, and cannibalism than any other class of Europeans that has visited that country as yet'. The arrival of the Catholics formed a happy contrast: the Bishop, insulted and threatened with death (at the behest of the English missionaries) simply replied 'Why treat me thus ... I want nothing from you; I have not come here to cheat you out of your land, as the English Missionaries have done, neither would my Society allow me to do so'. Dillon comments, 'What an example for English missionaries of virtue to adopt ...'.

In his third letter he renewed his attack on the missionaries as land-grabbers: one of them, Fairburn, formerly 'a Sydney joiner', had refused even to hand his lands over to the Society. If the mission claims were allowed by the government, those of the company and of private settlers like the 'curious character' M'Donnell and 'the expelled missionary' White would also have to be admitted. He added a further charge: members of the Church Missionary Society were the first to introduce 'nameless abominable crimes', for which Yate and Filley had been dismissed in 1836.[10]

Such was the partial image of the Mission which Dillon projected; he also gave Russell his version of the history of the New Zealand Company and its origins:

U

In 1837 some Roman Catholic noblemen and gentlemen, with others, turned their attention to New Zealand, with the intention of colonizing: however, the notorious E. G. Wakefield, got among them. Several gave up the business in disgust, not wishing to have their names classed with that of a man who qualified himself for the New Zealand direction by a three years' residence in Newgate, for the crimes of abduction, etc., etc., etc . . . [but] a few persons of desperate fortune with Mr. Wakefield kept the business up in the public mind.

Wakefield had influence, being for example the 'old school-fellow' of Lord Durham. As a result, 'this forward, intruding man, having been permitted into the councils of Lord Durham, now thinks he ought to be consulted in all matters connected with the colonies by the officers of your Lordship's department'.

Wakefield's friends had abducted two Maoris from a French whaler at Havre, passing them off as a prince and a great chief. One died; the survivor, 'Nightee' [Naiti] sold land at Port Nicholson to a member of the Company, 'Dr. Evans, of Hampstead (a man of not the best character)'. A map of this land was displayed in the Company's office, 'on which the shores of this port were divided into sections of 100 acres each, although the link of a surveyor's chain never passed over it . . . Whether the sections contained volcanoes, swamps, bogs, salt or freshwater lagoons, sand banks, etc., etc., etc., no person in England could tell.' But the land found purchasers, 'the public having been misled by the representation of the jobbers, who pretended to have the support of this Government, and were to have a charter'. Wakefield's brother, who had 'also qualified himself for the high situation by two years' imprisonment in Lancaster Castle', was to be governor of the new colony.

Regarding this brother Dillon also wrote with venom:

> This genius was a clerk in an attorney's office, and formed a clandestine marriage with the daughter of Sir —— Sydney, who would not consent to see his daughter or son-in-law; the lady died broken-hearted; the attorney's clerk joined a banditti here, and went over to Portugal to establish the authority of Donna Maria, where in a few months he was dubbed a Colonel, which title he now attempts to maintain, although that service has been broken up.

These arguments against the Company—the low quality of many of its leaders, the dishonesty of its propaganda (including the use of the alleged French threat), the plight to which settlers would be reduced through its misrepresentations—were elaborated in detail and with relentless hostility. In the second letter Dillon expresses satisfaction that the government has tabled its correspondence with 'the New Zealand Land Pirates' in the House of Commons: this has made intending settlers aware of the Company's real standing.

Alongside all this denunciation Dillon presented his own solution for the New Zealand problem. The country should certainly come under the control of a European Power, both because of its commercial possibilities and in the interests of the Maoris. But which Power should it be, and what course of action should be taken to ensure control? To these questions he gave a clear answer: 'The New Zealanders have a much greater respect for the English than for any other nation, and would be most happy to surrender up the Sovereignty of their country to the British Crown, if assured of protection'. (Already events were bearing him out: two months before he wrote the first signatures had been placed on the Treaty of Cession; but news of Hobson's success had not yet reached England.) As for land already in European hands, Dillon suggested that it might be resumed, with reimbursement of their actual expenditures to the purchasers; this, he said, was the policy that Governor Bourke had followed at Port Phillip.

He had, too, his own candidate for governorship of the new colony —Sir Augustus d'Este, the illegitimate son of the Duke of Sussex who, he claimed,

> informed me, in 1832, that he would be most happy to go out as Governor to New Zealand; he also informed me in August last (1839), that if the Government offered him the situation of Governor to New Zealand he would accept of it under the Crown, and there is certainly no man in Europe more fitted for it; he is the real friend of men in their natural state; his house is open to receive them, and he now corresponds with several Chiefs of the North America tribes; he is amiable . . .

As a member of the Royal family, he would be welcomed by the Maoris—a shrewd point.

When he wrote his final letter to Russell, at the end of July, he knew that Hobson's mission had been successful and that New Zealand was now a British colony. In his last sentence, therefore, he abruptly descends from the clouds: 'I hope that . . . you will be pleased to consider my claim for employment (or one of the many situations that must be filled in the new colony at New Zealand)'.

These letters—with their mixture of shrewdness and bombast, of encyclopaedic knowledge and patent misrepresentation—were unlikely, at any rate, to assist Dillon in gaining his final request. They showed him at best a politician *manqué*, at worst a crotchety man with a head full of grievances. They gave proof, if proof were needed, that he would be an intolerable officer in any colonial government. Yet they were not entirely ignored at the Colonial Office. The originals carry notes by Sir James Stephen (now Permanent Under-Secretary), R. Vernon Smith M.P. (Under-Secretary of State), and Lord John Russell himself. On the first letter Vernon Smith wrote: 'I do not think it altogether useless tho' I do not propose to make any immediate use of it'. A copy of the first letter was sent to the Church Missionary Society, on Russell's orders, and in due course the Committee rejected its accusations as in part exaggeration, in part untruth.[11]

Dillon published parts of these letters under the title *Extract of three Letters addressed to the Right Honourable LORD JOHN RUSSELL, Secretary of State for the Colonies, on the subject of Colonizing New Zealand A.D. 1840*; there is no printer's name, no place or date of publication, but Dillon writes elsewhere that he sent a copy to Vernon Smith in December 1840. He also, of course, sent copies to prominent people and to the press, and the *Sydney Gazette* reprinted them with the unflattering editorial comment: 'If for nothing else than the tone of gross exaggeration which pervade [sic] the letters they will be perused with some interest'.[12]

IN THESE years Dillon had domestic as well as other anxieties to occupy his mind. During the autumn of 1839 he and his family were out of London for several months, probably staying at Brighton for his wife's health.[13] Mary Dillon, always a shadowy figure, was in the last stages of a lingering illness, probably tubercular, and on 20 December 1840 she died.[14]

Dillon did not allow his wife's illness to interfere with his publicity campaign. In November the *New Zealand Journal*, published in London by the New Zealand Company, reprinted an article from the Hobart *Colonial Times*, based on the *Letter . . . to an influential character*, which not only contained several statements which Dillon thought misleading but—much worse—implied that he was dead. He at once wrote (2 December 1840, from the Jerusalem Coffee House):[15]

> Mr. Editor,— In your interesting journal of the 21st ult., there is a paragraph which would lead my friends and the public to believe that I have embarked on the voyage to kingdom come sometime past; *this*, I beg leave to assure you, is not the case as I am in the prime of life and in enjoyment

An Uneasy Londoner 289

of good health, thank God, with an excellent appetite, and plenty to eat and drink; and as a proof of my earthly existence I have delivered this note in *propria persona* at your office, which you will oblige me much by inserting in your next number, so as to convince my friends that I am still to be found at my post.

I also beg leave to state that I have not resided for twenty years in New Zealand, but have had more intercourse with the country from the year 1808 up to 1838 than any other European.

Many of the articles mentioned in my prospectus in your last number are the products of the islands in the tropics near New Zealand, and not of the latter islands I meant New Zealand as the depot for such produce when procured by the Company's traders at the adjacent islands.

It was natural that Dillon should wish to preserve his credibility by disclaiming misleading statements; he also attacked a chart of New Zealand by Lieutenant Macdonnell, R.N., dedicated to Spring Rice. He alleged that Macdonnell had used data from Cook and the French explorers and 'gave them as his own surveys'; the officers of the Company's own ship *Tory* had nearly lost the ship, and condemned the chart in letters published in the *New Zealand Journal*, and as a result of Dillon's representations to the publisher of the chart, Wyld of Charing Cross, Macdonnell—who had visited only Hokianga, for trade not survey—had admitted that Dillon was correct.

The letter was subscribed 'Your obedient Servant, C.P. Dillon', and this was no accidental error: in preparing his letters to Lord John Russell for the press he had altered the 'Peter Dillon' of the originals to 'C.P. Dillon'—the title chevalier had become so much a part of him that he could not forbear reference to it even when signing his name, and henceforth he used this form.

ON 1 JANUARY 1841 Dillon received some further, and favourable, public notice. On that day two prints by George Baxter, the celebrated colour printer, were issued as a memorial of the martyrdom of the Reverend John Williams at Eromanga, in the New Hebrides, in 1839. With them was issued a descriptive brochure—prepared with Dillon's aid—which included 'an account of the islands [Eromanga and Tana] when visited by Captain Cook and Captain Dillon'. Dillon no doubt revelled in the glory of being thus bracketed with Cook, a life-long hero of his, though he would not have thought the comparison inappropriate. Moreover in the text of the brochure, the compiler's introduction to his account referred to him as 'now the Chevalier Sir Peter Dillon'.

Dillon had admired John Williams for his courage and humanity, his understanding of island people, his experience as a navigator. Other members of the London Missionary Society had been his friends or won his admiration. But in his mind these stood out from the horde of little men, greedy, narrow-minded, cruel, boastful and self-satisfied, who were imposing themselves and their puritanical creed upon the islanders, taking the joy out of life, spreading dissension in the name of Christ, corrupting the islands society. Worst of all these little men— worse than the land-grabbers of the Church Missionary Society— were the Methodists in Tonga. The threat in his letter to the Reverend John Thomas at Vava'u had not been idle; Dillon was determined to expose him and his colleagues, as opportunity allowed. According to William Diaper, he had brought back to England a rope said by that beachcomber to have been used, at the missionaries' direction, to flog a white man. Diaper said that on Vava'u two bad missionaries

> ... had framed the laws first, and the kings and chiefs ratified them afterwards. Through these laws, enacted by the most narrow-minded bigots— men of very little or no education, and less brains—they had ... managed to ruin one poor white for life, by flogging him with a piece of whaleline, with three overhand knots in it, laid on by a powerful savage ... the only wonder is, that it did not, there and then, cut the very life out of him!

Still according to Diaper this man, Robert Stevens of Suffolk, died— years afterwards but yet as a result of the flogging—'in the care of a *good* missionary, old Mr Turner ... [who] from all accounts, had always been a man of great humanity'. Still according to Diaper, Dillon took this rope to England, 'where it was exposed; but, as Dillon was thought to be somewhat of a reprobate—principally by the Sanctified—no notice was taken of the truth'.[16]

Now, late in 1940, Dillon heard of an incident in Tonga which gave him an opening. In June H.M. sloop *Favourite* was at Tongatapu, where the Christian chief George Tupou—Taufa-ahau—was attempting to use his traditional title and the limited rights it gave him as the basis of a modern kingship. To the missionaries who backed him, his opponents were not only heathens but also rebels against their lawful ruler. With extreme unwisdom, they urged the commander of the *Favourite*, Captain Croker, to land a party to aid George Tupou, and, with even greater folly, he consented. In the ensuing fighting, Croker and two of his men were killed. Dillon wrote to Lord John Russell explaining that it was the folly and wickedness of the missionaries which had cost these British lives.[17] He seems to have got no satisfactory reply, but he was not prepared to let the matter rest. He wrote to the Secretary of the Admiralty, the Irishman Richard More O'Farrell, M.P. for Kildare, and in December 1840 printed the letter 'on the defeat of Her Majesty's Ship *Favourite*, and death of her Commander'.[18] He portrayed the heathen Tongans as 'innocent and unoffending', their 'only crime . . . that they would not embrace a religion that had already caused more bloodshed and cruelty, than any other event recorded connected with the Friendly Islands'; in contrast, George Tupou was 'the bloodthirsty ursurper', 'the satanic-like monster', and his missionary supporters correspondingly cruel and merciless. To their lust for power many Tongans had already been sacrificed, and the death of Croker and his men was the final tragedy provoked by their brutality.

This thesis he argued at some length, and supported it by printing his 1837 letter to the Reverend John Thomas at Vava'u and a letter, which he had probably received at Sydney just before his return, from the whaling surgeon Joseph Meyrick, who had been at Vava'u at that time.

The Wesleyans had not taken the Thomas letter lightly. Their Committee first heard of it towards the end of 1838, when they received a copy from William Ellis of the London Missionary Society, to whom Dillon had sent it. Ellis suggested that Dillon might 'appear again before the public as a voyager in the South Seas', and the publication of his views could damage all the missions there.[19] The Committee naturally agreed, and decided that nothing would meet the case except an on the spot examination of each of Dillon's charges by someone from outside the Tongan mission. The Reverend Joseph Orton, of Van Diemen's Land, was asked to visit Tonga for this purpose, accompanied if possible by the Reverend Joseph Waterhouse.[20]

When Dillon finally published his charges, the Society was thus ready to defend itself—but by a curious irony, the principal witness for the defence was missing. According to John Thomas, he would have been none other than the Captain Croker whose death Dillon was lamenting:

> . . . at 4 o'clock Cap. Croker came on shore for the purpose of collecting information respecting the conduct of Peter Dillon formerly of the Jess, of whom he had heard much of a most disgraceful nature in various places,

and after seeing his Letter to me the Captain was more convinced than ever that P. Dillon's infamous proceedings ought to be brought to light, feeling satisfied . . . that it would tend to the triumph of truth and righteousness in the earth, as well as the glory of God. He assured me that should God spare him to return to England again, that he would expose the calumny of that most infamous liar, and scandalous calumniator to the British public.[21]

The publication of Dillon's letters stung the missionaries into defending themselves publicly, and David Cargill, home on leave from Fiji, published his *Refutation of Chevalier Dillon's Slanderous Attacks on the Wesleyan Missionaries in the Friendly Islands* (London, 1842). Cargill, an intellectual among the missionaries, was perhaps not Dillon's match as a controversialist—except when preaching to the converted. With regard to King George's claims to authority he merely stated, with surprising ignorance of Tongan society, 'Tubou is a lineal descendant of the ancient royal family of Tongatabu; and . . . his title to the government of that Island is just and valid'; any attempt to resist him was 'treason and rebellion'.[22] Those who opposed the 'King' were

> more than rebels; they were intended regicides, and appeared in arms . . . if possible to execute their design of exterminating Christianity, by either driving the King and his adherents into exile, or, with unprovoked and atrocious cruelty, by putting them to death in one indiscriminate slaughter.[23]

This does not really deal with the arguments that Dillon had raised. Nor is the Reverend John Thomas's character necessarily vindicated by Cargill's evidence as to his industry:

> If the Chevalier had had such opportunities as I have had, of seeing Mr. Thomas, rising at four A.M., and leaving home at that early hour, to visit and preach at several islands before his return in the evening, if he had seen him travelling on foot, under a burning sun . . . if he had seen him returning home in the evening, bathed in perspiration and panting with the fatigue of his unsurpassed labours . . . he would have been obliged to acknowledge the man, whom he has misrepresented, as . . . one of the best and most efficient friends the islanders of Tonga ever welcomed to their shores.[24]

Cargill's tract was typical of many works of missionary apologetics, with its glow of self-righteousness, its over-written account of missionary hardships and sacrifices, and its refusal even to consider the social and political implications of missionary endeavour. It was typical, too, in its uncharitableness towards the critic.[25] Dillon, it is suggested, had been guilty of many forms of misconduct: there was the exchange of tobacco pipes 'for what I am reluctant to mention'—

the prudish hint of sexual sin is plausible enough, but quite implausible is the insinuating remark 'Perhaps Chevalier Dillon knows something about a proposal to commence a traffic in slaves in Polynesia, by purchasing Fijian captives, and selling them in some of the slave-markets on the coast of South America.[26]

MEANWHILE Dillon was still urging his claims to an official appointment by letter and interview. At the end of March 1841 he wrote—in his own hand, not as usual by an amanuensis—from the Jerusalem Coffee House to Vernon Smith, whom he addressed wrongly as 'Secretary of State for the Colonies'.[27] One of his most typical letters in matter and manner, it deserves to be quoted in full:

Sir!
I had the honour of sending in December last for your inspection three printed letters regarding New Zealand addressed by me to the Right Honourable Lord John Russell, since then a friend of mine Charles Lushington Esqr M.P. late chief secretary to the Bengal Government informs me that he has mentioned my case and claims to you which are as follows.

I have been in intercourse with New Zealand from 1809 up to 1828 and of course seeing the great intercourse carried on between British subjects and the natives. I pointed out to the Duke of Wellington the necessity there was of having a British consul or resident sent there. His Grace concurred in this opinion and promised that I should have this appointment as a reward for my having obtained an additional national honour for Great Britain by putting at rest a question which had for half a century agitated the friends of Humanity and the Literary World, namely the Discovery of the fate of the celebrated Comte De La Perouse's expedition.

This appointment was given during my short absence on the Continent to a Mr. Busbey a Scotch Stocking weaver by trade, who had never seen New Zealand or its inhabitants in his life[28] and knew no more of the Native Language, manners and customs, than the man in the Moon, but he had some Parliamentary influence and I had none.

I remonstrated with Lord Goodridge [Goderich] on this act of injustice towards me who was in every way qualified for the situation and entitled to it as a just reward for my services and the sacrifice of my fortune whilst humanely engaged in endeavouring to rescue from slavery and the hands of savages the talented Comte de La Pérouse and his gallant crew. His Lordship replied that it was certainly a great mistake but that justice would be done me and that I should be fully compensated by one of the first vacant situations in New South Wales or Van Diemen's Land this promise was never fulfilled.

Under the above circumstances may I beg the favor of your kindly and humanely obtaining for me one of the following situations for New Zealand Viz. Colonial Treasurer, master attendant & captain of the Port, Post Master chief superintendent of native reserves and native protectors or to be appointed New Zealand Colonial agent in London. I understand Mr. E. G. Wakefield is endeavouring to procure the latter appointment.

I am told that a person who was in the pay of Government lately made a survey of the Island of St. Helena and has had the Colonial treasureship of New Zealand offered him as a reward for his service, and that he will not accept of it, whereas I who have made a survey of La Perouse's Island, New Zealand and most of the Islands in the Pacific, am passed over, neglected, unnoticed and unrewarded for the great national service I have rendered, and thereby have obtained the grateful thanks of the French Nation for Great Britain.

I will feel obliged by the honour of an interview with you at your earliest convenience.

I remain Sir your
obedient servant
C. P. Dillon

This letter, and those which followed, display Dillon's ignorance of official procedures. His letter went round the office, and his claims were checked against the files. On his approaches to Lord Ripon (Goderich) it was noted: 'There is no record of any other answer to him than those which held out no prospect of employment'. Another minute, apparently by Stephen for the guidance of the clerk drafting the reply, read: 'Answer that there is not at present any official vacancy to which the writer could be appointed, nor has Lord Russell the definite prospect of any such vacancy'. Dillon was written to in these terms—the polite and guarded language of the Civil Service saying that he had nothing to hope for.

To Dillon it was obvious that he was being victimized by petty officials. Although Vernon Smith's reply began 'I have laid before Lord John Russell your Letter of the 30th Ultimo', he had strong doubts as to whether in fact Lord John had ever seen it. If he had seen it, would he not have been certain to have recognized the justice of the case? Long ago, over the *Phatisalam* trouble, he had voiced his belief that these things went by favour, even by nepotism, and more recently he had ascribed Wakefield's success to schoolfellowship with Lord Durham; indeed, to so self-conscious a personality, the personal factor in affairs must have seemed the overriding one. So now, since he could not reach the Secretary of State through his subordinates, he would

An Uneasy Londoner

take the opposite tack: he would write to a man who could be expected to influence Lord John—his elder brother, the Duke of Bedford.

He began: 'My Lord Duke, The following is a brief statement of my Services, the just claims I have on the British Government, and the very unjust manner in which I have been treated'.[29] Once more he traversed the principal events of his career, with some comments of interest: at Dillon's Rock 'I saved my life, to be useful to the friends of humanity and science'—pure Dillon!; in New Zealand in 1814, where the missionaries dared not approach, 'at the risk of my life I undertook to make a peace, and establish the Missionaries there . . . and effected a peace that has not since been broken . . .'; it was through the neglect of his own affairs that he 'gave my agents at Calcutta an opportunity of becoming bankrupt' and lost the *St Patrick* and twenty-three years savings, over £30,000—he had earlier said £20,000. The French promises of reward for discovering the fate of La Pérouse 'have not yet been realised, consequently I am reduced from a state of affluence to one of absolute poverty'.

He goes on to say that all these circumstances were mentioned by Polignac to Wellington, then Prime Minister, and the Duke had promised him the Consulship or Residency in New Zealand; later he had called on Lord Goderich, with a letter from Amherst, the Governor-General who had known him in India; Goderich 'was affable' and said that while New Zealand was not available, Dillon would 'be appointed to the first civil situation vacant in the New South Wales Colonies'. But years went by with nothing done: 'I had no friend or great man to push my claims forward at the Colonial Office . . . In despair, I went out to New Zealand in 1834, with the honorary appointment of French Consul, and . . . engaged in commerce'. Since returning he had twice applied for the post of Colonial Treasurer in New Zealand, supported on the second occasion by Charles Lushington, M.P., and Fitzstephen French, M.P. for County Roscommon —but the appointment had gone to a Mr Sheppard who 'never saw New Zealand or distinguished himself in any way whatever . . .'.

Such was his fortune: what of other navigators? Ross, Back, Parry, Franklin, Richardson were now all knights, with lucrative posts, as a reward for northern voyages which had never excited the interest that the fate of La Pérouse did. By settling this question, Dillon had 'showed the superior skill and perseverance of the British seamen over that of the celebrated French navigators . . . sent on this service'— d'Entrecasteaux, Rossel, Baudin, Duperrey, d'Urville . . . A merchant captain, Douglas, had just been knighted for services to our traders in China;

> ... and I, whom nations a few years past disputed about, as to which should have the honor of claiming me as their subject, am now left destitute and unnoticed, at a time when my services could be eminently useful ...

There was precedent for cancelling an appointment in favour of a more deserving candidate: when Governor Bourke had appointed a relative of his own named Brenan to a post in New South Wales, Lord Glenelg had overridden this action, saying 'he had his own friends to provide for, and persons who had claims on the Government for past services'—conduct 'very just and worthy of imitation'.

Finally, Dillon asks the Duke to bring his case 'before Lord John's own eyes'. If he should still be turned down, 'I shall then abandon all further representations to Her Majesty's Minister's, and quit my country for ever'.

Cannily unimpressed by this touching appeal, the Duke replied with a recommendation that Dillon should take up his case direct with the Colonial Office. Once more Dillon wrote to Vernon Smith, asking that the case be placed before Russell for his 'own inspection'; then, he had no doubt, Lord John would order justice to be done. If, however, he could not secure an official post in New Zealand, he would like a land grant there, 'such as was given [to various persons] in New South Wales ... for services rendered'. A minute on the letter instructs that he be told that no vacancies exist and that land grants have been discontinued.[30]

Old friends were not forgotten. Before Vernon Smith could reply, Dillon had written again—in fact, the very next day—commenting on recent dissensions at Port Nicholson; these, he said, were caused by the activities of Mr Haswell, 'a former Middlesex magistrate, who, for many good reasons, could no longer live in England' and had gone 'clandestinely for New Zealand, with the appointment from Wakefield and Co. of protector of the native land reserves, etc., etc..'. This job 'reminds all who know him here, of the protection afforded to Miss Turner by Mr. Wakefield, and that of the wolf to the sheep, so far as the poor natives are concerned'.[31]

Once more he printed the latest round of letters, with Russell's final reply of 21 August. On 2 September he sent a copy to James Stephen (addressed as 'Stevens'), together with his pamphlet on New Zealand and his earlier printed letters to Russell. In the covering letter, he urged Stephen to read an article in the current *Quarterly Review*, drawing his attention to two points—the arrangement with the New Zealand Company on land acquisition (a 'barefaced job') and the proposal of Port Nicholson as capital ('Totally unfit for the head settlement . . .'). He expressed the hope that the 'new ministers'— Peel as Prime Minister and Stanley as War and Colonies—would order an inquiry into the land settlement with the Company.[32] Why this approach to Stephen, a man whom he had reviled in previous years? Stephen himself suspected that Dillon 'suppose[d] that I should feel some personal gratification—in the New Zealand Company being discountenanced, they having made me the subject of frequent and bitter censure'. In any case, like so much of Dillon's correspondence, the letter was filed and no action taken.

EVER SINCE his return to Europe at the end of 1838, Dillon had maintained his contacts with France and with French Catholic missions. Immediately on his arrival from the Pacific, he had gone to Paris to present Bishop Pompallier's letters to Adélaïde d'Orléans, the King's sister. He had hoped, through her intervention, to gain final satisfaction of his claims against the French Government and then to be able to return to New Zealand, perhaps as French Consul and certainly better off. But to his lasting regret, he fell ill in Paris, and could only pass on the letters through a third party.[33]

In February 1839 Dillon took steps to bring himself and his plans before the head of the Marist Order, Father Colin.[34] He gave a full account of his contacts with Bishop Pompallier at the Bay of Islands and the services he had been able to render him. He then made suggestions as to the most convenient routes for the missionaries to reach the Pacific, but not on the lines of his earlier discussions with Solages (above, p. 236). It was time-wasting to send them to Valparaiso to wait for a ship for Mangareva or New Zealand; better to travel from London to Sydney, whence there was constant shipping to New Zealand. He gave details of the fares: £70 from London to Sydney, £10 from Sydney to Hokianga or the Bay of Islands—cabin fares for the priests; accompanying workmen could be taken from London to Sydney for only £25. His friend Mr Daniel Cooper[35] was in the shipping business and would be glad to provide passages; in fact, priests going to Australia had already travelled on one of Cooper's ships, and the Roman Catholic titular Bishop in London had told him that they had been very well treated. Cooper had a ship sailing at the end of May.

This news apparently interested the Mission, for a party of five priests arrived to take passage on her. Soon after they reached London, Dillon suffered from one of his recurrent bouts of illness, and on recovering found that they had been persuaded by the Reverend Thomas Heptonstall, OSB, to sail on another vessel 'on which I would not send a dog for which I had any friendship'. This infuriated him. He wrote bitterly to Colin: was he not the first person to suggest Catholic missions in the South Seas? had he not entered into an engagement on the Marists' behalf with Cooper? who was Heptonstall to interfere?[36] Eventually the difficulty was smoothed out, with the help of the son of the French Consul; Cooper lowered his price to £60 and the missionaries sailed on the *Australia*.[37]

During the autumn of 1839 Dillon was out of London, for his wife's health and perhaps his own; on his return he again took up his correspondence with Father Colin, telling him that he had heard from the Cape Verde Islands that the missionaries were having a happy voyage; in April he was able to report that they were in Sydney and about to leave for New Zealand.[38] He offered advice on the development of the New Zealand mission: let the Marists send out a few missionaries with a good knowledge of English; he himself knew several English and Irish priests in Paris who would be glad of such a call.

He returned in these letters to an old theme: his own potential usefulness to France and to the mission. He had followed up the letters to Madame Adelaïde by writing to other prominent French citizens, but nothing had happened.[39] Could Father Colin use his influence to have him appointed as French Consul to the Pacific Islands, with a salary? No one else, he was sure, could serve France so well. In October it would be thirty-one years since he first visited New Zealand, and there he possessed a large property at Tauranga, 'where the only foreigners are those in my service'. In one of the Society Islands he had 1,200 head of cattle, besides horses and donkeys.

In January—a few days after his wife's death—he had declared his intention of himself sailing for New Zealand in one of Cooper's ships in April; but as the months passed this project faded. He continued to place his services in London at the disposal of the mission, receiving Father Colin's warm thanks and support. When Dillon was applying for the consulship, Colin told him, the mission had written several times to Marshal Soult, the Foreign Minister, asking that a consul should be appointed; but despite the Minister's interest, nothing had so far been done. 'We shall be happy if our letters can be useful to you, and I am very much inclined to think, Sir Captain, your nomination to this consulship which your precedent services deserve so well, would be very advantageous to our dear Mission.'[40] They were deeply grateful for Dillon's help to Pompallier, and no less so for his aid in despatching the recent party of missionaries to New Zealand.

Late in 1840 the Marists faced a difficult situation in England, and Dillon again proffered his help. Over £1,300 of the Mission's money had been entrusted to the banking house of Wright and Company, whose head, John Wright, was a prominent Catholic layman. Now the firm had failed. Dillon believed that it was on Heptonstall's advice that the money had been placed with Wright, whose reputation had once been high but who had 'latterly associated himself with men of desperate fortune such as no honest man would be seen in company with two of these fellows were named Wakefield who had been in prison the one for two and the other for three years . . .'. Had he been approached initially this mishap would not have occurred: 'I regret exceedingly the misfortune that has befell the money of our poor Mission, the Missionaries were several days in London before they called on me, had they come to me on their arrival I would have advised them not to put one franc in Mr Wright's hands . . .'. Dillon offered his own and Cooper's services to try to recover the money, and this offer was gladly accepted: 'how your noble conduct has touched me', wrote Colin to them jointly. Dillon kept the mission informed of progress, and in June 1841 was able to report that Cooper had received on their behalf a payment of five shillings in the pound.[41]

In these same letters Dillon began to unfold a scheme for the expansion of the Marists' work in the Pacific. He sent Colin two copies of his Tongan pamphlet—'a printed letter addressed by me to the Secretary of the Admiralty here on the subject of the murders committed by the English missionaries at the Friendly Islands'.[42] He asserted that after the defeat of Croker's party the Tongans had 'banished their cruel oppressors the missionaries' from Tongatapu. They were now asking for French missionaries and the protection of the French Crown. He had already written to Madame Adélaïde on the political aspect: 'if His Majesty Louis Philippe would now come forward I could procure for him the sovereignty of Tonga and all the Friendly Islands at the trifling expense of a few thousand francs'. Now he pleaded with Colin to take advantage of 'the chance thrown into our hands by God'. A ship of 150 to 200 tons could be bought in

England when the next mission party was being sent to New Zealand; she could be at Pompallier's disposal for the expansion of the mission, and by using her also for trade much of her running costs could be covered.

Two months later he wrote again. Perhaps a French colonizing company could be formed to buy land in Tonga—under Dillon's guidance, though he feared there was 'a cruel prejudice' against him at the French Naval Ministry. The mission should also begin work in Fiji: 'je suis beaucoup attaché aux habitants des îles Fejees qui sont les plus civilisés et les plus vertueuses de tous les sauvages'. At about the same time he seems to have written to friends in Tonga telling them to advise the chiefs not to let the Wesleyans return, and to expect Roman Catholic missionaries soon.[43] In June he made a further suggestion: now that New Zealand had become British, perhaps the Marists should abandon it and concentrate on Tonga and Fiji, where they could benefit France as well as the Catholic faith.[44]

Colin gave Dillon's proposals careful consideration. After reading the printed letters, he had decided to send missionaries to Tonga, and had passed Dillon's views to Marshal Soult, with a request that they should be placed before the government, as they were only for the good of France, and he greatly appreciated Dillon's support: 'Souffrez, Monsieur le Capitaine, que je vous exprime de nouveau ma vive reconnaissance pour la zèle vraiment admirable qui vous porte à sacrifier votre repos pour le bien des Océaniens et de notre Mission'.[45] The proposals to start work at once in Tonga and in Fiji struck him as sound: he told Dillon that it was hoped to send out a large party of missionaries in the autumn, of whom some would be designated for these two island groups; Colin felt sure that they would make great progress, being backed by Dillon's powerful influence with the natives. But he rejected out of hand the suggested withdrawal from New Zealand: the Mission was happy to work under the British, and the prospects for evangelization were good.[46]

In September the promised party, led by Father Forest, arrived in London. Dillon had corresponded with Colin about their travel plans, and now met them and took them to Cooper's office. But from now on his charges, as he now regarded them, gave him trouble. They inspected Cooper's ship on which they were to sail, and found it too small.[47] They arranged to travel to Wellington on another ship, at considerably greater cost; they also bought the wrong trade goods. The party was also smaller than Dillon had hoped, so that there would be no missionaries for Fiji. Behind the other difficulties he saw the sinister figure of Father Heptonstall.[48]

Despite these disappointments, the correspondence with Colin continued to flow. Dillon sent news of the missionaries as he received it from New South Wales and New Zealand, or from meetings with merchant captains at the Jerusalem Coffee House and similar resorts; he sent word of impending sailings of Cooper's ships, and repeated his pleas for missionary expansion in the Islands. On Colin's side, the mounting evidence of his correspondent's irascibility does not seem to have reduced the warmth of his feelings towards Dillon, nor his admiration of the Chevalier's devotion to the cause.

DILLON's poverty may not have been so absolute as he claimed; indeed, he seems to have been living in modest comfort. After 1841 he lived at 3 Chapel Street, Belgrave Square—probably a better address than Charlotte Street, certainly a considerable advance on Camden Town. He must have been a well-known figure in City offices and coffee-houses and the like where those with South Seas interests foregathered; from 1843 he was on the Committee of the Aborigines' Protection Society, where he would have known men of light and leading like Thomas Hodgkin and the Buxtons. He dined with well-to-do friends, used the Colonial Club in St James's Square, dressed with respectability and even some dandyism—asking Father Colin at Lyons to get for him two black silk cravats of the best quality 'as those made in London are very bad'.[49] Apart from the French pension, he may well have received a fair (if highly irregular) amount from commissions—for example, from Daniel Cooper. But while his income sufficed for him to live reasonably well in London, with occasional trips as far as Dublin, it was not enough for his more ambitious plans. He often refers to his desire to visit the Marist headquarters in Lyons, but was unable to make the trip, possibly for lack of money. Still less could he fulfil his perennially cherished desire to return to the South Seas.

But this constant need for cash would seem the reason for Dillon's surprising appearance as author, or at least editor, of a work on Russian history. Late in 1842 he published a book entitled *Conquest of Siberia and History of the Transactions, Wars, Commerce &c. &c. carried on between Russia and China, from the Earliest Period.* According to the title page it was 'translated from the Russian of G. F. Muller . . . and of Peter Simon Pallas'—Dillon's own name nowhere appeared. He signed him-

v

self merely as 'The Editor', as in the lengthy dedication to Sir Henry Pottinger, who in August 1841 had reached Macao on his way as Minister Plenipotentiary to China.

What led Dillon to tackle so unexpected a subject, so far removed from his own experience? The recently concluded 'Opium War' (which Dillon had expected some ten years earlier) had of course increased popular interest in China; it is also possible that Dillon and Pottinger—an Irishman of his own age, with long service in India—knew each other. But there was nothing in the recent war with a bearing on Russo-Chinese relations. One can only surmise that Dillon's reading had led him to think that such a book would be profitable. He had indeed showed some interest in Russian expansion in the North Pacific as long ago as 1829—the heyday of the Russian American Company, whose interests extended to Hawaii and to Fort Ross some thirty miles north of San Francisco; but there is nothing to show that this was a continuing interest.[50]

The book itself is as puzzling as Dillon's choice of its theme. Muller had been Professor of History at the St Petersburg Academy of Sciences and official historiographer of the Russian Empire in the mid-eighteenth century; Pallas had also been in the Academy's service and had led a famous expedition in Siberia; both had written extensively—but in German, not Russian.[51] The answer to the puzzle is essentially simple: at bottom the book was a fraud, though a fraud of a type not very uncommon at that time.

In the 1770s an English clergyman, William Coxe, later a prolific historical compiler, had visited Russia as a tutor and had met Muller, Pallas and other scholars; on his return he produced a book based on translations from these two, and others, with some material of his own. This *Account of the Russian Discoveries between Europe and Asia. To which are added, the Conquest of Siberia and the History of the Transactions and Commerce between Russia and China* appeared in 1780 and reached a fourth edition in 1804. Dillon's book consists almost entirely of passages taken *verbatim* from Coxe, to whom no acknowledgement was made; these passages were arranged in a new order, with brief references to more recent events. Since Archdeacon Coxe lived until 1828 and was very much a standard author—indeed, this same book of his is still very occasionally cited—this seems to have been taking a risk.

Nevertheless the book was printed by Nichols and published by Smith and Elder of Cornhill, both very reputable firms. It seems to have been successful, for a second edition was published by Allen and

Company in 1843.⁵² This edition was identical with the first except for the awkward insertion of four words in the title, which reads: *Conquest of Siberia, by the Chevalier Dillon, and the history* . . . It seems that Dillon was trying to take credit for the authorship of the first part of the book. If this claim was being made, it was unwarranted: the account of the conquest is taken straight from Coxe.

BUT THIS Russian diversion clearly did not diminish Dillon's intense interest in current happenings in the South Seas, and he must often have pondered his chances of more active employment. Early in 1844 he thought he saw his opportunity.

Since 1838, visiting French naval officers had issued a series of threats and demands against the government of Queen Pomare in Tahiti. This government was strongly under the influence of British Protestant missionaries, and especially of the British Consul, George Pritchard, and was undoubtedly arbitrary in its efforts to exclude French Catholic missionaries. This and other grievances were made the excuse for shows of force against the local authorities, who were practically defenceless; at the same time a French party was fostered, playing on the discontent of Tahitians and non-mission Europeans with the strict Puritanism enforced by the London Missionary Society. The campaign of intimidation reached a climax in September 1842, when Admiral Du Petit-Thouars gave Queen Pomare—then on the point of confinement—the choice of paying an impossibly large indemnity or accepting a state of war. In confusion and distress, fearing a bombardment of Tahiti, the Queen consented to the establishment of a French protectorate.

Pritchard had been absent during this coup, but early in 1843 he returned on H.M.S. *Vindictive*, Captain Toup Nicolas, and soon reasserted his influence over the Queen. He and Nicolas refused to recognize the protectorate, and designed a new flag for the Queen, embodying a crown—Du Petit-Thouars had incorporated the French tricolor into her standard. When the Admiral returned in November 1843 with news that the French Government had ratified the protectorate, Pomare refused to haul down her new flag, whereupon Du Petit-Thouars landed troops, deposed the Queen, and annexed Tahiti.

News of this event appeared in the Paris press of 18 February 1844 and in the London papers two days later. In March Dillon wrote to the Foreign Secretary offering his services. Pritchard, he declared, would never be reconciled to the French, nor they to him. He himself, on the other hand, if the post were free, could perform most useful service.

V

He spoke Tahitian fluently and had considerable influence with the people as 'the adopted son of the most powerful chief in the Leeward Island[s]'. He would be acceptable to the French on account of his discovery of the fate of La Pérouse. As for references, 'I am a Gentleman by Birth and Education, descended from one of the oldest families in Europe . . . The Earls of Derby, Mountcashel [sic], Amherst, Lords Combermere and Middleton are my friends', and these gentlemen could be referred to on his suitability for appointment.[53]

Early in April he presented letters of support from Mountcashell and Combermere, and was granted an interview at the Foreign Office. He pointed out that he could do more there than another man on the small salary of the post, as he already possessed property in the islands. But—again—he was informed that other arrangements had been made.[54]

The Foreign Office had, in fact, decided to transfer Pritchard to Samoa; but before this decision had been taken, he had got into fresh quarrels with the French and had been deported from the island by the new régime. He arrived in London in July 1844, and his story created a violent public sensation. The crisis led Dillon to renew his application. He pointed out that he had foretold these new troubles, offered to give the Foreign Office the inside story of the disputes, and repeated his claim of acceptability to the French: 'Although a foreigner Charles the Tenth of France appointed me as his consul for those Islands in 1829'.[55] His offer was again declined.

While he was thus striving to secure an official British appointment, he was maintaining his links with the Marists. They were having more difficulties over passages: in November 1844 arrangements were being made through a shipping agent named Filby, 'le meilleur ami des Maristes'; by January 1845 another priest opines that Filby is crooked and has overcharged; 'Le Chevalier Dillon nous en offrait un pour £45 mais je pense que son navire n'a qu'une existence bien future . . .'.[56] At the end of the year Dillon wrote several letters to Father Colin, on plans to sail to Sydney: 'At Sydney I possess several houses and pieces of land that I wish to sell'; in the Society Islands there were the cattle to dispose of . . .[57] But he did not go. Perhaps he had not the money, perhaps he had still some lingering hope that he might receive what he thought his due rewards in Europe. In any case, travel was becoming more difficult for him as the years took toll of his strength.

During 1845 he seems to have continued to live in London—he attended several meetings of the Aborigines' Protection Society—but in 1846 he went to Paris with his daughter Martha, settling at 23 Rue des Postes, near the Irish College. In the autumn he wrote to the Marquess of Normanby, the British Ambassador:

> Pray pardon the liberty I take in begging of your Lordship the favour of an Interview before I leave Paris which will be in a few days. I am the Captain Dillon . . . who was so unfortunate as to discover the fate of the French Expedition commanded by the unfortunate but far famed Count de la Perouse.
> On this subject I solicit the favour of an interview . . . [58]

By now the phrase 'so unfortunate as to discover', which he had struck out in a moment of anger years before, to express his disgust with the French Government, had become no more that a cryptic summary of his own vision of the latter half of his career. When, as he saw it, his life might have taken one of two directions—that of prosperity in commerce or of fame as a public figure—he had chosen the latter. It had been a disastrous choice. The fame had been transient, the poverty had had no end.

Now it was too late to change. He was nearing his sixtieth year, and in October 1846 had been 'a martyr to the gout for months', though he thought he was getting rid of it.[59] There were small things still to do, and these he attended to. Martha had devoted her life to him, as housekeeper, amanuensis, translator, and companion. When he died, his pension would cease, and she would be left in penury. He asked Normanby to intercede with the French authorities on his behalf, and hers. Had his wife survived him, she would have received half his pension for life; she was dead, and Dillon wished this half-pension to go to Martha. The Ambassador passed on this request in December 1846, and in January it began to receive official consideration.[60]

At 3 p.m. on 9 February 1847, at 23 Rue des Postes, the Chevalier Peter Dillon died.[61] Briefly, his name was again before the public. *La Presse* on 12 February and *Le Moniteur* on the thirteenth published a notice: 'le capitaine Dillon, célèbre par ses voyages de découvertes dans l'océan Pacifique, est mort subitement . . .'. A notice was also published in *Galignani*, which was copied in Dublin by *Saunders Newsletter* on 18 February and in Auckland by the *New Zealander* on 10 July 1847; the translation in the Dublin paper runs:

> We regret to announce the death of Capt. Dillon, whose voyages and adventures among the natives of the islands in the Pacific are familiar to every reader, and who, it will be remembered, discovered and brought to

France the remnants of the Astrolabe, the sole relics of the unfortunate La Peyrouse and his companions, died on Tuesday almost suddenly.

A concise and matter-of-fact obituary: but 'voyages and adventures ... familiar to every reader' would surely have pleased the Chevalier.

WHEN DILLON died Martha was left in Paris almost penniless. Unlike her father, she spoke and wrote French with ease; but now that he was dead, she no longer had any place in that great city. Her life had been bound to his; she had obeyed his exacting demands, accepted his tantrums. Now that he was gone, she decided to join her grandfather, Patrick Moore, in Sydney.[62]

She renewed her father's request that half his pension should continue to be paid to her, but eventually this was refused. The authorities did, however, grant her a free passage on a warship as far as Valparaiso, whence it was expected that she could make her way across the Pacific, and this offer she accepted. Before she left Paris she presented to the Irish College some of Dillon's books and his precious copy of Máximo Rodríguez' journal, which had been returned to him at A. B Lambert's death in 1842.[63] Then she set out for Toulon to join the *Poursuivante*, with a letter from Palmerston requesting British consuls to extend their assistance to her.[64]

For the first time she was to see two places, Valparaiso and Tahiti, which had meant much in her father's life; her voyage must have been haunted by memories of his stories. If, as is very likely, she had as shipmate from Toulon to Valparaiso the newly appointed French Consul to Hawaii, irony was laid on with a heavy hand; he was a Frenchman, but his name was Dillon.[65] At Valparaiso, where her father had lost the *Calder* and bought the *St Patrick* over twenty years before, there was no ship bound for New South Wales, but British consuls in Chile and Tahiti exerted themselves for her, and the French navy again came to her rescue and gave her a passage on a man-of-war to Tahiti.[66] Here, amid scenes which Dillon had regarded from his youth with particular affection, his daughter waited for a trading ship to Sydney. The French authorities put her up in the rooms of a naval captain, P. F. Ribourt, who apparently had to move out; he gives us a glimpse of Martha which, whatever its evidential value—one would think of the slightest as regards the manner of Dillon's death—and however ill-natured, suggests at least that she was not utterly disconsolate:

The father having died from the effects of an unlimited number of bottles of Champagne, the daughter has set out in her turn to seek her fortune, stopping all along the way to try out the power of her charms. So far the display of her person has not had much effect . . .[67]

She sailed on the *Courier* on 17 July 1848 with two French priests as fellow-passengers, and reached Sydney at last on 28 September. But her reunion with her grandparents and her brothers Peter and Joseph Napoleon was brief: she died on 17 October 1849, still barely thirty years of age.[68]

Neither of her brothers survived her by many years. Joseph Napoleon—'Nap'—married Mary Ann McPherson in 1851 and died four years later at the age of thirty-three; Peter died in 1857, aged forty-two.[69] Nap left one son, named after him Joseph Napoleon, who became the only legitimate descendant of the Chevalier. This boy was brought up by his widowed mother in straightened circumstances. In 1878 he wrote to the French Consul-General in Sydney, and later called on him. He explained that, owing to his upbringing, 'I had not found out till lately all about my Grandfather' but now believed that as Peter Dillon's sole heir he was entitled to half of the French pension.[70] In due course he learnt that this was not so. He lived on as a working man in Sydney and brought up five children, none of whom married. In the 1940s two of them—John Peter and a third Joseph Napoleon— were living in a Sydney suburb with a French name, Sans Souci;[71] they still possessed the Chevalier's Cross of the Legion of Honour.[72] Perhaps in the Islands, in Fiji or Tahiti or New Zealand, Dillon left descendants who achieved at least a local fame, became chiefs or teachers or successful traders; but this we do not know.

FOR A MAN of Dillon's ambition and pride, this was a meagre heritage. He would assuredly have desired to found a notable family; but he would also have asked that his own life should be remembered, his exploits extolled to future generations, and in this he has been more fortunate. No history treating of the European opening of Oceania can omit his decisive action in following up the clues to the fate of La Pérouse, no history of early contact in Fiji the tense adventure at Dillon's Rock. His name is scattered on the maps of the Islands— Dillon's Rock itself and Koro-i-pita in Vanua Levu, Dillon Bay in Eromanga, Dillon's Anchorage at Lakeba, Dillon Head on Vanikoro. For many years after his death the missionaries whom he had so savagely attacked made unflattering references to him in their books and journals; but Islanders who had been his friends proudly showed passing seamen the gifts they had received from him. In 1832 the natives of 'Mallicola' (Vanikoro) greeted Captain Tregurtha, of the Hobart whaler *Caroline*, seven or eight leagues from the island, by holding up 'a fiery oakum wig' and shouting ' "Peter, Peter" . . . it was some days before I acquired a clue to their what appeared to me strange conduct. I had a work of Dillon's voyage in search of La Perouse . . . The natives of Mallicola had dubbed him Peter, and cherished his memory by ochr'd beard and wig'.[73]

The man in all his contradictions stands out in the pages of Bayly's Journal: irascible to the point of violence, but readily recalled to his senses. 'There is no one that ever sailed with him, that will call him humane, except the South Sea Natives, whom he always treated kindly'—and indeed he had a flair for true friendship with Islands people. He was big in physique in regions where physical size in a leader was almost a moral virtue, and with his flaming red hair could not fail to impress. But he owed more of his success to his capacity for involvement, for instance in his obvious enjoyment of the game of honorifics such as 'Brian Boru' and 'the Fejee Admiral', his boisterous humour, in a word his blarney. And when, as an Elder Brother of Trinity House, Bayly recollected in tranquillity the stirring days of his youthful service on the *St Patrick*, the violences are not disguised, but the stress is on the skilled seamanship, the decision and resolution in adversity, which make Peter Dillon, not George Bayly, the hero of *Sea-Life Sixty Years Ago*. Forty years after Dillon's death 'the Vagabond', Julian Thomas, who knew the South Seas and seems to have visited Vanikoro itself, wrote: 'Peter Dillon was evidently a notable man, one to inspire affection as well as fear. I take him to have been the most remarkable character known in the South Seas'[74]—a large claim, but not implausible.

The Chevalier Peter Dillon was not a 'great man' in the conventional sense, and his life as a whole was a failure, not only in conventional terms but as it must have seemed to himself: the one brief flush of glory after Vanikoro, but for the rest of his years

> all the voyage of his life
> Was bound in shallows and in miseries.

But if he was not a great man, he was surely a great personality, and had great gifts of courage and vitality. The interest of his life, as against the events upon which it impinged, lay in his capacity for agony and for ecstasy, in the intensity of his response to the demands of the self and of humanity, in his awareness both of the moment and of history. And this is life itself.

Appendix I

BOOKS, PAMPHLETS AND PRINTED LETTERS BY PETER DILLON

1. *Narrative and Successful Result of a Voyage in the South Seas performed by order of the Government of British India, to ascertain the Actual Fate of La Pérouse's Expedition, interspersed with Accounts of the Religion, Manners, Customs and Cannibal Practices of the South Sea Islanders*
Hurst, Chance and Co., 2 vols, London, 1829.

2. *Mémoire addressé à M. le Préfet d'Île Bourbon par le Capitaine Dillon, 7 septembre 1829*
Poussielgue-Rusand, Paris, 1829.
The printed version is a shortened copy of the original, and on this account is misleading on at least one point. May antedate No. 1.

3. *Voyage aux îles de la Mer du Sud, en 1827 et 1828, et Relation de la Découverte du Sort de la Pérouse.*
Chez Pillet Ainé, 2 vols, Paris, 1830.
Translation of No. 1 above, but with a different dedication.

4. *Reis naar de eilanden der Zuidzee, gedurende de Jaren 1827 en 1828. Behelzende het Verslag der Outdekking van het lot van De La Pérouse, door den scheepskapitein Peter Dillon voormalig, Bevelherber van het Engelsche O.I. kompagnieschip The Research. uit het fransch vertaald.*
G.J.A. Beijerinck, 2 vols, Amsterdam, 1830.
Translation of No. 3, with the same appendixes etc.

5. *À Son Excellence le Président du Conseil des Ministres, Et aux Membres composant le Conseil de S.M. le Roi de France.* [July 1831].
Imprimerie de Pillet Ainé, Paris, [1831].
An address, together with appendixes; first a French version, then an English; large 4to, 20 pp. and cover. Often referred to by Dillon as *Memoir*, and so cited as short title in notes to text.

6. *À Son Excellence Le Comte Sebastiani, Ministre des Affaires Etrangères, 17 septembre 1831.*
Paris, 1831.

7. *Extract of a Letter from the Chevalier Dillon, to an influential character here, on the advantages to be derived from the establishment of well conducted Commercial Settlements in New Zealand. Dated London, May 1 1832.*
London, 1832.

Appendix I

8. *Extract of a Letter* . . . [as above, No. 7].
   [London, 1839].
   There are significant differences between the two editions. See note 5 to Chapter 18 above.

9. [Letters to Lord John Russell on Tonga.]
   About end of 1840; not necessarily printed; see note 17 to Chapter 18 above.

10. *Extract of three Letters addressed to the Right Honourable LORD JOHN RUSSELL, Secretary of State for the Colonies, by the Chevalier Dillon, on the subject of Colonizing New Zealand. A.D. 1840.*
    London, ?1840.

11. *Letters addressed by the Chevalier Dillon to His Grace the Duke of Bedford the Right Hon. Lord John Russell, and Vernon Smith, Esq., M.P., regarding his claims for services performed in New Zealand.*
    London, ?1841; foolscap, no printer's name, date, or place of publication.

12. *Letter to Richard More O'Farrell* [sic: O'Ferrall], *Esq., M.P., Secretary to the Admiralty, Whitehall, London, from the Chevalier Dillon, late French Consul for the Islands in the South Seas, on the defeat of Her Majesty's Ship, Favorite, and death of Her commander, Captain Croker, at Tongataboo, one of the Friendly Islands, where he volunteered his services to the Wesleyan Missionaries to massacre the innocent and unoffending natives, whose only crime was, that they would not embrace a religion that has already caused more bloodshed and cruelty than any other event on record connected with the Friendly Islands.*
    London, ? December 1841.
    Contains Dillon's letter to Reverend John Thomas on affairs in Tonga (see above, pp. 271-4 and pp. 290-3). David Cargill, in *A Refutation of the Chevalier Dillon's Slanderous Attacks* . . . (London, 1842), states that this pamphlet was printed in December 1841; but there is some evidence that it (or a pamphlet very like it) appeared in 1840—Dillon sent a copy of some printed letters on Tonga, addressed to the Secretary of the Admiralty, to the Marists in February 1841. Also contains Joseph Meyrick's letter to Dillon, Vava'u, 16 January 1838.

13. *Conquest of Siberia and the History of the Transactions, Wars, Commerce, etc., etc., carried on between Russia and China from the Earliest Period.*
    Smith and Elder, London, 1842.
    'Translated from the Russian of G. F. Muller . . . and of Peter Simon Pallas . . . ' (actually taken from the English of William Coxe), anonymously edited by Dillon; see above, pp. 301-3.

14. *Conquest of Siberia, by the Chevalier Dillon, and the History* . . . [etc. as above].
    Allen, London, 1843.
    Second edition of No. 13, with significant alteration in title; see above p. 303. [This list does not include letters to the press, anonymous or over Dillon's name; some of these are cited in the text.]

Appendix II

DILLON'S ROCK

THE precise site of Dillon's Rock—some might prefer to call it Savage's—cannot be identified with absolute certainty. The coast alternates between low but rugged promontories and broad bays, with mangrove around the estuaries; a typical late Tertiary volcanic coast, with any number of little knobs formed by lava outcrops. From Dillon's *Narrative* it must lie between the broad-topped hill of Korolevu (830 feet, 253 m.) and the shores of Naurore Bay, between half and three-quarters of a mile to the north.

This at once rules out the feature often pointed out to travellers on launches going through Monkey Face Passage as 'Dillon's Rock', a lava knob near the end of an eroded rocky spur at the north-west point of Naurore Bay. Apart from the fact that there is nothing here to suggest a defensible point near a village, it is much too far away from the scene of action near Wailea, Dillon's 'Vilear'.

R. A. Derrick's account in his *History of Fiji* (Suva, 3rd ed. 1957, 46) is highly condensed. It speaks of Dillon's party burning houses on Korolevu (where there is no evidence that any ever existed) and thence retreating to 'Black Rock—a high isolated rock near the shore'. But it is clear from Dillon's *Narrative* and the picture in it, which he must have approved (Plate 1 in this book) that his rock was in a 'plain' and some distance from the shore. Derrick may have been confused by Dillon's reference to landing 'at the Black Rock' (*Narrative*, 1, 9). From the relations of beach, mangrove, and village, there can be little doubt that Macdonald and Dods are right in identifying this point with that named 'Beqa' on the accompanying sketch-map, a good landing place. The only doubtful point is that Dillon says this rock was 'a little way to the eastward of the river', and it is west of the Wailea River, if that is what he meant. But several small streams come down to the coastal flats west of Beqa, and this degree of confusion is surely allowable in the highly agitated circumstances. At all events, and with no disrespect to Derrick's contribution to Fijian history, his evidence on this specific matter may be disregarded.

In 1969 Professor Davidson and Dr Deryck Scarr visited the area; they concluded that Dillon's Rock lay towards the seaward end of the low but uneven peninsula of Koro-i-vita (which might be loosely identified as 'Peter's place') lying to the north of the Naviqiri-Wailea track, of which the highest point was named on an old map of 1907 'Koro-i-vita'. This name, so

Appendix II

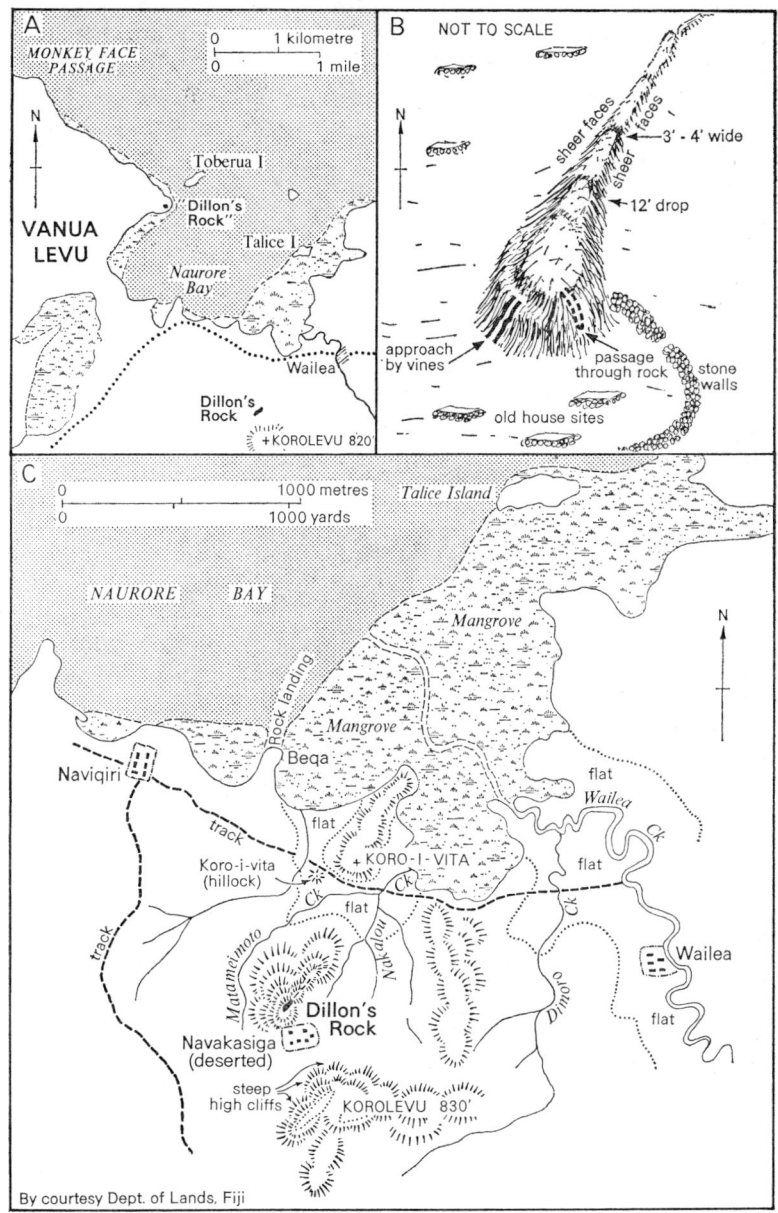

4 The location of Dillon's Rock

far as can be ascertained, seems to have been attached rather vaguely to the immediate locality as being within the general area of the exciting event of 1813, and perhaps more definitely the place where the first brush with the Waileans, and the burning of houses, took place; it may not represent a genuine old name. None of the Fijians questioned by Macdonald and Dods advanced any but the first of these explanations. On the same 1907 map there is another place marked 'Koro-i-vita (hillock)', lying to the south of the same track; but this is a mere hillock, as the name implies, about ten feet high and some forty feet in diameter. It would be quite indefensible, while the ridge running out to sea seems too close to the shore to square with Plate 1, is too wide for easy defence and has convex sides providing dead ground, with mangrove close-to at the seaward end, both features providing ample cover for the attack. Davidson and Scarr were led to their conclusion partly by the position of the ridge just north of the track leading along the shore west from Wailea; but tracks can change.

Later in October 1969 and April 1970 Mr P. D. Macdonald, then Chairman of the Fiji Public Service Commission, and Mr Robert Dods, then Commissioner, Northern Division, carried out a detailed search in the area, and reported to Professor Davidson in a long letter from Mr Macdonald on 20 May 1970, with maps, photographs, and sketches. Their conclusion was that Dillon's Rock was a feature about 430 yards north-east of the Korolevu summit and under three-quarters of a mile from the nearest mangrove-free shore; this is shown as Savage's Rock on the Lands Department cadastral maps.

It is impracticable to summarize the very close and lengthy reasoning which led Macdonald and Dods to their conclusion. One cannot expect a man in Dillon's position to narrate with precision his actual cross-country movements while under attack from hundreds (if not the 'thousands' of the *Narrative*) of exceedingly hostile savages; but their reconstruction fits very well with Dillon's own account. One might expect the detail of the actual terrain on which the stand took place to be more imprinted on Dillon's memory (and on those of Martin Buchert and Joe the Lascar, whom Bayly interrogated); and here the fit seems to me extraordinarily good.

At the northern end the Rock rises almost sheer for seventy to eighty feet of jagged lava; at the southern end, where it widens into a tiny plateau, the last twenty or thirty feet are negotiable at two points, by vines and by a narrow passage between the rocks, wide enough for only one man at a time. This passage ascends from an old village site, with the remains of a stone enceinte. The access for more than two or three people at a time could only be by the long northern spur, as it were the tail of the tadpole-shaped ridge, which for much of its length is only three or four feet wide and broken by a twelve-foot drop. It is thus eminently defensible.

Mr Dods had been a senior draftsman in the Lands Department, and from the top of the Rock drew a sketch-plan of it. This was done *before* he had seen the drawing from the *Narrative* reproduced in Plate 1, and allowing for the inevitable foreshortening of the northwards spur in the picture, it does indeed seem to match very well. The distance from Rock to shore in Plate 1 seems about right for the actual ground distance, difficult as such things are to judge.

Appendix II

The main, if not the only, difficulty about this site lies in its distance from the shore and the bearing of this on what Dillon could see of the movements of people to and from the *Hunter*. This may not be so serious a difficulty as it may appear at first sight. He says that he 'did not lose sight' of Dafny (sent with a safe-conduct to ask for the release of four of Robson's eight Fijian prisoners) 'until he got on the ship's deck' (*Narrative*, 1, 16). This may not be literally true but (apart from a few feet of dead ground at the beginning) he would surely have seen any violent incident between Rock and shore, and once the boat's people went aboard, he could take it that Dafny was one of them even if he had been unable to recognize him at that (unknown) distance. Dillon does not say that he saw the eight Fijians leave the ship, but that he saw the boat put off from the ship and soon get 'close to the landing-place, where we counted the eight prisoners landing from her' (*Narrative*, 1, 21). The distance on this identification was more than half a mile but definitely less than three-quarters and surely it should have been possible at this distance to count eight men getting out of a boat, especially as he was expecting to see four.

On the whole I am as reasonably sure as one can be in these matters that the Macdonald-Dods interpretation, as shown on the accompanying sketch map, is correct. The original of Mr Macdonald's documentation will be kept with Professor Davidson's drafts of this book in the Department of Pacific and Southeast Asian History, at the Australian National University; photocopies of the letter and maps will be deposited in the Fiji Archives.

Notes

1
THE SETTING

1 George Birkbeck Hill (ed.), *Boswell's Life of Johnson*, revised L. F. Powell (Oxford, 1934-50), IV, 308.
2 Quoted in John Dunmore, *French Explorers in the Pacific* (Oxford, 1965-69), I, 110.
3 Jean-Jacques Rousseau, 'A dissertation on the origin and foundation of the inequality of mankind', *The Social Contract & Discourses* (London, Everyman's Library, 1913) 214.
4 John Hawkesworth, *An Account of the Voyages undertaken by the Order of His Present Majesty for making Discoveries in the Southern Hemisphere...* (London, 1773), III, 353.

2
PACIFIC APPRENTICESHIP

1 Folio 13, no. 93—*Pensions*—ANM BB4 1003. This is, in form, a French official record; but it is not clear whether the information was obtained—or confirmed—from Martinique, or whether a statement by Dillon was simply accepted. There is no reason for doubting its accuracy.
2 Dillon to Chairman and Deputy Chairman, East India Company, 13 November 1828—IOL, Miscellaneous Letters Received, 1828, IV, no. 166; 'Dillon (Peter)' *Dictionnaire de biographie française*, XI (Paris, 1967).
3 Dillon to Chairman and Deputy Chairman, East India Company, 13 November 1828, *loc. cit.*
4 e.g., in Dillon to the Minister of Marine and Colonies, 5 January 1827—ANM BB4 1003—where he wrote: 'The person who addresses you is Captain Peter Dillon... a relation of the Dillon Family of Martinique'.
5 On the Dillons of Martinique, see: 'Dillon (Arthur, comte)', *Dictionnaire de biographie française*, XI (Paris, 1967); Marquise de La Tour du Pin, *Journal d'une femme de cinquante ans 1778-1815* (6th ed., 2 vols, Paris, 1913), *passim*; William Henry Dillon, *A Narrative of My Professional Adventures (1790-1839)*, ed. Michael Lewis (London, Navy Records Society, 1953), I, xvii-xx, 242; Frédéric Masson, *Napoleon at St. Helena 1815-1821*, trans. Louis B. Frewer (Oxford, 1949), 49-57.
6 See below, note 53 in Chapter 15.
7 Dillon, *Narrative*, II, 377— '... to Europe, from which place I had been absent about two and twenty years' (written under date 10 May 1828).
8 George Bayly, *Sea-Life Sixty Years Ago* (London, 1885), 183-4.
9 Dillon, *Narrative*, I, 217-18; Margaret Steven, *Merchant Campbell 1769-1846: a study of colonial trade* (Melbourne, 1965), 101.
10 Dillon to Chabrol, 7 August 1828—ANM, BB4 1003; *Government Gazette* (Calcutta), 16 October 1826.

11 Prince of Wales Island Gazette, 25 June 1808; Everard im Thurn and Leonard C. Wharton (eds), The Journal of William Lockerby, Sandalwood Trader in the Fijian Islands during the years 1808-1809 . . . (London, Hakluyt Society, 1925), 39.
12 Im Thurn and Wharton (eds), Lockerby, 36, 39. Lockerby's Journal, together with the long introduction by Sir Everard im Thurn, provides the most important source for this period of Fijian history.
13 Sydney Gazette, 27 November 1808; D. R. Hainsworth, 'In search of a staple: the Sydney sandalwood trade 1804-09', Business Archives and History, V (1965), 16.
14 Dillon, Narrative, I, 4.
15 Sydney Gazette, 27 November 1808.
16 Gregory M. Dening (ed.), The Marquesan Journal of Edward Robarts 1797-1824 (Canberra, 1974).
17 Dillon, Narrative, I, 1. He places this period of residence in 1809, rather than 1808-09; but the circumstances of his leaving the General Wellesley may well have given him cause for minor falsification.
18 Government Gazette (Calcutta), 16 October 1826.
19 The Perseverance sailed from Huahine, in the Society Islands, on 14 November 1808 (John Davies, The History of the Tahitian Mission 1799-1830, ed. C. W. Newbury (Cambridge, Hakluyt Society, 1961), 125). She reached Sydney on 20 February 1809 (Sydney Gazette, 26 February 1809).
20 Published in the Sydney Gazette, 5 March 1809. These lists were issued by the Secretary's Office. The originals do not survive. Dillon's signature on the occasion of his marriage in 1814 can be read as 'Peter Dellon' (St Philip's Church Register VII, ML D364).
21 Sydney Gazette, 9 April 1809.
22 Hainsworth, op. cit., 18; Steven, Merchant Campbell, 183, 244.
23 Blaxcell to Macarthur, 6 November 1809—Macarthur Papers, IV, ML A2900.
24 Sydney Gazette, 17 September 1809; Blaxcell to Macarthur, 6 November 1809—loc. cit.
25 Sydney Gazette, 19 March 1809; Blaxcell to Macarthur, 10 May 1810—loc. cit.
26 Davies, Tahitian Mission, 115-25 passim.
27 Sydney Gazette, 17 July 1808; see also Davies, Tahitian Mission, 110.
28 Sydney Gazette, 22 October 1809.
29 The Deposition of Peter Dillon. In a complaint preferred by the Revd. S. Marsden against Mr Theodore Walker late Master of the Mercury Schooner, 20 November 1813—Supreme Court, New South Wales, Criminal Papers, 1152.
30 ibid.; Dillon, Narrative, I, 197, 213. For Jemmy, see also: John Rawson Elder (ed.), The Letters and Journals of Samuel Marsden, 1765-1838 . . . (Dunedin, 1932), 81-2; Robert McNab, From Tasman to Marsden. A History of Northern New Zealand from 1642 to 1818 (Dunedin, 1914), 127. Marsden refers to him as 'Jem'.
31 Deposition of Peter Dillon . . . , 20 November 1813—loc. cit.
32 Elder (ed.), Samuel Marsden, 59.
33 The Deposition of Jacob Williams, 20 November 1813—Supreme Court, New South Wales, Criminal Papers, 1152.
34 Deposition of Peter Dillon . . . , 20 November 1813—loc. cit.
35 Davies, Tahitian Mission, 135-6; Sydney Gazette, 5 May 1810.
36 Sydney Gazette, 5 May 1810.
37 ibid., 21 July 1810.
38 ibid., 5 May 1810. This issue contains a fairly full account of the voyage.
39 Burnsides was not listed in the Sydney Gazette among the passengers leaving in the Boyd. His presence on board is mentioned, however, not only by Dillon but also by Garnham Blaxcell (Blaxcell to Macarthur, 10 May 1810—loc. cit.).
40 Dillon, Narrative, I, 217-18.
41 Deposition of Peter Dillon . . . , 20 November 1813—loc. cit. Dillon merely states that he received this information 'later'. It seems most likely, however, that it was at this time, as two of the vessels in New Zealand at the time of the attack on Te Pahi's island reached Sydney before or while he was there—the Perseverance on 28 April, the New Zealander on 30 May.
42 Elder (ed.), Samuel Marsden, 62.
43 Sydney Gazette, 30 June 1810.

44 ibid., 21 July, 10 November 1810.
45 ibid., 25 May 1811.
46 ibid., 21 July 1810.
47 ibid., 25 May 1811; Davies, *Tahitian Mission*, 137.
48 *Sydney Gazette*, 18, 25 May 1811.
49 Colin Newbury, '*Te Hau Pahu Rahi*: Pomare II and the concept of inter-island government in Eastern Polynesia', *Journal of the Polynesian Society*, LXXVI (1967), 495, 512.
50 Declaration of Mr Peter Dillon, n.d. [November 1813] HL MSS. 54/41.
51 Dillon to Aberdeen, 16 March 1844—FO 58/31; Dillon to Solages, 17 September 1829—AMAE: Océanie: Mémoires et Documents, I. There is slight doubt as to the identity of his adoptive father. Except for one statement all the evidence points to Tapoa. The exception occurs in the letter to Solages. The copy cited, which is a French translation of Dillon's original, refers to Queen Pomare IV as the 'petite fille' of this man. This would point to Tamatoa, of Ra'iatea. Tapoa became the father-in-law of the Queen, who married his son.
52 J. M. Orsmond, 14 December 1823—SSJ, lxxi.
53 Dillon to Foreign Office, 9 April 1844—FO 58/32.
54 *Sydney Gazette*, 30 May 1812.

3

THE PATH TO 'DILLON'S ROCK' 1813

1 Declaration of Mr Peter Dillon, n.d. [November 1813] HL MSS. 54/41.
2 J. S. Cumpston, *Shipping Arrivals and Departures: Sydney, 1788-1825* (Canberra, 1963), 78, 90.
3 Dillon, *Narrative*, I, 1; Deposition of Peter Dillon, 6 November 1813—*HRA*, I, VIII, 103-4.
4 Dillon, *Narrative*, I, 1.
5 Deposition of Peter Dillon, 6 November 1813—*HRA*, I, VIII, 104; *Sydney Gazette*, 23 October 1813.
6 These are three contemporary narratives of events during the *Hunter*'s stay at Naurore Bay. They are contained in: Dillon, *Narrative*, I, 1-31; Deposition of Peter Dillon, 6 November 1813—*HRA*, I, VIII, 103-7; *Sydney Gazette*, 23 October 1813. Quotations in this chapter are from Dillon's *Narrative*, except where another source is given.
    Dillon was the writer or informant in each case. His accuracy was questioned many years later, but on doubtful grounds. The 'Dillon's Rock' episode alone was independently checked; George Bayly obtained accounts of it from both Dillon and Martin Buchert; and George Bayly, *Sea-Life Sixty Years Ago* (London, 1885), vii-viii.
7 Dillon uses the word 'Nanpacab' (Bekavu), which is the name of an island in the Dreketi River. For the identification of Dreketi and Bekavu, see Everard im Thurn and Leonard C. Wharton (eds), *The Journal of William Lockerby, Sandalwood Trader in the Fijian Islands during the years 1808-1809* ... (London, Hakluyt Society, 1925), 62.
8 *Sydney Gazette*, 7 November 1812.
9 This episode is described in the Deposition of Peter Dillon, 6 November 1813—*HRA* I, VIII, 104.
10 Dillon, *Narrative*, I, 31. He wrote, in the *Narrative*, that he was 'now preparing' such a history. The book was perhaps never finished. Efforts to locate the manuscript have been unsuccessful.
11 On Savage, see: Im Thurn and Wharton (eds), *Lockerby*, lxvi-ii, 95; Basil Thomson, *South Sea Yarns* (Edinburgh and London, 1894), 288-326; and Basil Thomson, *The Fijians: a study of the Decay of Custom* (London, 1908), 27-32. Thomson, however, grossly exaggerates the importance of Savage's role.
12 *Sydney Gazette*, 28 May 1809; Dillon, *Narrative*, I, 11, 25.
13 Questions à faire au Matelot Prussien—ANM BB4 1003. The questions (and their answers) are in a folder labelled 'Mr Chaigneau'. They were presumably put to Buchert by Eugène Chaigneau in 1827.

Notes 319

The spelling of Buchert's name presents a problem. George Bayly, who knew him and could spell, wrote 'Buchert' (Bayly, *Sea-Life, passim*); Dillon, who was an atrocious speller, usually wrote 'Bushart'; other variants are 'Buschart', 'Bushard' and 'Busshart'. The document cited merely refers to him as the 'Matelot Prussien'.
14 Thomson, *South Sea Yarns*, 312-14.
15 This episode is described in the Deposition of Peter Dillon, 6 November 1813—*HRA*, I, VIII, 104-5.
16 *Sydney Gazette*, 23 October 1813.
17 The location of the sites at which the incidents described in this section occurred presents considerable difficulty. For a discussion of the problem, see Appendix II, below.
18 Deposition of Peter Dillon, 6 November 1813—*HRA*, I, VIII, 105.
19 *ibid.*
20 *ibid.*, 106.
21 George Bayly, 'Journal of Voyages to various parts of the World written by Geo^e. Bayly for the amusement of such of his friends as feel themselves disposed to read it', I, 56—HL MSS ML, 145-6 and 146A.
22 Bayly, *Sea-Life*, 17.

4
A MAN OF CONSEQUENCE IN AUSTRALIA 1813-16

1 Macquarie to Castlereagh, 30 April 1810—*HRA*, I, VII, 275-6.
2 *Sydney Gazette*, 23 October 1813.
3 Dillon, *Narrative*, I, 27.
4 *ibid.*, I, 24; 'Cox, William', *ADB*, I, 258-9.
5 Deposition of Peter Dillon, 6 November 1813—*HRA*, I, VIII, 103-7; see also Glenholme to Dillon, 5 November 1813; Dillon to Glenholme, 6 November 1813—*ibid.*, 111.
6 *Sydney Gazette*, 13 November 1813. For the correspondence relating to this subject, some of which arrived subsequently, see Macquarie to Bathurst, 17 January 1814 (and encls)—*HRA*, I, VIII, 96-103.
7 Macquarie to Bathurst, 17 January 1814—*HRA*, I, VIII, 97.
8 *ibid.*
9 Depositions of Abraham Hendrick, John Jones, Thomas French and John Randall, 16 November 1813—*HRA* I, VIII, 107-11.
10 The Deposition of Peter Dillon. In a complaint preferred by the Revd. S. Marsden against Mr Theodore Walker late Master of the Mercury Schooner, 20 November 1813—Supreme Court, NSW, Criminal Papers, 1152; Declaration of Mr Peter Dillon, n.d. [November 1813]—HL, MSS., 54/41.
11 Bathurst to Macquarie, 12 July 1815 (and encls)—*HRA*, I, VIII, 622-3; Macquarie to Bathurst, 18 March 1816—*ibid.*, IX, 66-7.
12 Published in *Sydney Gazette*, 4 December 1813.
13 *Sydney Gazette*, 18, 25 December 1813.
14 *ibid.*, 13, 27 November 1813, 22 January 1814.
15 John Rawson Elder (ed.), *Marsden's Lieutenants* (Dunedin, 1934), 45.
16 John Rawson Elder (ed.), *The Letters and Journals of Samuel Marsden, 1765-1838*... (Dunedin, 1932), 62.
17 Dillon to Polignac, 31 March 1830—AMAE: Océanie: Mémoires et Documents, I.
18 Elder, *Lieutenants*, 55-6.
19 Elder, *Letters and Journals*, 62.
20 Elder, *Lieutenants*, 49-50.
21 Knopwood Diary, 12 April 1814—Archives Office of Tasmania (photostat).
22 R. J. Solomon, The Evolution of Hobart. A Study in Historical Geography with Special Reference to Urban Fabric and Function, *circa* 1804-1963 (unpublished Ph.D. thesis, Tasmania, 1968), 219.
23 John West, *The History of Tasmania* (Launceston, 1852), I, 50-1.
24 Knopwood Diary, 15 April, 20, 21 May 1814.

25 Elder, *Lieutenants*, 56. On the *Spring*, see: Campbell to E. Lord, 21 March 1814—Letter Book, January 1814-March 1815—CSO 4/3493; Report of ships and vessels cleared outwards, 16 February-31 March 1814—CSO X698.
26 Elder, *Lieutenants*, 56; Kendall's Journal—Marsden MSS., Hocken Library, Dunedin.
27 Dillon, *Extract of a Letter from the Chevalier Dillon . . . on the advantages to be derived from the establishment of well conducted Commercial Settlements in New Zealand* (London, 1832), 7.
28 Elder, *Lieutenants*, 67. For Kendall's tragic story, see Judith Binney, *Legacy of Guilt* (Auckland, 1968).
29 Kendall's Journal. Substantial extracts from this Journal are printed in Elder, *Lieutenants*; and where these are cited reference is given to that book. Where the reference is to the Journal itself, the relevant passage is to be found only in the original manuscript, which is among the Marsden MSS., in the Hocken Library, Dunedin.
30 Elder, *Letters and Journals*, 63-5; Elder, *Lieutenants*, 75-9.
31 Kendall's Journal.
32 *ibid*.
33 List of convicts transported to New South Wales Britannia Transport December 1796—Convict Indentures . . . Ships 1796-98—CSO 4/4000; T. J. Kiernan, *Transportation from Ireland to Sydney: 1791-1816* (Canberra, 1954), 12-13, 54-60.
34 Petition of Patrick Moore, 22 January 1810—In-letters, 1810, CSO 4/1846; Hayward to Colonial Secretary, 26 August 1839—Papers received re land, CSO 2/7931; *Sydney Gazette*, 4 June, 13 August 1809, 27 September 1817.
35 Petition of Patrick Moore, 22 January 1810—*loc. cit.*; *Sydney Gazette*, 23 December 1815, 18 October 1817; Moore to Colonial Secretary, 25 October 1828—Papers received re land, CSO 2/7931.
36 Personal information from J. P. and J. N. Dillon, great-grandsons of Peter and Mary Dillon, 1946; St Philip's Church Register, VII, ML D364.
37 *Sydney Gazette*, 13 July 1811.
38 St Philip's Church Register, VII, ML D364.
39 Elder, *Letters and Journals*, 137.
40 *Sydney Gazette*, 11 March 1815.
41 Inquest on James O'Burne, 20 May 1815—*HRA*, 3, II, 122-3.
42 Knopwood Diary, 19 May 1815.
43 St Philip's Church Register, VII, ML D364.
44 *Sydney Gazette*, 23 December 1815.
45 For the movements of the *Spring* between Sydney, Hobart Town and Port Dalrymple, see: Report of ships and vessels cleared outwards, 1 July-30 September 1815—CSO X699; *Sydney Gazette*, 9, 23 September 1815; Knopwood Diary, 25 September, 1 November 1815. For the visit to Kangaroo Island, etc., see: *Evidence respecting the Soil, Climate, and Productions of the South Coast of Australia, Between the 132nd and 141st Degrees of East Longitude* (London, 1832), 47-8; Dillon to Hay, 15 August 1832—CO 13/1; Dillon to Hay, 7 October 1832—CO 323/168.

5
CALCUTTA AND THE 'COUNTRY TRADE' 1816-23

1 Report of ships and vessels entered inwards, 1 April-30 June 1816—CSO X699. These were the only arrivals from Hobart Town in May; there was one arrival in April—the *Tweed*, also from Calcutta, on 27 April. There was one arrival from Port Dalrymple, the *John Palmer*, on 19 April (Entries of colonial vessels, 1 April-30 June 1816—*ibid*.).
2 Report of ships and vessels cleared outwards, 1 April-30 June 1816—CSO X699. The *Bridgewater* sailed at the same time; but the Dillons were not listed among the passengers who reached Calcutta in her (*Government Gazette* (Calcutta), 5 September 1816).
3 Log of the Brig *Lynx* 1816-17—ML A2006.
4 See, especially, Walter Hamilton, *A Geographical, Statistical, and Historical Description of Hindostan and the Adjacent Countries* (2 vols, London, 1820), I, 48-65.
5 *Bengal Hurkaru*, 5 September 1826; Combermere to Canning, 31 March 1844—FO 58/31.

Notes

6 These relatives were there in the Marquis of Hasting's time (1813-22)—Dillon to Polignac, 31 March 1830—AMAE: Océanie, 1822-43: lettres et documents; see also Dillon to Laborde, 3 August 1830—ANM BB4 1003.
7 Dillon, *Narrative*, I, 84-5.
8 *Government Gazette* (Calcutta), 6 February 1817.
9 Dillon to J. Pratt, 13 October 1820—ATL Micro MS 310. For the connection between Campbell & Company and John Gilmore & Company, see Margaret Steven, *Merchant Campbell 1769-1846: a study of colonial trade* (Melbourne, 1965), 218-23, 240-2.
10 On the Barretto family, see: *Bengal Past and Present*, (Calcutta), II, (1908), 366-7; R. S. Whiteway, *The Rise of Portuguese Power in India 1497-1550* (2nd ed., London, 1967), 46, 71, 310.
11 Alfred Spencer (ed.), *Memoirs of William Hickey* (4 vols, 10th ed., London 1948), II, 381-2, III, 1-72 *passim*, IV, 328-9.
12 C. H. Philips (ed.), *The Correspondence of David Scott Director and Chairman of the East India Company relating to Indian Affairs 1787-1805* (2 vols, London, Camden Society 3rd Series, LXXV-VI, 1951), I, 123, 178, 199.
13 Records of St John's Church, Calcutta; *Bengal Past and Present, loc. cit.*
14 *Bengal Past and Present*, II, 366-7.
15 Information on the composition of business firms, committees etc. is contained in *The Bengal Directory and General Register* . . . (Calcutta, annually). The admission to partnership in Joseph Barretto & Sons of Da Cruz and Brightman was announced in the *Government Gazette* (Calcutta), 12 September, 17 October 1816. A Luis Barreto —probably the same man—was also a partner in Antonio Lourenço Barretto & Company, of Macao and Canton. For biographical information see especially Holmes & Company, *The Bengal Obituary, or a Record to Perpetuate the Memory of Departed Worth* . . . (Calcutta, 1848).
16 For the voyage of the *Greyhound*, see: *Hobart Town Gazette and Southern Reporter*. 28 February, 4 April 1818; *Sydney Gazette*, 18 April, 13 June 1818. For Dillon's presence as first officer, see [Hobart Town] Port Certificate Book, 1817[-1822], Crowther Collection, Hobart; Ships Musters, 1816-21, 102—CSO; for Thomas Ritchie, see *ADB*, II, 382-3.
17 For Benkulen or Bencoolen, see W. Marsden, *The History of Sumatra*, London, 3rd ed., 1811, 450-2 (Oxford in Asia Reprints, Kuala Lumpur, 1966).
18 Dillon (*Narrative*, I, 110) refers to conditions at this time of year; the reference can refer only to his experience in the *Greyhound*.
19 *Hobart Town Gazette*, 28 February 1818.
20 Knopwood Diary, 25, 26 February, 6, 14, 17, 20, 28, 29, 30 March 1818—Archives Office of Tasmania (photostat).
21 *Hobart Town Gazette*, 4 April 1818.
22 Knopwood Diary, 3 April 1818.
23 *Sydney Gazette*, 18 April, 13 June 1818.
24 *ibid.*, 18 September 1819.
25 *Calcutta Journal*, 2 October 1818.
26 Martha was aged ten months in December 1819—Ship's Musters, 1816-21, 201—CSO 4/4711.
27 *Prince of Wales Island Gazette*, 7 August 1819.
28 *Hobart Town Gazette*, 29 September 1821; J. S. Cumpston, *Shipping Arrivals and Departures: Sydney, 1788-1825* (Canberra, 1963), 118. The name *St Michael* first appears in *The Bengal Directory and General Register* in the issue for 1820. She may have been renamed by Dillon. He later renamed one of his ships *St Patrick* (see below, note 12 to chapter 6).
29 Horton to J. Orton, 19 June 1839—MMS.
30 *Prince of Wales Island Gazette*, 7 August 1819.
31 Dillon, *Narrative*, II, 379-82.
32 *Sydney Gazette*, 4 December 1819.
33 Secretary to 'the Commander of the Ship St Michael', 10 August 1819; Secretary to Town Major, n.d.; Acting Secretary to Town Major, 1 September 1819- : IOL, Prince of Wales Island, Letters and Orders in Council, 1819-20 (H.3), nos 604, 605,

22. For a description of Penang at this period, see A. Prinsep, *Journal of a Voyage from Calcutta to Van Diemen's Land* ... (London, 1833), 4-13.
34 *Prince of Wales Island Gazette*, 7 August-11 September 1819.
35 *Hobart Town Gazette*, 13 November 1819. The account of events in Atjeh begins: 'The St. Michael brings us the following intelligence'. Dillon seems certain to have been the informant.
36 *Prince of Wales Island Gazette*, 11 September 1819.
37 *Hobart Town Gazette*, 13 November 1819.
38 *ibid.*, 13, 27 November 1819; *Sydney Gazette*, 4 December 1819.
39 Ralph S. Kuykendall, *The Hawaiian Kingdom 1778-1854: Foundation and Transformation* (Honolulu, 1938), 42, 76.
40 Dillon to Colonial Secretary, 16, 18 December 1819—CSO, In-letters, 4/1743
41 Ships Musters, 1816-21, 201—CSO 4/4771.
42 *Hobart Town Gazette*, 29 September 1821.
43 *Sydney Gazette*, 29 December 1821; J. E. Calder, 'Captain Peter Dillon', *The Mercury* (Hobart), 29 January 1881.
44 George Bayly, *Sea-Life Sixty Years Ago* (London, 1885), 78.
45 Dillon to J. Pratt, 13 October 1820—ATL Micro MS 310. Two words which I have completed in square brackets have lost their final letters through deterioration of the paper. The letter contains a note regarding Pratt's reply and the enclosed letter from McCabe.
46 *Government Gazette* (Calcutta), 1 February 1821; *Hobart Town Gazette*, 18 August 1821.
47 Memorial of Peter Dillon of Calcutta Master Mariner to H. E. Lachlan Macquarie, 24 November 1821—CSO 4/1749.
48 *Government Gazette* (Calcutta), 8 March 1821.
49 The fullest account of events between the departure of the *Phatisalam* from Madras and her wreck is in the *Hobart Town Gazette*, 18 August 1821. This gives the 'substance of a letter received ... from Captain Dillon ... addressed to an inhabitant of this Town [probably James Kelly, the harbour master and pilot]'. Some additional facts are contained in two letters from former passengers in the ship: Jackson to Dillon, 8 October 1821; Smith to Dillon, 21 October 1821—*Sydney Gazette*, 29 December 1821. See also J. E. Calder, 'Captain Peter Dillon', *Mercury* (Hobart), 29 January 1881.
50 Memorial of the Chevalier Peter Dillon to the Rt. Hon. E. G. S. Stanley, Secretary of State, 22 June 1833—CO 201/235. For a list of those drowned, see *Sydney Gazette*, 29 September 1821.
51 Dillon to Murray, 23 December 1829—CO 201/206.
52 Dillon to Cimitière, 6 August 1821; Cimitière to Smith, 6 August 1821; Memorial of Peter Dillon, 24 November 1821; Extracts from Log Book of *Little Mary*—CSO 4/1749.
53 *Sydney Gazette*, 8, 22 September 1821.
54 *Hobart Town Gazette*, 18 August 1821.
55 Memorial of Peter Dillon, 24 November 1821—CSO 4/1749.
56 For his subsequent possession, and sale, of the cargo, see: Dillon to Lord, n.d.—Calder Papers, ML FM4/728; *Sydney Gazette*, 10 November 1821.
57 *Hobart Town Gazette*, 22 September 1821; *Sydney Gazette*, 10 November 1821.
58 *Sydney Gazette*, 29 September 1821.
59 *ibid.*, 2 January 1823.
60 For the initial discussion regarding liability for the expenses directly arising from the shipwreck, see: Kenworthy to Dillon, 11 September 1821; Dillon to Kenworthy, 14 September 1821; Cimitière, to Dillon, 11 October 1821; Dillon to Cimitière, 11 October 1821; Memorial of Peter Dillon, 24 November 1821—CSO In-letters, 4/1749, between pages 125 and 141; Dillon to Colonial Secretary, 26 January 1822—*ibid.*, 4/1759. The discussion continued, however, for many years.
61 Dillon to Kenworthy, 14 September 1821—CSO 4/1749.
62 Robinson (Secretary to Lieut-Governor) to Dillon, 27 August 1821—Letter book of Henry Edward Robinson, 1819-24, ML A 1356; *Hobart Town Gazette*, 18 August 1821.
63 *ibid.*, 25 August 1821.

Notes 323

64 Criminal Court Book commencing February 1822, 81, 82—CSO 4/1264; Dillon to Murray, 23 December 1829—CO 201/206.
65 *Hobart Town Gazette*, September 1821; *Sydney Gazette*, 8 September 1821.
66 J. E. Calder, 'Captain Peter Dillon', *Mercury* (Hobart), 29 January 1881. See also, for the general background, *The Proceedings in the case of His Majesty's Attorney-General, J. T. Gellibrand, Esq.*.. (Hobart Town, [1826]).
67 Horton to Orton, 19 June 1839—MMS.
68 *Sydney Gazette*, 29 December 1821. On Thomas Simpson, see G. H. Crawford, W. F. Ellis and G. H. Stancombe (eds), *The Diaries of James Helder Wedge 1824-1835* (Hobart, 1962), 88.
69 *ibid.*
70 *Hobart Town Gazette*, 29 September 1821.
71 *Hobart Town Gazette*, 22 September 1821; *Sydney Gazette*, 10 November 1821.
72 Dillon to Lord, n.d.—Calder Papers, ML FM4/728; Knopwood Diary, 6 January 1822; *Sydney Gazette*, 10 November 1821. Cargo taken to Sydney by Dillon included 4,650 gallons of rum and 93 gallons of brandy. According to Knopwood, Lord's brig *Jupiter* landed '5000 Gall of Spirits & quantity of other Stores' from the *Phatisalam* at Hobart Town.
73 J. E. Calder, 'Captain Peter Dillon', *Mercury* (Hobart), 29 January 1881; *Sydney Gazette*, 10 November 1821.
74 Dillon to Cimitière, 11 October 1821—CSO 4/1749; Dillon to Murray, 23 December 1829—CO 201/206.
75 *Sydney Gazette*, 10 November 1821; Dillon to Murray, 3 November 1830—CO 201/215.
76 Registrar General's Office, Sydney.
77 James *v*. Dillon—Supreme Court of Civil Judicature: Judgment Rolls, 1822, 3 & 4 Terms, NSW State Archives SB5; *Sydney Gazette*, 2 January 1823.
78 Memorial of Peter Dillon, 24 November 1821—CSO 4/1749.
79 List of part of the crew of the ship Phatisalam provided for by Captain P. Dillon..., n.d.—CSO 4/1749; Memorial of Patrick Moore, n.d.—*ibid.*, 4/1763, Dillon to Murray, 23 December 1829—CO/201/216.
80 Dillon to Lord, n.d.—Calder Papers, ML FM4/728.
81 Moore to Goulburn, 7 March 1822—CSO 4/1759; Memorial of Patrick Moore, n.d.—*ibid.*, 4/1763.
82 James *v*. Dillon (deposition of T. D. Rowe)—Supreme Court of Civil Judicature: Judgment Rolls... SB5.
83 *Sydney Gazette*, 8 February 1822; *Government Gazette* (Calcutta), 25 April 1822.
84 Bayly, *Sea-Life Sixty Years Ago*, 99; *Sydney Gazette*, 6 March 1823. The tonnage of the *Calder* was variously stated. Dillon subsequently described her as of 'burden 250 tons' (*Narrative*, I, 270); and I gave this figure in 'Peter Dillon: the voyages of the *Calder* and *St Patrick*' (*Pacific Island Portraits*, ed. J. W. Davidson and D. Scarr, Canberra, 1970, 9-30). I now think that the entries in the [Hobart Town] Port Certificate Book, 1817[-1822], Crowther Collection, Hobart, and the [Sydney] Report of ships and vessels entered inwards, 1 October-31 December 1822 (CSO X701), which both describe her as of 200 tons, are nearer the truth. Both figures, however, look like approximations.
85 For the voyage from Calcutta to Hobart Town, see: *Government Gazette* (Calcutta), 4, 11 July 1822; *Hobart Town Gazette*, 28 September 1822; Dillon, *Narrative*, II, 380-1.
86 For accounts of Hobart at this time, see: George William Evans, *A Geographical, Historical, and Topographical Description of Van Diemen's Land*... (London, 1822), 47-62; Edward Curr, *An Account of the Colony of Van Diemen's Land*... (London, 1824), 3-9; R. J. Solomon, The Evolution of Hobart, (unpublished Ph.D. thesis, University of Tasmania, 1968), I, *passim*.
87 Horton to Orton, 19 June 1839—MMS.
88 *Hobart Town Gazette*, 28 September, 5, 12 October 1822.
89 Knopwood Diary, 10 November 1822; *Sydney Gazette*, 22 November 1822.
90 *ibid.*, 18 October 1822.
91 *ibid.*, 22 November 1822.
92 For the origin of these figures, see: Report of ships and vessels entered inwards 1, October-31 December 1822—CSO X701; The Church Missionary Society in

a/c with Revd. Samuel Marsden, 4 October 1814—HL, MSS 54/50; Dillon to Goulburn, 12 May 1823—CSO 4/1771.
93 James v. Dillon—Supreme Court of Civil Judicature: Judgment Rolls, 1822, 3 & 4 Terms, NSW State Archives SB5; *Sydney Gazette*, 2 January 1823. I have removed a typographical error from the report of the judge's remarks.
94 *Sydney Gazette*, 2, 9 January, 6 February 1823.
95 ibid., 6 February, 6 March 1823.
96 Dillon to Goulburn, 30 April 1823; Dillon to Goulburn, 12 May 1823 (no. 2)—CSO 4/1771.
97 Dillon to Goulburn, 12 May 1823 (no. 1) (and minute for reply)—CSO 4/1771. For the composition of the crew, see: [Hobart Town] Port Certificate Book. 1817[-1822], Crowther Collection, Hobart; Ships Musters, 1823, 304—CSO 4/4774.
98 For the *Calder's* company and cargo, see: ibid.; and Report of ships and vessels cleared outwards, 1 July-30 September 1823—CSO X701.
99 *Sydney Gazette*, 1 January 1820.

6

TO SOUTH AMERICA AND THE SOUTH SEAS

1823-25

1 Dillon to Marsden, 6 August 1823—Hocken Library, MSS.
2 For Hongi Hika and his campaigns, see especially: S. Percy Smith, *Maori Wars of the Nineteenth Century: The Struggle of the Northern against the Southern Maori Tribes prior to . . . 1840* (2nd ed., Christchurch, 1910); Harrison M. Wright, *New Zealand, 1769-1840: Early Years of Western Contact* (Cambridge, Mass., 1959); Judith Binney, *The Legacy of Guilt: a life of Thomas Kendall* (Auckland, 1968).
3 Dillon to Marsden, 6 August 1823—HL, Marsden, MSS.
4 For Marsden's action, and inaction, regarding his former servant (James Ring), see Brisbane, Forbes and Scott to Bathurst, 10 August 1825 (and enclosures)—*HRA*, I, XI, 717-81 *passim*.
5 Dillon to Bedford, 4 August 1841—*Letters addressed by the Chevalier Dillon to His Grace the Duke of Bedford, the Right Hon. Lord John Russell, and Vernon Smith, Esq., M.P. . . .* [London, 1841], 1.
6 Gross Return of British and Foreign imports at the Port of Callao, 1 December 1823-4 February 1824—FO 61/2. This refers to the *Calder's* arrival at Callao from 'Concepción'; Talcahuano is the port for Concepción.
7 Robert Proctor, *Narrative of a Journey across the Cordillera of the Andes, and of a Residence in Lima, and other parts of Peru, in the years 1823 & 1824* (London, 1825), 120.
8 Dillon, *Narrative*, II, 330.
9 The summary was published in the *Government Gazette* (Calcutta), 26 October 1826.
10 For accounts of Valparaíso at about this time, see: Maria Graham (Lady Callcott), *Journal of a Residence in Chile during the year 1822* (London, 1824); J. Miers, *Travels in Chile and La Plata* (2 vols, London, 1826); Robert Proctor, *Narrative*. See also: Vicuña Mackenna, *The First Britons in Valparaíso* (Valparaíso, 1884); R. A. Humphreys (ed.), *British Consular Reports on the Trade and Politics of Latin America, 1824-1826* (Camden Society Third Series LXIII, London, 1940); 'Hardey' [Oswald Hardey Evans], 'Perilous Havens'—ML FM4/25.
11 Bayly, *Sea-Life Sixty Years Ago* (London, 1885), 91.
12 The renaming is referred to by George Bayly, who served in her (ibid.).
13 Dillon to Hay, 15 February 1834—CO 201/244; and 'P.D.' to the Editor, 10 October 1826—*Bengal Hurkaru*, 12 October 1826.
14 For the cargo carried by the *Calder*, see *Sydney Gazette*, 3 March 1825. Her date of sailing from Valparaíso is unknown. However, she reached Tahiti on 13 September 1824 (W. P. Crook, 14-15 September 1824—SSJ lxxvi) and is likely to have taken between 30 and 35 days on the passage.
15 *Calcutta Journal of Politics and General Literature*, 26 March 1822; Dillon, *Narrative*, II, 88, 284.
16 Bayly, *Sea-Life*, 80.

17 George Goyau, *Les grands desseins missionnaires d'Henri de Solages (1786-1832)* (Paris, 1933), 54.
18 Dillon to Chairman and Deputy Chairman, East India Company, 13 November 1828 (copy)—ANM BB4 1003.
19 Dillon, *Narrative*, I, 270.
20 W. P. Crook, 14-15 September 1824—SSJ lxxvi.
21 *Bengal Hurkaru*, 2 October 1826; *United Service Journal*, 1829, Part 2, 589-93.
22 J. M. Orsmond, 14 December 1823—SSJ lxxi.
23 George Bayly, Journal, I, 41 (for details see chapter 7, note 2, below); Bourne to Tidman, 1 November 1841—AL.
24 John Williams, *A Narrative of Missionary Enterprises in the South Sea Islands* ... (Fourteenth Thousand, London, 1839), 82.
25 Dillon, *Narrative*, I, 273.
26 *Australian*, 10 March 1825.
27 *Government Gazette* (Calcutta), 16 October 1826.
28 *Sydney Gazette*, 3 March 1825.
29 'John Henry Eagleston's Journal' (transcript), 343—Peabody Museum, Salem.
30 P. Dillon, *Mémoire addressé à M. le Préfet d'Ile Bourbon par le Capitaine Dillon, 7 Septembre 1829* (Paris, 1829); see also Goyau, *Les grands desseins missionnaires*, 59.
31 For Whippy's arrival in Fiji, see: [William Cary], *Wrecked on the Feejees* (Nantucket, 1928), 28; correspondence relative to David Whippy, *passim*—Central Archives, Suva, MS 165; Eagleston's Journal, 283; J. Calvert, Journal, December 1860—January 1863—MMS.
32 Dillon to the Editor, 12 October 1826, *Bengal Hurkaru*, 14 October 1826. Apart from this letter there are two other sources for Dillon's visit to the New Hebrides: a report in the *Sydney Gazette*, 3 March 1825; and an account by Dillon, obviously based on a journal kept at the time, in the brochure (1841) described in note 1 to Chapter 7. Nearly all quotations in the present narrative are documented in: J. W. Davidson, 'Peter Dillon and the Discovery of Sandalwood in the New Hebrides' *Journal de la Société des Océanistes*, XII (1956), 99-105.
33 R. Gerard Ward, in 'An intelligence report on sandalwood', *The Journal of Pacific History*, III (1968), 178-80, raises the possibility that the existence of sandalwood in the New Hebrides was known some years earlier. If this were so (which is by no means certain), the knowledge was clearly possessed by few.
34 William Hall, Abstract of a Journal, 3, 9 February 1825—HL, MSS, Vol. 67.
35 John Rawson Elder (ed.), *Marsden's Lieutenants* (Dunedin, 1934), 201; Binney, *Legacy of Guilt*, 161-2.
36 Hall, Abstract of a Journal, 9 February 1825. For the movements of the war parties, see Binney, *Legacy of Guilt*, 161-2.
37 *Sydney Gazette*, 3 March 1825.
38 *Australian*, 10 March 1825.
39 *Sydney Gazette*, 3, 10, 17 March 1825.
40 *ibid.*, 17 March 1825.
41 *ibid.*, 10 March 1825.
42 Dillon to Goulburn, 12 March 1825—CSO 4/1785; Bayly, *Sea-Life*, 78.
43 *Sydney Gazette*, 3, 17 March 1825.
44 Bayly, Journal, I, 24.

7
DILLON IN MID-PASSAGE 1825-26

1 For Dillon's method in compiling his journal, see George Bayly, *Sea-Life Sixty Years Ago* (London, 1885), 166-7. The extract relating to his visit to the New Hebrides is printed in a brochure entitled: *Two Specimens of Printing in oil colours: one representing the reception of the Rev. John Williams at Tanna, in the South Seas; the other, the massacre of that excellent missionary on the island of Eromanga . . . Executed by George Baxter . . . With a description, by J. Leary, . . . and an account of the islands when visited by Captain Cook and Captain Dillon* (London, 1841), 5-6. Dillon's *Narrative* consists, in large part, of journal extracts. He writes (I, 79): 'The subsequent occurrences of the voyage I shall give in the form of a diary, as they actually took place and were put on record in the journal of the *Research* . . .'.

2 George Bayly's 'Journal of Voyages to various parts of the World...' is in two volumes, containing in all some 550 manuscript pages. Only a relatively small part of the first volume (I, 23-75) deals with his voyages with Dillon. The writing of the first volume was apparently completed by 1831, since this date is given on the title-page. It also contains a note dated 14 August 1832: 'Lord Byron returns Mr Bayly's Journal with many thanks for the perusal of it...'. (This was George Anson Byron, the 7th Baron, who had succeeded his more famous predecessor in 1824.) The Journal is in the Hocken Library—MSS M1, 145-46; typescript copy 146A. For Bayly's book, see note 1, above.

In this chapter I have given a reference for quotations from Bayly's Journal and from *Sea-Life* only where the passage is a long one or where I have taken it from a section of the original account remote from the incident being described. The remaining quotations can be readily located, since both the journal and the book are written in narrative form.

3 Bayly, *Sea-Life*, 77.
4 Ships Musters, 1824-25, 489—CSO 4/4775. Bayly (*Sea-Life*, 82) states that there were eight Europeans and only four 'Tahitians' in the crew. The Ship's Muster shows a greater number of Tahitians and other evidence supports the larger figure.
5 *Sydney Gazette*, 3 March 1825; 'Busby, John', *ADB*, I, 188-89.
6 Letter from Dillon, 4 December 1825, *Sydney Gazette*, 15 March 1826.
7 This is an inference. Kendall began to perform clerical duties in Valparaiso on 10 April 1825 (John Rawson Elder (ed.), *Marsden's Lieutenants* (Dunedin, 1934), 217). Bayly (*Sea-Life*, 91-2) states that she arrived 'about a fortnight' before the *Calder*; this is clearly an error.
8 Return of British trade at the ports within the consulate of Valparaiso, 1 January-30 June 1825—FO 16/2.
9 Letter from Dillon, 4 December 1825, *Sydney Gazette*, 15 March 1826. The next two quotations from Dillon are from the same letter.
10 'Hardey' [Oswald Hardey Evans], 'Perilous Havens'—ML FM4/25.
11 Bayly, *Sea-Life*, 111-12.
12 *ibid.*, 79.
13 Dillon, *Narrative*, I, 270-1.
14 Bayly, *Sea-Life*, 121.
15 Dillon, *Narrative*, I, 102.
16 Bayly, Journal, I, 24, 74.
17 Diary of Reverend William White, 10 January 1825—Trinity College, Auckland.
18 S. Percy Smith, *Maori Wars of the Nineteenth Century*... (2nd ed., Christchurch, 1910), 329-75.
19 Bayly, *Sea-Life*, 135.
20 Dillon, *Narrative*, I, 248.
21 Bayly, Journal, I, 53.
22 Dillon, *Narrative*, I, 39-40.
23 Bayly, Journal, I, 59.
24 See N. L .A. Milet-Mureau (ed.), *Voyage autour du monde... de la Pérouse* (3 vols, Paris, 1797).
25 Bayly, Journal, I, 53.
26 H. Wallis (ed.), *Carteret's Voyage Round the World* (Cambridge, Hakluyt Society, 1965), I, 163, 198.
27 Bayly, Journal, I, 61-2. In *Sea-Life*, 161-2, Bayly describes Dillon as performing these actions at Santa Cruz. In locating the incident at Buka Passage, I have followed his earlier account. I think Dillon found his precedent elsewhere than in Carteret's narrative, as the latter appears to make no mention of these procedures.
28 Bayly, Journal, I, 63.
29 Bayly, *Sea-Life*, 173-74.
30 Bayly, Journal, I, 64.
31 Walter Hamilton, *The East India Gazetteer*... (2nd ed., London, 1828), I, 270.
32 Bayly, Journal, I, 67.
33 Bayly, *Sea-Life*, 183-4.
34 *ibid.*, 185-6.

Notes

35 Victor Jacquemont, *Letters from India: describing a Journey in the British Dominions of India, Tibet, Lahore, and Cashmere* . . . (2 vols, London, 1834), I, 82. On Saugor, see also Maria Graham, *Journal of a Residence in India* (Edinburgh, 1812), 132.
36 *Bengal Hurkaru*, 30 August, 5 September 1826; *Government Gazette* (Calcutta), 31 August, 4 September 1826; Bayly, Journal, I, 70, 73.
  The information published on 30 and 31 August was obviously obtained from Dillon. Unless it was sent overland from one of the places down-river at which he went ashore, the dates given by Bayly for the boat trip—and used by me in the text—appear to be in error by at least one day. Perhaps Bayly was using ship's time, noon to noon, not civil time, midnight to midnight.
37 Bayly, Journal, I, 73-4.
38 Bayly, *Sea-Life*, 193.
39 *ibid.*, 195-6.
40 *ibid.*, 114.
41 *ibid.*, 80.

8
THE SEARCH FOR LA PÉROUSE: PERSUADING BENGAL

1 John Dunmore, *French Explorers in the Pacific* (Oxford, 1965-69), I, 332-3.
2 Dillon, *Narrative*, words in title.
3 *Bengal Hurkaru*, 30 August 1826; *Government Gazette* (Calcutta), 31 August 1826.
4 *Bengal Hurkaru*, 5 September 1826.
5 *Government Gazette* (Calcutta), 31 August 1826.
6 On the Calcutta press, see: S. B. Chaudhuri, 'Early English Printers and Publishers in Calcutta', *Bengal Past and Present*, (Calcutta), LXXXVII, part 1, (1968), 68-77; Margarita Barns, *The Indian Press* . . . (London, 1940).
7 *India Gazette*, 4 September 1826; *Bengal Hurkaru*, 5 September 1826.
8 *Bengal Hurkaru*, 11 September 1826.
9 Bayly, Journal, I, 70.
10 *ibid.*; *Bengal Hurkaru*, 5 September 1826.
11 Bayly, Journal, I, 70.
12 Combermere to Canning, 31 March 1844—FO 58/31.
13 *India Gazette*, 14 September 1826.
14 *Bengal Hurkaru*, 5 September, 2 October 1826.
15 See above, 85-6.
16 *Bengal Hurkaru*, 2 October 1826.
17 *Government Gazette* (Calcutta), 26 October 1826.
18 *Bengal Hurkaru*, 26 September, 14 October 1826.
19 *ibid.*, 27 October 1826.
20 *ibid.*, 12 October 1826.
21 On the Asiatic Society, see: *Centenary Review of the Asiatic Society of Bengal* (Calcutta, 1885), *passim*; *The Asiatic Society* (Calcutta, n.d.), 1-8. On intellectual life in Calcutta, see, especially, David Kopf, *British Orientalism and the Bengal Renaissance: The Dynamics of Indian Modernization 1773-1835* (Berkeley and Los Angeles, 1969), *passim*.
22 *Bengal Hurkaru*, 7 September 1826.
23 Dillon to Lushington, 15 [sic] September 1826—ANM BB4 1003. This is a copy from Dillon's original, which I have not seen; I believe the date to be incorrect. Dillon printed the letter in his *Narrative*, I, 37-44, but with some editing.
24 *Bengal Hurkaru*, 5 September 1826.
25 Bayly, Journal, I, 73.
26 Dillon to Lushington, 10 October 1826—ANM BB4 1003.
27 Dillon, *Narrative*, I, 47-8.
28 *Bengal Hurkaru*, 26, 27 September 1826; *Government Gazette* (Calcutta), 28 September 1826; *India Gazette*, 28 September 1826.
29 V. C. P. Hodson, *List of Officers of the Bengal Army, 1758-1834* (London, 1946), 438-9; *Asiatic Researches*, XVI (Calcutta, 1828), Appendix xi.
30 *Bengal Hurkaru*, 13 October 1826.
31 On Hayes, see: Ida Lee, *Commodore John Hayes, His Voyage and Life (1767-1831)* . . . (London, 1912); 'Hayes, Sir John', *ADB*, I, 527.

32 *Bengal Hurkaru*, 14 October 1826.
33 Cordier to Minister of Marine and Colonies, 13 November 1826—ANM BB4 1003; Desbarrayus de Richemont [Administrator-General, Pondicherry] to Minister of Marine and Colonies, 18 November 1826—ANM BB4 507; *Asiatic Journal*, XXIII (London, 1827), 631; Georges Benoit-Guyod, *Sur les traces de Lapérouse* . . . (4th ed., Paris, 1945), 134.
34 *Asiatic Researches*, XVI (1828), Appendix x-xi; Dillon, *Narrative*, I, 48-50.
35 *Asiatic Researches*, XVI, Appendix x-xi; XVII (1832), 622.
36 Desbarrayus de Richemont to Minister of Marine and Colonies, 18 November 1826—ANM BB4 507.
37 Dillon to Arthur, 9 May 1827—CSO(VDL) 1/82/1870; Dillon, *Narrative*, I, 55-6; Combermere to Canning, 31 March 1844—FO 58/31.
38 Dillon, *Narrative*, I, 52. The *Narrative* (I, 52-78) describes the events of the following weeks and prints relevant documents. Facts taken from this source are not separately documented.
39 D. G. Crawford (compiler), *Role of the Indian Medical Service 1815-1930* (London, 1930); Amitabha Mukherjee, *Reform and Regeneration in Bengal 1774-1823* (Calcutta, 1968), 175-7.
40 On Chaigneau and the appointment of a French observer, see: Combermere and Harrington to Cordier, 16 November 1826; Chaigneau to Cordier, 18 November 1826; Dillon to Chabrol, 23 April 1828; Ministry of Foreign Affairs (Le Garde des Sceaux) to Minister of Marine and Colonies, 23 April 1829—ANM BB4 1003; Cordier to Minister of Marine and Colonies, 8 January 1827—ANM BB4 507; Benoit-Guyod, *Lapérouse*, 111-16.
41 Dillon to Minister of Marine and Colonies, 21 January 1827 (encl.); Dillon to Chabrol, 7 August 1828—ANM BB4 1003; Desbarrayus de Richemont to Minister of Marine and Colonies, 18 November 1826—ANM BB4 507; *Hobart Town Gazette*, 21 April 1827; Dillon, *Narrative*, I, 102.
42 Tytler to Arthur, 1 May 1827—CSO(VDL) 1/82/1870; *Hobart Town Gazette*, 28 April 1827; Dillon, *Narrative*, I, 64.
43 John Savage, *Some Account of New Zealand; particularly the Bay of Islands, and Surrounding Country* . . . (new ed., Wellington, 1939); 'Savage, John', *ADB*, II, 419.
44 Dillon to Minister of Marine and Colonies, 5 January 1827—ANM BB4 1003.

9
THE SEARCH FOR LA PÉROUSE: THE VOYAGE OUT

1 Dillon to Minister of Marine and Colonies, 21 January 1827 (encl.)—ANM BB4 1003; *Bengal Hurkaru*, 17 November 1826; *Colonial Times and Tasmanian Advertiser*, 13 April 1827; Dillon, *Narrative*, I, 83.
2 *ibid.*, 103. Dillon's *Narrative* (I, 89-302; II, 1-171) is the principal source for this chapter. Since it is a chronological account of the voyage, facts taken from it are not ordinarily documented, except when they are taken from a different part of the narrative. Information in other sources which are cited is often supplemented by the *Narrative*.
3 Dillon to Minister of Marine and Colonies, 21 January 1827—ANM BB4 1003.
4 Supreme Court, 1 May 1827—CSO(VDL), 1/82/1870. For details of these records see note 18, below.
5 Dillon to Tytler, 26 January 1827 (copy by Tytler)—CSO(VDL) 1/82/1870.
6 *Hobart Town Gazette*, 28 April 1827.
7 Tytler to Arthur, 2 May 1827—CSO(VDL) 1/82/1870; see also Dillon, *Narrative*, I, 100.
8 Dillon to Chairman and Deputy Chairman, East India Company, 13 November 1828 (copy)—ANM BB4 1003.
9 Supreme Court, 1 May 1827—CSO(VDL) 1/82/1870; *Hobart Town Gazette*, 28 April 1827; see also Dillon, *Narrative*, I, 114.
10 Tytler to Arthur, 2 May 1827—CSO(VDL) 1/82/1870.
11 *Hobart Town Gazette*, 28 April 1827.
12 For Van Diemen's Land affairs at this period see especially: R. W. Giblin, *The Early History of Tasmania*, II: *The Penal Settlement Era, 1804-18* [scil. *28*]: *Collins, Sorell and*

Notes 329

    Arthur (Melbourne, 1939), 371-632; William Douglass Forsyth, *Governor Arthur's Convict System: Van Diemen's Land, 1824-36* . . . (London, 1935), 1-23, 169-203. Among earlier works see especially: Henry Widowson, *Present State of Van Diemen's Land* . . . (London, 1829); Henry Melville, *The History of Van Diemen's Land, From the year 1824 to 1835, inclusive* . . . , ed. George Mackaness (Sydney, 1965); John West, *The History of Tasmania* (facsimile ed., Adelaide, 1966), I, 86-124.
13 Dillon also made this request in writing: Dillon to Arthur, 6 April 1827—CSO(VDL) 1/82/1870.
14 Dillon to Tytler, n.d. [21 March 1827] (copy by Tytler)—CSO (VDL) 1/82/1870. For the date of this letter and Tytler's, see *Hobart Town Gazette*, 28 April 1827.
15 Tytler to 'His Excellency the Governor of Hobarts' Town', 6 April 1827—CSO(VDL) 1/82/1870.
16 *Hobart Town Gazette*, 14 April 1827.
17 *Colonial Times*, 13, 20 April 1827.
18 SC(VDL) 41/2. This document contains the charge, the verdict and the sentence. It is the only reference to the case that has been found among the records of the Supreme Court. A copy of Chief Justice Pedder's judgment is, however, contained in CSO (VDL) 1/82/1870, 126-36, under the heading 'Supreme Court May 1. 1827'. No verbatim record of proceedings appears to survive, though Dillon apparently possessed one, 'taken in short-hand by an expert stenographist, and notarially attested as correct' (*Narrative*, I, 138). He quotes a few brief passages from it; he cannot, however, be entirely relied on not to have omitted phrases that he found embarrassing. The Hobart Town papers published summaries of the case, with some direct quotation.
19 *Hobart Town Gazette*, 28 April 1827; Dillon, *Narrative*, I, 135.
20 *Hobart Town Gazette*, 28 April 1827; Dillon, *Narrative*, I, 137.
21 *Hobart Town Gazette*, 28 April 1827; Dillon to Tytler, 26 January 1827, n.d. [21 March 1827] (both copies by Tytler)—CSO(VDL) 1/82/1870.
22 *Tasmanian*, 17 May 1827.
23 *Colonial Times*, 11 May 1827.
24 *ibid.*
25 Supreme Court, 1 May 1827—CSO(VDL) 1/82/1870; *Hobart Town Gazette*, 5 May 1827.
26 *Colonial Times*, 4 May 1827.
27 J. S. C. Dumont d'Urville, *Voyage de la Corvette L'Astrolabe* . . . *pendant les années 1826-1827-1828-1829* . . . *Histoire du Voyage* (5 vols, Paris, 1830-33), V, 9-22; *Sydney Gazette*, 16 January 1828.
28 Memorial of 'the Undersigned' [Lord and others] to Arthur, n.d.; Memorial of Peter Dillon to Arthur, n.d.—CSO (VDL) 1/82/1870.
29 Arthur to Colonial Secretary, 8 May 1827—*ibid.*
30 Tytler to Arthur, 2 May 1827—*ibid.*
31 Tytler to Colonial Secretary, n.d. [5 May 1827]; Blake to Colonial Secretary, 4 May 1827; Dillon to Arthur, 9 [*scil.* 8] May 1827—*ibid.*
32 James Stephen to Arthur, 31 July 1824—Papers of Sir George Arthur, IV, ML A2164.
33 Minutes of Executive Council, 9 May 1827—EC (VDL) 4/1; Arthur to Secretary of State, 10 May 1827—GO (VDL) 25/3. Arthur to Colonial Secretary, 8 May 1827—CSO (VDL) 1/82/1870—unless it is wrongly dated, shows that Arthur had decided to release Dillon before the meeting of the Executive Council.
34 For example, see Dillon to Chairman and Deputy Chairman, East India Company, 13 November 1828—ANM BB4 1003.
35 On the loan, see: Dillon to Arthur, 6, -, 30 April 1827; Dillon to Colonial Secretary, 16 April 1827; Bethune to Colonial Secretary, 27 April 1827 (with minute by C.S.); minutes of Arthur, 19 April, 11 May 1827; Stephen to Colonial Secretary, 14 May 1827—CSO(VDL) 1/82/1870; Minutes of Executive Council, 16 April 1827—EC (VDL) 4/1; Arthur to Secretary of State, 10 May 1827—GO (VDL) 25/3.
36 Dillon to Arthur, 9 [*scil.* 8] May—CSO(VDL) 1/82/1870; *Sydney Gazette*, 6 June 1827; Dillon, *Narrative*, I, 250, 295; II, 104, 138.
37 *Australian*, 6 June 1827.
38 *Gleaner*, 26 April, 17 May 1827.
39 *Sydney Gazette*, 1, 4, 6 June.

40 For Tytler's movements, see *Gleaner*, 26 May 1827.
41 Dillon to McLeay, 31 May, 4 June 1827—CSO 4/1933.
42 Dumont d'Urville, *Histoire du Voyage*, V, 19-21; *Sydney Gazette*, 16 January 1828. The letter was dated 18 July; it reached Hobart Town on 23 December.
43 J. D. Lang, *New Zealand in 1839: or Four Letters, . . . on the Colonization of that Island and on the Present Condition and Prospects of its Native Inhabitants* (London, 1839), 58.
44 S. Percy Smith, *Maori Wars of the Nineteenth Century* . . . (2nd ed., Christchurch, 1910), 375-92 *passim*; Dillon, *Narrative*, I, 232-4.
45 William Williams, Journal, 24 July 1827 (typescript)—ATL, q 920.
46 Lawrence M. Rogers (ed.), *The Early Journals of Henry Williams . . . 1826-40* (Christchurch, 1961), 62.
47 Additional Instructions from Marine Board, n.d.—ANM BB4 507.
48 John Thomas, Journal, 21 August 1827—ML FM4/1433.
49 John Martin, *An Account of the Natives of the Tonga Islands, in the South Pacific Ocean . . . Compiled and arranged from the extensive communications of Mr. William Mariner . . .* (2nd ed., London, 1818), II, 94.
50 John Thomas, Journal, 20-21 August 1827—ML/FM4 1433; John Thomas, Calendar and Diary, 15-26 August 1827—ML A1959.
51 Mrs Thomas's Journal, 31 August 1827—ML/FM4 1440.
52 John Thomas, Journal, 24 August 1827—*ibid.*
53 John Thomas, Calendar and Diary, 26 August, 19 December 1827—ML A1959.
54 See, for example, Basil Thomson (ed.), *Voyage of H.M.S. 'Pandora' . . . being the narratives of Captain Edward Edwards, R.N., the commander, and George Hamilton, the surgeon* (London, 1915). Edwards's position for Fatutaka was in error by 17' in longitude and 6' in latitude (*ibid.*, 67).
55 Dillon, *Narrative*, I, 294-5; II, 92, 104.

10
VANIKORO

1 For lists of the articles obtained at Tikopia and Vanikoro, certified by Dillon and his officers as to the date and circumstances of their acquisition, see *Bengal Hurkaru*, 12 April 1828.
2 Dillon, *Narrative*, I, 33; II, 267-8. Dillon's *Narrative* (II, 112-315) is the principal source for this chapter. Facts contained in it, and quotations from it, are documented only when they are, partly or wholly, from another part of the *Narrative*, as with the present reference.
3 Dillon, *Narrative*, II, 130-1, 175.
4 See *ibid.*, 306.

11
RETURN FROM VANIKORO

1 Lawrence M. Rogers (ed.), *The Early Journals of Henry Williams . . . 1826-40* (Christchurch, 1961), 84.
2 John Marmon, 'La Perouse in New Zealand—a wondrous story', *New Zealand Herald*, 6 November 1881. This article is one section of Marmon's memoirs which bore the general title 'The Life and Adventures of John Marmon, the Hokianga Pakeha Maori; or, Seventy-five Years in New Zealand'. Sections of this work, with significant editorial differences, appeared during 1880-82 in the *New Zealand Herald*, *Auckland Evening Star* and *Otago Witness*.
3 Dillon, *Narrative*, II, 321-9 *passim*.
4 See Dillon, *Narrative*, II, 191, 196, 206, 257.
5 *ibid.*, 236.
6 *ibid.*, 272, 400-3.
7 *Sydney Gazette*, 5, 7 December 1827; Rogers (ed.), *Henry Williams*, 85.
8 William Williams, [Private] Journal, 11 November 1827—ATL MSO 91; Rogers (ed.), *Henry Williams*, 88-9.
9 John Rawson Elder (ed.), *Marsden's Lieutenants* (Dunedin, 1934), 144-5, 258.

Notes 331

10 Dillon, *Narrative*, II, 341; see also Rogers (ed.), *Henry Williams*, 91-2.
11 Dillon, *Narrative*, II, 359-63; Dillon to McLeay, 1, 15 January 1828—CSO *Register of Letters Received* 2343 (the *Register* contains a note of the subject of the letter and of the action taken; the letters themselves seem to have been displaced); see also Dillon to McLeay, 15 January 1828 (no. 2)—CSO 4/1973.
12 *Sydney Gazette*, 25 January 1828.
13 See *ibid.*, 2, 4, 16, 23, 25 January 1828; *Australian*, 2, 16, 23, 30 January 1828; *Monitor*, 3, 21, 24 January 1828.
14 Dillon, *Narrative*, II, 363-4; J. D. Lang, *An Historical and Statistical Account of New South Wales* (2 vols, 3rd. ed., London, 1852), I, 19; *Sydney Gazette*, 16, 25 January 1828.
15 *ibid.*, 25 January 1828.
16 *Australian*, 30 January 1828.
17 Dillon, *Narrative*, II, 106, 128.
18 *ibid.*, I, 270; John Thomas, Calendar and Diary, 26 August 1827—ML A1959.
19 See Anon. [Dillon] to Editor, 4 June 1827—*Australian*, 6 June 1827.
20 *Hobart Town Courier*, 5 January 1828, quoted in *Sydney Gazette*, 16 January 1828.
21 J. S. C. Dumont d'Urville, *Voyage de la Corvette L'Astrolabe . . . pendant les années 1826-1827-1828-1829 . . . Histoire du Voyage* (5 vols, Paris 1830-33), V, 9-22.
22 *Monitor*, 21 January 1828.
23 *Sydney Gazette*, 16 January 1828.
24 *ibid.*, 4 February 1828.
25 Dillon to Chairman and Deputy Chairman, East India Company, 13 November 1828—ANM BB4 1003.
26 For the cholera epidemic, see *Bengal Hurkaru*, 23 April, 15, 26, 31 May 1828.
27 For an account of economic conditions, see Amales Tripathi, *Trade and Finance in the Bengal Presidency 1793-1833* (Calcutta, 1956), 192-251.
28 *Bengal, Past and Present* (Calcutta), II (1908), 366-67; *Government Gazette* (Calcutta), 3, 28 May, 5 July, 20 September 1827.
29 Dillon to Chabrol, 15 August 1828—ANM BB4 1003; Dillon, *À Son Excellence M. le Président du Conseil des Ministres, Et aux Membres composant le Conseil de S.M. le Roi de France*, 5 July 1831 (Paris, 1831). Apparent confirmation of Dillon's statements is given in a notice referring to several members of the Barretto family as 'deceased or absent' persons (*Government Gazette* (Calcutta), 7 January 1828).
30 On Dillon's financial position, see: Dillon to Chairman and Deputy Chairman, East India Company, 13 November 1828; Dillon to Orléans, 6 August 1830; Dillon to Aberdeen, 7 October 1830—ANM BB4 1003.
31 Dillon to Trotter, 6 April 1828—ANM BB4 1003.
32 Chaigneau to Dillon, 7 April 1828—*ibid.*
33 The resolution is printed in Dillon, *Narrative*, II, 374-7; see also Prinsep to Chester and members of the Marine Board, 21 April 1828 (and encls)—ANM BB4 1003.
34 Cordier to Dillon, 9 April 1828—*ibid.*
35 Dillon to Wilson, 7 May 1828—Asiatic Society Archives, Calcutta.
36 *Government Gazette* (Calcutta), 15 May 1828.
37 *ibid.*, 23, 26 July 1827. On 27 August the *Gazette* reported the return of Tytler.
38 *Bengal Hurkaru*, 8, 10, 11, 12, 25 April 1828; *Government Gazette* (Calcutta), 7, 10, 14, 17 April, 8 May 1828.
39 *Government Gazette* (Calcutta), 10 April 1828. A letter criticizing Dillon's comments on Tonga was published on 5 May.
40 *Bengal Hurkaru*, 16 April 1828.
41 *ibid.*, 12, 25 April, 24 May 1828.
42 Dillon to Flavigny, 15 February 1829—ANM BB4 1003; Dillon, *À Son Excellence M. le Président du Conseil . . .*, 5 July 1831.
43 See Dillon to Wilson, 7 May 1828—Asiatic Society Archives, Calcutta; Dillon to Chabrol, 7 August 1828—ANM BB4 1003. Some of the drawings are in the Archives Nationales (ANM BB4 1003); they are signed by J. A. Jackson, Calcutta.
44 *Bengal Hurkaru*, 13 May 1828. Dillon writes '*Mary Anne*'; I have preferred the spelling used in the advertisement by her owner and agents.

12
IN QUEST OF RECOGNITION:
LONDON AND PARIS 1828-29

1 As in the preceding four chapters, quotations not otherwise identified are from Dillon's *Narrative*.
2 *Asiatic Journal and Monthly Register for British India and its Dependencies* (London), XXVI (July-December 1828), 645.
3 Dillon to Dart, 30 October 1828—IOL, Miscellaneous Letters Received, 1828, IV, no. 166.
4 Dillon to Chabrol, 7 August 1828 (and encls)—ANM BB4 1003. The enclosures included a 'List of articles belonging to the French frigates La Boussole and, L'Astrolabe . . . procured by Captain Dillon at Tucopia and Mannicola'.
5 Dillon, *Narrative*, II, 241-2.
6 *Sydney Gazette*, 25 January 1828. Chaigneau had also praised Dillon in writing to the French (see Chaigneau to Minister for the Navy, 19 July 1827—ANM BB4 1003).
7 Dillon to Chabrol, 15 August 1828—ANM BB4 1003.
8 Dillon to Pratt, 13 October 1820—ATL Micro MS310. See above, 65.
9 *Asiatic Journal*, XXIII (January-June 1827), 625-31, 657, 673; XXIV (July-December 1827), 619-20, 778-9; XXV (January-June 1828), 144, 350, 375; *Moniteur* (Paris), 9, 10, 12 April 1827.
10 *Asiatic Journal*, XXVI (July-December 1828), 381-2, 443-52; *Literary Gazette* (London), 12 April 1828 (quoted in Dillon, *Narrative*, II, 400-2); *Gentleman's Magazine* (London), XCVIII (September 1828), 263; *Moniteur*, 4 October 1828. See also Séguier (French Embassy, London) to Minister for the Navy, 12 March, 14 April, 22 September 1828—ANM BB4 1003.
11 On the Jerusalem Coffee House see Bryant Lillywhite, *London Coffee Houses* (London, 1963), 289-94.
12 Dillon to Dart, 30 October 1828—IOL, Miscellaneous Letters Received, 1828, IV, no. 166. Other evidence suggests that this was probably written on the 29th.
13 Astell and Loch to Aberdeen, 30 October, 20 November 1828; dinner invitations, 30 October 1828—IOL, Miscellanies, no. 67, 1828.
14 Dillon to Chairman and Deputy Chairman, East India Company, 13 November 1828—IOL, Miscellaneous Letters Received, 1828, IV, no. 166.
15 Secretary of State to Lieutenant-Governor, 28 April 1828—GO (VDL) 1/7.
16 Dillon to Laborde, 18 March 1831—Dillon, *A Son Excellence M. le Président du Conseil . . .* (Paris, 1831), appendix—hereafter cited (as by Dillon) as *Memoir*.
17 Polignac to Hyde de Neuville, 31 October 1828—ANM BB4 1004.
18 Dillon to Chabrol, 15 August 1828; Duperré to Minister for the Navy, 3 December 1828; Minister for the Navy to Minister for Foreign Affairs, 22 December 1828 [draft]—*ibid*.
19 *Asiatic Journal*, XXVI (July-December 1828), 577-81, 643, 715-16; XXVII (January-June 1829), 190-1.
20 Dillon to Chairman and Deputy Chairman, East India Company, 13 November 1828—IOL, Miscellaneous Letters Received, 1828, IV, no. 166.
21 Dart to Dillon, 20 November 1828—ANM BB4 1003; see also Astell and Loch to Aberdeen, 20 November 1828—IOL, Miscellanies, no. 67, 1828.
22 On Dillon's financial position see Dillon to Aberdeen, 6 October 1830 (encl.)—ANM BB4 1003; Dillon to Stuart de Rothesay, 7 May 1830—ML FM3/209.
23 Minister for the Navy to the King, 14 December 1828 (draft); Minister for the Navy to Minister for Justice, 8 January 1829 (draft)—ANM BB4 1003; Dillon to Stuart de Rothesay, 7 May, 20 May 1830—ML FM3/209; Dillon, *Memoir*.
24 Dillon to Billing, 15 January 1829—ANM BB4 1003.
25 *Morning Chronicle*, 15 January 1829; Dillon to Editor, 15 January 1829—*ibid*., 21 January 1829.
26 Dillon to Stuart de Rothesay, 7 May 1830—ML FM3/209.
27 Jean-Baptiste A. Hapdé, *Expédition et Naufrage de Lapérouse, recueil historique de faits, événements, découvertes, etc., etc., . . . et l'énumération authentique de tous les débris du naufrage* (Paris, 1829).

Notes

28 Dillon to Flavigny, 15 February 1829; Minister for the Navy to the King, 22 February 1829; Ordonnance du 22 février 1829 ... Pensions—ANM BB4 1003; Dillon to Stuart de Rothesay, 7, 20 May 1830—ML FM3/209.
29 For example, see *Moniteur*, 27 February 1829.
30 Procés-Verbal: Commission Supérieure des Invalides de la Marine, 27 May 1829; Note de 4e Direction (Fonds et Invalides) à 1e Direction, Ministry for the Navy, 17 July 1829—ANM BB4 1003.
31 Dillon to Hyde de Neuville, 27 March 1829—*ibid.*

13
DILLON'S NARRATIVE

1 George Birkbeck Hill (ed.), *Boswell's Life of Johnson*, revised L. F. Powell (Oxford, 1934-50), III, 19.
2 Dillon, *Narrative*, I, 31, 255.
3 Hill (ed.), *Johnson*, IV, 219.
4 Dillon, *Narrative*, II, 1.
5 *A Voyage round the World, performed in the years 1785, 1786, 1787, and 1788, by the Boussole and Astrolabe, under the command of J. F. G. de la Pérouse: published by order of the National Assembly, under the superintendance of L. A. Milet-Mureau* ... (2 vols, 4to and 3 vols 8vo, London, 1799). This version of the *Voyage Round the World* was republished, in 3 vols, in 1807.
6 Dillon, *Narrative*, I, xx, xxiii, xxv, xlix.
7 For Dillon's relations with Tytler, see *ibid.*, I, 50-170 *passim*; for the passages quoted, see *ibid.*, I, 63n., 87, 138-9, 148-9.
8 James Burney, *A Chronological History of the Discoveries in the South Sea or Pacific Ocean* (5 vols, London, 1803-17). Apart from his copies of *A Voyage round the World* ... *under the command of J. F. G. de la Pérouse* ..., and J. J. Labillardière's, *Voyage in search of La Pérouse* ..., he also possessed John Hawkesworth's *An Account of the Voyages* ... *successively performed by Commodore Byron, Captain Carteret, Captain, Wallis, and Captain Cook* ... (3 vols, London, 1773), narratives of Cook's second and third voyages, of the voyage of Bougainville, and probably other works on exploration.
9 For some of the principal references to the history of the Pacific in Dillon's *Narrative*, see I, 4, 191-5 *passim*, 203-5, 215-25, 259-60, 266, 288-9; II, 292, 313.
10 John Martin, *An Account of the Natives of the Tonga Islands, in the South Pacific Ocean* ... *Compiled and arranged from the extensive communications of Mr. William Mariner* ... (2 vols, London, 1817). Chapter 1 of Vol. II of Dillon's *Narrative* is based on chapters 17-22 of Mariner's *Tonga*.
11 Dillon, *Narrative*, II, 42-3.
12 *ibid.*, II, 132-8.
13 See the references to Dillon in three books by Raymond Firth: *We, the Tikopia: A Sociological Study of Kinship in Primitive Polynesia* (London, 1936), 408; *Social Change in Tikopia: re-study of a Polynesian community after a generation* (London, 1959), 32-4; *History and Traditions of Tikopia* (Wellington, 1961).
14 Dillon, *Narrative*, I, 271-3; II, 103-4, 138.
15 *ibid.*, I, 242.
16 *ibid.*, I, 187-9, 296-7.
17 *ibid.*, I, 219.
18 *ibid.*, I, 227.
19 *ibid.*, I, 211.
20 *ibid.*, II, 161, 299.
21 *ibid.*, II, 122-3.
22 *ibid.*, II, 302-4.
23 *ibid.*, I, 244-6.
24 *ibid.*, II, 350-1.
25 *ibid.*, II, 322-3.
26 *ibid.*, II, 334-5.
27 *ibid.*, II, 328, 330.
28 *ibid.*, I, 175, 253-4; II, 321, 328-30.

334 Peter Dillon of Vanikoro

29 ibid., I, 201-2.
30 James Cook, *A Voyage towards the South Pole, and round the World, performed in His Majesty's Ships the Resolution and Adventure, In the Years 1772, 1773, 1774, and 1775* (3 vols, London, 1777), I, xxxvi.
31 Dillon to Stuart de Rothesay, 7 May 1830—ML FM3/209; Dillon to Laborde, 3 August 1830—ANM BB4 1003.
32 Dillon to Court of Directors, EIC, 23 May 1829—IOL Miscellaneous Letters Received, 1829, II, no. 168.
33 ibid.
34 On the publishing trade at this period, see especially: Thomas Constable, *Archibald Constable and his literary correspondents: a memorial* (3 vols, Edinburgh, 1873); Henry Curwen, *A History of Booksellers, the old and the new* (London, 1873); Samuel Smiles, *A publisher and his Friends: memoir and correspondence of the late John Murray* (2 vols, London, 1891); Royal A. Gettmann, *A Victorian Publisher: a study of the Bentley papers* (Cambridge, 1960).
35 See the list of 'New and Popular Works recently published by Hurst, Chance, and Co., 65 St. Paul's Church-yard', January 1830, appended to: [Maslen, T. J.,] *The Friend of Australia . . . By a Retired Officer of the Hon. East India Company's Service* (London, 1830). Dillon's book was the first title listed.
36 Thomas Constable, *Archibald Constable*, III, 422; *Notes and Queries*, no. 49 [5 October 1850], 290
37 *United Service Journal and Naval and Military Magazine*, 1829, part 1, 674-9; part 2, 589-93.
38 *Asiatic Journal*, XXVII (July-December 1829), 320.
39 *Edinburgh Journal of Natural and Geographical Science*, I (1829-30), 350-52.
40 *Asiatic Journal*, New Series, I, 205-12.

14
A CHART FOR CATHOLICISM 1829-30

1   Dillon to Stuart de Rothesay, 7, 20 May 1830 (and encls)—ML FM3/209; Dillon. *À Son Excellence M. le Président du Conseil des Ministres . . .* (Paris, 1831)—hereafter cited as 'Dillon, Memoir'.
2   On the Irish College, see: Patrick Boyle, *The Irish College in Paris from 1578 to 1901* . . . (London, 1901), 78-87; Richard Hayes, *Old Irish Links with France* . . . (Dublin, 1940).
3   Georges Goyau, *Les grands desseins missionnaires d'Henri de Solages (1786-1832): Le Pacifique—L'Ile Bourbon—Madagascar* (Paris, 1933), 1-30; Ralph M. Wiltgen, 'Founders of the Prefecture Apostolic of the South Sea Islands', *Verbum SVD*, XI (1970), 54-78.
4   Wiltgen, 'Founders', 57; Goyau, *Les grands desseins missionnaires*, 48, 54.
5   Goyau, 61.
6   Dillon to Solages, 7 September 1829 (MS. copy)—AMAE: Océanie, 1822-43: lettres et documents. A copy of the printed version of this letter is also in this series; the latter has a number of minor changes and omissions.
7   Goyau, 61; Wiltgen, 'Founders', 60.
8   Goyau, 62 (my translation).
9   Wiltgen, 'Founders', 61, 63; Goyau, 64.
10 Dillon to Stuart de Rothesay, 7 May 1830—ML FM3/209.
11 See, for example, Dillon, *Voyage aux Iles*, I, xliii, lii, lx; II, 216, 345-61; Dillon, *Narrative*, I, xlix; II, 329, 407-36.
12 Dillon, *Memoir*.
13 Goyau, 74 (my translation); Dillon to Polignac, 31 March 1830—AMAE: Océanie, 1822-43: lettres et documents.
14 ibid.
15 Dillon to Murray, 23 December 1829—CO 201/206.
16 Dillon to Polignac, 31 March 1830—AMAE: Océanie, 1822-43: lettres et documents.
17 Dillon to Polignac, 20 July 1830—ML FM3/209.

Notes 335

15
IN THE WAKE OF SUCCESS 1830-34

1   Dillon to Hay, 15 November 1830—CO 201/215.
2   '... his destitute children whom he has left in N.S. Wales and for whose provision and support he has not advanced a farthing for many years'—Bourne to Tidman, 1 November 1841, AL 1833-44. The LMS was not of course likely to take a charitable view of Dillon, and he seems to have retained the respect of his father-in-law Peter Moore.
3   Vaudrenil to Jourdan, 9 August 1830—AMAE, Lettres politiques: Angleterre, 631 (June-Sept 1830).
4   *Robson's London Commercial Directory . . . For 1830* (London, 1830). In 1831 Arnot produced a Hindustani grammer which, like Dillon's book, was printed by the EIC's printer, J. S. Cox.
5   Some of Dillon's letters at the PRO appear to be in the same hand as one of Arnot's in the India Office archives.
6   Dillon to Stuart, 28 May 1840: in the possession of Sir Thomas Ramsay, St Kilda, Victoria. He also gave a copy to the Duke of Wellington, to whom he had been mentioned by Polignac and whom he apparently met when trying to secure an appointment in New Zealand.
7   Dillon to Murray, 5 April 1830—CO 201/215.
8   *ibid*. John Benett, M.P., whom Dillon cited, was Aylmer Lambert's brother-in-law.
9   Hay to Lack, 3 May 1830—CO 202/24.
10 Hay to Dillon, 11 May 1830—*ibid*.
11 Hay to Dillon, 22 June 1830—CO 202/26. Dillon had asked in his first letter to Murray that the reply should be sent to 2 South Place for forwarding; he thus had contacts with Arnot and Forbes before his return from Paris. In a later letter he asked that the reply be left at the Foreign Office; as often in later years—before the 'penny post'—he was using the diplomatic bag for his official communications.
12 Dillon to Sutart, 18 May 1830—Ramsay Papers. [In 1830 the independent British merchants at Canton (i.e. those not belonging to the EIC) presented a petition to the House of Commons, protesting against the humiliations imposed upon them by the Chinese authorities—E. Holt, *The Opium Wars in China* (London, 1964), 42-43.]
13 Memorial of Peter Dillon of Calcutta, Master Mariner, to His Excellency Lachlan Macquarie, 26 November 1821; Dillon to Murray, 23 December 1829, with enclosures—CO 201/206. The address given in this letter was that of the East India agents Fletcher, Alexander and Co., King's Arms Yard, Coleman Street.
14 Twiss to Dillon, 8 January 1830; Twiss to Bankes, 8 January 1830—CO 202/24.
15 Twiss to Dillon, 8 February 1830—*ibid*.
16 Hay to Dillon, 7 July 1830; Hay to Bankes, 7 July 1830—CO 202/26. [As will be seen, at this stage much of Dillon's prolonged correspondences with the Colonial Office landed on the desk of R. W. Hay, who must have felt a much-tried man.]
17 Dillon to Hay, 20 October 1830—CO 201/215.
18 Dillon to Hay, 1 November 1830—*ibid*.
19 Dillon to Murray, 3 November 1830—*ibid*.
20 Dillon to Hay (two letters), 5 November 1830—CO 201/215.
21 Dillon to Hay, 15 November 1830—*ibid*.; Hay to Stuart Wortley, 17 November 1830—CO 202/26. In the latter Hay pointed out that Dillon was disingenuously disputing the amount of the *Little Mary* charter; he had himself proposed the same sum as proper when he thought it would be paid by the government.
22 Dillon to Goderich, 11 December 1830—CO 201/215.
23 *Nouvelle Biographie Générale* . . . (Paris, 1857-66), s.v.
24 Dillon to Goderich, 15 January 1831—CO 201/223. It is not clear whether his book had brought him any money, as he had certainly hoped it would.
25 Howick to Dillon, 28 January, 14 February 1831—CO 202/36; Dillon to Howick, 31 January, 10 February 1831—CO 201/223.
26 Dillon to Aberdeen, 5, 6 October 1831; Dillon to Backhouse, 7 October 1831—FO 27/423.

336   *Peter Dillon of Vanikoro*

27 Dillon to Orléans, 3 December 1830—ANM BB4 1003; Secretary of Commandants of Duke of Orléans to Dillon, 24 December 1830; Talleyrand to Dillon, 28 December 1830—printed in Dillon, *Memoir* (1831), for which see note 32 to this chapter.
28 Talleyrand to Dillon, 17 January 1831—Dillon, *Memoir* (1831)—cf. note 32 to this chapter.
29 Dillon to Backhouse, 31 December 1830, 12 February 1831—FO 27/423; Granville to Sebastiani (French Foreign Minister), 20 January 1831—Dillon, *Memoir* (1831).
30 Dillon to Laborde, 18 March 1831—Dillon, *Memoir* (1831).
31 Granville to Backhouse, 14 March 1831—FO 27/427; Dillon to de Rigny, 31 May 1831—ANM BB4 1003.
32 Dated from 18 rue Vivienne, 5 July 1831; there are two copies in ANM BB4 1003. It is here cited as 'Dillon, *Memoir* (1831)', a term which he himself used.
33 He said that in June he had from sheer desperation written to Polignac for a loan, but had received no reply. [In June that unfortunate Prince must have had other things on his mind.]
34 Dillon to Minister of the Navy, 15 July 1831; Dillon to Minister of the Interior, 13 July 1831—ANM BB4 1003; Dillon to Sebastiani, 17 September 1831 (cf. note 37 to this chapter). [Despite the careful repudiation of Polignac, such remarks (like the charge against Sir George Murray in London) were not likely to advantage Dillon in Paris.]
35 Dillon to Macleay, 3 August 1831—CSO 31/10511 (N.S.W. Archives office refce X30); Dillon to the Rev. J. J. Therry, 3 August 1831—printed in Eris M. O'Brien, *The Life of Archpriest John Joseph Therry* . . . (Sydney, 1922), 324-5. I have been unable to find evidence of the nature of the relations between Peter Dillon and the Dillons of Mount Dillon.
36 Emile Michel, 'La tentative de colonisation Belge aux Nouvelles-Hébrides et aux îles Fidgi et Salomon . . . ' , Institut Royale Colonial Belge, *Bulletin des Séances* XIX (1948), 138-49. Contacts of uncertain date between Dillon and Belgian representatives in London are indicated by the inscription in the Turnbull Library copy of his *Narrative*: 'A. Castelain Esquire, Belgian Consul, London, With the author's, compliments'.
37 *À Son Excellence Le Comte Sebastiani, Ministre des Affaires Etrangères*, 17 septembre 1831 (Paris, 1831).
38 This point is based on the *procès verbal* of a meeting of the Conseil d'Amirauté on 23 February 1831: ' . . . et dans un petit nombre d'années cette découverte n'aurait plus excité qu'un simple intérêt de curiosité'—ANM BB4 1003.
39 He said he would nominate one of the following: M. Lafitte; Comte Bertrand (whose wife was a Martinique Dillon); Admiral Sir Sydney Smith.
40 They were not actually in India. [Perhaps Dillon used the vague 'aux Indes'.]
41 Sebastiani recommended that Dillon's expenses on the book should be paid: Sebastiani to Minister of Marine, 21 December 1831—ANM BB4 1003.
42 Dillon to Stuart de Rothesay, 14 March 1832—Ramsay Papers.
43 Listed in PRO index 22842 (FO Register of Correspondence); originals not located.
44 Correspondence in CO 201/229.
45 Dillon to Hay, 15 August 1832—CO 13/1/ Cf. above, 52-3.
46 *Evidence respecting the Soil, Climate, and Productions of the South Coast of Australia, Between the 132nd and 141st Degrees of East Longitude* (London, 1832), 47-48.
47 Dillon to Hay, 15 August 1832—CO 13/1.
48 Dillon to Hay, 7 October 1832—CO 323/168.
49 Dillon to Russell, 11 April 1840—CO 209/7.
50 Dillon to Goderich, 9 May 1832—CO 201/229. His 'friends' may have been those who two years later supported his flax venture.
51 Hay to Dillon, 12 May 1832—CO 202/28.
52 The Memorial of the Chevalier Captn. P. Dillon late of the Honorable East India Company's Service, 14 May 1832 (two days after Hay's letter)—CO 201/229.
53 Most of these had Irish connections: the mother of Lambert and of his sister Lucy Benett was the heiress of Viscount Mayo; the family of Viscount Dillon of Castello-Gallon also belonged to Mayo, and Browne seems to have had intimate personal and political connections with them. Staunton was the son of Sir George L. Staunton who had been on Macartney's Embassy, and had himself been President of the

Select Committee at Canton; he had been in the chair at a meeting of the Royal Asiatic Society on 7 April 1832, when Dillon had introduced a Maori (*Sydney Herald*, 12 November 1832, from *Bengal Hurkaru* of 5 July). Staunton also had links with Irish society, having a home in County Galway—biographical details from C. R. Dod, *The Parliamentary Companion* and *Electoral Facts* for various years. [Respectable as Dillon's backing was, it seems rather lacking in range.]

54 Dillon to Hay, 30 July 1832—CO 201/229.
55 Dillon to Hay, 30 July 1832—CO 201/229; Hay to Dillon, 3 August 1832—CO 202/28.
56 Hay to Dillon, 1 October 1832—202/29.
57 Dillon to Hay, 25 September 1832—CO 201/229.
58 *ibid.*
59 *Nautical Magazine*, 1833 (September), 529; [E. G. Wakefield], *The New British Province of South Australia* (London, 1834), 21.
60 Dillon to Hay, 26 June 1833—CO 201/235.
61 The Memorial of the Chevalier Peter Dillon dated 22 June 1833—*ibid.*
62 Dillon to Stanley, 2 October 1833—*ibid.* Dillon bitterly resented the intrusion of Stephen, 'this young man' 'who never took the trouble of reading my Dossier'—Dillon to Spring Rice, 27 February 1835—CO 201/250.
63 Dillon to Earl, 12 November 1833—CO 201/235; Dillon to Earl, 8 January 1834 —CO 201/244.
64 Dillon to Hay, 8 January 1834—*ibid.*
65 Dillon to Hay, 15 February 1834—*ibid.* [This is a confused reference to the confused state of affairs in the Falklands leading to the murder of Matthew Brisbane in August 1833, by mutinous Argentine convicts—see V. F. Boyson, *The Falkland Islands* (London, 1924), 93-104.]
66 Dillon to Wright, 20 April 1834—CO 208/1. I have been unable to discover the identity of the backers for this venture.
67 Dillon to Chaigneau, 24 May 1834—ML B 149. One of these letters, to the Minister of Foreign Affairs, 24 May 1834, is in ANM BB4 1003.
68 Dillon to Lefevre, 2 May, 10 June 1834—CO 201/244; the second of these is the earliest dated from the Jerusalem Coffee House, Cornhill.
69 Dillon to Hay 27 February 1835—CO 201/250.

16

INTERLUDE IN NEW ZEALAND 1834-36

1 On 21 June, according to *Sydney Gazette*, 28 October 1834. There are some details of the voyage in A. G. Bagnall and G. C. Petersen, *William Colenso* (Wellington, 1948), 29-31.
2 *Sydney Gazette*, 27 October 1834.
3 *Australian*, 28 October 1834.
4 R. Therry, *Reminiscences of Thirty Years' Residence in New South Wales and Victoria* (London, 1863), 179-81. Therry misquotes. [There were two editions in 1863, the second correcting some appalling howlers in the account of Dillon's Vanikoro expedition.]
5 *Sydney Herald*, 19 March 1835.
6 Dillon to ——, 4 March 1835; he also wrote, 28 February 1835, to Parisor, chief of the historical section of the Ministry, [giving details of the seizure by Fijians of the French bêche-de-mer trader *L'Aimable Josephine*, with the massacre of most of her crew and her subsequent wreck, in July 1834. Both letters are in ANM BB4 1003. See R. A. Derrick, *History of Fiji* (Suva, 3rd ed. 1957), 59-60, and cf. *Hobart Town Courier*, 17 April 1935.]
7 Dillon to Spring Rice, 27 February 1835—HRA, I, XVIII, 69-70; R. W. Hay to Bourke, 9 August 1835—*ibid.* [This is the last we hear of the £245.]
8 Brown to Henry Williams, 23 July 1835—in W. H. Gifford and H. B. Williams, *A Centennial History of Tauronga*, (Dunedin and Wellington, 1940), 43.
9 Rev. A. N. Brown's *Journal March 21 1835 to October 27 1836 Matamata*, entries for 27-28 July and 3 August 1835—transcript in ATL. Dillon is one of three traders whom Brown mentions by name; others are simply 'a European'.

x

10 W. R. Wade, Journal 14 August 1835—ATL f MS 1834-39P.
11 Gordon Browne of Mahurangi (Mercury Bay), August 1835, in R. A. A. Sherrin and J. H. Wallace, *Early History of New Zealand* (Auckland, 1890), 371.
12 Browne to Mair, 18 January 1836; Dacre to Mair, n.d.—Mair Papers, City of Auckland Public Library.
13 National Archives of New Zealand, British Resident, correspondence, 1832-39, 2, 41.
14 Laura L. Jackson, *Annals of a New Zealand Family: the household of Gilbert Mair* . . . (Dunedin, 1935), 34; *Otago Daily Times*, 27 June 1917 ('Mrs William Bedlington: New Zealand's First-Born European').
15 *Sydney Gazette*, 31 March 1836.

17
FINALE IN THE SOUTH SEAS 1836-38

1 *Commercial Journal and Advertiser*, 30 March 1836.
2 *Sydney Gazette*, 2 April 1836.
3 *Commercial Journal and Advertiser*, 7 May; *Sydney Herald*, 9 May; *Sydney Gazette*, 10 May 1836.
4 Report of the Case of John Adair . . . , 6 February 1837—Governor's Despatches, 1837, . . .
5 Molé to D'Eckmühl, 30 January 1837—ANM BB4 1003. [As so often with Dillon's affairs, the timing went awry.]
6 *Sydney Herald*, 2 February 1837.
7 *Colonist*, 31 March 1836; advertisement dated 6 February in *Sydney Herald*, 9 February 1836.
8 Dacre and Wilks to Mair, 11 February 1837—Mair Papers, City of Auckland Public Library.
9 Dacre and Wilks to Mair, n.d.—*ibid*.
10 Dillon to J. J. Therry, 3 August 1831—printed in Eris M. O'Brien, *Life and Letters of Archpriest John Joseph Therry* . . . (Sydney, 1922), 324-5.
11 *Truth* (Sydney), 29 December 1925; CSP, 37/2935.
12 R. Therry, *Reminiscences of Thirty Years' Residence in New South Wales and Victoria* (London, 1863), 107-09; J. Mudie, *The Felonry of New South Wales* (London, 1837), 185.
13 Spring Rice to Bourke, 22 June 1834—State Archives of New South Wales, Governor's Despatches, 1834. The pardon may have been granted in 1831 but not communicated until 1834.
14 *Sydney Herald*, 20, 23 March 1837. Dillon is still styled 'French Consul for the Pacific'. [Charles X's appointment had lapsed with the Revolution (above, 240); whether or no Dillon was himself responsible for such honorific attributions, his vanity, perhaps his eye to the main chance, and doubtless his character for Irish blarney, ensured that he would not be over-hasty in disclaiming them.]
15 *ibid.*, 3 April 1837.
16 Attorney-General to Dillon, 18 March 1837—CSO 37/2935. [The last sentence seems a very odd argument from a lawyer.]
17 Luke Dillon to Colonial Secretary, 26 March 1837—*ibid.*
18 Rough draft by E. Deas Thomson, 27 March 1837—*ibid.*
19 For the pardon, Russell to Gipps, 11 May 1840—Governor's Despatches, 1840. According to Roger Therry, who is not always accurate, Luke married, under an assumed name, the daughter of a Dieppe inn-keeper; when the virtuous father heard of his son-in-law's past, he persuaded the wife to leave him, taking their children with her. Before this blow his ebullience collapsed, and he died in a French asylum (Therry, *op. cit.*, 109).
20 Dillon to Russell, 11 April 1840—CO 209/7.
21 *ibid.*
22 [E. Lucett], *Rovings in the Pacific, from 1837 to 1849* . . . (London, 1851), I, 303-4; II, 19-21.
23 Dillon to Colin, 22 March 1842—APM Z 208.
24 Dillon, *Narrative*, I, 283-5; II, 97.

Notes 339

25 For Tongan politics at this time, see S. Lātūkefu, *Church and State in Tonga* (Canberra, 1974), 28-49, 58-67.
26 D. Cargill, *A Refutation of the Chevalier Dillon's Slanderous Attacks on the Wesleyan Missionaries in the Friendly Islands* (London, 1842), 30-1.
27 *Sydney Herald*, 16 April 1838.
28 Cargill, *Refutation*, 29. In the pamphlet which Dillon devoted to his attack on the Protestant missions (see note 30), he claims to have taken 30 depositions at Tongatapu and Vava'u, mainly from Europeans.
29 R. P. Mangeret, *Mgr. Bataillon et les missions de l'Océanie centrale* (Paris, 1884), 2 vols, I, 59-79.
30 In 1840 or 1841 (see No. 12 in List of Dillon's publications) Dillon printed this attack in a letter to Richard More O'Ferrall; a French translation is printed in A. du Petit-Thouars, *Voyage autour du monde* ... (Paris, 1840-46), II, 414-19. Du Petit-Thouars obtained it in Valparaiso from an acquaintance, 'homme d'esprit et de judgment' and violently opposed to the [Protestant] missions. His identity is unknown: he was not, apparently, Joseph Brémond, a French carpenter whom Dillon took aboard the *Jess* in Tahiti, and probably neither J. A. Moerenhout nor Thomas Ebrill. Parts of the letter are printed in French in Mangeret, *op. cit.*, and in English, from the printed text, in Cargill, *Refutation*. [The extracts here given are from Davidson's original draft, and differ in spelling (only) from the printed version cited at the beginning of this note: the source of Davidson's text is not given.]
31 This passage refers to the succession of Taufa'ahau as ruler of Vava'u, in place of Finau Ukualala's son Matekitonga, who was only a boy. According to Wood (*op. cit.*, 47), Finau had before his death nominated Taufa'ahau.
32 According to William Diaper, Dillon obtained a rope which he claimed to have been so used (on a white man) and took it to England as evidence; see below, 340.
33 This refers to the war of early 1837—see S. S. Farmer, *Tonga and the Friendly Islands* ... (London, 1855), 297.
34 Dillon wrote 'Since writing the above a few days past I have received the following account of the fleet now rendezvousing at the Hapaee's ...'.
35 Cargill later claimed (*Refutation*, 18) that there was a rumour that Dillon himself had supplied the 'heathen' with knives for the massacre of the Christians.
36 According to Joseph Meyrick, writing in January 1838, Dillon's threat to Thomas, designed to frighten him into stopping the war, did achieve this result (cf. above, 291).
37 Cargill to General Secretaries, 6 July 1838—MMS, Fiji, 1835-39.
38 Cross and Cargill to General Secretaries, MMS, 27 December 1837—*ibid*. The only chart generally available was probably Arrowsmith's *Chart of the Feejee Islands*, 1814, on which, for Viti Levu, only the north and north-east coasts were shown, inaccurately; the survey of the south and south-west coasts by H.M.S. *Victor* (1836) was almost certainly unknown and unavailable to Dillon.
39 Letter of 13 October 1836, quoted in Report of the *Wesleyan Methodist Missionary Society for the Year ending April, 1838*, 50.
40 Cargill to General Secretaries, 6 July 1838, MMS, Fiji 1835-39.
41 *ibid*. Cargill gathered this on a visit to Oneata in February 1838.
42 D. Cargill, *Refutation*, 30.
43 *ibid.*, 21.
44 Cross and Cargill to General Secretaries, 27 December 1837, MMS Fiji 1835-38.
45 J. Hunt, *Memoir of the Rev. William Cross* (London, 1846), 95.
46 *ibid.*, 96.
47 *ibid.*, 97. David Whippy responded.
48 R. A. Derrick, *History of Fiji* (Suva, 1946), 67.
49 J. S. C. Dumont d'Urville, *Voyage au Pôle Sud et dans l'Océanie* ... (Paris, 1841-46), IV, 221.
50 Dillon to —— [Scratchley?], 18 February 1839—PM 2208. Pompallier had recommended Moerenhout as Consul in Tahiti in October 1837.
51 W. R. Wade, *A Journey in the Northern Island of New Zealand* (Hobart, 1842), 134-6

340   *Peter Dillon of Vanikoro*

18

AN UNEASY LONDONER: PETITIONS AND POLEMICS 1839-47

1   T. F. Cheeseman's Journal says she left Sydney on 13 May, was at the Bay 1-8 and 12-15 June, rounded Cape Horn at the end of July, and reached Rio de Janeiro on 11 September, where Dillon 'left us'—ATL f MS 1836-41P.
2   J. D. Lang, *New Zealand in 1839* (London, 1839), 58; her portrait was painted by R. A. Oliver.
3   Dillon to Palmerston, 28 January 1839—CO 209/5, 230; dated from East India House, Leadenhall Street.
4   Dillon to Glenelg, 31 January 1839—CO 209/5; from Jerusalem Coffee House. At about this time Dillon sent the Colonial Office a copy of the resolutions of the Kororareka Association—CO 209/3.
5   *Extract of a Letter from Chevalier Dillon to an influential character here on the advantages to be derived from the establishment of well conducted Commercial Settlements in New Zealand* (No. 7 in list of Dillon's publications below). On the strength of the date 'May 1 1832', library catalogues generally date this pamphlet 1832, as does T. M. H. Hocken's *A Bibliography of the Literature relating to New Zealand* (Wellington, 1909), although his own copy was of the 1839 edition, and on page 1 this has a footnote by Dillon giving 1834 for the earlier edition. But this may be a slip since Dillon elsewhere gives 1832, as in the letter to Wright of the NZC here quoted. For a summary, see 252-4 above.
6   Dillon to Jno. Wright, 20 April 1839—CO 208/1; dated from 92 Charlotte Street. He later claimed that Dr Evans of the NZC asked him to join 'his party' but that he had declined—Dillon to Russell, 29 July 1840—CO 209/7.
7   Copy in CO 208/291. Dillon seems to have made some enquiries about these cattle, which he landed in the Islands in 1824, from 'the chief' (Tapoa?) through the LMS; he gathered that John Williams had taken and sold some of them—R. Bourne to D. Tidman, 1 November 1841—AL, 1833-44.
8   Based on an account of the advertisement in the *Australian*, 11 February 1840.
9   Dillon to Russell, 8 April 1940—CO 209/7. There is reference to previous correspondence which I have not seen.
10 Dillon to Russell, 29 July 1840. In fact, homosexuality was common in Polynesia, as Dillon must have known.
11 Dandeson Coates to Vernon Smith, 14 May 1840—CO 209/8.
12 *Sydney Gazette*, 20, 22 May 1841.
13 Dillon to Colin, 25 January 1840—APM 2208.
14 The Register of Deaths at Somerset House gives the details: 'Mary Dillon, 42 years, wife of Peter Dillon, Captain, of a Decline; Peter Dillon present at the Death 15 Alfred Street [Bloomsbury]'.
15 *New Zealand Journal* 21 November and 5 December 1840.
16 William Diapea [sic], *Cannibal Jack: The True Autobiography of a White Man in the South Seas*, printed from the manuscript in the possession of the Reverend James Hadfield (London, 1928), 239-40. [The only references by Dillon to such an exhibit are in a note to his letter to the Reverend John Thomas—'One of these terrible ropes is in my possession, brought from the Tonga Islands, and may be seen by the humane British People' (*Letter to Richard More O'Farrell*, 4 December 1840, 6) and another note, presumably by Dillon, attached to Joseph Meyrick's statement that the officers of H.M.S. *Conway* were given pieces from a line with which King George had flogged eleven men and five women in one morning; the officers held a whitewashing enquiry 'not on board H.M.S.—but at the dwelling of the Grand Inquisitor'. The note reads confusingly 'To be shown in England as instruments of conversion, such as are used in that country by King George the Fourth, Mr. T's quondam friend'—an ironic reference to Dillon's allegation that Thomas claimed to be 'a friend of King George, (who was himself a Missionary,)'—*ibid*, 11, 5. All this is confusing enough without Diaper's tale, which looks like a conflation of some other beachcomber's story with Dillon's well-known anti-missionary activities.]
17 I have not found these letters, but the *Australian* (20 May 1841) states: 'We have to acknowledge the receipt of certain documents, purporting to be addressed by the Chevalier Dillon to Lord John Russell, relative to the conduct of certain Wesleyan

Notes 341

Missionaries in the South Sea Islands, and more particularly in Tongataboo, with reference to the unfortunate affair of Captain Croker, and H.M. Ship Favorite'. The documents were not published, [doubtless a measure of prudence].
18 Copy in University College London Library.
19 Ellis to Wesleyan Missionary Society Secretaries, 8 October 1838—MMS, Friendly Islands.
20 Secretaries to Orton, 21 December 1838—*ibid*.
21 John Thomas's Journal, 9 June 1840—*ibid*.
22 *Refutation*, 4-5.
23 *ibid.*, 9.
24 *ibid.*, 25.
25 [It must be admitted that as regards self-righteousness, over-writing, and uncharitableness, Dillon's letter to Thomas had given a provocative lead.]
26 *ibid.*, 30, 35.
27 Dillon to Vernon Smith, 30 March 1841—CO 209/13.
28 But his father had, as Dillon knew.
29 Dillon to Duke of Bedford, 4 August 1841, from Jerusalem Coffee House; copy in hand of amanuensis but with Dillon's signature, CO 290/13. Later printed in *Letters addressed to His Grace the Duke of Bedford* . . . [and others; see No. 11 in list of Dillon's publications, below]; a copy was sent to James Stephen on 21 September 1841.
30 Dillon to Vernon Smith, 11 August 1841—CO 209/13.
31 Dillon to Vernon Smith, 12 August 1841—*ibid*. [Dillon seems never to have realized that all this back-biting might well ruin such poor chances as he had of official advancement.]
32 Dillon to Stephen, 2 September 1841—*ibid*.
33 Dillon to ——, 18 February 1839: APM Z 208. The addressee was perhaps George Scratchley in Paris, but it was clearly intended to reach Father Colin, head of the Marist Order, in Lyons. It is in French—presumably written by Martha Dillon from her father's English draft.
34 *ibid*.
35 Dillon seems at this time to have had fairly close relations with Cooper, and probably earned some money from occasional work for him. Cooper, transported for life, reached Sydney in 1816 and received an absolute pardon in 1819; like Dillon's father-in-law, Peter Moore, he was a member of the Emancipist Colonists' Standing Committee in 1821. He had a highly successful business career, eight years of it in partnership with Solomon Levey; his interests included the timber trade at Hokianga, whence doubtless his link with Dillon. From 1835 onwards—after Levey's death— he is shown in London Business directories as a merchant with City offices at Copthall Chambers, although he signed a Sydney address to Bourke in 1836.
36 Dillon to Colin, 25 January 1840—APM Z 208. He also wrote to Bishop Polding in New South Wales; I have not seen this letter, referred to in Heptonstall to Colin, 7 December 1841—*ibid.*; it should be, I think, in the Manly Archives. Thomas Heptonstall, OSB, 'Vicar-General in England to Dr. Polding', was a cousin of Bishop Polding, who had appointed him as his business agent in London; he helped Ullathorne and his party before they left England. See H. N. Birt, *Benedictine Pioneers in Australia* (London, 1911), I, 288-9.
37 Or *Australian*, for which Cooper was agent; he may himself have owned a Sydney whaler of the same name.
38 Dillon to Colin, 24 April 1840—APM Z 208.
39 Lamy, Mme Adélaïde's secretary, informed him that his papers had been laid before the King: Lamy to Dillon, 25 February 1840—*ibid*.
40 Colin to Dillon, 2 May 1840—*ibid*. Like most of Colin's letters to Dillon, this seems to have been drafted by Fr Poupinel; the practice seems to have been to draft in French and then translate into English. In this case both versions survive; the translation, though often awkward, is not literal.
41 Dillon to Colin, 25 November 1840; Colin to Cooper, 22 December 1840; Dillon to Colin, 10 June 1841—all APM Z 208.
42 Dillon to Colin, 9 February 1841—*ibid*.
43 Dillon to Colin, 10 June 1841—*ibid*.
44 *idem*.

45 Colin to Dillon, 10 May 1841—*ibid.*
46 Colin to Dillon, 6 July 1841—*ibid.*
47 Dillon was particularly upset by this; he had a document signed by a number of seafaring men, affirming that Cooper's *Eleanor* was fit 'to carry passengers to any part of the known world', and sent it to Colin, 28 October 1841—*ibid.* [Of course the priests, perhaps mostly of rustic origins, may have had a landlubberly approach; but is it uncharitable to think that Dillon may have been looking to a commission from Cooper?]
48 *idem*; and Dillon to Colin, 25 October 1841—*ibid.*
49 Dillon to Colin, 14 October 1841—*ibid.*
50 Dillon to Solages, 7 September 1829—AMAE: Océanie, 1822-43.
51 On Muller and Pallas see J. R. Masterman and Helen Brower, *Bering's Successors, 1745-1780* . . . (Seattle, 1948).
52 On 21 January 1843 Dillon, in Dublin, sent the printer's bill—£39 3s—to the publisher—ML A2, p. 55. The second edition is not recorded in the British Museum catalogue; there is a copy in the India Office Library.
53 Dillon to Aberdeen, 16 March 1844—FO 58/31.
54 Dillon to Aberdeen, 4, 9 April 1844; Dillon to [FO], 9 April 1844; Mountcashel to Aberdeen, 1 April 1844; FO to Dillon, 13 April 1844—all FO 58/32.
55 Dillon to Aberdeen, 18 September 1844—FO 58/32; Dillon to Aberdeen, 3 October 1844—FO 58/33.
56 Dubreul to Epalle, London, 11 November 1844; Epalle to Poupinel, London, 12 January 1845 (reference to Dillon's ship in futurity); Epalle to Colin, from London 31 January 1845 and from Cape of Good Hope 2 May 1845—all in APM OMM 411.
57 Dillon to Colin, 21, 27, 31 December 1844 APM Z 208.
58 Dillon to Normandy, 30 September 1846—FO 146/306. For the 'so unfortunate, phrase, see above, 248—[it was now sixteen years old.]
59 Dillon to ——, 19 October 1846; probably to Thomas Hodgkin, Secretary of the Aborigines' Protection Society, as it refers to several of the Society's current affairs.
60 Draft letter by Direction du Personnel en Division des Invalides (of Ministry of Navy), 23 January 1847—ANM BB4 1003.
61 The *Acte de décès* gives his age as 60, birthplace Martinique; among the witnesses was Denis Sheehan, Bursar of the Irish College-Ville de Paris, *Extrait du registre des actes de décès de la 12ᵉ mairie*.
62 Most of this and the following paragraph is based on a *Note du Personnel militaire et des mouvements de la Flotte*, 26 January 1849, and a copy of a letter from the Minister of the Navy to the French Consul-General at Sydney, 2 November 1878, in the *Dossier Personnel de Dillon (Pierre)*, Service des Archives du Ministère, Paris.
63 Georges Goyau, *Les grands desseins missionnaires d'Henri de Solages 1786-1832*, (Paris, 1933), 54.
64 Secretary of State for Foreign Affairs to H.M.'s Consuls, 5 June 1847.
65 A note in the file of movements referred to in note 62 above implies that G. P. Dillon and his family travelled on the *Poursuivante*.
66 Tahiti: British Consulate Papers, 1840-55—ML MSS 24/3; *ibid.*, 1847-53.
67 Ribourt to Bouillon, Papeete, 28 March 1848—*Bulletin de la Société des Études Océaniennes* (Papeete), No. 65, March 1939, 134-40.
68 *Sydney Morning Herald*, 19 and 20 October 1849, and Dillon family records. Her age is given as 26, but the muster of the *St Michael*, December 1819, shows her as 10 months old—Ships Musters, 1816-21, 201-CSO 4/4771.
69 *Sydney Morning Herald*, 5 April 1851, 21 May 1855, 27 July 1857; and Dillon family records.
70 J. N. Dillon to 'the French Consul', 26 July 1878; Consul-General to Minister of the Navy and Colonies, 15 August 1878—*Dossier Personnel de Dillon (Pierre)*. Joseph Napoleon was probably misled by his grandfather's categorical statement '. . . and half that amount to my family in case they should survive me'—*Narrative*, II, 397).
71 *Sun* (Sydney), 4 March 1973. A sword often described as having belonged to Dillon is in Vaucluse House, Woollahra (Sydney), but there is no evidence at all that it was his.
72 A. J. Villiers, *Vanished Fleets* (London, 1931), 185.
73 The *Age* (Melbourne), 19 November 1887.

Index

Index

Aborigines' Protection Soc., 2, 281, 301, 305
Acapulco, 6, 83
Adair, Rev. J., 265-6
Adams, John, of Pitcairn, 86
Adams, Dr J., 131-2
Adelaïde d'Orléans, 278, 297-9
Ahuturu, 9
Aitutaki I., 101, 164
Amherst, Lord, 204, 242, 246, 304
Arthur, Sir G., 140-2, 146, 148-50, 152, 200, 211, 215, 227
Asiatic Soc., 57, 58, 124, 129, 144, 204, 213
Astell, W., 211, 213, 246
Atiu I., 86, 87, 164
Atjeh, 62, 72
Auckland, 105
Australia, 7-8, 43

Babahey, 168
Bacon, Maj. A., 251, 257
Banks, Sir J., 8, 242
Barnes, Peter, 75
Barrettos, 57-8, 60, 71, 72, 77, 88, 92, 201-2, 248
Batavia, 59
Bathurst, Lord, 140
Bayly, G., 94-117 passim, 120, 192, 308
Bay of Islands, 11, 21-4, 45-9, 78-82, 91-2, 96, 103, 106, 154-61, 190-5, 223, 229, 261-4, 278, 280, 284
bêche-de-mer, 26, 31, 88, 106, 254, 277
Bedford, Duke of, 295
Bedford, Rev. W., 104, 142, 215, 227
Belgium, and Fiji, 249
Bellingshausen, T. von, 58-9, 62
Benkulen, 58-9, 62
Bertrands, 14, 149, 209
Betham, Sir W., 192-3, 211
Bethune, W. A., 141, 148
Blake, J. R., 130-1, 138, 151-4, 192

Bligh, W., 10, 19, 42, 138
Borabora I., 20, 23, 26-7, 269
Botany Bay, 10, 11, 107, 118
Bougainville, L.-A. de, 7, 9, 85
Bourke, Sir R., 259, 287, 296
'Brian Boru', 106, 115, 118-33 passim, 136-8, 158, 161, 179, 191, 194-6, 238, 308
Brightman, E., 58, 71, 72, 120, 202
Brisbane, Sir T., 71, 244, 276
Bua, Fiji, 12, 15, 17, 88
Buache, J., 10
Buchert, Martin, 28-41 passim, 76, 106-7, 125, 127, 130, 148, 161, 169, 170-89 passim, 195-6, 215
Bunster, Capt. W., 49, 52-3
Burma, 120, 127, 202, 205
Burnsides, A., 14-15, 17, 23-4
Buru I., 111, 112, 152
Busby, James, 254, 264, 293
Busby, John, 96

Calcutta, 14, 55-8, 83, 114-15, 118-33 passim
Callao, 82
Campbell & Co., 15, 18, 57
Campbell, R., 15, 17, 43, 70, 153
Cargill, Rev. D., 270, 275-6, 292-3
Carteret, P., 7, 109, 170, 187, 189
Chaigneau, E., 130, 135, 142, 166, 170-89 passim, 192, 203, 207, 208, 212, 258
Chandernagore, 127, 203, 249
Charles X, 212, 214, 217-18, 237, 240, 241, 263, 277, 304
Chile, 82, 83, 98, 102, 111, 113
China, 56, 243, 301-2
Christian, Fletcher, 85, 138
Church Missionary Soc., 91, 285-6, 290
Cimitière, G., 66-7
Cochrane, Lord, 98

345

Colin, Fr, OM, 297-301, 304
Colonial Office, 242-6, 254-7, 260-2, 293-6
Combermere, Lord, 56, 84, 121, 129, 174, 204, 205, 304
Commerson, P., 9, 12, 25
Cook, Capt. James, 7-10, 11, 12, 19, 82, 85, 102, 123, 138, 161, 166, 208, 220, 231-2, 242, 276, 298
Cooper, D., 297-300
Cooper, R., 92-3
Cordier, J., 127, 129, 203
'Country Trade', 54-6, 83
Cox, Charles, 34, 38, 44
Coxe, Rev. W., 302-3
Croker, Capt., 290-3
Crook, W. P., 60, 85
Cross, Rev. W., 275-7

Dafny, T., 36-7
Dalrymple & Co., 15, 16
Dampier, W., 123, 138, 161, 222
Dart, J., 211-12, 213
d'Entrecasteaux, B., 108, 127, 208, 217, 220, 239
de Lesseps, B., 217
d'Este, Sir A., 251, 287
d'Haussez, Baron, 238, 241
Diaper, W., 290
Dillon Bay, 91, 307
Dillon, J. Napoleon, 71, 307
Dillon, Luke, 249, 267-8
Dillon, Martha, 60, 66, 67, 134, 205, 240, 248, 258, 305-7
Dillon, Mary, 51-2, 63-72, 134, 156, 205, 240, 280-1, 284, 288, 305
DILLON, PETER: birth, 5, 10, 13; character, 1-2, 12, 14, 16-17, 76-7, 94-117 *passim*, 134, 147, 198-9, 207, 216, 219-34 *passim*, 246-7, 279, 301, 308-9; *Narrative*, 154, 169, 174, 192, 202, 207, 219-34 *passim*, 239-40, 246; marriage, 51; death, 305
Dillon, Peter (son), 52, 307
Dillon, Sir W., 149
Dillons, of France and Martinique, 13-14, 209, 215, 269
Dillon's Rock, 28-41 *passim*, 295, 307, Appx II
Drake, Sir F., 138
Dudman, J., 130, 137-8, 153, 192
Du Petit-Thouars, 303

D'Urville, D., 162-3, 168, 198-200, 205, 215-16, 218, 233, 234, 241, 258, 260, 295
East India Company, 11, 12, 54-6, 60, 61, 147, 150, 205, 211-14, 232, 235, 241-58 *passim*, 269, 281
Ebrill, T., 100
Ellis, Rev. W., 234, 291
Eromanga I., 90-1, 100-1, 289
'Eua I., 162-3
Evans, G. W., 59

Fa'anuhe, of Ra'ieatea, 28, 45, 50
Falkland Is, 123, 257
Fakafanua, of Tonga, 165-7
Fenuapeho, of Tonga, 27, 86, 101
FIJI: 6; sandalwood, 11, 12, 15-18, 28-41 *passim*, 87-8, 237-8; and Belgium, 249; in 1837, 275-8
'Fingal, Marquis of Wyemattee', *see* Titore
flax, N.Z., 238, 251, 253, 258, 263, 269
Flinders, Matthew, 58, 84
Florence, J., 76, 83, 91, 93, 110, 114
Forster, J. R., 89
Fodger, Capt. M., 26, 28, 45
Freycinet, L. de, 123
'Frinch', Mr, 64, 210
Futuna I., 89, 167

Galignani, 235
Gellibrand, J. T., 141, 144, 148, 152, 155
George Town, V.D.L., 66-7, 244
George Tupou, of Tonga, 270-4, 290-2
Glenelg, Lord, 296
Goderich, Lord, 246, 254, 293-5
Golovnin, V. M., 89
Gower's Harbour, New Ireland, 109-10
Graham, J., 32, 34
Granville, Lord, 247-8, 250
Griffiths, Dr J., 151, 153, 195, 201
Griffiths, Jonathan, 69

Hall, W., 46-9, 78, 92
Hapdé, J. B., 216
Harrington, J. H., 124, 128-9
Hauraki Gulf, 79, 102, 238
Hawaii, 8-9, 10, 11, 63, 202
Hawkesworth, J., 232

Index 347

Hay, R. W., 245, 251, 254-7
Hayes, Cdre J., 126-7, 129
Helmick, L., 143
Henry, Capt. S. P., 100-1
Henry IV, funny to Fijians, 132
Hickey, W., 57
Hinaki, 103, 104
Hobart Town, 48-9, 52, 68-70, 73, 140-1, 198-200
Hobson, W., 284, 287
Hokianga, 191, 194, 262, 289
Hongi Hika, 49, 50, 78-80, 92, 158, 193-4, 285
Hooghly, 61, 113, 117, 133
Howe, G., 141, 152
Howe, R., 152, 200
Howick, Lord, 247
Heptonstall, Fr T. P. OSB, 298, 301
Huahine I., 8, 20, 22-3, 26, 101
Hunter Is, 66
Hyde de Neuville, Baron, 212, 217, 218

Ireland, 13, 119-20, 183, 242

Jackson, J., 69-70
James, Capt. J., 67-9, 71-2, 74
Jemmy, of Tahiti, 21, 157
Jenny, *see* Teehuteatuanoa
Jerusalem Coffee House, 211, 281, 288, 293, 301
Jervis Bay, 48, 71
'Joe the Lascar', 31, 40, 106-7, 125, 169, 171
Johnson, Samuel, 5, 219
Josephine, Empress, 13
'Joseph Baretto's I.' (Ono-i-Lau), 88, 92
July Revolution, 241

Kaba, Fiji, 31, 33, 76, 276
Kajeli Bay, 111-12, 113
Kangaroo I., 52-3, 66, 251
Kauri, *see* spar trade
Kelly, J., 68, 200
Kemp, A. F., 141, 148
Kent, Capt., 190, 195-6
King George's Sound, 65
King, J., 46, 78
Knopwood, Rev. R., 49, 52, 140
Kororareka, N.Z., 49, 106, 154, 157, 160, 190, 195, 196, 280, 285

Lafitte, J., 246, 250
Lakeba I., 87, 275-6
Lang, Rev. J. D., 92
Langi, of Tonga, 92, 100, 119, 163
Lambert, A. B., 242, 255, 306
La Pérouse, J. F. G. de, 1, 2, 10, 107-8, 116, 118-33 *passim*, 142, 145, 162, 165, 170-89 *passim*, 199, 200, 202, 205, 207-18 *passim*, 219-20, 233, 238, 247-8, 260, 261, 266, 280, 293-5, 305, 307
Launceston, 67, 73
Levuka, 88, 277
Lima, 82, 230, 237, 242
London Missionary Soc., 11, 18, 82, 85, 238, 290-3, 303
Lord, E., 49, 52, 69-70, 72, 141, 148, 150, 242
Louis Philippe, 246-8, 263, 299
'Luis', the Chinaman, 36, 40
Lushington, C., 125, 126, 174, 293, 295

Macarthur, J., 21
Macleay, A., 249, 260
Macquarie, L., 42-4, 46, 68, 71, 79, 244
Mafi Hape, 163-4
Magellan, 6, 7, 138
Mai, of Borabora, 26-7
Mair, G., 263-4, 266, 268
Makogai I., 68, 238
'Mallicolo', *see* Vanikoro
Manila, 6, 12
Ma'ofonga, Tonga, 163, 165
Maoris, 8, 21, 24, 78-82, 91, 102-6, 155-9, 252-3, 269
marihuana, 135
Mariner, W., 163-4, 223-4, 233, 234, 278
Marist Order, 297-301, 304
Marquesas, 6, 8, 11, 95, 237
Marsden, Rev. S., 18, 21, 22, 45-9, 74, 78, 80, 91, 102, 133, 159, 198, 230, 239, 259
Marsh, H., 63
Martin, I., 86
Martinique, 13, 14, 209, 212, 269
Matavai, Tahiti, 19, 85
Maungatapu, N.Z., 262, 264, 265, 269, 279
McCabe, J., 64-5
Meath County, 13, 51, 149
Melvin, L. W., 102

Mendaña, A. de, 6, 7, 10, 82, 109, 123, 138, 170, 187, 189, 238
Meyrick, J., 270, 278, 291
missions, Protestant, 11, 18, 19, 25, 46-9, 193, 228-30, 265-79 *passim*, 280, 284-5, 289-93, 303-4
missions, Roman Catholic, 235-40 *passim*, 269, 270-1, 280, 281-2, 285, 297-301
Moehanga, 132, 158-9, 160, 230
Moore, J., 51, 52
Moore, P., 51, 71, 72, 76, 306
Mo'orea I., 25, 26
'Morgan McMurragh, H. E.', 106, 115, 118-33 *passim*, 136-8, 143, 158, 181, 191, 194-5, 204
Mossman, J., 95, 97-8, 104, 110, 130, 138, 153
Murray, Sir G., 240, 244-6
Muscat, 11
musket trade, 19-20, 78-9, 80, 83, 91, 99-100, 103-4

Napoleon, 14, 209, 210
Naulivou, of Bau, 31, 34, 88, 238
Naurore Bay, 15, 29-34, 44, 312
Ndeni I., 188, 189, 227
'Nero', of Vanikoro, 177-8, 181, 188
New Caledonia, 8, 91, 189
New Guinea, 10, 106, 110
New Hebrides, 6, 7, 8, 89-91, 123
New South Wales Corps, 42, 43
NEW ZEALAND: 2, 6, 8, 11, 21, 23-4; first mission, 46-7, 49-50; in 1814, 76-82; 96; in 1826-27, 102-6, 155-62, 190-5, 223, 226, 228, 238; projects for, 250-6, 259-64 *passim*, 282-7
New Zealand Company, 280, 282-7, 297
Nicolas, Capt. T., 303
Norfolk I., 27, 28, 29, 50
Normanby, Marquis of, 1, 304
North-West Passage, 9, 10
Nott, Rev. H., 25, 27, 85-6, 100
Nuku'alofa, 270

O'Ferrall, R., 141-2
Ogea I., 87, 167
Ono-i-Lau I., 87-8, 170
Oriental Institution, 242
Ousely, J. R. 126

Palmerston, Lord, 282
Paris, 216, 218, 306-7
Paterson, Col. W., 42
Pedder, J. L., 140, 144-50, 200, 215
Peel, Thomas, 282
Penang, 15, 61-2, 205
PERIODICALS:
 Annales Maritimes, 218
 Asiatic Jnl, 211, 213, 233
 Australian, 92, 259
 Bengal Hurkaru, 85, 119-20, 123-6, 132, 204
 Colonial Times (V.D.L.), 141, 143-4, 221, 288
 Edinburgh Jnl of Natural and Geographical Science, 233-4
 Galignani, 305
 Gleaner (Sydney), 152
 Government Gaz. (Calcutta), 56, 123, 126, 143
 Hobart Town Gaz., 62, 145, 152, 200, 215
 India Gaz., 121
 Literary Gaz., 211
 Main-sheet, 259
 Monitor (V.D.L.), 200
 Morning Chronicle (London), 215, 218, 284
 Nautical Mag., 256
 New Zealand Jnl (London), 288-9
 Quarterly Rev., 296
 Sydney Gaz., 18, 23, 44, 55, 67, 71, 73, 77, 92, 123, 152, 198-9, 259, 288
 Tasmanian, 141, 152
 Times, 233
 United Services Jnl, 233
Peru, 6, 82
Phillip, A., 10, 11
Pitcairn I., 85-6, 122-3, 233, 237
Polignac, Prince, 212, 237-41, 248, 295
Polynesian voyaging, 87, 164, 225
Pomare (Bomarey), Maori chief, 101, 104-5, 302
Pomare, Royal Family of Tahiti, 19-37, 101, 302
Pompallier, Bishop, 270-1, 278, 280, 285, 297, 299
Pondicherry, 113, 128, 131
pork trade, 11, 18, 20, 47, 86, 100
Port Dalrymple, 49, 52, 244
Port Jackson, 11, 152, 154
Port Nicholson, 286, 296

Index 349

Pratt, Rev. J., 64-5
Pritchard, G., 303-4
Purdy, J., 87

Quiros, P. F. de, 6, 187

Raffles, Sir S., 62
Ra'iatea I., 8, 19, 20-1, 26, 86, 101, 283
Rammohun Roy, 130, 142
Rangoon, 129
Rarotonga I., 86
Ratia, of Tikopia, 170-89 passim, 191, 192, 194
Read, Capt. G. F., 54
Reibey T., 18, 20-1, 25
Richardson, Dr, 156-7
Ritchie, Capt. T., 58-60, 63
Robson, Capt. J., 18, 28-41 passim, 44
Rodríguez, M., 82-3, 123, 242, 306
Rongomatane, 86
Ross, G., 95, 97-8, 103, 112, 130, 148
Ross, J., 200, 215
Rotuma I., 128, 165, 167, 168, 170
Rousseau, J. J., 5, 9
Royal Asiatic Soc., 213, 256, 263
Ruatara, 47-50
Russell, J., 130-1, 170-89 passim, 192-3
Russell, Lord John, 285-9, 293-6
Russia, 300-3

sandalwood, 11-12, 15, 17, 18, 26, 29-31, 84, 88, 90-1, 95, 100-1, 254
Santa Cruz I., 6, 7, 10, 109, 170, 177, 188, 238
Saugor, 114
Savage, Charles, 31-7, 76
Savage, Dr. J., 132
Scott, D., 57-8
Sebastiani, H. F. B., 250
Seru of Bau (Cakobau), 276-7
SHIPS: (*, Dillon in command; †, Dillon sailed in)
Active,* 46-51, 52, 64, 77-9, 158, 161, 169, 194
Aguila (Spsh), 82
Aimable Josephine (Fch), 266
Anastasia, 260
Ann, 46
Astrolabe (Fch, d'Urville), 162, 199, 270

Astrolabe (Fch, La Pérouse), 125, 186, 306
Australia, 298
Bounty, H.M.S. (Bligh), 10, 19, 20, 25, 85-6, 122
Boussole (Fch, La Pérouse), 125, 186, 211
Boyd, 23-4, 44, 47, 79, 159
Bridgewater, 54
Britannia, 51
Briton, H.M.S. 85
Buffalo,† H.M.S., 278-9, 280
Bussorah Merchant, 267
Calder,* 72-6, 78-93 passim, 94-8, 122, 123, 147, 197-9, 202, 237, 306
Campbell Macquarie, 50
Caroline, 308
Chalcedony (Amcn),† 264
Clyde,† 14-15
Conway, H.M.S., 278
Courier, 307
Daphne, 45
Dordogne (Fch), 240
Eliza (Amcn), 16
Elizabeth,* 31-3, 40, 43, 44, 50, 52
Endeavour, 24-5, 27, 28, 45
Endeavour, H.M.S. (Cook), 8
Favourite, 15-16
Favourite, H.M.S., 290-1
Fire-fly,† 206
Futta Salem, see Phatisalam
General Wellesley,† 15-16, 59, 66, 88
Glory, 67-9
Governor Macquarie, 191-2, 195, 196
Greyhound,† 58-60
Haweis,† 70
Herald, 191-3
Hibernia, 23
Hunter,† 18, 28-41 passim, 44-5, 50, 57, 219
Jean Bart (Fch), 264
Jess,* 265-79 passim
Jupiter (Spsh), 82
Lady Hungerford,† 72
Larne, H.M.S., 105
Little Mary, 67-71, 240, 244
Lynx, 54
Mary Ann,† 205-6, 207
Mercury,† 18, 20-5, 27, 159
Nandey, 201
Nereid, 251
Pandora, H.M.S., 167

350   Peter Dillon of Vanikoro

Perseverance,† 17-18, 20, 29, 57
Phatisalam,* 63, 64-72, 76, 84, 93, 108, 151, 240, 244, 256, 260-1, 294
Port-au-Prince (Fch), 164
Poursuivante (Fch), 306
Prince Regent,† 259, 278
Queen Charlotte, 45, 50
Raietea, 270
Research,* 94, 126, 129-31, 133, 134-69 passim, 190, 194-5, 197, 223, 227, 229, 237, 248
Robulla,* 261-4, 265
Spring,† 49, 52-3, 54
St Michael,* 60-3, 69, 70
'St. Patricio', 119
St Patrick,* 83, 91, 94-117 passim, 120, 126, 130, 135, 143, 147, 157, 171, 190, 201-6, 237, 295, 306, 308
Tagus, H.M.S., 85
Ternate, 129
Tory, 26, 28
Trial, 26, 28
Uranie (Fch), 123
Venus, 22, 23
Vindictive, H.M.S., 303
Slater, O., 11-12
Smith, Capt. D., 68-9
Smith, Capt. J., 69-70
Solages, Henri de, 235-40 passim, 269
Sorell, W., 68, 70, 73, 140
spar trade, 80, 81, 91, 103-5, 279
Speck, Capt. S., 134, 142
Stanley, E. G. S., 256-8, 297
Stephen, A., 140, 144-50
Stephen, J., 140, 150, 245, 256-7, 288, 296-7
Stewart, C., 187, 188, 195, 258, 263
St Helena I., 14, 207, 209, 210, 294
Stuart de Rothesay, Lord, 243, 247, 250, 251
Surville, J. F. de, 10
Swan River, 282-3
Swift, Jonathan, 7, 175
Sydney, 11, 12, 42-4, 71, 197-201

Taha'a I., 8, 27, 86, 101
TAHITI: 7-9, 11; early politics, 19-20, 22, 25-7; Spanish at, 82, 85, 100-1, 123, 237; in 1830s, 269-70; Anglo-French crisis, 303-4
Tahuata I., 11, 18
Tait, J., 21-2, 24-5

Takai, of Lau, 87, 92-3, 100, 106, 119, 276
Talcahuano, 82
Talleyrand, 247
Tamaki Strait, 104-5
Tana I., 89-90, 289
Tapoa, of Borabora, 20, 23, 26, 27
Tasman, A. J., 6, 8
Tariou, of Aitutaki, 135
Taufa'ahau, see George Tupou
Tauranga, 262-3, 278, 298
Teehuteatuaonoa, 85, 122, 233
Te Pahi, 22, 24, 46, 80, 158
Terra Australis Incognita, 6, 7, 8
Te Whareumu, 193, 195, 196
Thames, Firth of, 11, 12, 29, 80, 93, 102-6, 157, 161, 262
Therry, Fr J. J., 249
Therry, R., 259-60, 267
Thierry, Baron de, 264, 265
Thomas, Rev. J., 163, 165, 166, 270-4, 290-3
Thomas, Julian, 306
Tikopia I., 40-1, 106-8, 123-5, 134-69 passim, 170-89 passim, 195, 224-5, 248
Timor, 11, 113
Titore, 158, 160, 181, 193, 194, 196, 285
Tokoroa, 103-4, 105
TONGA: 6, 8, 11, 87, 162-6, 170;
    Mariner on, 223-4, 234, 237;
    Thomas affair, 270-4, 291-3, 299-300
Tongatapu I., 11, 18, 87, 153, 163, 166, 270-5, 290-3
Towai, 80, 92
Trafalgar, 13
Treacherous Shoals, see Tytler's
Tuamotu Is., 6, 8, 85, 100
Tupou, of Tonga, 164
Tytler, R., 129-33, 134-69 passim, 178, 192, 201, 203, 221-2
Tytler's Shoals, 177

Valparaiso, 83, 84, 91, 97-8, 113, 237, 297, 306
Vancouver, G., 19, 63
VAN DIEMEN'S LAND: 6, 8, 28; in 1813-14, 48-9, 66-70, 73, 127; under Arthur, 140-51, 242-3
VANIKORO I.: 2, 41, 107-9, 116, 122, 125-9, 143, 148, 153, 168, 170-89 passim, 199, 200, 208, 308

Vernon-Smith, R., 288, 293-4, 296
Vonasa, of Wailea, 29-30

Wade, Rev. W. R., 259, 263, 278
Wahooey, 135-6
Waikato, 103, 104, 157
Wailea, 28-41 *passim*, 44, 312, 314
Wakefield, E. G., 251, 256, 280, 282, 286, 297, 299
Wales, W., 89
Walker, Capt. T., 21-4, 28, 45
Wallis, S., 7, 9, 19, 85
Wellington, Duke of, 209, 210, 293, 295

whaling, 10-11
Whangaroa, 23, 158
Whetoi, 158, 196
Whippy, D., 85-9, 106, 108, 277
White, Rev. W., 158
Williams, Rev. H., 80, 86, 161, 190-1, 193, 230
Williams, Rev. J., 164, 289-90
Williams, Rev. W., 161, 193
Wilson, H. H., 128-9
Wilson, W., 36-8
Worth, W., 75

Zenteno, J. I., 83, 98
Zenteno, M., 98, 130

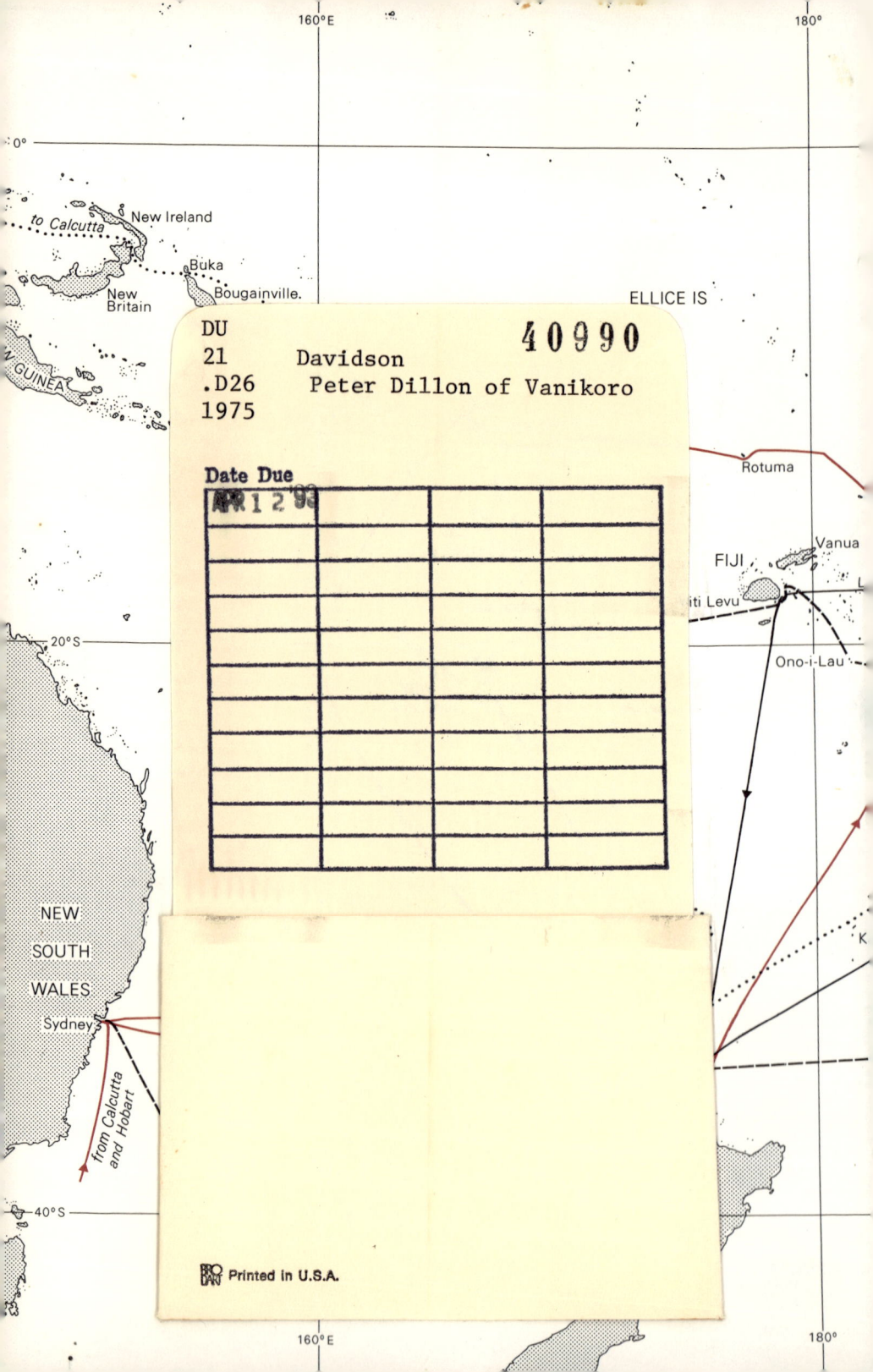